SO I HAVE THOUGHT OF YOU

The Letters of Penelope Fitzgerald

So I Have Thought of You

The Letters of Penelope Fitzgerald

EDITED BY TERENCE DOOLEY

Preface by A.S. Byatt

FOURTH ESTATE • *London*

Will dich im Traum nicht stören,
Wär schad un deine Ruh.
Sollst meinen Tritt nicht hören –
Sacht, sacht die Türe zu!
Schreib im Vorübergehen
Ans Tor dir: Gute Nacht
Damit du mögest sehen
An dich hab' ich gedacht.
An dich hab' ich gedacht.

CONTENTS

PREFACE BY A.S. BYATT

Penelope Fitzgerald and I taught together in the 1960s at the Westminster Tutors, an institution which prepared students, almost all female, for the long-abolished Entrance Exams to Oxford and Cambridge. We sat together in the small staff room on sagging sofas, amid a rich and pervasive smell of old upholstery and decaying dogs. Penelope was contradictory. She could appear vague and self-effacing and was. She could also say formidably knowledgeable and percipient things about literature. She was generous and exacting. She once rebuked me for not understanding that one of her pupils had a touch of genius. It was a concept that meant a great deal to her, which I did not understand at the time. It did not occur to me, young as I was and obsessed with literature and small children, that she might herself have more than a touch of genius. I don't know if it occurred to her. I didn't know her very well. She was interesting to know, but not easy to get to know well.

Her son-in-law, Terence Dooley, points out wisely in his introduction to this collection of letters, that friends and relations of novelists are not always best pleased when they first discover that, and what, the novelists have been writing. I was surprised, and pleased, as I struggled on with my own children and my own teaching and my own need to write, to see that Penelope had become a novelist. I had not been surprised to be told that she had written a biography of Burne-Jones. She was just and scholarly. I had not read her other biographies. When she won the Booker Prize with *Offshore* I was delighted, and immediately read it. (I did not know that this prize was to be such a trouble and such a problem to Penelope, until I read Terence Dooley's account of it.) I think I then read almost all her books, more or less as they came out. I admired them. They had a finished, separate quality. They were works of art, in excellent prose. They were funny and terrible. I did not ask whether they had anything to do with her life – whether she had owned a houseboat that sank, or a bookshop. There was something self-sufficient about even those early works. The writer knew exactly what belonged in a particular tale, and how to arrange it. I admired the craft, still without thinking of genius.

She said to me about *Human Voices* that she wished I would write something in the *TLS* or somewhere to point out that it was based on a German poem, by Heine, 'Der Asra'. I hadn't noticed that, and I don't know how she expected anyone to do so. 'Asra' to me was Coleridge's transposition of Sara in his diaries and love letters. But I felt challenged, and I reread *Human Voices*, and I read 'Der Asra', a perfect, moving, chilling, brief poem and I saw that Penelope Fitzgerald was not an English lady writer – in a lot of these letters she is putting on an act as one – but someone with an austere, original talent, unlike anyone else writing in this country at this time. I don't think I then said 'genius' to myself. It isn't a word I much use.

In the light of these letters we can see what parts of Fitzgerald's own life served as raw material for the earlier novels. This makes me, as a writer and reader, feel uneasy. The connections, the sources, are there, and yet there is something hermetic, something completed, about good novels of the kind Fitzgerald wrote. Deliberately personal novels like Dundy's *The Dud Avocado* or Jong's *Fear of Flying* almost take off from their authors' lives and flow back into them. Fitzgerald had made messy life into finished art – even if it was a finished observation about the messiness of life.

It was when I read the last three novels, *Innocence*, *The Beginning of Spring*, and *The Blue Flower*, that I came to understand – hindered by the fact that I had met her long before I read them – that she was a great writer. Each is different; each takes a whole world of history, knowledge, politics and literature and turns it into something at once suggestive and complete, full of newly created people and newly connected ideas. One is Italian, one is Russian, one is German. All are about tragi-comic, fallible human beings living personal lives in a world that is political and spiritual, which is sketched in with the sureness of an artist who knows *enough* (which means a very great deal) to know exactly what details of daily life, or philosophical thought, to put elegantly in place to make a whole. This is perhaps most remarkable of all in Von Hardenberg's Prussia. She told me once she had read the records of the salt mines from cover to cover in German to understand how her hero was employed – and then in a few sketched details she places the mines, in his daily life and in his thought about the scientific and spiritual world.

It was at this point only that I read *The Knox Brothers*, her biography of her father and uncles. I read the book looking for its author, not for its subjects. And I have come to see how much the austere perfectionist – with a wicked sense of humour – is descended from that family of bishops, saints, dons, idealists, intellects. She effaces herself, referring to her birth only as that of a 'daughter', and her observations (only about twice, moreover) as those of 'a niece'. I'm not sure I've read a better-written biography. The quality of the writing is derived partly from an exact, matter-of-fact, wildly funny wit in the descriptions. The other part comes from a scrupulous respect for the spiritual lives, as they themselves saw them, of the four brothers. Hermione Lee once asked her in an interview if she would say anything about her feminist or political beliefs. Fitzgerald corrected her; she hoped the readers would be interested in her *spiritual* beliefs.

The Knox Brothers opens with their grandfather, the missionary Thomas French, who travelled and died taking Christianity to the Afghans and the North West Frontier. Penelope Fitzgerald comments:

> Today he would certainly be asked: why not leave these people to their own beliefs? Why press on them something they did not ask for and do not want? To this his reply would be: 'The viewing of the unseen world instead of the visible things of time – this cannot be a shallow matter; it must be deep or not at all – no halves in such a business.'

The four brothers, in very different ways, inherited this absolute vision. Ronald Knox became a Catholic and distressed his father, an Anglican bishop. Wilfred made unworldly, precise vows of poverty and celibacy and joined the (Anglican) Oratory of the Good Shepherd. Penelope Fitzgerald comments sharply on people who saw him as a delightful eccentric, unconcerned like the birds of the air:

> This idea was particularly irritating. Wilfred was the young man who had chosen his ties in the Burlington Arcade, and he loved good wine, good tea and the best tobacco. But renunciation must never be seen in terms of loss.

Dillwyn, a mathematician who helped break the codes of the Enigma machine, was as resolute an unbeliever as those two brothers were believers. Penelope respects that. She describes him in 1916, recruiting Ronnie – 'an unlikely figure in clerical garb' – to Naval Intelligence:

> To Dilly, all the long-drawn out [family] suffering over his youngest brother was a matter of unrealities; we pray, no one answers, the Churches dispute to the death over how to go on speaking to someone who is not there.

It is in Dillwyn's logical and startling company that 'his niece, confined for what seemed an eternity to a boarding school at nearby High Wycombe', makes a rare appearance. He brings her back late, and confronts the outraged housemistress, who said 'Rules are made to be kept', with the answer: 'But they are defined only by being broken.'

It has rightly been said that Penelope wrote wonderfully about children. Terence Dooley makes the caveat that she liked children, not when they were babies or infants, but 'when they had reached the age of reason'. ('Ronnie's niece' makes another appearance, rebuked by Evelyn Waugh for wanting to leave Ronnie's sixtieth birthday party early 'to look after her baby'. Waugh 'snapped "Children! Nonsense! Nothing so easily replaceable."')

She tells us, of the Knox family, when their mother was sickening: 'There was an atmosphere, so frightening to children, of things not being quite right, and of discussions behind closed doors.' She says of her father that 'the blow of this death was one from which, in a very long life, he never quite recovered. It gave him, at twelve years old, a spartan endurance and a determination not to risk himself too easily to life's blows, which might, at times, have been mistaken for coldness.'

The children in whom Penelope, as a writer, is most interested are indeed – like the Knoxes – like Penelope herself: beings who combine clarity of thought with a sense of the existence of the unseen world. They are also perfectionists. The boy actor, in *At Freddie's*, practising a jump from a wall again and again may well have died in the search for perfection. Both Hardenberg and his young brother have the same absolutism. They inconvenience others, damage them even, yet are to be loved and understood and respected. There is something of the same quality in the midget child in *Innocence*, and by extension in the young Italians in that book. The quality is indeed a form of innocence. There is a comic version of it in the boy, observed by Penelope's father at Rugby, who stopped the school clock with an accurately aimed squash ball. It turned out that the boy had been practising the shot for two years. The headmaster called this 'un-English'.

> Eddie did not agree. The patient, self-contained, self-imposed pursuit of an entirely personal solution seemed to him most characteristically English.

It is in this sense – for she resembled her family, and knew it, as well as observing it clearly – that Penelope Fitzgerald is an English novelist. She is not a novelist of manners, though she observes them wickedly, nor of class, though she understands it. She writes very English versions of European metaphysical fables, embodying them in idiosyncratic reality.

I spoke to her, possibly for the last time, at one of the award parties for the Cohen Prize. She looked distracted, as she usually did at parties. I asked her if she was writing, and she looked at me searchingly and asked: 'How do you think of a novel?'

I don't know how she thought of the ones she wrote. I don't know what they can have been like in the planning – they seem as though they *had to be* as they are. She made it appear a question of extreme difficulty. I do not think reading her letters will really answer it either – though they illuminate other things. Instead, their reader will enjoy being in the company of Penelope's courtesy and intelligence. And then will ask for him or herself: 'How do you think of a novel?' And understand the difficulty of the question.

INTRODUCTION

I: Family and Friends

Penelope Fitzgerald was shy and awkward with anyone who was not an old friend or a family member. If writers are often monsters of egoism, she was not. Confident only in her fearsome sense of artistic rightness and in her abundant knowledge, she had no great conceit of herself; she feared herself ineffective socially, a voice unlikely to be heard. In person, one felt her reserves of sharp kindness, intelligence and sympathy. She was stern. She willed one to come up to the mark. She could be devastatingly funny.

In letters she could say all that she wanted to say, and couldn't quite face to face. She did so in a way that was truthful, witty and persuasive, but above all focused on the person she was writing to. She intended to be entertaining, to offer consolation or to celebrate. She is vividly alive in these letters, and, because she has their recipients so clearly in mind, their characters become clear to us too. Though she writes eloquently, she is unselfconscious and unguarded – it is quite evident that she wrote without thought of publication. It was part of her modesty that Penelope left no instructions about what should or shouldn't be published after her death. I think these letters will give her readers, without the frisson of gossip and malice, a rounded picture of what she was really like, a sense of the passage of her days, an impression of her career and interests, and the same pleasure they gave to those who first opened them.

Who could have predicted a time when the epistolary art would cease to be a part of ordinary communication, and would pass into history? Every morning when Penelope first sat down at her writing-table she attended to her correspondence. What is collected here must be a small fraction of what she in fact wrote and sent.

Her fame came so late in life that there was no reason for anyone to keep her letters, apart from affection, and she lost her personal records, including her husband Desmond's and her (copiously illustrated) letters, written when he was serving overseas, when the family's houseboat, *Grace*, sank for the second and last time, in 1963, which also made it difficult to trace Hampstead and Suffolk friends from the earlier, more prosperous periods of her married life. There is therefore a hole in the middle of this collection which engulfs her work as a programmes assistant at the BBC, the early years of her marriage, her editorship of *World Review*, her child-bearing and -rearing years, and her financial disasters. The years when, as Cervantes said to explain his own long silence, she was living her life: the years before she came to write.

I was fortunate when I began on this book to be given two meticulously kept series of letters: that of Chris Carduff, Penelope's American editor at Addison Wesley and then at Houghton Mifflin, and that of J. Howard Woolmer, bookseller and bibliographer, who corresponded with Penelope about the Poetry Bookshop in Bloomsbury and who brokered the sale of her papers to the University of Texas. A third and most fascinating series was sent to me by Hugh Lee – known as 'Ham' for his perceived acting abilities – and covers the early war years when Penelope was just down from Oxford and working for *Punch* and then for the Ministry of Food. She had met Ham through her childhood friend, Jean Fisher. They formed part of a set of young Oxford graduates, the men training to be officers, those women who had not joined up drafted into the ministries. It was a time of *amitiés amoureuses*, with Penelope an ever-sympathetic confidante when these went wrong, and an unquenchable babbling brook of light-hearted, fantastic invention. The letters are full of gaiety and exuberance, and, despite the sombre times, are without the darker notes of her later writing. They give a rare glimpse of what the children's generation never know about their parents: what they were like when they were young and silly and brimming with hope.

They break off about the time Penelope was falling in love with Desmond Fitzgerald, himself a recent Oxford graduate, and, like Ham's group, a year younger than her. A few months after they married he went off to fight with the Irish Guards in North Africa. He was awarded the MC for holding Hill 212 in the face of terrible odds, a battle that led to the capture of Tunis. He would have received the Victoria Cross, but for the dreadful technicality that he was the only surviving officer. 'It was lonely on that hill,' he wrote later in his *History of the Irish Guards*, the hill now marked by a large white cross bearing the names of those killed there and the words *Quis separabit?* Ever after he suffered nightmares, and he found it difficult to adapt to civilian life.

Twenty-three years pass between the last letter to Hugh and the first to Tina, her elder daughter. There was never any distance between Penelope and the page, so that to read one of the flimsy blue airmail forms in her beautiful blue italic hand, one and a half pages with an arabesque border of afterthoughts, and every corner filled, was and is to feel her beside you. And, I wondered, thinking back to 1970, when I first read one over Tina's shoulder, and remembering the delightful letter itself, and all it contained, how many of them she might have saved from all our travels and moves. Happily, there were a good many, scattered through drawers, cupboards and attics, interleaved with a miscellany of memories. They begin the year after *Grace* sank, when she was putting her life back together after eight years of free fall, and afford glimpses of her early literary adventures. We also see her imagination taking flight in her places of retreat: St Deiniol's library in Hawarden, with its Burne-Jones connections, and the abbey on Iona, and on the package holidays she was now able to take, thanks to Desmond's job with the travel firm Lunn Poly, despite the desperate scrimping – hair dyed with tea bags, Green Shield stamps saved for small comforts – that plagued her everyday life. We also get, as in the series of letters to her younger daughter, Maria, a most moving portrait of motherhood, which always took precedence over literature for Penelope.

I was talking one day to Maria about the (often furious) parental rows she remembers from the early years of her childhood, over bills unpaid, repossessions looming, and Desmond's drinking, and about how secure the children nonetheless felt in the love of two kind, intelligent and funny people who simply couldn't manage the world, despite their best efforts, so that it mattered less that they never knew where they would be living next, or where they would be going to school, there was a kind of adventure in it, when she suddenly absented herself and returned a little later from her cellar with a heavy black plastic bag. Inside was the complete set of letters her mother had written to her while she was up at

Oxford, the only time in fact that they lived in different cities. All were in their postmarked envelopes, significant in that the letters are almost all undated as to year, and so exist in a seasonal but otherwise indeterminate present. There are two or three letters a week for each of her nine terms at the university and they provide an unusually detailed portrait of her state of mind at an unsettling period of her life when much was changing, and make on the whole for sadder reading than those to Tina:

'*Autumn: Departure of Daughters*'

Oh my dark & light brown daughters
When you go to find new faces
Our place & me are put in our places
Our place may take what name it pleases –
It stares & stares, and all it sees is
That it is not a home.
Oh my dark & light brown daughters
When you go to find new places
Our place must face that it has no faces –
Tidiness, emptiness and peace is
All it has, and all it sees is
That it is not a home

Penelope put this poem away, in a drawer, without showing it to anyone, except these daughters. Its note continues to be sounded from time to time throughout the letters to her youngest child, the last to go away to find new places.

Now in her mid-fifties, she was working terribly hard: a full week's teaching in two different jobs, three days at Queens Gate, Kensington, two days at Westminster Tutors, vast piles of exam-board marking as well as her own, with only Saturdays to spare for the mountainous research and writing of her first two books, the Burne-Jones and Knox Brothers biographies. After a difficult start (teaching R.E. at the stage school Italia Conti, remembered in *At Freddie's*) she had become a valued and inspiring English teacher, the texts she was studying with her pupils – Jane Austen, but also Lawrence, Conrad, Forster, Joyce and Beckett, much modern poetry, philosophy, theory, history of art (we still have the tattered, meticulously annotated paperbacks) – all no doubt fuelling the future motor of her fiction. For, almost imperceptibly to her family, as she rarely spoke of work in progress, she was at last becoming what her old friends had always thought she would be: a writer, and this was confirmed by the acceptance of *Edward Burne-Jones* in 1973. It should have been an exciting and exhilarating time; intellectually and creatively it must have been, but personally it was a time of anxiety, loneliness and fear.

There had been ten years of comparative stability. Desmond and she had repaired their finances, made a rather stylish island home in their Clapham council flat, and seen their three children into and through Oxford. After the disasters of the previous decade, this had taken a great deal of persistence and bravery. Now they could say to each other: look, we have come through. A historian by training, he was able to help her in her research and they travelled happily together, at weekends and in the holidays, all over England, and to France, interviewing and absorbing atmospheres. In 1974 it became clear, though both delayed facing it (and their local GP was no help whatsoever), that Desmond was unwell. Penelope states barely in one of the later letters to Maria that she could not imagine living without one of her daughters nearby. The extent of her father's illness, when it was eventually discovered, was kept hidden from Maria until she had completed her finals, but then she had to be told of his operation, in the reticent terms used in those days, which didn't make anything any better.

Tina and I had married in 1973, and now we bought a three-storey house off Battersea Rise – the 25 Almeric Road of the letters – so that her parents could come and live with us. Desmond continued to go to work, growing frailer and thinner, but still as funny, endearing and patient. He died in the summer of 1976. In the first of the letters to her old friend, Maryllis, Penelope describes the morning of his death, at home, the district nurse reading to him: 'such a kindly person, not much of a nurse but a very good woman, and she helped me to see him out of this world and read a Bible chapter, absolutely naturally, as only a West Indian could do'. In the same letter she reflects: 'the truth is I was spoilt, as with all our ups and downs Desmond always thought everything I did was right'.

Penelope kept four close friends from her childhood and youth: Maryllis Conder ('Willie'), Jeanie Fisher (later Lady Talbot), Rachel Hichens and Janet Probert. Marriage, child-rearing, work and geographical distance separated them for long years after the war, but Jeanie and Maryllis in particular became a great support to her in her widowhood.

'Your mother has been my dearest friend,' wrote Willie to Maria. They met at Wycombe Abbey, 'a terrible place', as Penelope remembered it. She was thinking of its aping of boys' boarding schools, the sport, the cricket, the rituals, but it was principally terrible to both of them because of their home-sickness: they cried themselves to sleep for the first three weeks of every term. English Literature, however, was inspiringly taught ('under Daisy') and was a shared consolation. They would both go on to study it at Oxford, though Penelope's great enthusiasm was Art and Maryllis's Music. They sat together in class, laughed at the same absurdities, and Mops (as Penelope was always known to friends) would help Willie with her essays. At the end of their last term at Wycombe, Penelope's mother, Christina, died. Her father, Evoe, was too grief-stricken to speak of her, and she went to stay with Maryllis and her family in Devon. 'It was a painful visit,' Maryllis said, 'but she told me later that it had helped her.' During the war, as young women, they would meet unfailingly every week for lunch. 'How clearly I can see her walking down Sloane St with me in her cherry coat.'

It is a strange thing that some good friends (and even family members) don't always welcome the transformation of a person known so well into a successful writer, almost as if they had been hiding something from them and had now to be seen in a different light. Maryllis emphatically didn't fall into this category, but devoted a corner of her study to Penelope's books and drawings, her idiosyncratic Christmas cards which gave such pleasure. She also kept a selection of her letters ('in my Mops letters file box'), which covers the last twenty-five years of her life. 'You know what a wonderful letter-writer she was.'

Willie and her husband Mike had restored a beautiful small Jacobean manor house, 'Terry Bank', near Kirkby Lonsdale. It had always been in the Conder family and still retains some of its original furniture. It is a tranquil place in a serene setting. Here, or to their converted lighthouse on Alderney, they invited Penelope every year. 'We had some very happy times together, unforgettable'. In the dramatic hillside garden they created on the bank behind the house they planted the Himalayan Blue Poppy (Meconopsis baileyi: The Blue Flower) in her honour. The letters provide a remarkable record of friendship and a continuing conversation. They discuss their children and grandchildren, plantings in their gardens. There is the occasional glimpse of Penelope's busy literary career. They sympathise with each other over their ailments. Maryllis wrote to Tina after Penelope's death that her mother had appeared to her at night in her room to console her and to tell her not to worry. It sounds the sort of thing she would do.

Another loving friendship of a whole life is detailed in the letters to Rachel Hichens (and her daughter Elizabeth Barnet, Penelope's goddaughter). Each married a Cornish vicar, and they were and are rich in good works in a way with which Penelope had almost complete sympathy, only regretting that she couldn't match it herself. Rachel was the daughter of the writer Alfred Ollivant. She and Penelope met through their mothers' friendship, in Hampstead, when they were both about six years old. She told her daughter that she believed Penelope's childhood to have been overshadowed by her mother's illness. She worked at Bletchley Park during the war, where Dillwyn Knox was working on breaking the German codes. (He often tried to recruit his niece to help him, but unsuccessfully.) After both women married, they saw each other only occasionally, but Elizabeth often stayed with her godmother in London as a young woman, and found her and her family 'so interesting'.

Mary Knox, Penelope's stepmother (and illustrator of *Mary Poppins*, daughter of E. H. Shepard, illustrator of *Winnie the Pooh* and *The Wind in the Willows)* was only seven years older than Penelope, something that might have been resented, but wasn't. They were frequent companions, so that letters were not really necessary. Nonetheless, many were written, though sadly only a few have survived. I hope they show how dear she was to Penelope, and to all the family.

These collections, which I am most grateful to have been given, depict Penelope as she was with those she loved, but inevitably those who 'answered some of her long marvellous letters but kept none' have had to be omitted: Jean Fisher, her friend from prep school, a source of practical kindness and help, as close a friend as Maryllis, if not quite such a kindred spirit – books were off limits; Rawle, her brother, to whom she pays tribute in *A House of Air*; finally her son, Valpy, of whom she writes in a never completed late essay, with perhaps rather whimsical and unjust exaggeration: 'I'm not sure that he knows how to write a letter, and I think it possible that he doesn't read them.' She took the greatest possible pride in his achievements, as in those of her daughters. The last paragraph of her essay reads:

> Once when we were living on the Suffolk coast and the mechanics of daily living had got altogether too much for me, Valpy who must have been about thirteen, looked at me thoughtfully and said he'd take me out for a row. We had a proofed canvas boat, the *Little Emily*, down on the marshes. She was anchored to a stake in the bank. Quite often one or other of the local boys would 'borrow' her and leave her wherever they felt like it. We had to go looking for her in the maze of reeds and narrow waterways. However, that afternoon she was lying patiently in her proper place. We got in and Valpy rowed for an hour or so under the immense shining East Coast sky, a watercolours sky. We went as far as the old pumping mill, through great banks of flowering sedge with grey leaves as sharp as saws. We rowed back, tied up, took out the rowlocks and walked home without saying anything, because nothing needed to be said. I felt more at peace then I think than I had ever done before.

II: Writing

For someone who was not at all business-like, Penelope managed her literary career decisively and with acumen. She would never employ an agent, and money is rarely mentioned in these letters. She was concerned first that her projects would be published, then that the books would look right, be error-free, reviewed, read and understood. About her writing she kept her own counsel, but she relied on her editors for much reassurance, help, advice and friendship. In finding four publishers in as many years (this was necessitated by the scope of her interests, and her shifts between the genres) she had only her talent and persistence to recommend her. She was probably introduced to Michael Joseph, who published her first book, *Edward Burne-Jones*, by Jean Fisher, whose cousin was the managing director of the firm. By a lucky coincidence, she had printed the first story of Raleigh Trevelyan, the editor who first read her biography, in her magazine *World Review* in the early '50s. They admired each other's writing and became friends. Sadly, publishers' archives are parlously preserved in these days, and I haven't been able to trace any of her letters to him. The book's status is an awkward one, because, as Penelope remarks, as a non-member of the art history establishment she wasn't really allowed to have written it. Literary biographies are usually written about writers. It was patchily but well reviewed and, despite remaining the standard work on its subject, since no-one has discovered more about Burne-Jones, nor written as entertainingly about his loves and sorrows, nor with such enthusiasm and skill about his art, it is nonetheless the least read of her books, the only one now out of print, and never to have been available in America. This is a pity, for its non-readers have missed many wonderful vivid scenes, as when Robert Browning, woken by his geese, sees from his windows Burne-Jones desperately trying to prevent his mistress-muse, Mary Zambaco, from throwing herself off the bridge over the Regents Canal. Penelope's correspondence with the eminent American Burne-Jones scholar, Mary Lago, shows like minds, whose interest in one subject draws them on and outwards, at the most unexpected tangent, to the next. The seeds of several of her later projects are in this vast, living, late-Victorian world.

The biography, though, didn't sell, and her next project didn't sound any more commercial to the rather middlebrow publishing house of Michael Joseph (as Raleigh Trevelyan recently recalled, they preferred to publish books about horses and dogs). It was politely turned down. But there were good reasons to believe Macmillan might be interested in *The Knox Brothers*, for Harold Macmillan had been much influenced by the Catholic chaplain, Ronald Knox, as an undergraduate at Oxford, and they always remained friends. He appears in the book as 'C'. Harold Macmillan's letter of congratulations to Penelope is most touching: 'you have brought out marvellously well the characteristics of these remarkable men . . . you have made it all so living and, to me, in my old age deeply moving'.

The first of the revealing sets of letters to editors that form the core of this book is to Richard Garnett at Macmillan: 'All writers are intimidated by all publishers,' she remarked to him, and he sounds more intimidating than most, though Penelope politely stood up to him, in part by quoting his brusqueries back to him: 'It worried me terribly when you told me I was only an amateur writer, and I asked myself how many books do you have to write and how many semi-colons do you have to discard before you lose amateur status.' And again: 'I recall that my heart sank when you said "I have the right to expect accuracy".' Garnett was a scrupulous editor, but Penelope won most of the skirmishes over accuracy, even over how best to explain the complex workings of the Enigma decoding machine.

To describe the Knoxes' many achievements required an overview of several quite distinct disciplines and milieux. Sons of Bishop Knox of Manchester, two of her uncles became priests of quite different stripe. Ronnie, much to his father's distress, was the most public convert to Catholicism since Newman. A Christian apologist famous between the wars for his witness, he was much in demand in the newspapers and on the radio. He also wrote much-praised learned theological works, was renowned as a wit – his book *Let Dons Delight* being a particular favourite with the public – translated the Bible, and, while chaplain at Oxford, penned a best-selling series of detective novels. Wilfred, the least known of the brothers, was an Anglican chaplain at Cambridge, wrote profound devotional works, and inspired a generation of clergymen. Penelope's father Eddie (or 'Evoe', his chosen sobriquet), the longest lived of the family, dying in 1970 at the age of ninety, made humour his speciality, writing graceful light verse and prose for *Punch*. Collected every Christmas in volume form, it was very popular. He edited the paper between the wars and brought it to its highest point of success and circulation. Dillwyn began as a brilliant classicist, and editor of the Herodas papyri. His subsequent career, though shrouded in mystery at the time (Penelope had to break the Official Secrets Act to write about it), has probably had the most long-lasting effects of all the Knoxes' achievements, as he was instrumental in breaking the German codes in both wars. The letters to Mavis Batey, his assistant at Bletchley Park, illuminate this aspect of Penelope's research.

She began the book a year or so after her father's death, as a memorial to him and her uncles, rarely mentioning herself, and even then only as 'the niece' and 'the daughter'. Her research had the good effect of reuniting her with her cousins, and igniting a warm friendship in particular with Oliver Knox, Dilly's son, which would last until the end of her life. *The Knox Brothers* is a skilful and original family biography, interleaving four contrasting stories with a wealth of feeling and detail. It also captures a whole period of British life, the memory of which was beginning to fade in very different times. This was immediately appreciated, and, with its appearance, in 1977, Penelope could be said to have arrived. With her *Burne-Jones* she had repaid a debt to an artist who, in an epiphanic childhood moment, when the sun shone through his stained-glass window, 'The Last Judgement', in Birmingham cathedral, had awoken in her a sense of ideal beauty in art. In *The Knox Brothers* she captured a quality of mind, personality, temperament and values that defined her. When Francis King seemed to mock the brothers' sometimes unremitting brilliance and sanctity, she replied 'I loved them'. Now she need no longer consider herself the daughter or the niece. Free of that long shadow, she could delve into herself. She would essay fiction.

In fact she had already begun, but in a recognisably Knoxian mode, with a comic detective story, perhaps a false start. We do not know quite how she came to offer *The Golden Child* to Colin and Anna Haycraft at Duckworth, as the firm cannot trace the correspondence relating to the book, but she certainly, and soon, came to regret it. In September 1977 she wrote to Richard Garnett at Macmillan:

> I thought quite well of the book at first but it's now almost unintelligible, it was probably an improvement that the last chapters got lost, but then 4 characters and 1000s of words had to be cut to save paper, then the artwork got lost (by the printer this time) so we had to use my roughs and it looks pretty bad, but there you are, it doesn't matter, and no-one will notice . . . everyone has to do the best they can.

But Duckworth were known for the ruthless editing of manuscripts, in the service of a house style: the *nouvelle*; indeed they were said to have improved Beryl Bainbridge's first novels by this process. With Penelope it ever after rankled, yet even in its truncated form *The Golden Child* has much to amuse, with its egomaniacal establishment villains, and its unpromisingly named sleuth, Professor Untermensch. He, like Dilly Knox, is an expert decoder, in this case of Garamantian hieroglyphs, which Penelope draws herself, and with which she has a great deal of fun, as in their corresponding phonemes: Poo, Sog, Hak, Mum, etc.

If the book itself has to be decoded, it is not Penelope's fault, and it was enjoyed when it appeared in 1977, in the same year as *The Knox Brothers*, though it was only mentioned in round-ups of crime fiction, a category to which it does not quite belong, as it has serious points to make about fakery, and about the corruption and denaturing of art through money and politics.

Penelope seemed to have taken the mutilation of *The Golden Child* philosophically, but she would have worse to contend with from Duckworth, as the correspondence with Colin Haycraft about her next book demonstrates all too clearly. With the money from *The Knox Brothers* she had embarked on a long-dreamt-of voyage to China. From the perspective of all that distance, she had the revelation all writers await. She saw as in a blinding light how to transmute the events of her own life into serious fiction. The first fruits of this earth-tremor was to be *The Bookshop*.

No woman is a hero to her son-in-law, and yet, when I first came across this book (till then unaware of its very existence) lying in bound-proof form on her kitchen table, where it had been written, and took advantage of Penelope's temporary absence to read it in one sitting, I did have a sense of 'What? And in our house?' I had no doubt that this was the real thing, and still feel grateful for the stolen privilege of being one of the first people to read it. Ever after that Penelope had an extra dimension of mystery to me. I immediately wrote her a note to express my amazed and delighted appreciation; it would have been too embarrassing to confess in person. I was touched, much later, to come across the never-referred-to note among her papers in Texas.

The Bookshop is not especially autobiographical, but it does seem to grind an axe in its depiction of Southwold as 'Hardborough', an exemplar of provincial mean spirit, the petty exercise of power, and philistinism.

It is eloquent on the great beauty of the region, only spoilt for her by the loss, through the family's insolvency, of 'Blackshore', their home, the large former oyster warehouse on the Hard, on which the bookshop was modelled. (But an earlier loss, the failure of her magazine *World Review*, which, in the end, 'hadn't been wanted' must surely also underlie the book.) The real bookshop, in the High Street, remained open for many years, ably run by Mrs Neame, the old friend of the book's dedication, whose assistant Penelope became, after her financial misfortunes. In reality, the family made a good many kind supportive friends there, though mainly among the intellectual bohemia of nearby Walberswick, including the Freuds, Sampsons and Fiennes. The moral atmosphere of the book, perhaps also some of the form (each chapter a scene), comes, as is mentioned in the blurb, from the *Scènes de la Vie de Province* of Balzac's *Human Comedy*, which she studied with Tina, to help her with her 'A' level. The style, however, with its dry compassionate humour, could already be nobody but Penelope. It is still one of her most popular books, particularly abroad, in Europe and America, where it is seen as a very English classic. It has just been reissued in France with the misleading, but certainly striking, title *L'Affaire Lolita*. It was reviewed, in 1978, with respect and enthusiasm, and, with almost unheard-of good fortune for a first novel, shortlisted for the Booker Prize.

With all of this Duckworth should have been well contented. However, with hindsight, Penelope should have thought better of entering a small pool of lady writers, all sharing some of the same traits, one of whom – Anna Haycraft (her pen-name Alice Thomas Ellis) – was also the nominal fiction editor. With Colin she got on, admiring his jovial eccentricity and classical scholarship. She had hoped he would accompany her to the Booker dinner, but he did not, adducing the improbable lack of a dinner jacket. Shortly after this it was inexplicably implied to Penelope that Duckworth had a surfeit of elegant *nouvelles* and she should return to crime-writing, which would sell better. Though we see Colin Haycraft hastily backtracking, the damage was done. She was deeply hurt. She would take her next novel to Collins. Here at last she fell on her feet: she had found a publishing home.

It is impossible to overstate Penelope's energy and creativity in the late 1970s. There would be five novels in as many years, as well as an enormous amount of work on two biographies, each dear to her heart as projects, both of which she had to abandon, one from scruple, the other in the face of determined resistance from publishers. Although she would say little to friends or editors about her fiction (and that little misleading, for the novels must speak for themselves), the letters are full of fascinating detail about the unwritten biographies.

'The Poetry Bookshop' was the first conceived of these, and its intended theme is, if anything, more compelling and urgent today: the loss, through the unforeseen side-effects of modernism, of the lyric voice of English verse – the voice that spoke to the ordinary reader's heart, the loss therefore (by now almost complete) of the mass audience for serious poetry. The book would have concerned itself with the rehabilitation of the Georgians, whose headquarters was at Harold and Alida Monro's poetry bookshop in Devonshire Street (now Boswell Street) in Bloomsbury. Yeats, Frost, Edward Thomas, Lawrence, Wilfred Owen, even Eliot, all passed through its portals, but Penelope was especially interested in the minor figures: Monro himself, Anna Wickham, F. S. Flint and Charlotte Mew, with their, as she discovered, often tragic and tormented lives, who never quite made it, but each produced a handful of perfect lyrics. How one regrets this book, which she did not abandon until all four of her publishers had turned it down in succession. Yet fragments of it survive, first in the story of Harold Monro, in her introduction to J. Howard Woolmer's scholarly bibliography of publications of the Poetry Bookshop, especially of its beautiful illustrated rhyme sheets, a treasured childhood memory of Penelope's. Her letters to Woolmer trace the development of a warm transatlantic relationship between bookseller (albeit a very grand one) and collector, which becomes a meeting of minds as we see them sharing the details of their research. He most generously gave her some of the precious rhyme sheets when he realised she couldn't afford them, and put her in the way of more money, most necessary to impecunious authors, by persuading her to sell her papers to Texas, and thus no doubt saving many of them, for she was modestly careless in such things.

To Richard Ollard, her great support and ally at Collins over the next years, we owe the eventual publication of the other fruit of 'The Poetry Bookshop' research: her wonderful dark biography *Charlotte Mew and*

Her Friends, which reads so much like one of her novels. Ollard, like Raleigh Trevelyan also a distinguished writer, was senior literary editor at Collins, and perhaps the last of the 'gentleman publishers'. They suited each other; she could rely on him. 'You can always consult Richard if anything worries you,' his assistant, Sarah, told Penelope. They became friends, as they remained to the end of her life. With him (as with several other correspondents, notably Francis King who gave her much encouragement) she discussed, in a spirit of high comedy, her difficulties and adventures in the preparation of her life of Leslie (L. P.) Hartley. The book, which sounded more promising than 'The Poetry Bookshop' to publishers, was still promised to Colin Haycraft, despite their rift.

What became of it? She had to overcome the implacable opposition of Lord David Cecil, Hartley's literary executor, even to begin it. Cecil had been the love of Hartley's life. Long married, he didn't perhaps wish to acknowledge the basis of their youthful friendship. Anthony Powell kindly intervened to persuade him that Penelope would be the ideal person to tell Hartley's story with the tact needed, and she worked hard on the book for three years from 1977. It wasn't so much the gondoliers, the murderous, manipulative man-servants, the oceans of gin, the snobbery (all those duchesses), the extreme right-wing politics, the pot-shots at swans from his house on the River Avon, that dissuaded her from proceeding, but the affection she developed for his loving sister, Norah. How could she present the dissipation of his achievement of the '40s and '50s, the coarsening of his clear, careful voice (an echo of it is audible in *The Bookshop*, as Haycraft points out) in a good light? Could she betray the memory of their own friendship, of his support during her first literary career, her editorship of *World Review*, when she often published him, by the honest depiction of his long decline, all too visible in the desperately feeble novels and stories of his later years? She couldn't, and wouldn't. Somewhat wistfully, she gave up on the project in the early 1980s. These letters give a strong sense of what a biography it might have been.

The book she did deliver to Richard Ollard in 1979 was *Offshore*. Here one feels distinctly in Fitzgeraldland, or, in this case, afloat on the brackish, swirling, hardly benevolent waters of a great tidal river, uncertainly tethered to a land that has brought no luck. Though the characters couldn't be more English, the tragicomedy of their fates (tragi-farce she called it) sounds notes more common in European fiction. It was sometimes painful to read for her family. All art, the adult characters invented or composite, there is much in it that was recognisably the case: 'Grace', the houseboat, probably bought for its name as much as its cheapness, appears as itself, as does Stripey the cat, and the two little girls are called Tina and Maria in the manuscript. Reality dances with imagination in a treacherous way, games are being played with remembered facts, though not with the feelings beneath them. In the third chapter, Nenna, who is as distanced from Penelope as she is like her, finds her thoughts becoming 'a kind of perpetual magistrate's hearing' about her marriage and her motives for her actions. After many ordeals, the drama is resolved in irresolution. The boat never actually goes down.

Offshore was enthusiastically reviewed, shortlisted for the Booker, and then, against all expectations, won it. But what should have been a triumph had decidedly mixed results.

The Booker has an honourable reputation for selecting the best and most interesting novels of the year, even if they don't always win, and it is now a venerable and respected institution, guaranteeing a (sometimes vast) increase in sales for the winner, and boosting reputations; but that only began to happen a year or so after Penelope won. Then, shamefully, in the early years when the prize ceremony received fairly shoddy television coverage, the lucky six authors shortlisted, whose only sin was to have written praiseworthy novels, were lined up as in a coconut shy to be insulted by media pundits, who gave no very convincing impression of having read the books in question. That year the firm favourite was *A Bend in the River* by V. S. Naipaul, a fine novel that Penelope later recommended for another prize. It would have been an equally worthy winner, but it is said, with truth, that judging literary competitions is like comparing gazelles with tigers. Journalists had already written their pieces, and were affronted by not even having heard, in most cases, of Penelope. What followed could be described as a field day of ignorant and exceedingly unfair indignation. *The Critics* on Radio 3 (which had praised *The Bookshop* to the skies), called the result a disgrace and a very bad day for modern fiction, or something of the kind. 'When I got to the *Book Programme*, soaking wet because I'd had to be photographed on a bale of rope on the Embankment, R[obert] Robinson was in a very bad temper and complained to his programme executive "who are these people, you promised me they were going to be the losers?"' wrote Penelope to Francis King. 'I'll never forget the *Book Programme*,' Penelope wrote to Richard Ollard; 'I was delighted to hear that you are printing off a few more *Offshores*. I thought it had got shipwrecked altogether by so many unpleasant remarks.'

It may have set back her career. Her next two novels, though liked, did not receive the appreciation they deserved. Hasty readers and reviewers missed the depths of *Human Voices* and *At Freddie's*: it was too easy to take them only for the dazzling entertainments that in one sense they are. Her ellipses and puzzles often led them to wonder if she had left something out, if the apparent holes in her plots were accidental, but really she intended her readers to work, to solve the mysteries the stories hinge on for themselves. She tried to define *Human Voices* for the blurb that Richard Ollard was writing, and makes clear its complexity:

> It is really about the love-hate relationship between 2 of the eccentrics on whom the BBC depended, and about love, jealousy, death, childbirth in Broadcasting House and the crises that go on to produce the 9 o'clock news on which the whole nation relied during the war years, heartbreak &c, and also about this truth telling business.

The original title, 'Ten Seconds From Now', seemed only to refer to the urgency and danger of the times, to the effort of the whole nation to avert evil by upholding the truth, in which Penelope participated as a programmes assistant at the BBC. The preferred title, 'Human Voices', taken from Eliot's 'Prufrock', is apt both in its reference to the disembodied broadcasters, and to the pain of young love: for 'human voices wake us and we drown'. Another poem also underlies the book, as she points out helpfully or unhelpfully to Ollard in the same letter: '(Incidentally, as no-one reads Heine I suppose no-one will understand the name Asra, but that's by the way.)' Annie Asra, the heroine of *Human Voices*, like all Penelope's female protagonists, represents her in some aspects. Heine's poem 'Der Asra' is about a slave slowly dying for love of his mistress. All his tribe, the Asra, in fact die if they fall in love, and Annie is clearly a member of it. The unsuitability of the people we fall in love with is one of Penelope's themes. She goes so far as to wonder, in one of her novels, whether men and women are ever quite the right thing for each other. However, she certainly believed in love unto death.

At Freddie's was originally called 'What! Are They Children?', but although the precocious boy actors are its ultimate focus, it is also about the theatre and its *monstres sacrés*, unhappy love, life's casualties, and the impossibility of teaching children what they don't require to know, what they don't already intuit as necessary to them. The teachers in the novel, Pierce and Hannah, quickly realise that it is only their support and kindness that their charges need. It is interesting that their backgrounds in some respects mirror Desmond's and Penelope's. Pierce is an Irish Catholic; Hannah is from Ulster (where the Knoxes have their roots). Shakespeare's 'King John', with its murder of innocents, is the play being rehearsed in the book, for Freddie is a serious headmistress. The character derives from Miss Freeston, head not of Italia Conti, where Penelope began her teaching in the early 1960s, but of Westminster Tutors, the eccentric Oxbridge crammer where she was still teaching. However Freddie is given some of the traits and fearsome reputation of Lilian Baylis, the much-loved dragon of the Old Vic, the theatre that flew the flag for Shakespeare in London for so many years.

Penelope wrote to Richard Ollard about the cover design for *At Freddie's*:

> I wanted a high wall with a broken basket of fruit at the bottom of it, having evidently fallen, one of the Covent Garden baskets. That gives some movement, because it's evidently fallen from somewhere. I did think of the stage children as to some extent expendable products, like the fruit.

Ollard, the fourth publisher to do so, politely turned down 'The Poetry Bookshop' project four times. In the face of Penelope's lively persistence, which makes for entertaining reading, and with the reduction of its focus to a study of the life of Charlotte Mew, and how it gave rise to her few, haunting poems, in the end he gracefully bowed to the inevitable. She wrote to him as the publication date neared:

> the interesting things about CMew are that: 1. she was a poet, otherwise I shouldn't bother to write about her 2. she was a lesbian 3. she was unhappy 4. she has a curious lifespan as a writer, from the nineties to the 1920s . . . I fear none of the papers would be interested in an extract about a lesbian who didn't make it . . . The interest, to me, is that she's a divided personality who had to produce so many versions of herself at the same time. Perhaps we all do.

Chris Carduff, in his first assignment as an editor, oversaw the Addison Wesley edition in the US, and sensibly and logically enriched it with a selection of Mew's poems.

It is curious how many successful writers have been drawn to write wonderful books about unsuccessful ones. *Charlotte Mew and Her Friends* (but she had so few) is a tragic, deeply literary book, of similar length and structure to her novels. It was her last biography. From now on, nonetheless, all her fiction would include people who had really existed. The two worlds were merging.

In the letters to Richard Ollard, as befitted their flourishing friendship, she discussed freely the upheavals in her life provoked by the decision of my wife and myself to move to the country and bring up our children there. Now she would live between Somerset and London. In Theale she gardened, helped sometimes with Fergus (though she wasn't terribly good with babies and toddlers; she preferred children to have reached the age of reason), relaxed as much as she ever did, and we hoped that she would be able to write. However she found that 'I personally can <u>only</u> write in London, I love the noise and squalor and the perpetual distractions and the temptation to take an aircraft somewhere else', and so Jean Fisher helped her to find a base, at 76 Clifton Hill, St John's Wood, in the house of a friend of a friend where she lived in 'a kind of attic, overlooking the tree-tops, with gold wallpaper'. This arrangement worked well until 1987, when her work for the writers' association PEN International and the Arts Council, her research at the British Museum reading room for her books, and her tireless reviewing, kept her more and more in London, and her daughter Maria and son-in-law John generously agreed to convert the coachhouse of their new house in Bishop's Road, Highgate for her. They looked after her there for the rest of her life.

During the years at Clifton Hill she was taking her writing in a new direction. An examination of her manuscripts in the Harry Ransom Humanities Center at the University of Texas seems to indicate that, however intense the thought and technique that went into them, her first four novels almost wrote themselves. Her pure fiction is entrancing, but now she was attempting to combine this with the novel of ideas, the metaphysical novel. She had been considering writing about Italy, and specifically Florence, for a decade, the book that after many evolutions became *Innocence*. An early version of the Ridolfis appears in a first draft, which was to have been about the great Florentine flood, and might even have been intended to be a detective story. It is Francis King she credits with putting her on track: 'you'll hardly remember, having been to so many other places since, that you told me the story of the Italian family and their dwarfs yourself'. This cruel legend or parable from the 1560s is retold by Penelope with a wealth of vivid apparently historical detail as the first chapter of *Innocence*, shedding its mysterious light and darkness over the Shakespearean comedy of tangled loves, with the rumbling of politics beneath, set in a 1950s Italy seemingly known and recreated from within. The Ridolfis of those earlier days were midgets. When their daughter's companion starts outgrowing her her legs must be cut off at the knees.

The twentieth-century Ridolfis retain 'a tendency to rash decisions, perhaps always intended to ensure other people's happiness'. Stuart Proffitt, who took over as her editor on Richard Ollard's retirement, suggested 'Happiness' as a title, but Penelope remarked that the novel could as easily be called 'Unhappiness'. The happiness in question is marital. Constant misunderstandings drive the lovers, Chiara and Salvatore, together and apart. By the end their young stormy marriage seems to have been saved by a hair's breadth, to be provisionally permanent. Salvatore throws up his hands:

'What's to become of us? We can't go on like this.'
  'Yes, we can go on like this. We can go on exactly like this for the rest of our lives.'

As well as telling a story, Penelope now sought to evoke a culture, and an historical period. Every page gives evidence of a lightly worn, instructive and relevant erudition: about viticulture, law, medicine, architecture, the cinema, fashion, economics, and, above all, politics. For Gramsci, the influential communist reformer who wrote of the ethical society, is the historical figure introduced here, his ideas appealing to Penelope in much the same way as did those of William Morris. Lastly, one should point out the striking, if idealised, resemblance of Chiara to Penelope herself, particularly in the cover-picture she chose for *Innocence*, one of Pontormo's angels, from his *Annunciation*. The virtues of her new method were immediately recognised by the critics, and her reputation began to grow: she was again shortlisted for the Booker, the third of her four novels to be so honoured.

Through vicissitudes of archive-keeping, the letters to Stuart Proffitt about this and her next two novels have (I hope temporarily) disappeared. However, for *The Beginning of Spring*, her next novel, we do have the letters to Harvey Pitcher, author of *The Smiths of Moscow*, credited by Penelope as having been vital to her research. These, like many of the letters in the 'Writing' section, show how meticulous and indefatigable she was in this aspect of her work, with what a sense of adventure and enjoyment she undertook it. On one level *The Beginning of Spring*, first called *Nellie and Lisa*, is once again a brilliant tragicomedy of marital misunderstanding, memorable like *Offshore* for its depiction of children not unlike her own. The spring is also the Russian revolutionary spring, for she chose historical periods, which seemed to promise change, emancipation and spiritual rebirth. The novel's first conception also dates back at least a decade. In Texas is a notebook entitled *The Greenhouse*, with an early draft of the story of the English expatriate printer which takes the firm on into the May Revolution itself, but this proved unworkable. Pitcher's book and *The Times*' Russian Supplements of the period provide the realistic detail, but the uncanny imaginative power that makes a countrified chaotic Moscow almost tangible surely springs from a deep knowledge of and affinity with Russian literature, especially the Tolstoy of *Resurrection* and *Master and Man*, whose idiosyncratic Christian socialism infuses the novel. More than this, in *The Beginning of Spring*, uninsistently, symbolically, mysteriously, the presence of the supernatural is felt, and it will continue to startle and unsettle (as do the ghosts of the future in the birch wood here) in her last two novels and late stories.

Her next novel, *The Gate of Angels*, is also set in the first decade of last century, on the cusp of the modern era. It revolves around an accident, which may have been caused by a ghost, and culminates in a miracle. Fred, the Cambridge scientist, and Daisy, the London nurse down on her luck, live in minutely recreated social spheres which are set never to collide. Yet 'Chance is one of the manifestations of God's will' and they wake up naked in a Samaritan stranger's bedroom, having been knocked off their bicycles by a carter who has vanished into thin air. (This incident was a real one, recounted in *Edward Burne-Jones*.) Penelope is at her most formally experimental and teasing in her late fiction, but she gave some clues as to the interpretation of this novel to an enquiring reader, Bridget Nichols:

> The Gate of Angels is about the questions of faith and generosity
> . . . Dr Matthews is a portrait of Monty James. I set my novel in the
> Cambridge of 1912 because that was the height of the so-called
> 'body/mind controversy', with the scientists of the Cavendish in
> controversy with professing Christians, championed by James who
> was then Provost of Kings.

Dr Matthews, like M. R. James, tells ghost stories, and, in one of Penelope's intertextual serious games, tells one here to explain the bicycle accident to himself by means of a local haunting. He adds plausibility to it, by seeming to ground it in his own youthful experience, telling it in the first person, something James never did. 'Do I believe in such things?' Matthews asks himself, and goes on: 'Well, I am prepared to consider the evidence, and accept it if I am satisfied.' That places retain the evil that was done in them, and that apparently ordinary people, like Daisy, for whom the gate of Angels opens, may have some healing force of goodness in them, these were certainly things that Penelope believed. She also wants us to accept the miraculous as part of life.

The Gate of Angels was the fourth of Penelope's books to be shortlisted for the Booker, and it was on three other shortlists. Though it did not win, it received wonderful reviews, especially from other writers, and sold very well. Much was now expected of her. It was extraordinary enough to have started on a literary career so late, to have run it entirely on her own terms, only writing what she chose, never faltering either in excellence or variety; but perhaps the most remarkable thing of all was that her next and last novel, published when she was seventy-eight, should have been generally hailed as her masterpiece, and, despite its complexity and intellectual scope, become a bestseller on both sides of the Atlantic.

If *The Blue Flower* is certainly a novel and a work of the imagination, it is a most original one in that its hero and most of its characters were real people, yet it transcends the genres of biography and historical fiction: it seems to be an enquiry into what it means to be alive. With imperfect German but great concentration on what was germane to her artistic purposes, Penelope studied Mähl and Samuel's *Complete Works, Diaries, and Letters* (including letters to him) *of Novalis*, the Romantic poet. It took her two years, and gave her ample material to write the story of his tragically curtailed life, if that had been her intention, but it wasn't. What fascinated her was the blue flower itself. She is on record as saying that in an ideal life she wouldn't have gone to Oxford to read English, but would have become an artist. Much of her writing in *World Review* (and her first book, *Burne-Jones*) was on art. In the '70s, one of her many projects was a book on flower symbolism in the original pre-Raphael painters of the Quattrocento. In this she saw a Christian mysticism that went to the heart of her beliefs. It appears from the very chaotic drafts of *The Blue Flower* in her archive in Texas (where also is the folder on flower symbolism) that she wanted to incorporate the anachronical story of the discovery of the blue poppy in the high Himalayas in the early twentieth century by Colonel Eric Bailey – from whom it derives its botanical name, Meconopsis Baileyi – and a mysterious Jesuit priest. All this is the pollen that led her to the poet Novalis and his incomplete mystical novel *Heinrich von Ofterdingen*, the beginning of which she quotes teasingly in the wonderful seventeenth chapter 'What is the Meaning?': ' . . . I long to see the blue flower . . . ' In Novalis, the flower is a remnant of the golden age when plants and animals spoke and told their secrets to mankind. In a dream he sees it mutate into a sweet girl's face: 'Du hast das Wunder der Welt gesehen.' You have seen the wonder of the world.

Fritz, the young poet who has not yet rechristened himself, but is already for those around him a genius in whose presence 'everything is illuminated', finds his meaning and wisdom in Sophie, an absolutely ordinary Saxon girl, yet one who has moral grace, whose likeness cannot be taken, who is indefinable. If love is the answer to the first question expressed as a chapter-heading, how is it altered by the second: 'What is pain?' Sophie has 'opened the door' to Fritz, but now she succumbs to tuberculosis, undergoes appalling operations without anaesthetic, dies. Fritz is of little comfort or practical help to her during this time, though after her death he takes the symbolic name Novalis and writes his great philosophical poem *Hymns to the Night* in her memory.

Almost incidentally to its high themes, *The Blue Flower* recreates the whole fabric of life in eighteenth-century Prussia, food and drink, taxes and laws, roads, landscape, seasons, philosophy and salt mining, and establishes the characters of the twenty or so people closest to Fritz in the course of his *bildung*, with their own concerns and point of view, characters at every stage of development, so that for every reader there is one who speaks to his or her heart. Inexplicably it missed every British prize list when it came out in 1995, but the reviews were outstanding, again especially from other writers, and in the end-of-year round-ups it was book of the year, with 25 mentions, and went on to sell 25,000 copies in hardback.

Stuart Proffitt, Penelope's editor for her last four novels, did much to promote and advance her career, and her gratitude to him (and their warm friendship) is evident in the letters that survive. Her dream had been to be published in paperback, and this was realised with the advent of Collins' Flamingo imprint. It meant even more to her to see a stranger reading one of her books, and laughing at one of her jokes on the tube – a modest ambition perhaps, but one achieved. Her letters to Stuart demonstrate his devotion and kindness. She was distressed when he felt obliged to leave HarperCollins on a matter of principle not unconnected with the new owner. Still, Flamingo's excellent care of her continued under the new team of Philip Gwyn-Jones, Karen Duffy and Mandy Kirkby. They found time to escort her to the readings, signings, events and festivals, which she was becoming too frail, and would have been too shy, to attend alone. Another devoted editor who was to achieve much for her now came back into her life.

Several publishers, including the redoubtable Nan Talese at Doubleday, had already attempted to 'break' her in America, without great success. It was feared, and Penelope herself thought, that she was 'too British'. Chris Carduff had returned to publishing after some years spent editing *The New Criterion*, and was now employed at the Boston firm of Houghton Mifflin. He persuaded his boss, Janet Silver, to publish *The Blue Flower* in the US in 1997. It received a most enthusiastic and erudite review from Michael Hoffman, the lead and front cover of the *New York Times* Books section. That year for the first time the National Book Critics Circle Award was opened to foreign authors and Penelope won it, beating Roth's *American Pastoral*, DeLillo's *Underworld* and Charles Frazier's *Cold Mountain*. She particularly appreciated winning this prize, as it is judged by 700 book reviewers. There was some grumbling, as at her Booker Prize, for here again she was an unknown David against Goliaths, but it was politer, and soon to be silenced by a chorus of praise. *The Blue Flower* went on to sell 100,000 copies, and all her other novels followed it into print in America, permitting a timely retrospective of her career. Each of her books was admiringly reviewed as somebody's favourite. *The Bookshop*, in particular, after twenty years, but recapturing the 1950s, was now recognised as a British classic.

In fact her novels had brought back all the periods of her active non-writing life, of her long literary silence. *Human Voices* described her young woman's war service at the BBC, and the unique role that institution played in the upholding of truth and the national spirit in those years; *Innocence* recalled the 1950s, her young married years, when she was publishing Alberto Moravia and the younger Italian writers in *World Review*; *The Bookshop*, the failure of her early literary hopes and

experiment in country-living in the late 1950s; *Offshore*, so redolent of the
early 1960s and London's river, her lowest point; *At Freddie's*, her first
teaching job, and the London stage in the days before the National
Theatre, when, incidentally, she was beginning her self-apprenticeship
to become a writer. Neither should her last three 'historical' novels,
including *The Blue Flower*, be assumed to be free of autobiographical
elements: Nellie in *The Beginning of Spring*, Daisy in *The Gate of Angels*,
Fritz's mother, all have aspects of Penelope, and her child characters
always owe much to her own children. In choosing her periods she was
chiefly guided, as she declared in interviews, by the wish to write of
moments of optimism and ideological ferment, 'when people really
thought things might get better', when the debates between science and
religion, revolution and the unalterable, had not yet apparently ended
in atomic bombs, tyranny and unbelief.

From the first, as we see everywhere in these letters, Penelope was
most conscientious in undertaking the duties inherent in being a writer
of reputation. Though she never enjoyed committees, she worked for
PEN, the Arts Council, and later became Fellow of the Royal Society for
Literature. A cause near her heart was that biographers should be
recognised by grant-awarding bodies as creative writers. She was
successful in fighting for this, as in her energetic support of Public
Lending Right, which very belatedly ensured that writers were paid for
the lending-out of their books by libraries. Her friendships with Francis
King, Sybille Bedford and Michael Holroyd originated in this work. She
met J. L. Carr, Thomas Hinde, Edward Blishen and A. L. Barker (known
as Pat, author of short stories of fine sensibility, not to be confused with
the equally estimable novelist Pat Barker) through her tutoring of fiction
courses for the Arvon Foundation. She encouraged and advanced the
careers of other writers not only through her tireless reviewing (there
was almost no English paper she didn't write for, reviewing regularly for
the *Evening Standard*, the *London Review of Books*, the *TLS*, the *Tablet*, the
New York Times and the *Washington Post*) but also by judging for most
of the literary prizes, biography, poetry and fiction, including, twice, the
Booker. She argued fiercely for Roddy Doyle's *The Van*, and Magnus
Mills' *The Restraint of Beasts*, managing to get them both onto the
respective shortlists. Among other young writers she championed were

Glyn Maxwell, Candia McWilliam and Claire Messud. Among those who reviewed her, or whom she reviewed, and who are represented in this collection are Hilary Mantel, the biographer Richard Holmes and Sir Frank Kermode.

From 1995 onwards, as she entered her eighties, though she continued to work as hard as ever, and retained her all her formidable intellectual acuity, Penelope's health and mobility began to decline. She suffered badly from rheumatism and from the slow weakening of her heart. She was no longer able to get to the British Museum reading room where she had spent so many happy years in research, following the circuitous trails which led to her biographies and later novels. The beautiful round reading room itself closed, and she couldn't contemplate transferring her affections to the new British Library. Now for the first time she began to complain of a lack of inspiration. It troubled her that she had accepted a generous advance for a new novel, the idea for which stubbornly refused to come to her. In the meantime she wrote, to commission, her wonderful introductions to *Emma*, *Middlemarch* and, repaying the debt to friendship, J. L. Carr's *A Month in the Country*, and also her amazing last three stories. How to classify her short fiction? Are they fables, parables, folk-tales, poems even? She insisted that each demanded more effort to write than a novel. They range across the whole world in setting, from New Zealand to Tasmania, Mexico, Istanbul (twice), Brittany, Jerusalem (by implication), Iona, far Somerset, the Home Counties, London, and across four centuries.

Though under no external pressure to repay her advance, in 1999 she gratefully accepted her publishers' suggestion that she collect her stories into a volume. The title, *The Means of Escape*, was supplied by Janet Silver of Houghton Mifflin, who considered that the story provided a unifying theme, which Penelope doubted, feeling rightly that the stories are as unsettlingly different from one another as are her novels. Two at least of them could have been novels. Christian motifs proliferate throughout them: the uninvited guest, the unfaithful servant, the unawakened soul, the buried talent. There are ghosts and hauntings. There are two great cries of protest: 'She belonged to the tribe of torturers. Why pretend they don't exist?' and 'Make no mistake, you pay for every drop of blood in your body.' Yet there is always the faith that good will prevail. Through character or fate, self-knowledge and grace may be gained or regained. There remains, against all odds, the possibility of salvation.

The Means of Escape was written during the concentrated struggle to perfect *The Blue Flower*. It is rich enough to have become the vicarage novel that Penelope was perhaps always on the verge of writing. The story is characterised by a black humour. Evil uncomprehended by innocence flickers through it – a stench, a hood, an elected silence. The shameless may escape, the dutiful never.

The Likeness was to have been a novel based on the Ionides family from *Burne-Jones*. It is now a romantic high comedy, based on misunderstanding. *The Axe*, Penelope's first published fiction, from 1975, is both a memorably chilling ghost story in its own right and a brilliant 'take' on Melville's *Bartleby the Scrivener*. *At Hiruharama* is an example of the anecdote or tall tale, which evades the narrator as it assumes a moral and pictorial solidity of its own. *The Prescription* is a violent fable about dishonesty. *Not Shown* hints at an English murder.

Penelope's three great last stories were written and published in 1997 and 1998. They are absolutely ambiguous; yet there is an urgency to be understood in them. They seem to be about inspiration at different stages of life: the human cost of joy. *Desideratus* sees a resourceful boy wrest the coin he has been given from the pallid ghost of his weaker self. He must earn his talent through travail. *The Red-Haired Girl*, unwilling model to an uncomprehending painter, tells him, before she disappears, what he's missed in his search for the picturesque: 'You don't know what I want and you don't know what I feel.' In *Beehernz*, a famous conductor who has become a hermit to block out the noisy music of the world, hears a young woman sing a folk setting of Goethe's *Gefunden*: 'I went in the woodland/Nothing to find' but it goes on 'I saw in the shadow/A stone-flax stay'. Too long a prisoner of his mute keyboard, he has recaptured his visionary sense, symbolised by a blue wayside flower, the linseed.

Though all attempts to describe and define a life are doomed to failure, it is tempting to see Penelope's as describing a dramatic arc from dazzling early success, a promising career as literary editor, a comfortable, if hubristic, establishment in Hampstead, down to destitution and humiliation, the half-way house for the homeless, and thence ever upwards, by dint of hard work, study and inspiration, until at eighty she was at the peak of her achievement, reputation and earnings, passing for the first time, as she ruefully remarks in the letters, into a higher tax bracket. Her one final ambition was to see in the new Millennium. This also she achieved. Several of the series of letters follow her right up to the days before her first stroke, when she was eighty-three, busier than ever, reviewing for papers on both sides of the Atlantic, judging a prize, preparing a new American edition of *The Knox Brothers* (a family of which she was by now the most remarkable member) and proof-reading her stories, *The Means of Escape*, for publication by Flamingo and Houghton Mifflin. She survived a month longer, able to talk a little to her children, until she suffered two further strokes and died on 28 April 2000. She is buried in the churchyard of St Mary's, Hampstead.

It occurred to me, during my researches for this book, to wonder where she worshipped when, at her lowest point, she lived offshore on *Grace*. The boat is described in the book as being moored on Battersea Reach; in reality it had been moored at Dakin's yard, World's End, but directly opposite St Mary's Battersea. Inside that lovely eighteenth-century church, the first thing that one sees, among a wonderful collection of modern stained-glass windows, Blake and the grain of sand, Turner, Franklin and the promise of happiness, on the left side of the door is a large and beautiful blue flower.

Terence Dooley

A NOTE ON THE TEXT

Penelope's handwriting is clear, graceful and original, her own creation. In her youth it was a simplified italic, each letter carefully formed and rarely joined up to the next. Later, the characters connect more often, though never for a complete word; it gives an artistic impression. It is a pleasure to read and transcribe, because there is never any doubt about what she has written.

Her punctuation has been preserved, with its occasional inconsistencies, or survivals from an earlier era (Mrs: for Mrs), its underlinings for emphasis or titles, its capitals for jokes. The ampersands, which looked so well in the blue ink italic, look like so many snails in black print, therefore they are now *and*. She wrote *thankyou* as one word, and I have not altered this.

Individual letters haven't been cut, save in one or two cases where the fun being had at someone's expense would never have been intended to be read by that person. She sometimes misspelt names; these have been corrected where possible.

I have kept the correspondences separate, in this way the nuances of the different relationships and the tone of voice may be better appreciated. A rough chronology has been followed in both sections. Penelope rarely included the year in her dates, so internal ordering has been more than usually difficult. It is now as accurate as we can get it, relying on family knowledge and internal evidence.

I.

FAMILY AND FRIENDS

Hugh Lee ('Ham')*

27a Bishop's Road
London, N6
21 February [*c.*1990]

Dearest Ham – No-one but you – absolutely no-one – would find any old letters in a suitcase of their father-in-law's at the bottom of the carcase of an old freezer. You're someone to whom things happen.

It's kind of you to suggest that I might write my autobiography but I shan't do that as I've written something about my family already and also about what (in the tedious little talks I sometimes give) I call my work experience – I used to regret that all the letters and photographs we had went down to the bottom of the Thames, but I see now I'm better off without them. The reason is that as my step-mother gets more and more hazy in her nursing-home (but this is a blessing to <u>her</u>, I truly think, because she doesn't <u>worry</u> as much as she used to do) we've brought home all the old papers from her flat and I'm beginning to go through them, and it's such a sad business, so many forgotten names, so much wasted effort, that I've decided I simply mustn't leave my children to go through what I've accumulated, I <u>must</u> give them to the NSPCC who bring a green bag round every week to collect the waste paper.

I don't know why I'm rambling on like this,

love to you both. – Mops.

I had to change my handwriting because the bank wouldn't accept my signature

---

* One of a set of London friends recently down from Oxford. PMF wrote to him as he was posted round the country in the early years of the war and after they resumed their friendship in the 1970s.

'*PUNCH*'
10 Bouverie Street
London, EC4
5 October [1939]

Dear Ham,

I spiritually drank your health the other day by ringing the bell (this is a very well-appointed office) and sending for all the books on ballet from the Art Room and a lettuce sandwich – I read them all through and could now maintain a conversation on the subject with almost anyone – but perhaps as a result of this indulgence I caught 'flu, and had to take a sinister lightning cold cure which has made me very hazy, and rather the colour of a cream cheese. On the other hand I feel even more sympathetic about your tooth-ache, and about Yorkshire too, I am told the wildernesses literally howl there.

I am waiting in agonies for the reports of Hitler's speech, as any reference to unknown weapons will hypnotize me with fear. The sub-editor from Lowestoft, who is sitting opposite me, has a permanent flush this morning, and is even glowering.

Putting aside the idea that he has been drinking, I think he has heard something to my discredit, or perhaps suspects me of making advances to him. I have discovered that he is a gadget fiend, and has made a penknife and magnifying glass combined, out of old razor-blades. A magneto would be nothing to him. He is now with angry gestures filling his pipe with tobacco, and I can't make up my mind whether to warn him that this will make me feel sick – owing to the lightning cold cure – or whether to collapse suddenly on the floor later on, which should teach him a sharp lesson, and prevent his smoking Craven Mixture for some time to come.

In spite of the somewhat ominous news I am in one of my optimistic moods, in which I feel that it will be a short war. Please concentrate on agreeing with this,

love,

Mops.

16 *Avenue Close**
Avenue Road, NW8
13 October [1939]

Dear Ham,

This is another letter which you needn't read if you don't care to
as it only expresses the fact that I am melancholy and terrified of the
celebrated Blitzkrieg. I start at noises in the street, sleep with my head
under the bedclothes, and listen to the owls hooting – they really do
hoot around this block of flats – with gloomy relish. When I get as
depressed as this though, I must get better soon, it's a law of nature –
but the really annoying thing is my fondness for doughnuts. An
organisation called the British Doughnut Association has sent us a
pamphlet announcing that a representative will call at the office with
some samples of the new type of doughnut to get our opinion – now
this was 3 days ago, and I suspect that the doughnuts have been
intercepted either by the Advertising Department or by the publishers,
or by the sub-editor from Lowestoft, who is something of a gross
feeder – at all events I have seen nothing of them, and I have an
unfortunate tendency to pin my hopes to small things.

I haven't seen Oliver,** for he has departed to Cambridge, I think
on a bicycle. I admire, and always have admired, the way he quarters
the countryside. He ought to be a Transport Officer really,

love,
Mops.

16 *Avenue Close,* NW8
[1939]

My dear Ham,

I hear you are being visited by Mrs Breakwell, which I suppose is a
refresher course in itself. She went flying down to Devon on full sail
with the bomb bags trailing after her. I should very much like a list of
the objects these bags contain.

---

  * PMF's parents' house.
** Oliver Breakwell.

Here is a photo of Oliver, Mrs B., Kate and me entertaining the famous French soldiers at an al fresco meal in Hyde Park. They ate cakes and drank lemonade which one of them declared, with a forced smile, was the champagne of England.

Oliver has become very wild and spends his time disappearing in a cloud of dust on his motor-bicycle and reappearing with a headache next day after an evening at The Nuthouse. The Nuthouse is a night-club, and I should say what the Daily Mirror calls a haunt. You frequent haunts, and Oliver accordingly frequents the Nuthouse.

The mulberry tree at the back of the flats has suddenly produced a large crop of fruits which, though you live in the country and don't realise it, is a very pleasant surprise in London, so we have made quantities of jam and jelly.

On second thoughts this seems a remarkably dull bit of news, so perhaps if I have sunk to this level I had better stop.

There seem to be rather too many bombers over your part of the island, so you might learn to dodge,

love,

Mops.

'PUNCH'
10 Bouverie Street
London, EC4
30 October [1939]

My dear Ham,

I don't know if you are still in Yorkshire. I can't believe that you are, everybody seems to be so mobile nowadays, and to flash to and fro past or through the metropolis leaving me glued to my desk. There is something to be said for remaining static, however, for it gives one an illusion of being nailed to the mast, or steadfast at the post. A message has just come through from the censor forbidding us to mention the state of the weather in any part of the country – the proprietor apparently takes this seriously and has qualms about the only too familiar snow scene which is appearing on the cover of the Christmas number. – The sub-editor from Lowestoft has lost a good deal of his timidity since he came into the office during a thunderstorm (did you have one in Yorkshire, presuming that you are in Yorkshire?) and found me crouching under the desk among the back numbers. Further, he actually came to dinner and made several independent, though not original remarks, until he was silenced by a large cigar which my father gave him. Though he draws a considerable salary he only has bread and cheese for lunch, and lives in Fleet Street to save tube fares – what can he be saving up for? I believe he is a Gauguin at heart and yearns for the South Seas, but isn't quite abandoned enough to go there until he has got enough for a return ticket.

I have no news at all, for I haven't seen Oliver and I missed Janet* on her last leave, though I believe she is going to abandon the Air Force if she can. I have a practicable idea however, which is to exchange the Magna Carta for all these aeroplanes instead of paying cash. It's at New York anyway, and the Americans seem to be fonder of it than we are,

love,

Mops.

Punch Office
10 Bouverie Street
27 November 1939

My dear Ham,

I can't bear to think of you being so uncomfortable. You ought to curl up on silk cushions like a cat and exist against a luxurious background. The only thing I can say from my brother's experience in camp, is that it gets better – that is, the discomfort – not worse, but I suppose this is due to a gradual dulling of the faculties, known as merciful oblivion. As everything is so horrid, I can think of nothing consoling to say, except that I am glad you are not in the Navy, and being sunk every day. Sean and Oliver and I were at the ballet the other night and very much regretted your absence, especially when the

---

* Janet Probert, a friend.

Lac des Cygnes was danced in a highly kitchy manner with clouds of dust and reverberating thuds.

Lowestoft sits opposite, basking in the warmth and sucking his pipe. I am getting very fond of him as we have a kind of tacit arrangement by which I hold him responsible for the bad news in the paper every morning, and he leads me to look on the brighter side of things. 'It is no good' he says 'being pessimistic.' With that, and a piece of chocolate, I am able to face the morning.

Please forgive this odious piece of paper. I love apologising for the quality of the paper and ink when writing a letter, as it is so perfectly pointless.

love,

Mops.

'PUNCH'
10 Bouverie Street
London, EC4
1 January 1940

My dear Ham,

Happy new year (the Sergeant Major here actually <u>says</u> 'the compliments of the season', but I never met anyone else who did). I think the gramophone records are wonderful, I didn't know either of them before, due to my ignorance, but I took to them like a duck to water and play them all day, and even try to sing them in the bath, which is disastrous of course, and it was better when I stuck to 'Run, rabbit, run' with my own variations; only I do love the records and it is now one of my premier ambitions to go to hear Otello in the flesh.

I went to an alarming dinner party at the Hoods the other night. For want of other conversation I told Mrs H. (quite accurately) that I couldn't abide bulldogs, and insulted the horrid but apparently precious specimen which she keeps. Now she is stalking up and down and saying that intelligence is all very well but other things are more important. I was terrified of Sinclair too. He looks so dry I want to wash him; but this may be my feline instincts coming to the top. Oliver was kind and covered up my social errors as well as he could. Jean is up in London today and we are all going to the Toy Symphony with Kenneth Clark conducting.

I gather a lot of rum was issued to the troops at Christmas, so I hope that if you didn't get leave you at least passed the time in a vaguely pleasurable daze. I was at Oundle, where I had to appear in a charade as a British slave dressed in a bathing suit and Mrs Fisher's fur coat, which, it seems, disgusted and appalled the audience. I am back at the office now and have made the room so hot, by the simple process of shutting all the windows, that Mallet has fallen fast asleep,

love, Mops.

Ministry of Food
Great Westminster House
Horseferry Road
London, sw1
11 June 1940

My dear Ham,

Thankyou very much for writing – I wish I could have come down last Sunday but I had to stay here and draft a message for the Minister to send to the National Association of Bee-Keepers – and though I have applied all the brains and training I have to the question I am unable to think of anything, though I am very fond of honey in the comb. I've got a new straw hat, such a one, with red roses, which seems vaguely connected with the subject somehow.

My ideas of Officers' Messes are based on lurid films and novels by P. C. Wren which I read under the bedclothes at school. They include quarrels of honour, with cards and glasses all over the floor, and horses jumping on, and off, the table, and also jackboots and being roasted alive by Roundheads. I do hope you are enjoying yourself. I suppose, however good and broadminded you are, there is some satisfaction in being an officer and superior by profession to so many people. Have you a comic batman, I wonder?

You will be pleased to hear that I haven't been to any films at all lately as I have a vague feeling that it is wicked, and I expect I shall gradually lose the habit and be able to despise films as you do, though I suppose not with the same fine scornful profile.

Rawle* is coming up to London on Saturday to get made into an officer – then we shall have to go through this saluting trouble all over again – but I believe I am a 2nd lieutenant now too as we have our own tasteless rifle corps to defend the Ministry against assaults and I seem to be embodied in it,

much love,

Mops.

Ministry of Food
Great Westminster House
Horseferry Road
London, sw1
29 June [1940]

My dear Ham,

How dare you resent anything to do with the rustics of Herefordshire? Little do you realise that my grandfather, the bishop, was curate of Kington in Herefordshire and I have spent my holidays there ever since I can remember, and it is in fact the only part of the country I can bear and the only part that makes me placid, with fat horses, fat haystacks, fat rustics and a happy lack of anything famous or distinguished. It is odd that you say that there are some trees that you take to be limes, there are some just outside our cottage, a kind of avenue, green as you say and charming, and one of our few discussions there – there aren't many subjects of conversation, you see is the great question of whether they are limes or not. Somebody always suggests hornbeams towards the end of supper.

Well, everyone here says

1. That Liverpool docks have been reduced to ashes.

2. That Chamberlain, Col. Lindbergh and Laval have got together and are arranging peace terms.

---

* PMF's brother, Rawle Knox.

3. That the Germans are arriving in motor launches and amphibious tanks on July 2nd.

4. That Halifax is to be dismissed and replaced by Lord Strabolgin. I want a dog more and more. I suppose the price of Pomeranians has gone up as all the dogs have been shot in Germany, but after the war I shall save up and buy one nevertheless. I have got into the frame of mind, you see – I don't know why – when I think the war will possibly come to an end one day.

I hope you come to London soon, through the agency of Cyril Falls or any other way,

love,

Mops.

> *Ministry of Food*
> *Great Westminster House*
> *Horseferry Road*
> *London, sw1*
> *8 July [1940]*

My dear Ham,

Thankyou very much for your letter, and I would have answered your first one before if I hadn't thought you wanted me not to – and I am very nervous of saying anything where people's feelings and sensibilities are concerned, which often makes me appear even stupider than I am.

I don't know exactly what you feel about me. I have always been very fond of you and very proud on the occasions when you broke your three silences and spoke to me, and I have always looked forward to seeing you when you come up to London. I hope I shall again. I don't know whether Oliver ever told you that ever since I broke my engagement* I have been mixed up in a rather stupid and unsatisfactory way, I suppose, but it is the only thing I can do, it goes on and on and it makes me appreciate my friends all the more.

---

* The last of several not very serious 'engagements'.

Oliver has left the flat to go and stay with Kate, and in the meantime Mrs B. gave an amazing party at which your sister was a tower of strength with the coffee, wine and cutlets and there was a strange babel of languages – Mrs B. pre-eminent in a torrent of mixed French and English, easily drowning the harassed player at the piano. Jouky was present, but did not sing.

I had a dreadful time at Guildford on Sunday with the L.D.V's.* The colonel lent me his very large horse to 'see the fun' – i.e. 50 men crawling about on a parachute scheme in the height of misunderstanding and confusion – but it bolted and scattered the people disguised as Germans – the colonel however referred to me afterwards as 'the little secret weapon' at tea-time.

I have never been to Somerset. What is it like?

love,

Mops.

> 16 Avenue Close,
> Avenue Road, NW8
> 20 July [1940]

My dear Ham,

Thankyou very much for your letter. It is difficult to follow you in your rapid course through Devon and Somerset but I hope that wherever you have pitched your tent now you are comfortable and at ease. I am sitting in the Breakwells' flat and Mamma is lying back on the sofa which is draped with an Indian carpet and telling Oliver he is repressed – she has just been appealing to a bus-load of people to throw away Oliver's stick, to show that she doesn't believe in the Guards and that French people are understanding and sympathetic.

I have nearly got the sack from my office but I had a last-minute reprieve and I am being protected by the Editorial Officer who is prepared to swear I am indispensable. Meanwhile I am sitting everyday and answering letters to the minister threatening to strangle him if the writers aren't immediately given more tea.

---

* Local Defence Volunteers.

Raven is in the Field Security now which gives him an excellent excuse for stopping all conversation as subversive ('it's my job now, you know') and talking about himself and his latest, and quite dreadful, French girlfriend – supported violently by mamma, of course.

We had our very last champagne party before the invasion the other day – I wish you had been there, as I am all for celebrating, and fiddling while Rome burns,

Hugh and Oliver send their love and Hugh adds that he owes you half a crown,

love,

Mops.

> *Ministry of Food*
> *Neville House*
> *Page Street*
> *London,* sw1
> 22 August [1940]

My dear Ham,

The lobster salad poisoned me, and there may be a moral in it somewhere. It was extremely nice to see you. You wouldn't, or at any rate didn't, tell me anything about what you have been doing, but you looked well and didn't repeat any stories about sergeants and I consider that these are two excellent signs. I missed however the moment at 5 o'clock on Sunday afternoon when you read through the cinema announcements and condemn them all in round terms.

Mrs B.'s French soldiers, I am relieved to say, are expecting to go back to their country next week and then perhaps an autumnal peace will descend on Stamford Court.

I went to a dreadful diplomatic party on Monday night. We had to eat more lobster salad, small biscuits and drink a weak decoction of punch, alleged to be prepared in the Czechoslovakian manner. This was in honour of the Czech minister to Paris and his wife, who had arrived in England and we all had to sit around on gilt chairs and listen to their tale of privations and desperate escapes. This lasted half an hour and was much interrupted by showers of tears from the wife which mingled with the enormous pearls she was wearing and shook the whole sofa till it tottered on its little gilt legs. The conversation was entirely in French and everyone seized the opportunity to make idiomatic exclamations. In the end it turned out that she had had no difficulties at all except losing a fur coat and having only room for nine when she was travelling with an entourage of eleven. But everyone seemed overcome at this disaster and the insult to the diplomatic corps. No-one paid any attention to me except the poodle. Fortunately the household has no bulldog.

I suppose it is quite useless for me to say that I hope you are not in too much danger, as you quite certainly are, and as you said the other night, it's necessary to talk about serious things, but also quite impossible,

Love,

Mops.

Ministry of Food
Neville House
Page Street
London, sw1
[September 1940]

My dear Ham,

I hope by this time you have heard all about Freddie and that he is safe and well, though his flute is lost, and he is very tired. I saw him in the Café Royal the other night with Kate and he looked the colour of cream cheese but otherwise just the same as usual. I haven't heard from Oliver about it as he is off down to the country for three weeks, but I am afraid it may have an even worse effect on him than on Freddie, as is often the case with catastrophes.

I wish you didn't always go to places where danger and boredom are mixed in equal proportions and I have a suspicion, though you don't say so, that you don't much care for your companions. It is bad enough being forced into uniform, every war does that, but every war doesn't drag you to uncongenial watering-places with unsympathetic spirits.

I hope you come to London soon, although it is true that the outer suburbs are falling down like a pack of cards, to the great joy of the town planners who are now revealed in their true colours as ghouls laughing over the wreckage and erecting garden cities with communal health centres, peoples theatres, and spacious boulevards. You may wonder how I know anything about town planning, but it so happens that Mr McAllister, my small short Scotch problem boss, is a mad town-planner, besides having stood for Parliament and appeared as a Tam o' Shanter in the pictures in the early days of the talkies. If you don't know what a problem boss is you should look at the Secretary's page in the Ladies Home Journal which tells you how to deal with them. Mr McAllister is what is known as a caution, it seems that he has been engaged at various times to practically all the short women doctors in Scotland, or all the ones shorter than he is.

I am falling out of favour with Mrs B. who calls me a frivolous little idiot because I had forgotten to post her 25 photographs of the French soldiers and also didn't appear (mercifully) in a colour film taken of them and her in Hyde Park at a picnic. I am afraid that during the winter hibernation she will come to dislike me intensely but you must support my cause, if you will.

Jean* is up today, but she is just fluttering through London as her parents' natural distrust of the metropolis has now greatly increased.

I now have to write an article on communal feeding for a paper called 'Our Empire'. I rang up 'Our Empire' a few minutes ago, but, ominously enough, it wasn't there,

much love,
Mops.

Ministry of Food
24 September [1940]

My dear Ham,

The news about Bill is dreadful, and as I don't quite know how well you knew him I, as usual, don't quite know what to say for fear of treading on your feelings, and so I shan't say anything at all.

---

* Jean Fisher, a friend.

I hope at least you are stagnating in Devonshire, that is the quality for which it is famous, and that there are apples, red cows, and the beautiful undulating landscape which I detest, and that your general stupidity, which I don't believe in, is in harmony with the pervading quiet. All the same it will be nice when you come back, if you do, to the quite alarming noises (alleged to be due to a new anti-aircraft weapon) of the London night.

Mrs Breakwell now hates me so much, and says such curiously far-fetched things, that I don't think it matters what I do at, or about, 24 Cornwall Gardens – but I forgive her everything, as she has to spend her nights in such appalling conditions.

Dear Ham, I wonder if by now you are imbued with an offensive spirit, or if after all you have decided to fold your hands.

We have had a large oil-canister bomb which came through my bedroom window, so that I have a twisted piece of metal as a souvenir, but I was not there at the time and so although all the windows in the flat collapsed I did not.

I am wretched as I have got a pair of red gloves against the winter, as they say, which make me sneeze continually. It isn't the colour, because my blue ones make me sneeze, too,

love,
Mops.

There is a photo of me somewhere, I went into the box-room to find it but a large naval gun blew in the window and I retreated in disorder, but I will find it and send it you though it is horrid.

Long Meadow
Longdown
Guildford
6 October [1940]

My dear Ham,

I have not heard any more about Bill, but Oliver and Fred are convinced that he must be a prisoner of war and are doing all they can to find out through the Red Cross and through some mysterious friends of Fred's in Spain.

Do tell me some more about Devonshire. I like to hear about all the counties and it seems to me that you visit most of them.

Our land-mine has been removed, parachute, tassels, and all, without damaging Avenue Close, but on the other hand a bomb seems to have fallen very near Cornwall Gardens. Mrs B., however, has sunk into her hazy September melancholy and not even the return of Oliver from Chequers seems to arouse her.

We are down in the country getting some fresh air – that means that we all sit indoors, owing to the hurricane outside, and eat too much, and try to prevent the dogs getting on to the sofas or making nests in the Sunday Times. I must soon stagger out, however, and pick some wet Michaelmas daisies.

In ending a letter from the country I notice that people always say 'I must rush now to catch the post' – however, I have already missed the post by several hours, so I must just send my love,

Mops.

Ministry of Food
Great Westminster House
Horseferry Road
London, SW1
15 October [1940]

My dear Ham,

Thankyou very much for writing and for saying you aren't going to West Africa, an idea which alarmed me considerably, though if you had really made up your mind to it I would have pretended to like it.

Similarly, Oliver seems so delighted about going to Egypt that it doesn't seem worth while saying how unhappy I am about it and Mrs Breakwell, poor Mrs B., keeps pointing at soldiers of all ranks in the streets and saying why can't he go. I secretly feel the same, but what's the use, because Oliver is pleased as punch, literally like punch, he is effervescent.

I have had my brother on a week's leave. He slept in the passage, and the Danish cook evidently regarded him as a soldier billeted on us and ran the carpet-sweeper over him remorselessly.

We have had two more bombs on the block, one of them on the show flat, which now has a sign Luxurious Flats To Let swinging over a crater. I think my brother was really glad to get back to the peaceful battery in Scotland. I do love having him on leave but a week is no good at all, a brother should be there all the time like the church and the post-office.

If you get leave do ring up and tell me how to pronounce Melhuish for I have never known,

love,

Mops.

Ministry of Food
Great Westminster House
Horseferry Road
London, SW1
28 October [1940]

My dear Ham,

It is one of my minor ambitions to write as good letters as you do, but short of that I must just say how very glad I was to see you when you were on leave, and I may add that Oliver seemed as gay as a lark when I went to visit him on Sunday at the Duke of York's barracks, where he was sitting among the ruins drinking a large cup of horrid sweetened tea. Mrs FitzG also came and delighted the sergeant with her furs, pearls and smart black hat.

I do not believe Oliver is going to Egypt for a month or so at least anyway and I hope this means the end of one cause of misunderstanding. The person most to be pitied is Mrs B.

I haven't got another job yet so I am still at the ministry under the shadow of dismissal. Now that I am going however the rest of the staff are rather kinder to me as they have a comfortable feeling of superiority. Perhaps I shall even get a leaving present from them. A cake-stand or the works of John Masefield. How I hate the poem about the tall ship and the star to steer her by! I believe that you oughtn't to dissipate your hate in all directions but ought to save it for the Germans, but I can't help it.

I wish you didn't always have such horrid billets. I can't read whether it is a 'hutted' or a 'dratted' camp. Both, I am afraid. You <u>must</u> start calling it the 'War House', by the way,

    much love,

    Mops.

> *Ministry of Food*
> *Great Westminster House*
> *Horseferry Road*
> *London, sw1*
> 13 November [1940]

My dear Ham,

I have just discovered that I don't know how to write out B.N.C.* in full, but hope this will get to you, or at least lodge in the Sheldonian and be found there, or perhaps be handed away next door with the leaflets after the university sermon. You are lucky really to be in Oxford, and although when I left I swore never to be sentimental about it I always am, in fact I feel my soul becomes a positive watermeadow, but if you say you get nothing to eat these memories may not be part of your troubles.

I have just had letters from both Jean and Janet, independently pointing out how nice you have been to them, at some length.

I do not remember a saddler called Forty anywhere near George Street. Perhaps you had your historic 4-in-hand fitted out there.

I looked very closely at the pages of 'Picture Post' last week to try and find you in one of the backgrounds of the photographs of Pat Kirkwood visiting Oxford. I didn't see you. I hoped you might be leaning over a bridge observing one of your 3 silences, or disappearing in a cloud of dust, or rather water, on your motor-bicycle.

I have heard nothing from Mrs B., and I am afraid the incident of the tinned lobster, with her usual autumn melancholy and Oliver's departure to Egypt, has made a breach between us.

My brother suddenly appeared yesterday in the course of taking his men from Aberdeen to Portsmouth, and gave me a sandwich and some

---

* Brasenose College Oxford.

good advice. The men, who are all very simple lowlanders, were
fascinated by the moving model of Mickey Mouse at Waterloo station
and stood open-mouthed, grasping their lunch-money in their hands.

I hear that Oxford is violently gay and in general suggests those bits
in comedy films where you see champagne glasses superimposed on
merry-go-rounds to suggest dissipation, so when I come up I do hope
you will be able to show me some of it,

Love,

Mops.

P.S. By the way, do you ever regret your 30 men? I should really like to
know.

> 16 Avenue Close
> Avenue Road, NW8
> 26 November [1940]

My dear Ham,

Thankyou for your note – our telephone is going to be restored
soon under the character of Primrose 1256 but I do not quite know
when this will happen – it is a graceful official promise – meanwhile
the porter's lodge is Primrose 6741, but I shall be in the London
Library on Saturday anyway. I do hope you will have time to tell me
about the telephone battle – it is the only military activity which has
aroused my deepest interest so far. I had a terrible leaving party at the
Ministry of Food – the messenger cried, and we had Dundee cake –

love

Mops.

> The British Broadcasting Corporation
> Broadcasting House
> London. W1
> 5 December 1940

My dear Ham,

I was sorry and regretful not to be able to call in at the Cumberland
the other day – by the way I consider you were what I should call

rather cagey about these marble halls all the weekend long, and I was very disappointed not to be allowed to have tea or to book a theatre ticket or a piece of scented soap in the vestibule. However. What is even sadder as far as I am concerned is that I don't believe that this dubious organisation will let me go off to Oxford, or rather they may let me off late on Saturday but too late to make it worth while. I have had to sign their grasping contract which says that I have to devote all my time attention and skill, within reasonable limits, to the service of the Corporation. I don't consider Saturday afternoon reasonable, but I suppose it is thought, or rather deemed, as they put it, reasonable by the B.B.C.

So far as I can see I shall miss you, and Jeanie, and Janet all at one swoop and you will have a gay and perhaps even hectic party, according to my notions of Oxford, without me. I am very depressed too and need cheering up, as Rawle's embarkation leave finishes on Thursday and I have horrid moments when I wake up in the middle of the night and calculate just how many minutes he has left just like the end of the holidays used to be. Well I mustn't complain as it is tiresome,

love,

Mops.

16 *Avenue Close*, NW8
[On Broadcasting House headed paper]
11 February 1941

My dear Ham,

Of course I should like to hear from you very much, as I have often wondered lately how you are and what you have been doing, and however surprised I may be at being called a harpy, I am always flattered at being wanted as a correspondent.

In London we are all preparing to snipe at the Germans out of the dining-room windows, and poor Mrs Breakwell is a fountain of tears. I have become very common, and drink cups of tea in the morning,

love,

Mops.

16 Avenue Close
Avenue Road, NW8
19 March 1941

My dear Ham,

Thankyou for your letter. I am glad you are so well and enjoying the spring in Devon

> The pleasant cow, both red and white,
> I love with all my heart;
> She gives me cream with all her might
> To eat with apple tart –

And I am glad too that you are pleased with your move to Taunton, but as I thought you were there already I cannot feel the surprise I should.

Poor Janet is recovering from her measles and will soon move to London, to her special post in the bosom, so to speak, of the Minister.

The BBC is not exactly tedious, in fact it is rent with scandals and there are dreadful quarrels in the canteen about liberty, the peoples' convention, &c, and the air is dark with flying spoons and dishes. Miss Stevens poured some tea down Mr Fletcher's neck the other day. He knew Freud who told him the term inferiority complex was a mistranslation and there was really no such thing. I have to eat all the time to keep my spirits up, so I am getting quite fat. We are doing a programme called 'These Things are English', with the funeral of George V, beer, cricket, people singing in the underground &c. I think the people singing only express their own fierce triumph in getting the better of the London Passenger Transport Board. Besides, they all sing 'I wouldn't change my little wooden bunk for anywhere else in the world'. We had a mock invasion the other day. We were overpowered in 5 minutes as the officers in charge of the defence forgot their passes and couldn't get into B.H.* We have heard from Rawle to say he is safe in India. How horrid you were to me Ham! But all the same you have my best wishes – love – Mops.

---

* Broadcasting House.

P.S. The windows of Marshall and Snelgroves are entirely filled with scarves printed 'Grim but Gay' and 'This is a war of unknown warriors', papier maché bulldogs, and photographs of Winston Churchill with an old-fashioned sporting-gun.

25 Almeric Road
London, sw11
14 May [1978]

Dear Ham,

Thankyou so much for your card and kind message – I don't know <u>why</u> I put an entry into the Somerville mag, indeed don't remember doing so, but I'm glad now that I did. I'm not quite sure why I've taken to writing either, but it's better than weaving, hand-printing &c in that it represents a slight profit rather than a large loss for the amateur; also it struck me that I was getting to the end of my life and would like to write one or 2 biographies of people I loved, and novels about people I didn't like, put it that way.

My husband died the summer before last, but I'm lucky in that my elder daughter and her husband moved me into the ground floor of their house (the mortgage company's house) in Battersea, so I don't have to feel alone.

I don't know where <u>anyone</u> is except of course Janet and Jean, and have only heard distantly about Jimmy Fisher when my nephew was articled as a solicitor to Theodore G. – I remember him playing Bach however, through I don't know how many years.

I'd love to come and see you and your wife, and I'll ring up next week if I may.

love,
Penelope

2 October [1978]

Thankyou so much for a happy day at the Vineyard, for lunch, and for the opportunity to meet some of your family, your tortoises and your pictures, also for making me feel that enormous numbers of years haven't passed, after all – you were so kind and hospitable, and, whatever I feel about Bloomsbury, believe me I'm heart and soul in the success of the Newsletter – love and best wishes – Mops

[25 Almeric Road]
[6 November 1978]

Thankyou so much for the kind congratulations.* Prize unfortunately is going not to me but to someone who doesn't need the £££ – my publisher asked if the runners-up couldn't all have £100 and a package trip to Bulgaria, like the Miss World contestants, but they were adamant – hope you had a good grape-harvest – I made chutney out of my 6 bunches.
 love Mops

25 Almeric Road
London, sw11
2 May [1979]

Dear Ham and Penny.
 Thankyou so much – it was a lovely dinner which more than made up for the melancholy of realising how many years had passed. I could hardly believe the photographs (all mine went down to the bottom of the Thames when our houseboat sank on Chelsea Reach) – especially of Mrs Breakwell – As I was going home on the bus I remembered her ringing up my father to tell him to come to a Greek restaurant to meet Cyril Falls (how did he come into it?) – 'It's a Greek name – D-E.M.O.S, DEMOS' – 'yes', said my father sadly 'I'm familiar with the word.' However, I'm writing not really to open the endless store of anecdotes but to thank you and say how much I enjoyed myself – only I was sorry not to see a little more of William –
 love,
 Mops.

* On being shortlisted for the Booker Prize with *The Bookshop*.

76 Clifton Hill
London, NW8
[postcard]
15 January 1983

Thankyou so much for Charleston material, on which I most sincerely
think you've done wonders, I wish you absolutely all success in spite of
my reservations about some of the personnel.* Next Sat (22nd) I'm
going to Somerset and could I think find a copy of a play written by
one of my uncles** about L. Strachey, M. Keynes and when they were
all at Cambridge (*c.* 1910), from which you might take a <u>short</u> extract,
if that's not too remote, I'm not quite sure what kind of thing is
wanted really, I'll send it unless you say no (and if it hasn't mouldered
away in the damp wet country) – love Mops

Theale Post Office Stores
Wedmore, Somerset
22 January [1983]

My dear Ham,
    Alas, I can't find <u>any</u> of my notebooks at Theale at the moment –
they <u>were</u> in the garage, which is in the process of being turned into a
hen-roost – so Dilly's play (which is very good really) isn't to hand, but
I'm not sure you were very taken by the idea anyway! – I enclose a
couple of paragraphs in the hope of their being of use, but shan't <u>of
course</u> mind a bit if they're not wanted – there's always the WPB,† as
my grandfather used to say –
    love Mops
    P.T.O.

* In his new role as editor of the *Charleston Newsletter*, having helped in the campaign to
save Charleston House, once Vanessa Bell's home.
** Dilly Knox.
† Waste-paper basket.

I don't for a moment say that Q. Bell* &c are <u>rich</u>, but I <u>do</u> say that they've turned their family, and connections, into an industry, with the help of Michael Holroyd (who is always so kind and polite to us all) – and I think it allowable to feel that they might support Charleston out of all the £££ and dollars that they have made out of digging out and publishing their family skeletons. That's all I meant! But I think there are some others who think as I do. –

76 Clifton Hill, NW8
31 January [1986]

My dear Ham,

Do send me Quentin B.'s <u>Bloomsbury</u> and I'll write something (how long?) in case it's any use to the <u>Newsletter</u> – only I can't guarantee to be rude as he's such a good writer – I think it was awe, rather than hatred, that we shabby long-ago Georgians felt – and I <u>did</u> think, although this of course isn't something to be mentioned in the <u>Newsletter</u> that Nigel Nicolson in particular has made enough money out of his ma's old letters discovered by chance in the attic, &c, to pay for Charleston without any public subscription, but I've come to see I was wrong.

I do hope PEN** is allowed to come in the summer, though hitherto Francis King† has always shepherded us in a large coach, and I don't know whether Michael Holroyd would be prepared to do that – perhaps he <u>would</u>. We'll see!

Unfortunately, since the Arts Council subsidy was withdrawn, PEN has to spend half its time raising £££, like everyone else.

Must now summon up energy to go and see new grandchild, who has arrived in Holland, from Nicaragua, and I do so very much want to, only it's so cold –

love

Mops

---

  * Quentin Bell.
 ** The writers' association.
  † Novelist and, at that time, PEN committee member.

76 Clifton Hill
London, NW8
21 February [1986]

Dear Ham,

I didn't mean to criticise the Alpine Gallery exhibition – I only thought, & still have to think, that <u>Freshwater</u>* is rubbish, but then it was only intended for home consumption – it was a very good exhibition, very well hung in a difficult gallery not too well suited to it, and I was only sorry to miss you and Penny.

While on the subject of criticism, I've sent a notice of <u>Bloomsbury</u>, but if you don't like it do throw it away, or cut bits out. I'm glad to have the new edition anyway, although I do think it was disimproved as they say in N. Ireland.

If you use it, and want a bit about me, could you say that I'm a biographer and novelist (a word I still prefer to 'fictioneer'). <u>Burne-Jones</u> is the only biography I've done that is of any kind of interest to the Friends of C., I imagine, as after all he did paint Mrs Stephen pregnant with Vanessa in one of his Annunciations. That came out in 1975, and then I was given the Booker award in 1979 for <u>Offshore</u>. What a long time ago all this was. I've got a new novel about Florence coming out this autumn, I think – that is if Collins survives all its frightful present disputes.

I must tell you that when we went to Rodmell some of the PEN members were very disappointed, feeling that V. Woolf 'couldn't have done very well'. They expected it to be a house like Barbara Cartland's –
   love, Mops

Best wishes for the cellars.

27a Bishop's Road, N6
29 October [1988]

My dear Ham,

Thankyou so much for taking time to write what, I daresay, is your 101st letter of the day – I quite agree about the judges,** and

---

* Virginia Woolf's play.
** Of that year's Booker Prize. *The Beginning of Spring* had been shortlisted.

Michael Foot* drifted alarmingly in his (supposedly) summing-up speech, telling us repeatedly that Walter Scott was 'another conservative'. Also the stately corridors of the Guildhall were lined with police, as Salman R.** claimed that a threat had been made against his life and he was in imminent danger, still there were plenty of people there and Ria and I enjoyed ourselves very much and were taken about in a car from the Collins fleet, for the last time I fear. All this is quite good for business. But now I have to write another novel.

I'm glad that the envelope sale went so well, but now they'll expect you to produce another brilliant notion, you'll see.

Tommy feels he would like a tortoise, but I suppose the spring would be the best time

much love to you and Penny

Mops

> 27a Bishop's Road
> London, N6
> 26 January [1992]

Dear Ham and Penny,

Thankyou so very much in the first place for a splendid lunch, although I only discovered at the last moment that the rabbit was done with chocolate, in an improvement surely on the Mexican style. – And it was a great treat to meet Katharine – who may well not spell her name like that at all, so forgive me – she was so interesting, and also interested in everything that everyone else was doing, a great gift, not a very common one though.

In respect to Wittgenstein, I do hope you liked Ray Monk's biography – I had to help judge the Llewellyn Rhys Prize, the year before last, and I thought it far and away the best book, even though some good ones were sent in, perhaps because Ray M. is a philosopher himself, although, as it turned out, a young and cheerful one – anyway he got the prize and I am sure he deserved it.

---

 * The politician and former Labour MP.
 ** Salman Rushdie.

On the other hand, in respect to Skidelsky, I consider that Ham in fact has been singularly patient with this absurdly irritating man – I daresay he knows a lot about Keynes, but he'd have to be ashamed of himself if he didn't. Thinking about Skidelsky, and even feeling irritated by him, is a waste of precious time. – What I should like to know is what you're going to undertake next. If only there was someone with your persuasiveness and ruthless energy to defend the Public Library Service. Here in dreaded Haringey, to which Highgate unwillingly belongs, they're going to close all 7 branch libraries, the music and the mobile libraries, because reading isn't a priority leisure resource. It's all very depressing. Last year we managed to get the closures put off and I had to go to a party with non-alcoholic champagne made with pears, at 10 o'clock in the morning.

I so much enjoyed seeing you, thankyou once again for asking me – love
Mops

I take it the tortoise isn't stirring yet

> *27a Bishop's Road*
> *Highgate, N6*
> 11 September [c.1995]

Dear Ham and Penny,

What a lovely lunch party – if I wasn't afraid you might think me sentimental, or perhaps even feeble-witted, I could say how happy it made me to sit and talk to people I'm so fond of and to see you both again, and Janet, (this ought to be easy enough but hasn't proved to be so at all), and then Alyson,* who I hardly expected to come but of course she did, calm and smiling as ever, though whether she really always feels so calm I can't tell. I enjoyed myself so much, and still haven't said anything about the lunch itself, which, after Penny had said, as a kind of afterthought, 'I must do some cooking', seemed to produce itself by magic and was so delicious.

---

* Alyson Barr, a friend of Ham's whom PMF had met separately through the William Morris Society.

Janet's energy, and genuine interest in everything, is wonderful – I had thought it a merciful dispensation of nature that I like things less and less (though a few things more and more) but Janet makes me feel that's not so, and I must try to wake up a little.

Thankyou again, it was a Sunday to remember –

love, Mops

Just looking at the photograph of Jonathan Pryce as L. S. (he is a parent at the church school where Thomas and Sophie go) – I've never seen Carrington but I <u>have</u> seen Lytton Strachey and I think the Pryce make-up (I last saw him as Fagin) is very successful. But I suppose it's an easy one to do. –

[summer 1996 – after PMF's 80th birthday party]

Dear Ham –

I'm so glad you and Penny enjoyed the party and it was lovely to see you – the last day of summer.

By 'one stroke' I meant the kind of bike people used to have, with an engine you switched on when you were going uphill.

I don't agree that the children in my novels are precious. They're exactly like my own children, who always noticed everything.

As to 'may' for 'might', it is frightful, and we must do all we can to eradicate it. I think it's American and <u>they</u> think it's the subjunctive. –

Love to you and Penny – Mops

– Hibernating time now I imagine.

27a Bishop's Road, N6
15 February [late 1990s]

My dear Ham,

Thankyou so much for sending me the evidence, which only confirms what I've always thought, that the intensely unpleasant atmosphere of Bloomsbury (which must have come close to choking poor Leonard, for example) has lingered on in what racing people call their 'connections'. There is a Byzantine feeling, they will all end up poisoning each other. <u>That</u> is the moral.

Your statement of course is surely very restrained, as there are so many things you might have mentioned – the colour photographs in the Newsletter for example – but it was better to leave it as you have, as an absolutely clear account of a deliberate decision to make you resign. They took advantage of your not being there. Their next step, I suppose, will be to elect somebody as Chairman, or President, or whatever, of the Friends, in spite of having said that they weren't going to.

Judging from the few societies I belong to, something like this always happens – (I think Alyson would confirm that it particularly does at the William Morris). – Another example would be the Arts Council where Lord Gowrie seems to have jockeyed Michael Holroyd off the literature panel for no reason whatever except a love of pushing and shoving. But I'm sure that you were right to resign <u>now</u> and, as I find it difficult to imagine you without something to organise – something worth while, I should add – I suppose and hope that you're looking round, or at least leaving yourself open for the next field of action.

I myself can't organise the (proverbial) whelk-stall and you know I would never try to give advice, but sympathy I do give. You worked so hard and I don't think they could have got it all started at all without you. I wonder if they mentioned <u>that</u> at their committee meeting.

love to you and Penny – Mops

P.S. Our urban fox has gone lame and lies pathetically on the compost box – I don't like to disturb it to put any more leaves in – It also seems to have lost part of its brush.

27a Bishop's Road, N6
26 June [late 1990s]

Dear Penny and Ham,

Thankyou so very much for inviting me yesterday and the royal treatment you gave me, a lift back across 3 counties. It was such a nice lunch, and although I must restrain myself from talking about the quails, I did want to tell you that they are very special as far as I am concerned because my mother, who'd always been used to plain living and hard thinking and a large vicarage family, and was presented at court, as people used to be then, after she was married, had her one and only chance of trying quail that day at the palace and missed it, because the tray was taken away while her back was turned.

I do so hope everything goes well on Friday. I was just looking through the old Charleston mags yesterday evening and I <u>still</u> think they were better. There was an enterprising friendly feeling about them, but I suppose that belonged to the earlier stages. And I did like your colour pix, Ham –

many thanks and love to all of you –

Mops

Tina Fitzgerald*

Flat 5 144 Earls Court Rd.
London, sw5
Thursday [Easter, 1964]

Dearest Tina,

I do hope the crossing was all right, as we had a very stiff breeze in the Earls Court Rd. s.w.5. But Daddy tells me that Mrs Taylor had brought half a bottle of brandy and a tea-spoon to quell any cases of sickness – I don't know if she had to resort to this.

Of course you are very much missed especially by Maria who finds me boring in the extreme, but I'm not quite so tired to-day and will try to amuse her a bit better. We've got her a slip with lace, which seems to be a status symbol at the school. Meanwhile she went to confession all by herself which was quite an effort.

It's a lovely day here but cold. I see it's raining in Barcelona but I think this is a good thing as it will surely clear up and be really sunny when you arrive.

Do remember to wash your stockings or socks every night and please if you can get some Spanish playing cards, the ordinary cheap kind, you will, won't you? Señor Ramos can easily get a pack from a bar or a fonda, but perhaps he is not very approachable.

Mrs Morris's baby does not seem to have arrived yet, and there is a terrible smell of cooking from Mr Morris's kitchen. Some new people are moving in downstairs. Mrs Ladas says that a large family with fierce Alsatian and 3 ponies have moved into the Wright's house and she feels that between them and the Pages she would have no peace at all. The Alsatian is always on the lawn.

---

* PMF's elder daughter. The letters follow her through school trips, language courses, vacation nannying jobs, to Oxford, and finally to her move to the West Country.

I am off now to the Post Office to send the eggs to Wangford – choc. drops for Ralph and I knitted a pair of bootees for Martha.* Ria has gone to play two-balls with Jane.

Hasta la vista y diviértete bien

much love mum

Flat 5 144 Earls Court Road
London, sw5
Easter Saturday [1964]

Dearest Tina,

I do hope you will get this letter in time before you leave on the long trek home. The Express says it is sunny in Barcelona, so I hope you're in for a good Easter.

Great distress as Maria has just eaten all the pips of her orange, so none can be planted.

We went down to see the Boat Race at Hammersmith Bridge but arrived too late – which didn't matter because Cambridge was winning easily it turned out. We took the opportunity to look at Godolphin school again and it certainly didn't look too bad. We also visited the Doll Museum – were taken round by the excessively kinky proprietor with a flickering oil lamp. He showed all the dolls sitting round like corpses 'having a fish tea' as he said with a queer laugh – Maria misses you very much, and is very obstreperous. Valpy back on Tuesday.

I have been asked to coach a Buddhist girl, but she wants to come here, so I can't do it; such a pity as it would have been money for nothing.

Longing to see you and hear about your trip. Hope you are keeping Miss Taylor in order.

love from Mum

X

* The future actor Ralph Fiennes and his sister, Martha, Christina's god-daughter.

Squalid Council Estate
[7 April 1965]

Dearest Tina,

I wasn't able to say the many things I intended in the Lighthills'
hall – just as well I expect – but I must say now that I miss you very
much – as we all do – and what to do without you I cannot think, but
I do hope you may get some amusement of it at least. I thought you
looked exceedingly nice when you went off in the white stockings. I'm
afraid I'm not at all successful, as a mother, in not getting on your
nerves: but I do love you very much. It's so queer with no voice
coming from your room.

Maria was asleep when I got back, worn out with the excitement
of your departure. I ought to go to see Mme. Aubrey in hospital
to-morrow, but it seems hard on her to drag her all that way. I'm not
quite sure what to do. One of my ivy plants looks as though it's dying:
I must sneak out by night and see if I can get some more earth from
the Agnes Riley gardens.

Please don't be depressed by the thought of our flat &c, I know it
isn't grand, but I am sure we'll be able to manage so she* doesn't
notice too much. The Lighthills' carpet doesn't meet properly in the
hall anyway. But I did rather fall for the Professor, he's just like a
professor in a comic. Anyway it was very kind of them and better by
far than struggling up from s.w.4.

I am dying to know what life is like in Avenue du Cèdre (only one
cedar presumably) and look forward very much to a letter; I've nothing
to say in this one as you see, but wanted to tell you how much I was
thinking of you. I feel so low, but this won't do, and is not the right
attitude of mind. I really want you to have a rest, and a good time if
at all possible, as you've been so very tired lately. – We'll send on the
Musical Express as I see it's all a great crisis as to whether Cliff is top
or not. I'm surprised he's celebrating with champagne – I thought he
was a non-drinker and non-smoker?

Poor Daddy aghast at the budget.

much love from us all Mum XXX

---

* Tina's French exchange partner, Milène.

185 Poynders Gardens, sw4
[10 April 1965]

Dearest Tina,

So glad to get your letter even though it was rather a sad one and while I think of it the Lighthills were very pleased that you had written to thank them, it was a good idea.

I think you are facing up very bravely to the horrors of staying in a large French family – so much more efficiently than I did for instance – I was always in tears and then I got hungry in the middle of the night and went and got some cold potatoes out of the kitchen and the Italian cook was accused of stealing them. José sounds nice, though.

I do hope all will be well at the ski-ing, perhaps the brother will be nice, though I don't feel inclined to bet on this. I think it <u>rather odd</u> of Madame to be away when you came – a relief in a way though, I suppose. You seem to be managing well with the French language though.

You say it's not like what you thought, but it does sound rather like a French family, all the same. I agree it's a pity they live in quite such style, but you'll do quite different things with her – sightseeing and packed lunches – and I'll try and cook something really nice in the evening and it'll be something quite different for her – also we'll give her something to do all the time, even if it's only getting birdseed from Woolies.

I do rather envy you going up into the mountains, I always feel so well there, and am <u>longing</u> to hear about the ski-ing – I'm amazed that Madame is ski-ing too, no dull domestic duties.

Maria and Daddy and I miss you very much. Maria recalls with nostalgia the time when <u>I</u> was away (so much preferable) and you cooked such nice things and had Cornflakes every day. She's bought a cuckoo clock with her gift voucher, which hiccups at the quarters as poor Daddy dropped it while trying to put it up, and there were many tears, but now all is well and she's gone to Titia's party in her new dress. What does Milène wear by the way?

We went to see Mme. Aubrey in hospital – grim ward with dying patients grasping for fumigation bottles – but Ria rather liked it.

much love
Mum
X

185 *Poynders Gardens, sw4*
15 April [1965]

Dearest Tina,

Thankyou so much for your lovely letters and the p.c.* I could hardly believe there'd be <u>another</u> breakdown in your trip, but you're getting an old hand now, and seem to deal with everything wonderfully well. I can't make out quite where you were for the ski-ing though – do they have a chalet of their own or what? Anyway if they're as rich as all this we couldn't compete anyway. And I think it would have been worse to stay with people who didn't do anything at all, perhaps. I'm glad there really <u>is</u> a cèdre in the avenue – can't say the same for Cedars Road, S.W.4.

Ria has gone off to spend the afternoon with Sylvia and is going again to-morrow, I'm glad really as it's less dull for her though I can't really approve of Sylvia and Mrs Donan, naturally enough, doesn't approve of <u>me</u> – so Daddy has to fetch her, from the back door of Lord Chelsea's house. Ria continues to fill notebooks with drawings of 'ladies' in topless dresses who, she says, are 'out to catch the boys', so I feel I must get her a Nice Book from the library as you advised, but I haven't the nerve to ask the one-man army at the Clapham Branch Library.

We went skating again and a kindly stranger ('let me introduce myself: I'm Dr Green') helped Maria – who of course took an objection to him – asked her to do the preliminary Foxtrot with him, so at last she's done one properly.

I've ordered some skimpy lino remnants for the loo and kitchen so that will be another small step forwards, and I'm collecting plants for the balcony. I've also been working very late each night on this (probably useless) Spanish grammar.

Tina, if you're getting me a present I would like one of these bowls and chopper like this [drawings] for chopping parsley and herbs and things – Josie will know what it is – it's to hâcher things in – but maybe they're very expensive

Much love and best Easter wishes Mum

---

* Postcard.

Poynders Jardin
[185 Poynders Gardens, sw4]
Good Friday [9 April 1966]

Dearest Tina,

Thankyou so much for your lovely letter, we thought it was marvellous of you to write at once without even having a snooze. Your journey out sounds exhausting in the extreme, and I would never have wanted you to go out if I'd known what it was going to be like, but I can only hope you're recovered and that the quiet room will drive away the hated miggy. – it sounds lovely. And I think you'd feel it was worth it if you saw Clapham S.W.4 at the moment – grey, rain falling, all of us exhausted in the middle of the spring clean – Maria washing the dolls clothes, to be put away finally, she says, me <u>having everything out</u> and poor Daddy left with taking the gas stove to bits and cleaning it – impossible to put it back – not like romantic processions, jasmine, oranges and paseos. I'm terribly sorry too that the Academia* was shut but I thought that Valpy's <u>duties</u> would include doing something about meeting the young ladies and they were due on that early train, weren't they, it was the same one that he came on?

Very exhausted as received mysterious letter from Randolph Vigne (at Stillic Press) who you may remember (or Not) was a freedom fighter in S. Africa and just escaped being hung and therefore does everything in a queer, urgent manner – saying I must take the famous ms. down to Holborn College, in Red Lion Square, at once. – but when I got there it was all shut and locked, with notes in milk bottle saying 'college on Easter vacation' – so I came back tired, wet and dispirited. However Rachel (name of old friend) writes enthusiastically, saying she's so glad I'm going to drive over to Exeter with her (I'd written to say that I <u>didn't</u> want to do this) and, strangely, to ask if Maria could bring a good dress, as she may have to go to a wine and cheese party!

We're looking forward keenly to hearing about Easter ceremonies &c and what you think of eulogio. Do you think José will turn up again from the Sierra de Córdoba? It was an excellent move to get someone to carry your luggage, even if he occasionally drinks out of a bottle, much love and Happy Easter Mum x

---

* The English school in Córdoba where Valpy was teaching English and where Christina was studying Spanish.

185 Poynders Gardens, sw4
9 April [1966]

Dearest Tina,

Thankyou so much for gorgeous technicolour p.c.s all of which
we'll keep por supuesto – I also read Daddy's letter, all keenly
interesting – I didn't know Valpy wore a <u>green</u> hood,* somehow I'd
imagined him all in black, with a skull and crossbones. I felt tremendous
relief when you told me that Angelines was very sweet and that you
feel sure they'll be happy – because it was clear that when Valpy went
back in the spring that the engagement must go on, it couldn't go
back, and (as Miss Gray would say) I trust your judgement absolutely
– as there can't be many people who notice things more acutely – and
after all she'll be your sister-in-law long after I'm dead and buried – so
it was worth your going out to Cordoba simply to find out how nice
she really was, apart from the holiday (not rest, you never seem to get
that) which I hope is doing something for your shattered health.

Maria says it is high time you came back to keep Daddy in order, as
he's getting too independent, and actually is asking how to turn on the
television. Meanwhile, wistfully thinking of the smell of orange-blossom,
I'm packing the grip to depart to Cornwall – Ria insists on taking
a large assortment of clothes, although I think only trousers are
necessary. It was pouring with rain in the market in Balham High Rd.
to-day – the water streaming down through their poor stalls and
fit-ups, pools of water among the lettuces and apples and all the cheap
dresses sodden and streaky and the stallholders covered with sacks and
newspapers shouting out 'It's a wash-out, dearie – eat your radishes
indoors! &c.' Needless to say the Battersea Easter Parade is going on
<u>whatever the weather</u> – but we shan't have to go to it this year.

Very many Easter wishes &c. &c.

I'm putting the mystic envelope you left with me on Maria's plate
to-morrow. It seems Father Sullivan sat grimly in his confessional but
no-one came while there was a long queue right round the church for
kindly Father Whatsit, the Dutch one – much love Mum X

---

* As a Nazareno in the Easter processions.

Playa Andalucía
Puerto de Santa María
Provincia de Cádiz
España
23 August [*c.*1966]

Dearest Tina,

We arrived safely to discover that you didn't need vaccination certificates at all – they'd just been declared unnecessary! I got very upset before we went away and said I wouldn't go at all, I felt I was really going to have a nervous breakdown, like other peoples' friends do, and Daddy and Maria were very fed up naturally, but there had been such a lot to do, then we had a nice flight to Gibraltar and the rock was lit up so we had a good view of it and not too much delay at the customs. The camp (called a Residential Club) is much more comfortable than we expected as we have a dwarf bath, with real hot water, and pine trees which keep the flies away, and green grass and flowers – there was a large bunch of luridly coloured flowers when we arrived with <u>well come</u> written on them. Everything is made of pinewood, with a built-in cupboard, but quite comfortable and the fashion in beachwear seems to be kibbutz hats so Maria's is just the thing. Daddy is sunburnt <u>already</u> but luckily I'd brought lots of stuff, Maria however seems to favour burying him in sand up to the neck. As usual, he's regarded as a high-grade executive by the manager who plies us with revolting Spanish champagne and when I admired the water jug he presented it to me (quaint Andalusian hospitality). Puerto de Santa María is rather nice, we walked in yesterday and went to one of those dark places with barrels to have some wine – we got a lift back fortunately. En España son muchos burros – Maria approves of these though a bit insular about absence of Golden Shred &c. She is being very patient about fusty old parents but I think it would be worse to try and find nice friends among the very mixed inhabitants and it is a lovely beach – waves, as it's the Atlantic, but so far the Woolies lilo rides triumphantly over them with its vulgar red stripes. Hope for bullfight ('murder on Sunday p.m.') in Puerto on Sunday.

We're <u>longing</u> for a letter from you although I suppose it's too early to hope for one yet. Have left some supplies in frig: by the way.

Much much love from all

Mum.

Love to Linda. How is Mrs Dent?

Playa Andalucia
Puerto Sta. Maria
29 August [1966]

Dearest Tina,

Thankyou so much for your letter, we did enjoy reading it. I see that Mrs Dent appears to have lost all control but I don't care at all if it gives you a better holiday, only I hope Mrs Dunant never gets to hear about all the spumante. It sounds lovely and it's a bit of luck that, after all, they were all nice. We're longing to see you, postcards, souvenirs, sun-tan &c. I hope you won't be completely tired of telling about it by Monday night. Amazed to hear about the sword dance.

We have got very fond of our little house among the pines, I do like the sound of the sea at night as you know and find it very easy to sleep here. Last night the proprietor (who's from Cordoba and wears a succession of silk suits, it's impossible to get Daddy sufficiently tidy to live up to him) and his wife, who is very nice but speaks only Spanish; he took her to England however while he was learning the business and she spoke rapturously of the C & A. She still has some things from there. <u>She's</u> from Seville, and says that all Columbus' crew were Sevillans, though from the prisons. Maria was threatened with a huge lobster but managed to get her something else. She has been very long-suffering having to be with us and always seems to enjoy everything – the bullfight went very well as everything happened – a bull jumped out of the ring, one was objected to and had to be lured out of the ring by some enormous brown and white oxen with huge bells, and then we had one very good fight where the man knelt down &c. It was a very magnificent occasion and the mayor arrived in a carriage & horses but unfortunately Maria thinks she didn't 'wind on' the film so I don't know if any record will remain. We are hoping you will show us Holiday Snaps of Tom, Rob, &c. &c. as well as much culture. I wonder if Rosalyn is the one with the large marble-like features?

much love and longing to see you

Mum

You will just water the plants, won't you?

Old Terry Bank
Kirkby Lonsdale
Westmorland
1 August [1967]

Dearest Tina,

I felt distressed at seeing you disappear, we all did, particularly as Daddy said the 2 young men sitting next to you looked very rough and we wished they were a nice English lady; but I daresay you could deal with them. Now I am waiting eagerly to hear what it is like at Courcelles-Chaussy and whether the Comtesse met you, oh dear I do think you showed considerable courage going off like that.

Meanwhile we transferred to Euston, (so sordid as it's still all kept up by scaffolding) and had to change at <u>Preston</u> (antique Victorian station with Corinthian pillars in wrought iron) and catch a local to Carnforth, Maria was very patient though we had 2 nuns in the carriage who watched every morsel we ate.

I'm now sitting in the (nice) church in Kirkby Lonsdale while Willie* practises the organ (100 years old and painted with flowers and crowns on top of the pipes) she is playing the piece Bach wrote on his death-bed which is rather nice I think. The organist who is teaching her is a stout little man, terribly strict, who won't permit her even to play for school services unless everything is perfect, so she has to come for an hour every day.

The pony is called Nutty, and is in a field opposite the house, and a TV set has now been acquired as otherwise the girls were never in, but

---

* 'Willie' was (Maryllis) Conder, a friend of PMF's.

they're asked after supper if they would <u>like</u> to watch, after they've
helped with the washing-up, I can see that Maria's amazed at this.
Hoping to go to Wordsworth's cottage this afternoon, it's only a little
way away at the other side of the lake. There are 2 nice Jack Russell
terriers and an old cat, which looks nice, like a black and yellow
fur rug.

Maria and Susan are out doing the shopping, but Maria is rather
cross because I haven't enough money for postcards. I hope she soon
won't be. We're thinking of you so much, darling Love Mum

Old Terry Bank
Kirkby Lonsdale
2 August [1967]

Dearest Tina,

In the excitement of going away I don't believe I ever gave Daddy
<u>our</u> address, I'm so vexed as he won't be able to write, or to forward
your letter, when it comes, but then I expect we'll be back in London by
that time, especially as poor Willie has had bad news about her mother
and may have to go to Norfolk to see her in hospital, but in spite of this
we are having a lovely holiday so far, wonderful mild sunshine, there's a
kind of arch out of the yard at Willie's house and you see all the hills
and clouds framed through it. Of course Ria's still in blue jeans, already
very muddy, and they are going out this morning with the pony,
Nutmeg, who clearly has everybody's measure exactly, and a lovely new
green bike Susan has which I daresay Ria will prefer, up the hill tracks.
We did miss you very much at Wordsworth's cottage yesterday, it was
lovely and sunshiny there too, it's built into the hillside so that you go
into the front door at one level and out of the back-door halfway up
the hill. Ria read out of the guide – but very firmly, and we also had
Dorothy Wordsworth's diaries, how they managed the cooking &c.
I can't think, but we saw W's gun, sandwich box, waterproof hat, skates
and the flat-irons and goffering irons and stew-pots they had, and
wash-jugs and basins – but all the walking – 12 miles to see Coleridge,
2 miles to get eggs – and they often seem to have felt ill – I didn't realise
until yesterday that Dorothy was insane for the last 20 years of her life

and Mary Wordsworth went on looking after her, even after Wordsworth died, she must have been a saintly woman. The cottage rent was £8 a year, their income was £80, and tea cost 15 shillings a pound, and there were locks on the tea-caddies. They had to make their own candles out of mutton-fat in candle-moulds, and yet they did all that reading and writing – Shakespeare and sermons aloud in the evening, and Coleridge came over and read aloud his new ballad – the Ancient M! – and she doesn't say what he thought of it!

We had a nice picnic by Grasmere and Susan and Maria swam in the lake and could see clear down to the bottom. Mrs Spyra seems far away.

Willie and Mike fell in love with the Gorges of the Tarn and want to go and live there for a year in a quaint cottage or auberge, sending the little girls to a French school. I do wonder what you are thinking of Froggyland this time

much love

Mum

Old Terry Bank
Kirkby Lonsdale
6 August [1967]

Dearest Tina,

To begin with, some little bits from the newspapers (obtained with great difficulty as they aren't delivered here)

1. Lord Robens has been more or less completely blamed for the Aberfan disaster, but sulks and more or less refuses to resign.

2. Dymock and Oldenshaw on the Fellows have made up their disagreement.

3. Harvey Smith's O'Malley has been nobbled at the Royal Lancashire Show – he has twice been let out of his box at night, although Harvey had secured it with string, and ate a lot of grass in the show grounds and couldn't jump properly next day. But Harvey S. won everything with Harvester. However it's felt that 'competitors' dislike Harvey Smith so much that an unsuitable element is being

brought into the gentlemanly sport. Of course we get all the Lancashire papers up here which report all this at length.

Maria is snoozing after more violent exercise – long walk taking turns with the pony and a swim in the icy cold lake above the house – the old Scotch Road where as I think I told you the Young Pretender retreated during the '45.

Also she had to help cook the supper and wash up! As poor Willie's mother is dying and she had to hurry down to gloomy Ipswich General Hospital to see her, leaving everything at sixes and sevens. But Susan, the 13 year old, is managing very well, especially as Mike who has returned for the weekend is queerly strict and has inspections to see that the rooms are tidy and makes everyone change for dinner. I feared he mightn't pass Ria's orange bloomer suit which looks a bit voyant in Westmorland. Many strange relations (vets from Canada &c) have arrived and help themselves freely to everything, even the sanatogen tonic wine and the spinach from the garden, but they're all quite childish and love playing ball in the yard after dinner so the girls are in fits of laughter.

Back to London to-morrow which I am afraid will be dull for Ria, but she can start revising her clothes to go to Italy: Willie rang up from Ipswich and asked us to stay longer, but I'm getting so asthmatic up here that I actually coughed up blood in the night (complain, complain) and anyway with all this trouble about her mother I daresay she'd like to be clear of visitors for a while, but it certainly is a nice place for Maria, and I'm getting very attached to Nutmeg.

Hoping to find a letter from you when we get back – very much love Mum

185 Poynders Gardens
London, sw4
9 August [1967]

Dearest Tina,

Many thanks for nice long informative letters, which we are reading eagerly. So glad the water is back, and I quite see there is nothing to do either in Metz, or on your day off, so it looks as though this time will have to be written off, except for the study of literature française. It was all very well for the Austrian girl as apparently she had some relations or friends in Metz. So glad too that the bites are somewhat better, but surely if you run out of medical supplies, such as elastoplast, the Comtesse would give you some? But perhaps the aristocracy don't have such things. Haemophilia?

Feel the anti-German thing is definitely bad, but agree that all must be attributed to living in Alsace-Lorraine (don't forget La Dernière Classe!) But perhaps better not to say so.

The whole valley of the Lune (where we were with Auntie Willie) has now flooded owing to heavy rains and cottages are being carried away, just a day or so after we left. I think Maria really did enjoy it, and felt pleased when she cantered briskly about on the pony and explained to Mike (who has a mania that town children can't do anything, and do 'damage' all the time) that 'Tina had taught her'. Fortunately asthma reduced my impulse to get everything cleaned up and enter him for the local Agricultural Show, which includes a shepherd's crook-jumping competition.

Alas, poor Daddy couldn't manage the paint-spray and didn't dare scrape off what he'd done, so the bath is not a great success, but hope it will pass – perhaps fit a dimming lampshade?

Alison is going to France for 3 days as Mr Packer doesn't like to be out of the country longer (why?) and so Ria may <u>have</u> to come up to Bedford with me to see Miss C., but still it won't kill her. Our tickets have now come from Lunns with an absurd brochure, advising you not to forget the name of your hotel, and to stick to English dishes. By the way, I should so much like to know what the food is like at Aubigny.

I'm going to goggle at the Royal Ascot show so that I can tell you whether Harvey Smith appears.

Meanwhile I have received a letter from Valpy (as I expect you have too) suggesting that you go to the Angie* family for the Easter holiday, as a kind of exchange, as it's so difficult to find a paying job, now this of course is for you to decide and you must write direct to Valpy about it, but I was rather taken aback as the fare, £30, is so high and the

* Angelines, who eventually became Valpy's wife.

journey rather formidable by oneself and, also, I'd rather thought of
our offering hospitality to Angie, which I do want to do, rather than its
all being an exchange – a kind of business arrangement? Also, quite
honestly, is the Angie family an easy one to live with? I'd thought more
of San Sebastian, or somewhere with a much cheaper fare, but I know
that without a job I shan't really be able to manage it: still we were
going to try the Franc ha Leal. You'll write to Valpy, won't you, and tell
me what you decide? Of course it is very sweet of him to make this
suggestion and I would do anything rather than hurt his feelings, for
many reasons.

Next week we must start our great pack – Daddy's new summer
coat is already looking rather crumply, but apparently it was a great
success in the office, so he keeps wearing it. I do hope your clothes are
all right, except the unfortunate sandals.

Workmen are trying to strengthen the wire around the playground,
but I expect the kiddies will be ready with blow-torches. Nothing will
keep them out.

Will write again soon – very much love from us all – X Mum

185 Poynders Gardens, sw4
15 August [1967]

Dearest Tina,

I can see you are well up on the news owing to the Comte's TV and
so will merely give a little sports and T.V. news – Michael Miles* has
been arrested twice at London Airport, once for being drunk and
disorderly and once for trying to get by with excess luggage, and at the
Dublin Horse Show O'Malley was not 'nobbled' and Harvey S. won
almost everything. We have just seen Cassius Clay on TV getting ready
to go to jail. But I think he's still appealing really. – Hope you didn't
feel any earth tremors – they seem to be much farther south. This
reminds me of Spain, and you won't forget to write to Valpy about his
scheme of your staying with the Angies?

* A TV broadcaster.

I sent the mosquito stuff, which I hope arrived, but was relieved to learn that you might be able to get some from Metz. Also very glad that Dr Gibbie's pills were of some use. So sorry Mme. was cross the one morning you overslept. Surely she must appreciate all the useful work you're doing, much more than the Hapsburg, I'm sure.

Maria is being very good although it is dull for her since all her cronies have left London and the Packers are now off on their mysterious trip to France, to see Mr Packer's old battle-grounds. She is helping me paint and decorate, but soon all this must be put aside and we must make lists and start ironing everything. I can't decide what to do about the plants – I'll try putting a plastic bag round the creeper, as I did last year.

I helped an old lady across the road this morning who told me she was 92 – she's lived in Clapham since 1880, when there were horses in all the stables. But she tells me 'there are still many kind hearts in Honeybourne Road'.

We went up to Grove Cottage for lunch on Sat: – Auntie Mary had a nice new navy-blue tablecloth. A mysterious Indian had come to tea unexpectedly and told them that Uncle Rawle has resigned from the Daily Telegraph (which I suppose will mean leaving the house they have now) and is making some other mysterious deal – perhaps with the Times of India? So I sent Miss Chamot there only just in time. I suppose I shall have to wait till I see William* to get details of this.

I don't think I've ever felt quite so exhausted as when we went to Oxford Street on Monday to get the olive-green bath-towels (vexatious expenditure).

Maria, clumping along in her Dr Scholl sandals, was most gallant and encouraging. But the first ones I bought turned out to be <u>spring</u> green when I got them to the light and so we had to take them back to the man and pretend to be dissatisfied customers. Then we couldn't afford the things in John Lewis's and the assistant humiliatingly recommended us to go to Wallis's. Meanwhile Maria had sunk onto a chair and a kind lady, apparently taking her for a waif, asked her

---

* Rawle's son.

if she felt well enough to go home. Nothing ever tasted better than the cup of tea that we made when we got back. I'm so jaded that I can't study any Russian, and am reduced to reading 'Diary of a No-body' for the 20th time. – Are you sure that Sabine is worse than 'Junie' in Britannicus?*

As you see I have nothing interesting to tell, but am enjoying your lovely long letters immensely, and Grandpa says they mustn't be lost on any account. Try to send Mme. de B.** a note if you can.

So glad they liked the Christina Rossetti. That was a very sad life, I think – to give up love, as she certainly did, for Christian principles, and having that dreadful Dante Gabriel as a brother – much love always, Mum

185 Poynders Gardens, sw4
[August 1967]

Dearest Tina,

You can easily imagine what it's like here when I tell you we are just packing and cleaning up before going to Elba to-morrow. I have been mending my sandals with plastic wood (unfortunately Woolie's only had 'antique walnut') and rather good new plastic soles, also from Woolie's: but Ria says they're horrible. I've also cleaned the oven and put clean sheets on the beds and checked over a very long itinerary – Daddy, very reluctantly, as he had lunch very late and no rest, is fixing up a curtain-rail for himself, and Maria has filled up his suitcase already with li-los, suncream &c. and he hasn't even started putting his clothes in.

Sporting news is depressing as this American runner, Jim Ryun, wins all the miles and half miles by practically a lap, and the others have given up trying, and the crowd actually attacked the Yorkshire team with umbrellas because they played so slowly – the bowler actually stopped to dry the ball between each over. – Michael Miles has apologised for

---

* Racine's tragedy *Britannicus* (1669).
** Marielle de Baissac, a friend and colleague of PMF's from Queens Gate School.

being drunk at the airport and giving the name of Hughie Green; and murdered Joe Orton was cremated in a maroon coffin at Golder's Green and Harold Pinter read a poem, part of which ran

> If you're sad that he's dead
> you'd make him sad
> that you'd missed the point
> of his best bad joke

When the wretched man was hit on the head with a hammer!

Lord Boothby's tasteless engagement to a lady croupier from Soho is condemned by all.

I expect Maria has written to you about our strange trip to Bedford to see Miss Charboneau – Mme. de Baissac (delighted with your letter, by the way, so I'm so glad you wrote it) has become rather Victorian Society and v. enthusiastic about the graceful railway arch at St Pancras – Bedford a dreary red-brick and green tree place full of Italian brickworkers – terribly embarrassing as Miss C. had prepared a vast lunch, liqueurs &c. which we couldn't possibly eat.

Yesterday we went up to Grove Cottage, grandpa looking rather frail but very spry; he has a new (mild) mania that Rawle may want to take Indian nationality, I do hope not.

I don't know whether I told you that I met Myrtle, my old pottery teacher – at the Hampstead Open Air Exhibition. She now has a studio and bookshop in Rosslyn Hill.

Ferdie pecked me sharply on the way to the Budgie Hotel – but he was greeted by the Hansel and Gretel lady as 'dear Ferdie, and Freddie'. Many other cages including cockatoo, and much excitement – must put Daddy and Ria to bed now: Daddy's dirtied up his new room already.

much love darling
Mum

[postcard]
22 August [1967]

Thankyou for lovely letters, but you were right as usual, we may be moving, as beach here is stony, though we are in a nice friendly hotel with plenty of pasta, and grapes growing round washing-line. We came here on a hydrofoil from Pisa – very rapid. Maria devoted to task of getting brown. Much love from all X Mum.

On board cronky ferry-steamer
23 August [1967]

Dearest Tina,

We're just crossing to the mainland for a day's outing. NOT on the grand hydrofoil we came on, but on the ferry boat, which I should say is an old British coastal craft fitted up by the so-called 'Tuscan Navigation Company' – We're going to take an excursion to Florence, from which I'm sure we'll return very hot and tired, but as I've never seen Florence and keep thinking I'm now somewhat declined into the vale of years (but that's not much) I may not have the chance to see it again, and Maria is an intrepid sight-seer, here we are. Our hotel, which is not an efficient place though nice in some ways, has FORGOTTEN OUR PICNIC but fortunately we were able to buy some of the inevitable ham rolls in the shoddy galley. Maria has had to take to lemon in her tea as the milk here is so terrible (worse than Froggyland I'm sure) and I'm not surprised when I see the cows, each one is miserably pegged to the ground with nothing at all to eat, except some withered corn stalks.

A nice thing in this boat has been that Bruno, the CEAT man, retrieved your letters from the Arcabaleno where as you so justly point out we're NOT staying, and we were able to read them on deck, going through the blue sea, past the misty islands (Ria wrapped in Daddy's jacket over her unsuitable skimpy 'flower-power' dress) which is lovely, and we do enjoy your letters, I hope you didn't mind my showing them at Grove Cottage as they gave such pleasure and Grandpa of course said 'they should be published'.

Well, as I said, our hotel isn't very efficient, being run by a peasant, his fiancée 20 years younger in a faded black dress, and alarmingly smart in the evenings, and a dwarf only 3 ft. high who is a nephew who helps out in the evenings. But the food is nice and so is the wine and the mineral water, which normally I can't bear, but this is called (of course) Fonte Napoleone and comes from a spring high up in the mountain. It's nice eating under the vines and the English people are not from Lunns, but decorous Erna Low clients with Nigelly sons who play ping-pong (also under the vines and glorious Bougainvillea) – they are clergymen and schoolteachers with open-necked shirts and panamas and one is actually reading Pendennis.

We've been to Napoleon's town house in the capital – the one he escaped in a brig from – he seems to have done himself very well and had lavish furniture and a bed covered with golden eagles imported from France. He amused himself for a few months organising the chestnut gathering, brickworks &c. – no trace of this organisation now I may say. Vulgar washbasin, also with eagles.

We are quite tired out to-day with yesterday's trip to Florence – we had to start at 6 and were back at 12, but it was a great success really, and Maria and me of course had never been there before. We crossed in the steamer this time, 2½ hours in bus with unintelligible commentary by Bruno (Italian version of Gilbert, under Daddy's thumb) and were shown everything in a few hours by an alarming countess who had lost everything (either in the flood or elsewhere) and was at the same time royalist and anti-clerical (you will cover your arms in the Duomo but not in Santa Croce – the Franciscans care nothing for nudities). We had lunch right on the hill overlooking the city, just like Henry James – that was lovely, and we finished up with the Uffizi (Maria still game though longing to take off Dr Scholls on the shining marble floors) and the Primavera &c. (all details remembered from Ria's art books) and there was a coffee-place on the roof where you could overlook the square and all the statues.

So glad mosquito stuff arrived and you are coping so wonderfully with the strange aristos. We do love your letters – forgive bad writing – love from all Mum

[postcard of Napoleon]
24 August [1967]

I'm sure you won't mind keeping these p.c.s for Ria's scrap book (unluckily we've only got a primary school geography book with an Arab on the cover. Why?) You won't be surprised to hear that we're sitting on the harbour front drinking cappucine (?) after fatigue of walking from one mountain village to another, about 3 miles, terribly hard on those wearing Dr Scholls exercise sandals. Lovely Spanish chestnuts, palms &c on mountains.

[August 1967]

Dearest Tina – I've just been allowed to add a page to Daddy's letter as we've just received your wonderful exam. news, I'm so <u>delighted</u>, not only in a school-teachery way but I did think you deserved it so, you worked so hard and were so well up to it, but I thought it might all be spoiled by the badly phrased questions, or by your being over-tired – it really <u>is</u> something to be proud of, an A over all the papers, and so many good things come from it – you're justified now in having asked to take the exam. earlier than the others, and in having chosen languages as your subject; and also I think you'll be justified in going to Miss Gray and asking for an advance from the 'Franc Ha Leal' for a study course in Spain at Easter, which I should hardly have thought we could have applied for otherwise, and Miss Kershaw will be really pleased, and she <u>has</u> tried to help, I know! Forgive this scrawl, I must congratulate you at once, this double A is not so easy to get, even by people who spend every vacation in France
    much love Mum
    AAAAAAAAA

[postcard]
[August 1967]

Sitting in the sun making cappuc(h)inos last – you'll sympathise
I'm sure

Please forgive me if someone has sent Napoleon's bed before, I
thought you'd like it

(Marie Walenska's as she was the only one who'd come.) Still talking
about your good news, though Maria speculating what Dish* will say
about terrible Epstein affair. Absurd rumours in Italian papers about
Aga Khan and Princess Margaret.

Glad Nancy ** was nice.

much love Mum

> Queens Gate, sw7
> 24 March [1968]

Dearest Tina,

Not really anything to say since you rang up last night but I thought
I'd just write a few lines. It's <u>icy</u> in this library as the heater doesn't
seem to work, so I've seized the opportunity to say that everyone who
is cold must go away – and all have left except a few faithful scribblers. –
But stay, Odious Mr Turner, the shady odd-job man who is running an
independent plumbing and decorating business from the basement,
has come in and said he'll fix it – I wish he wouldn't.

Needless to say I can't wait for your letter, as we all know that it is
'incredible' at the Maltbys. I wonder why? I'm so very glad you arrived
safely – I still think they might have made better arrangements. And I
wonder what your 'charge' as babies are called in the 'Nursery World' is like?

John Probst came yesterday and ate large quantities and took Maria
for a spin on his motor bike to Godstone, from which she came back
so cold that she had a sort of rash all over her cheeks. She <u>loves</u> going
fast – she always enjoys things so much. Probst is very ingenuous, and
told me exactly all the quantities of bread cheese and coffee he'd

---

 *   Paul McCartney.
**   The city.

ordered for his party the night before, with the exact prices, and how he'd decided to give a daffodil to everyone 'to be thoroughly out of date' as he quite brightly added. He's very sympathetic and always takes a great interest in everyone else, and apparently believes all that they say – he told me a long story about a Mrs Lazaretto ? a friend of his parents who was a second mother to him, and determined to have each of her <u>nine</u> children on Sept 26th (I think), so delayed her labour pain by the power of thought – this is <u>nonsense</u> – anyway he's off on a surveying course now, their degree seems very odd to me.

We went to Jeremy Court for lunch – Angie now tired of Peter Jones and says they are all jealous of her because she is a foreigner and can manage all the department better than they can, as they are common and haven't the power to command: so I think it's a good thing she's leaving there soon. I reminded Valpy about Huelva, I think he'll do something. He's a good boy and I'm sure he's happy, what else matters?

On Wednesday I make my annual pilgrimage to the school play with Miss Macrini – a small collation first at Lyons. Maria sportingly says she'll come too (it's As You Like It!) but I certainly shan't hold her to this.

It seems Daddy had to walk all the way from Victoria to Clapham – I really am sorry but money really is short – and now he says he's 'not certain' if he'll be paid on Friday – I think Lunn have given up paying altogether! My income tax problems are tiresome, as Mrs Lavender (immensely frail and ancient Bursar) is now alienated by my enquiries although I've hitherto been on excellent terms with her, and I still have to pay all the extra tax. Daddy must go round and see Mr Hassan, my Oriental sounding inspector, he's a big strong man and <u>he</u> must face Mr Hassan. Daddy says, why are you sometimes so bold and sometimes so timid – but don't you find that you're also like this.

I'm quite dismayed by my book-table. – I'll <u>never</u> get all these books read, and I'm still seeing double! Hard Times! Adolphe! Apologia Pro Vita Sua! Maria has started on Little Dorrit: she selected it herself – she says that she can't bear it when other people keep talking about books,

Well enough of this: what really interests me is to hear about you and the Maltbys.

much love dear

Ma

Sir Henry Lunn
Marble Arch House
World travel (!!)
Sunday [7 April 1968]

Dearest Tina – No air-mail paper so am using Sir Henry Lunn's shoddy lightweight office paper. – We miss you so much, but Maria pointed out firmly and quite correctly, on the station, that we mustn't stare, as Tina was getting just a little embarrassed by us. – We had to go and have coffee and buns in Lyons to cheer ourselves up.

Quite exhausted by emotions raised by Eurovision Song Contest: We felt sure Cliff should have won, though doubtful about his dress of nylon ruffles and dandy's velvet-effect suit. It was very odd Germany suddenly giving 6 votes for Spain, I'm sure it was a vote to promote trade. (Wollen Sie in Spanien gehen?) As usual I was quite wrong as the one I thought best got no votes at all, and Sandie Shaw looked frightful in ostrich-effect feathers and was hit by a piece of stage.

No letter for Valpy from The Economic Associates Inc: so I daresay he'll accept the Mobil offer, and I do think it will be best if he settles his mind and accepts it, and probably Don Rafael* will be impressed and pay for the wedding (and also expect Valpy to get jobs for his relations in oil companies). Anyway, we expect him back late to-night.

Maria has given me my first guitar lesson but I'm very slow and my fingers are so stiff. I've done your room out and the kitchen, with not much <u>visible</u> effect but I feel better as it was always a great thing to have the spring-cleaning started by Palm Sunday. – I can't stand these dried-up bits of palm, what would be the point of strewing them under anyone's feet? I do wish we still had bunches of pussy-willow. – Meanwhile I am continuing to read the Ruskin book slowly, as I'm enjoying it so much. How <u>ill</u> they all were – <u>all</u> Victorians I mean – and how much they talk about it, and what endurance they had all the same.

---

* Valpy's father-in-law.

It's very smelly here this morning and I do envy you the nice pure air and wide skies of Castile. – Maria is reading a historical romance in the Loo. – She sends all her love and so does Daddy.

Longing to hear from you –

Much love always – Mum X

Happy Easter and Much Love from us all

11 April [1968]

Dearest Tina,

Very relieved to get your letter, and realise that you were not poisoned by the Cornish pasties from the cook-shop. Not surprised to hear about many deficiencies of the trip – but at least they got you there which is more than our ridiculous Escort would have done to Córdoba. Hope the 2 chicas are under your control: I'm sure they are.

Valpy still out interviewing – I quite see that he feels the Mobil job would be terribly staid and settled to start in, and wants to go abroad – they've written him a terribly nice letter saying that they'd love him to come for his personal qualities – no matter about degree. Better perhaps are the Economic Associates (not the wild glamorous one) who have shorter smaller projects, but more secure I think. Anyway he's encouraged that he's gone off to Esso and says he'll say: 'Let me see now, what is it that you manufacture?' – We had a wild dinner last night with Diana and both feel poisoned. She brought back some lovely things from Bangkok – plastic flowers for idols, but they're bright and lovely.

Angie wrote that she went to help the nuns lay out her grandmother who died recently – as it would be useful practice – I suppose it is – more strangely, she suggests that Miss Walker is a bit of a Lesbian and was quite angry when Angie got engaged – which I think quite ridiculous – being educated in a convent evidently doesn't exclude these fantasies – I'll be glad when they're both safely married and settled.

Lovely fine weather here and we went to the Barbara Hepworth exhibition and ate sandwiches on the steps of the Tate. Still tearful

after seeing Luther King funeral on TV. It was so cosy – they didn't
care a bit that it was a muddle.

Reading book on American poetry – have learnt that 1. T. S. Eliot
first learnt to love poetry from Omar Khayyam – Funny you gave me
both. 2. The planters in the Southern states took the names of their
estates and their whole code of honour and genteel manners from
Scott's novels! This interested me a lot. No room left – will write again
XXX Mum

185 Poynders Gardens
London, sw4
13 April [1968]

Dearest Tina,

Thankyou so much for nice postcards, and we were glad you now
seem to have respectable escort, and seem cheerier, though exhausted.
I wonder what time the meals are? (Maria tells me dinner at 10).

Valpy went off gaily in the end, though much confusion over
various letters, contracts &c. I think he'll accept the Economic Unit:
I do hope so, as I'm sure it would suit him, with so many different
assignments. The Japanese girl is returning to Japan, so I think the
development of property in Oxford won't come off.

Maria and I have been having a good weep at Dr Zhivago, or rather
I <u>would</u> have cried if I'd been able to bear Julie Christie seen through a
blue filter: but I loved all the snow and the trains and Tom Courtenay's
tin spectacles. Now we're sitting by the fire (still cold though very
sunny) and sewing – Daddy is at the launderette you'll be surprised to
hear! Wish we were in blazing Spanish sunshine like you and very glad
you're going to Valladolid as all the best images are there. Longing to
hear about gay time, and bull-fight.

Maria has much depressed me by 1. Looking at Daddy and me
and saying: 'What a funny old couple you are!' and 2. Telling me that
studying art and literature is only a personal indulgence and doesn't
really help humanity or lead to anything, and, I suppose, really, that
is quite true: she said it very kindly. My life seemed to be crumbling
into dust.

Valpy and I went to the 8 o'clock mass on Maundy Thursday. Father Sammons got terribly out of hand with numerous processions and clouds of incense and many respectable men in blue suits and red sashes worn crossways. We finally left as I was getting worried about Ria while yet another elaborate procession was getting tangled up in the aisles.

Must finish making my nightie – in rather low spirits – much love Mum

Glad it's not turning out too badly XX

185 *Poynders Gardens, sw4*
12 October [1968]

Dearest Tina,

Just a note – to say we are missing you very much, but this is not really what I meant to say – I am here all by myself watching the Olympic opening, for Daddy is at the launderette and Maria has gone out to a gay dance, carelessly tossing aside another missive from Pope, containing a smiling photograph of the three brothers, heavily hair-creamed. She took Daddy to have the first fitting of his suit this afternoon, but the fly-buttons were not on straight, however it's to be finished properly in 3 weeks. Outside it is very wet and windy and the laundry is flapping against your window.

Valpy and Angie are coming to lunch to-morrow, I must keep off controversial subjects and be sensible, and try and get some wine, for there's none in the house. – My new bun-cosy is not quite the right shade of red – just off – so I've tried to <u>dye</u> it a little more crimson, and it too is flapping in the wind.

Very great difficulty in changing the ribbon of the typewriter – I don't think it's right yet. The booklet says, in four languages, that it's a very simple operation.

I did so wish I could have come up on Thursday – Maria says your room* is in the front quad, which is nice, surely, handy for people to

---

* At Somerville.

drop in? and that though small dark and smelly, as you predicted, it is also cosy and began to look really homely after you'd put out your things, and she says you'd like blue curtains, so I'll go up to the dreaded Oxford St. next Thursday and try and get the right colour. Did you mean to leave your Swiss cow behind? Well, you've had to settle in to a lot of very odd places, and are pretty expert by this time. I wonder what the Linguists' coffee party was like?

I went up to the paper shop where I was received with pathetic enthusiasm by the manager, and changed the Sunday Express to the Sunday Times, but I don't expect he'll remember.

Must now turn to tattered essays and hysterical postcards sent by my candidates. Aren't you sorry for them? At least you won't have to do that again!

Daddy back from launderette, it seems some boys came with their washing at 10 and when they weren't allowed in they smashed the windows with a tin and had to be taken away by the police! I wonder how you're managing with your washing, and indeed with everything – so much love dear old mum.

> 185 Poynders G[ardens]
> London, sw4
> 11 November [1968]

Dearest Tina,

To start with, and before I forget, here are 'A Room of One's Own' – which <u>was</u> in your room, and your New Poetry, which I regret, wasn't – and the 'Sunday Times' cutting about Yevtushenko, which you'll have seen of course, but I thought you might like for your 'memory lane' book.

Thankyou so much for a very nice Saturday – a real break for me, and it was lovely to see you and very kind of you and your friends to take me for granted, so to speak. But I can't help being very angry with your French tutor – very angry. It just seems to be not only <u>mistaken</u> but quite <u>irresponsible</u> for tutors (or even VI form teachers) to be unfair, unpleasant or bullying – it doesn't matter if they're stuffy,

old-fashioned or ridiculous, but surely it should be a kind of
partnership to study the language – to make anyone you're teaching
feel unhappy means you can't teach them anyway – if things aren't
right you could always talk to them privately – but she really <u>is</u> lucky to
have you to teach, as you're perfectly ready to do the work – I suppose
she's a 'sick woman', like Miss James, but it's <u>too bad</u>, the French system
is impossible, and I see the lycéens refuse to accept even the new reforms
and the lycées are in chaos and I'm not surprised I imagine Milène
alone in a grey classroom trying to write her entrée en matière as
usual. I'm so <u>glad</u> that you are now to have a rest and 4 weeks Spanish.

I'm sorry that the poor English school is so dull too – the truth
is, though I would never <u>dare</u> saying it in public, that the value of
studying literature only really appears as you go on living, and find
how it really is like life – that it all works – and it's a pity this can't
somehow be shown in the course, except I suppose in Marxist Free
Universities.

I'd love to know how your poetry circle party went. Seeing so many
bookshops has, actually, gone to my head a bit, and it's a good thing I
have a long staff meeting, on Monday.

Daddy says they've managed to transfer nearly all the Poly Lunn
customers onto other airlines, but of course the 'Turkish all-in holiday'
has to be cancelled – all the exciting ones really – they have to cut
back – I do so wish we'd gone last year, but the wedding made it
impossible. I suppose I shall never see Constantinople (as I choose
to call it) now.

Ria came home at 2.30! and said it had been an engagement party
with mums and dads, and vodka and lime, and she <u>couldn't</u> leave
earlier – John was affected by drink, and finally a parent gave them a
lift – it was in <u>Tooting</u> – Ria drank Dubonnet – I feel it is all beyond
me, and I am old and grey and full of sleep.

Well, I did enjoy it yesterday, I really did – If you decide to come up,
which wd. be nice, just send a P.C. won't you

Love Mum

Dearest Tina,

Yes I <u>was</u> worried about your headache and felt I was being tiresome asking about it, but I did enjoy the week-end and felt very much better on the Sunday (but this also made me feel worse because you weren't) – I would love to stay the night again, another time. When I was up at Somerville I was always extravagantly worried about something – now it soothes me, particularly when it's damp, dripping and cosy.

I hope you got P.C. I tried to persuade the V&A slides dept. (now in charge of amateurish lady in cardigan, and still behind piles of masonry and bits of statues) to send the slides off at once – but she said they couldn't be assembled till Friday.

I told Mrs Macintyre how much we'd enjoyed Donald's performance – she said anxiously <u>Didn't you think he gabbled?</u> I at once replied no I thought that <u>was an interesting part of the interpretation</u>. Mrs M. very pleased.

Just received the copy of Grandpa's book on the Church school – very nicely done in offset type, but no illustration or photograph of the school, which I think a pity. A bit of a shadow, because grandpa declares that this is the last thing he'll write, after <u>70</u> years writing! – but satisfactory to see it finished properly. I'm going to read it all carefully as soon as I've got a civilized time to do so.

Thankyou again darling, it was lovely to see you,
much love Ma

Dearest Tina,

Still wondering how the play is going and whether the ladies will squeeze or half squeeze into their low-necked costumes obtained from Dorchester-on-Thames. Donald Macintyre and company are returning at end of Feb to do special Twelfth Night in front of the unfortunate Middle Temple who are expecting a nice evening of Shakespeare with nice music; more dirt and filth is specially being sprayed on the costumes.

I felt very encouraged when in spite of my poor reading I got through to the finals of the Poetry Festival with the 'Kitchen Drawer' poem* – I was much helped by Daddy's loud applause from where he was sitting with the Sunday Times in the back row, and by a decent young poet with a thick head of hair and beard who came after me and said 'I did like the poem about kitchen drawers.' In the evening I had to read after Roger McGough who was very funny, and before a compassionate coloured poet, so didn't really feel at ease, and Daddy had gone home, after sitting through the whole read-in – (many of the contestants cheated and read very long poems about priests and sex and oppression and snow-queens), and tea at Lyons and a visit to Westminster Cathedral (where I was frightened by a new reliquaire, a martyr lying down wearing a surplice with black shoes and polished silver face and hands) so I had no-one to support me and missed you very much. That dreadful Glasgow man Leo Edlon was there trying to sell his tattily printed poems – he was at the reading you took me to in Oxford – he was accompanied this time by an unwholesome youth in a tiny blue corduroy outfit – however it all went off quite well as St John's has been done over very well by the inevitable BBC and the crypt has become a large bar with red wine and coffee. Yesterday, Monday, I took my VI form – Ted Hughes strangely mumbling with his eyes close to the paper read some animal poems and then lengthy extracts from this 'autobiography of the crow' he's doing, of himself really I suppose. (It seems so violent and not quite nice – better than the animals though). I took 2 Indians on the staff who drove me down in a mini and seemed to enjoy it. Well enough of this. – A further embarrassment this week, one of my pupils is the grand-daughter of the old lady in Suffolk to whom (as they say) Helen is cook! She tells me that her Granny is 'quite afraid of your brother because he is so clever'. I can't imagine what Rawle can have said, but I can see that the girl feels it's all awkward; if I go to see them should I sit above or below stairs?

* See p. 522.

Poor Ria very depressed (though delighted by the socks &c) but has gone to the Packers today and I hope this will cheer her up. I'll go now and cook a large dinner, in the hope that someone eventually comes in for it.

much love always and longing to hear all about everything
Mum x

(Valpy is still in Portugal, in luxury suite with bed which gives you a massage if you press a button)

St Deiniol's Library
Hawarden
Chester
10 July [1969]

Dearest Tina,

I have arrived here sneezing loudly, and shrunk from by everyone, but safely – it is very queer here – <u>very</u> – as strange, musty, smell about everything – I was only <u>just</u> in time (taking a taxi with a lady taxi-driver) for lunch – this was quite nice, with boiled chicken and ice-cream eagerly devoured, as by hospital patients – the guests, with the sub-warden, who seems to be in a coma, were seated round an imitation mediaeval oak table – of good quality – only the sub-warden had a silver napkin ring, we had paper ones – the guests are all men, and all decayed clergy-men – I'm the only lady, and I do think my skirts are too short – when I arrived at table they were discussing Austrian Baroque architecture, and the writings of Professor Asa Briggs – <u>there is nothing spiritual in them</u> – afterwards you go into a mouldering Gothic oak drawing-room for coffee – but everyone stays standing up, to show they don't intend to have a second cup – it turns out the place is really a theological college and everything is geared to the ordinands – but they were all away for the week-end – will be back in October, clearly a big event – I was offered a glass of cider at lunch – it was left behind by the <u>ordinands</u> – no TV in the 'common room' so as not to distract the ordinands – the croquet-lawn behind the library is to give a little recreation to the ordinands – After tea, which came into the common room on a trolley, with sandwiches and Battenberg cake, and teapots of that mysterious metal – some of the clerics helped themselves liberally, but I didn't like to – the sub-warden showed me the library – a wonderful wood-panelled Gothic library, but smelling frightfully of must – impossible, it seems, to work there during the winter because of the cold – what about these pipes? – they haven't worked since 1912 – the sub-warden explained <u>our library system</u> – you write your name on half of a ticket, then put the other half on the shelf where the missing book is – clearly nobody ever does this – clerics were tottering dangerously up and down the stairs and ladders. The latest Who's Who is 1927 – but there are quite a few dusty English Lit: books, and the sub-warden proudly showed me the files of The Victorian magazine – these may interest you – the chair I sat on collapsed <u>instantly</u>. My room is just like a Somerville first-year room, with a pink basketwork chair. It overlooks a gloomy churchyard, where a few ladies in hats are arranging flowers in jam-jars. However the church is pretty and the headstones look romantic in the bright evening sun. – The dinner bell has just interrupted me – I went down five minutes late, which I thought was about right, but they were half way through dinner already, the sub-warden absurdly presiding in a gown – a new, ancient deaf, cleric has arrived from the Canary Islands – he says that in 3 weeks he is going back to the Canary Islands – q. Why did he come at all? – another cleric said to me – <u>I saw you soaking up the sun on the back lawn</u> – I shall sit on the front lawn tomorrow – another cleric who seems to be wearing a wig (they've all <u>got</u> wives but haven't brought them) has asked me if I'd like to come to the Castle tomorrow to see the interesting chapel, but I shan't go, as he gives me hysterics.

It turns out the ordinands are all late vocations – men of advanced years – thank heavens they're away. We discussed <u>life-spans</u> at dinner – one of them said his father knew Newman well – On the other hand it must be admitted that it's beautifully quiet here, just the birds, and as all the clerics are really on holiday, I have the Gothic library almost to myself, and my room with a desk, and no-one disturbs you at all between meals, and I've done a lot of work already, and the whole house, including all the shelves on all the landings, is full of wonderful

old books, memoirs and novels (I'll have to give up the resolution to
stop reading Victorian things) and busts of Mr Gladstone; and the
clerics are very kind really and quite restful. – I've now actually had a
<u>bath</u> – the bathroom has a queer brass column to let down into the
plughole instead of a plug, and a brass soap dish with holes in it.

Thankyou so much for taking charge at the week-end – I really felt
proud as I said good-bye at having two such gorgeous daughters, in
fashionable nighties. Well, I shall certainly get all my work done here
easily, and shall rush back to see the twins: of course, I shall be able to
baby-sit, if you would like to go out. Do hope house-keeping money
&c is all right and I forgot to show you the plums – they were for
Sunday lunch. I don't think Ria will need to get very much.

much love darling,
Mum

St Deiniol's Library
Hawarden
Chester
14 July [1969]

Dearest Tina,

Thankyou so much for your letter, I was so pleased to have one as
all the clerics seemed to have one (many with Church Repair Fund on
the envelope) and they were glanced at amid the tapping of eggshells.
Many more clerics have arrived – some quite nice, including Father
something or other (Anglican I think) who is sportingly running a
hostel for religiously minded youth at Sussex University, with no money
and discouragement from free-thinking authorities. Unfortunately
he squints so hard that it's hard to tell if he's addressing you or not.
Others clearly think I shouldn't be here at all, and I do see that my
Swedish beach dress, which I'm defiantly wearing as it's nice on a hot
day, is too short for my years, but they'll just have to put up with it,
you and Maria both said it was all right. The Warden and his wife
come back on Tues: – hope she won't speak to me about this dress. It's
when I sit down it gets a bit short, so I try to draw in my old oak chair
rapidly at meal-time, but this won't do, as the clerics feel they ought to

<u>push in</u> my chair for me and worse still, half get up when I come into the room and bow frequently (like Daddy).

No TV in common-room though I think there's one in staff sitting room (all the maids are very kind and nice but wear very long skirts and white aprons) – and radio doesn't work – <u>hasn't</u> for many years I should say. There are some little figures in a glass case which I at first thought might be pin-football, but turns out to be <u>a model of St Deiniol's in the 13th century made entirely of edible materials</u> (i.e. marzipan). I asked the sub-warden when he meant to eat it and he replied <u>oh, not yet, we've only had it for three years</u>. Everyone nodded, and an ancient vicar who comes here every year said <u>we hope to keep it indefinitely</u>.

Bells go at 8.45, 11 (tea and digestive biscuit), 1, 4, and 7.30 but quick as I am into the old oak dining-room or common-room (for tea) I'm always last. Can it be they're sitting in there waiting for the bell?

The meals are very nice but <u>small</u> – the clerics finish their platefuls in 30 secs. flat – of course they're used to semi-starvation in country vicarages as I know well enough, and I suppose the ordinands are kept on a low diet – but I'm not complaining or buying biscuits (though you were quite right about this) because I'm steadily reducing round the waist.

It turns out that the Rev: Mr King doesn't wear a wig, but just brushes his hair forward, a human weakness – he's studying mediaeval Latin breviaries: but another little man has arrived from London University (studying nineteenth-century church documents and letters from some Tractarian, so he <u>says</u>) who really does wear a 'piece' and a Madras jacket from the C&A and tells me he uses Ambre Solaire: clearly he's regarded as worldly by the others.

<u>After lunch</u> Warden and wife have now arrived, and it's such a relief, as she's very nice – wears a long crimplene dress, but clearly doesn't mind what anyone else wears and is cheery and motherly – and has quite a lot to do I imagine because the Warden it turns out is <u>blind</u> and very stout – and she has to manage him as well as the ordinands. One of the clerics points out to me quietly that <u>all the drawers of the dressing tables are lined with pages of the Radio Times in Braille</u>. And this is true.

I'm so glad she's come – there was <u>much</u> more for lunch as a result and I can decline the invitations (from an ancient cleric) to visit

1. Mr Gladstone's seat in the parish church, on which Archbishop Benson collapsed and died.

2. The dog cemetery in the castle grounds where the tomb of Mr Gladstone's favourite dog may be seen.

I shall go to this later, and I'm always in and out of the parish church anyway, as there are fine windows by Burne-Jones – the west window is the last one he ever designed – and I want to see them both morning and evening, to get the different lights through them. I'm still mindful of not getting sunk in Victorianism – but I do do modern literature courses, indeed I find everyone else strangely reluctant to undertake them, so perhaps as I'm here it's all right to 'give way'.

When you say you can't stop laughing in church, is that because you've come to feel the whole thing is absurd? I do hope not! (I thought of this this morning when I was counting my blessings, one great one being that all 3 children are still believers, as we used to call it.)

It really is restful here and I shall easily get all my work done and a bit of Russian. It's a ridiculous but most peaceful and regular existence and very calming to the nerves. But I do worry about you and the twins in this heat, it must be so sticky pushing the pram. I shouldn't think it's any hotter on the Costa Brava.

I'll make a daring expedition now to post this in Hawarden sub post-office,

much love always

Ma x

Thankyou for getting in supplies: I've told Da that if an answer comes from Spain he must read it to you at once.

Beach Hotel
Attakoy
Thursday [summer 1969]

Dearest Tina,

I've decided in the end to write to Poynders G. as the post here doesn't inspire me with confidence – we do have a Guide Bleu (borrowed) which says that the post in the larger cities works 'as with civilised nations' but I don't believe this.

There is too much to see here, and Daddy is being very good and although he is <u>so</u> deliberate and keeps saying he'll just finish his cigarette or walk to the end of the beach (not much of an 'end' as the whole coast is strictly divided into lengths of greyish sand and bluish sea and each one is a private beach) – the next one, Turk Camping, is much gayer with loud songs and games but I am glad to be quiet here. Each room has a balcony where you can sit and have a glass of acid Turkish wine and it was built on the site of an old farm house so there are nice willow and plane trees, with leaves that make different noises in the night breeze.

You get into Istanbul on the public minibuses and taxis and more and more helpful and unintelligible people squeeze in as you get nearer to the city. You arrange what you're going to pay before you start so it's not worrying, and we're getting very good with the phrasebook. The Turkish for 'station' is 'tren' but what is 'train' I wonder? Old Istanbul is very dirty and seedy but tipico beyond words and rather like Spain used to be (except not the trouble about the girls). You have to look out as the porters carry vast loads of mattresses, chests of drawers &c through streets and there are horses and donkeys wearing blue beads against the evil eye, and everything including hair-cutting, bread-baking and furniture-making going on in the street. The watersellers have lovely water containers with luscious flowers, ladies and landscapes painted on the back, and a long tube through which water comes out ice-cold. I feel I <u>must</u> have one but Daddy is difficult and suggests it is <u>too heavy to carry back</u>, he was very reluctant too to buy a glass of water so I could snap him and now I've gone and let light into the camera by pressing the open button by mistake, I'm so miserable! Just when I'd taken a stunning picture in a Moslem cemetery, with children's graves with stone fezes on, and the father with a stone turban! I don't know what to look at next, as I've never seen Turkish architecture before and everything is different – a bit like Spanish I suppose. I think it's lovely in the mosques, the big ones are so empty and quiet and when you've taken your shoes off you shuffle over very old very soft lovely Turkish rugs with a green one here and there, grass green really, then there are very wide alcoves near the windows where people sit for hours mumbling over a Koran looking completely peaceful and it's so noisy outside. Travel description! We're going up the Bosphorus by boat this afternoon as there are some ancient fortifications and I know Daddy would like these. He calls the whole place Constantinople, and wants to trace the walls, and I feel it's his turn.

Still wondering about 10 o'clock feed – hope all went well!
much love Ma X

[St Deiniol's]
[1974]

[incomplete]

Daddy is bearing up very well really and I notice he keeps looking at the map, and working out the distances.

Poor Mary* has been called up for jury service, just as she's going to take her 2 weeks' holiday: admittedly she was going to spend it typing out 3000 envelopes to all the polytechnics, but she wanted to do this. I'm trying to get her to ask for a postponement, and I'm sure Rawle and everyone else will suggest the same thing. Certainly she's showing amazing energy, but the publishing business seems a bit difficult on one's own. I wonder how all these little presses manage – but then they do get grants from the Arts Council.

* Mary Knox, PMF's stepmother, had recently been widowed and had taken a secretarial job.

I see the Tories <u>say</u> they'll peg mortgages at 9½ per cent, but I shall have to read the small print carefully – I'm not sure it's not part of their obsession with getting council tenants to buy their houses on the grounds that all house owners are bound to vote conservative – but it does madden me that you and Valpy and of course 100000s of others have to pay so much at the beginning of your lives.

As for me I shall stay in my foul old nest till the time comes for me to put my head under my wing for good.

Back on Monday, Tues: Miss Freeston and Sainsburys! (A kindly minister asks if Daddy and me would like to come into Liverpool and see the big Marks and Spencers!) I don't mind that, but can't <u>bear</u> the idea of Puerto de las Reinas. Longing to hear about Paris – much love from us both xx Ma.

P.S. I read Criticón* last thing as a treat! – The Natural Man is getting quite critical and sarcastic! –

[St Deiniol's]
[postcard]
22 August 1974

Got your lovely letter, proudly put by silver plate, gong and visitors book in the Gothic hallway, lovely here and you're now allowed to make tea <u>all the time</u> in a Somerville-like pantry as well as general tea at !!, 4 and 10. Plenty of tec yarns in the yellow drawing-room for Daddy and we've got the rules for croquet out of the encyclopedia. I only wept <u>once</u> when Daddy didn't appreciate light through stained glass on Gladstone's Boat of Death where he lies in marble with Mrs G. Marvellous about the drier. Many amiable lunatics here, chatted and bowed to by Daddy. Best love in Paris, imagining you in Louvre XX Ma

---

* Tina was doing postgraduate work on *El Criticón*, a work by the Spanish philosopher Gracián.

[postcard from Alderney*]
20 July [1978]

I'm afraid this won't get to you in time but you will know I am really
on summer holiday when I tell you everything including my ears and
my shoes are full of fine white sand. Lovely here and they still go out to
milk the cows in the fields. Boat comes in from Guernsey to-day with
new supplies, big excitement. Mike has an outboard engine with a
string, which actually starts! This seems unnatural –
    Much love Ma. X

[25 Almeric Road, sw11]
[1979]

Dearest T and T**
    All well here, sun and rain, drainpipe working well, your geranium
is coming into bloom. Ria says I am not to make a fuss about my
Travel Arrangements, but I am v. worried. Paul Bloomfield's tea-party
was very mad, not to say macabre, cake made by mad daughter, I was
asked there to meet a silver-haired man in Olympic track outfit and
sneakers, he is called Lindsay Anderson and seems to be something to
do with films, perhaps Terry wd: know who he is, – the good news is
that Mary's landlord offered to sell her the flat for £10,000, £30 ground
rent – Mary's bank manager she says actually rubbed his hands –
of course he says it must be done through a bank loan, so that the
'excellent investment' as he calls it, will actually belong to the bank –
she is working hard at herb drawings and is well, came here to lunch
to draw herbs &c – I want to give a party in the autumn, for all these
Hampstead people who've asked me out, but Mary says yes and I could
ask the S——s (who are absolute death) and the vicar (with pectoral
cross, guaranteed to wreck any party) &c. – do you think she'd be hurt
if I suggested 2 different parties, I'd be glad to help with both of them?
I don't say my acquaintances aren't awful, but they are differently

* Where PMF was on holiday with Willie and Mike Conder.
** Christina was now married to Terence Dooley.

awful, and I had hoped to give them something hot to eat and even sit
down, do advise.

Two calls asking to buy frig.

Mary says my book-jacket for <u>Offshore</u> is terrible – as you know she
usually praises everything. Gloom.

Virginia Surtees rings up very madly and says we must all unite to
stop the M—— gallery (he's just sold this lovely Burne-Jones) as he is
only a <u>hairdresser</u> who has married one of his wealthy clients and knows
nothing about pix; also I've got to go to lunch to meet the Director(ess)
of Jewels at the Bmuseum – I know nothing about jewels and care less –
and now I owe her 1 dinner and 1 lunch, it's all so hopeless.

Don't know if this article would be of interest – prob: not as you've
finished it long ago – dreaded name of Ackermann appears!

I was knocked down by a bus queue and have a round bruise on my
arm, just like the mark of Cain,

much love ma

76 Clifton Hill, NW8
[postcard]
[April 1983]

It was a lovely Easter and like all inhabitants and visitors to Theale we
hated to go, but as you stood waving goodbye in the doorway in your
brown corduroy pinny you looked, we all of us suddenly felt and said,
very pretty, and a good deal better* – much love and thanks to you and
Terry XX Ma

Have not prepared anything for anywhere – feel I'm going rapidly
downhill.
P.S. Rosa Moyesii. I don't know who Moyes was, a Himalayan explorer
I daresay.**

---

* From morning sickness.
** Answer to botanical query.

76 Clifton Hill, NW8
11 May [1984]

Love and remembrance* for May 15th
    I'm sorry this is an oldish card, but it's the picture I wanted to send, a favourite of Daddy's too.
    Ma

76 Clifton Hill, NW8
[postcard of the cover of *Innocence*]
[July 1986]

So glad to hear news but I feel bewildered and wd. like to ask so many other things, looking forward to seeing you on Monday week but please let me know won't you if I can be of the least use** as really the things I'm doing are singularly unimportant now I come to look at them.
    Collins have printed these cards at vast expense, please leave it casually on the mantelpiece if there's room! And please could you look at the thunbergia in the greenhouse and fill up its water-dish, hope it has not passed away. No matter.
    Still sneezing. So glad the house will soon be rid of the dreaded mark-sheets and brown envelopes,
    So much love to you all
    Ma

76 Clifton Hill &c
12 January [1987]

Dearest Tina,
    They say it's going on for several days, and 'elderly people living on their own', old folk, like myself, are given useful advice, which is to

---

* For the birthday of PMF's grandson, Tina and Terence's son, Fergus, who died in 1982. The card was *A Boy Reading*.
** PMF had offered to help round the time of the birth of Tina's third child, Paschal.

keep warm, and to remember that it is warmer inside than out – not quite true here, where all the pipes have stopped working and Theo has gone down to work (which he never does on Mondays) because there is central heating at the College of Heralds. He left his bath full of water and Desmond and I found it had turned to solid ice – would be bath-shaped if it was taken out, which Luke would like. And that's the main point of this letter, to say how tremendous it was to see Lukey himself again, and more so, eating and bustling about and putting us all in our places. You and T have been so steady and patient with him all the way through and that's made him able to come through it, because it <u>was</u> an illness, even if it's never likely to come back again.

I wish I'd finished digging up the back garden before the great cold, as the frost would have got into the earth then and broken it up, but then there are so many things I ought to have done. I'm reading Virginia W.'s diaries again, not from the genius point of view, but all her little jealousies and miseries about the reviewers and the housekeeping and Leonard's rash, and going upstairs to tell him (where he sat solidly pipe-smoking and advising Labour Politicians) 'my book is hopelessly bad, I must destroy all the proofs at once' and Leonard steadying her down and saying 'you know you always say that, you know you say it every time'.

The lunch party on Sunday wasn't at all what I expected, not really a Virago one, but it would have been wrong not to go. Tim Hilton cooked enormous quantities – mussels, wh. I couldn't eat, but fortunately a little girl, a 5-year old, Lily, was also very critical of the idea of eating them and that, I hope, meant I wasn't noticed so much – pasta with a nice sauce, wh. I thought was the main course, then a beautiful leg of roast lamb with roast pots.cut small and mangetouts – the baby (9 months) sat there very gravely and good as gold, reminding me a little of Paschal – he has a cot in their bedroom and a wooden playpen in the corner of the living-room (bookshelf built all round the picture-rail, quite a good idea, but how to reach the books? But the bookshelves were all completely full) – one of the guests, in fact the mother of shellfish-rejecting Lily, was Jemima Thompson, now living at 34 Well Walk, where I was brought up, with a nice journalist husband from Newcastle looking like Philip Larkin, and her mother,

Ursula Thompson, but I don't know if you remember them next door at Chestnut Lodge or going to stay with them near Lulworth Cove, or the little brother Toby, now a psychiatrist. I walked back with Jemima through the freezing Hampstead streets (she was going to give someone a Greek lesson, having given up her job at Time Life when Lily was born) – enough of all this, you'll say.

Now a weather report on TV, showing those brightish clouds in the SW and very black ones in the SE, so hope it isn't, in Lukey's words 'terribly cold in Weston' you always manage to make things easy wherever you go, but still, with 2 tiny children, it <u>does</u> mean managing. – They keep saying it's the coldest night for 425 years – but can it be worse than those nights in Fergie's time, when the tree fell, and you all had to huddle into the living-room? Or indeed when Valpy was born, and all the patients crowded into my room because I had a new-born baby and so was allowed a coal fire? At least you're not in the shop and won't have to discuss the matter of the cold with an endless succession of people.

Desmond says he'll ring up a plumber and take him out 'for a few pints'. He (Desmond Maxwell) is not a bad sort really. I have one cold tap running (just), and a kettle of course. – He tells me (perhaps indiscreetly) that Theo's 'flat' at the College of Heralds, which Joan told me (and I think believes) was to sleep in while he was on official duty, in case the Queen wanted to make someone a lord in the middle of the night – is really just a spare office with a sofa, in case he can't manage to stagger home. And Joan bought some pretty tea towels for it!

I'm sure you don't realise, as one can't, working away at it, day by day, what an immense amount you've done at Moorland Rd, and how well everything is beginning to look. The hall, with the coloured glass, is such a good introduction to the house, then the other colours follow.

A letter from Broccoli Clark inc., Columbia, asking for my impressions of the Booker Prize. I think I might give them a few of my recollections, which would stop them being so painful, as surely nobody in England would be likely to read them.

I rang up Ria to congratulate her &, if everything doesn't freeze up, hope to have lunch with her to-morrow, when she doesn't have to lecture until 3.

We usually have the vegetable soup and French bread at Habitat and Ria recklessly takes more than one or indeed 2 of those miserable little squares of butter. I do hope nothing has frozen up in Bishop's Road, there is such a complicated balance to keep going there, and of course Tom-Tom hates the cold, but he has plenty of room to extend himself there.

Theo has come in, and is smashing the ice in the bath. BBC advises elderly people living on their own not to cut down on the food, so shall have my dinner, parsnips and bacon.

Now I'm going to ask you something which I hope you won't find mad or irritating or both, and that is, do you think that you and Terry could possibly find something else to go down on the living-room floor except the serape? I thought it was lost, and never expected to see it again, but since you've found it, and all the lovely colours (though not the right ones, I know) I should so very much like to keep it as what it really is, a bedspread, I haven't one here in London and of course not the Bishop's Rd bedsitter, (if John and Maria really feel able to do that) – it is the only thing I have left from Chestnut Lodge, as I wasn't allowed the opportunity to say what I wanted to keep from the sell-up at Blackshore, and all the things I cared about most were sold – well, all that's in the past, – but I carried the serape all the way from Mexico City, through N. York, then Halifax and back to Liverpool on the old <u>Franconia</u>, and it was never meant as a rug or a carpet, any more than your own heirloom patchwork quilt, and if it has to be on bare boards without any undercarpet I don't think it will last long, if it's walked over. Please don't think me mad, or even worse, stingy, but please could you take it up, I was wondering whether the green cotton dhurries would do instead, they're machine-made (the serape is hand-woven) and don't matter a bit: but I suppose they would be the wrong colour? Anyway I would be glad to contribute to another rug for your birthday, if I could please keep the serape, I think you can see from the way it's wrinkling up that it isn't really intended to go on a floor? It never has before. – I wish now I'd kept the undercarpet from Theale, but no matter. Don't be annoyed with me, truly I appreciate your goodness to me over so many years – it's just a weakness of old age to want to keep a few 'nice things' connected with the past and the serape as we said is 35 years old – I could never buy one like it now – and

I should so much like to keep it – perhaps it isn't a 'nice thing' to anyone else, but it is to me. so much love to you all Ma.

28 March [c.1988]

Dearest Tina, so many thanks for lovely Easter visit – Mary said on the way back in the train that she realised she'd overdone things with the envelopes and this holiday had made all the difference and I'm sure it has, and you know what it means to me to see you all, and I think it's gallant in the extreme of you and Terry to manage outings and expeditions to the beach as well as even more than the usual list of other things to do – but I think this has got beyond the stage of lists.

I hope dear Luke will change his mind about being tired of the human race, as he told me on the beach, or at least he'll kindly make a few exceptions.

I have been brushing my best black coat with a damp brush, and it looks all right, but then the hairs come back again, they appear to be growing out of the coat while my back is turned – (now hanging in the lower basement while some fanciful alterations are going on)

much love to all from Ma

[postcard of Paul Klee image]
[1988]

Dearest Tina – I'm sending you this although it's been up on the wall, because I thought you might like it – do you remember your knobblyhead?

I was so happy at Watchet, and loved the Vikings even in the adverse weather conditions. Thankyou for listening to my probably imaginary and certainly small and dull difficulties (I could feel how dull they were even while I was describing them) while you were at such a point of exhaustion and hateful headache and I can't tell whether it's gone away even now but I do hope and pray so, as it looked only just about bearable. Note that I'm not giving advice or talking about Nurofen or feverfew.

I got the train with 2 minutes to spare – wonderful, just like Round the World in 80 days – a train too grand to stop at Newbury, though they always do at Westbury, perhaps because there are so many Nobs there. The castors on my bed work very well – without them I know I should never have dusted behind it and perhaps I shan't now – but I know I could. Joan asks to know why I left my ironing-board behind? When it's hers and I only left it after a severe struggle of conscience. Too late now!

All my love to all the family and best wishes for

[incomplete]

29 November [1988]
– distraught –

Dearest Tina – Just off to dreaded all-day Commonwealth Fiction judging, followed by Kipper* exhibition (manias), still feel dreadful, but Ria much better and Sophie singing and chirruping. I'm in a terrible state because I wanted to ask you whether the weekend of 8 Dec would be any good, as there are various things (not important) I shd. be doing on 16th and 17th, but if Luke has part in play it's different and MY TELEPHONE HAS GONE DEAD.

Sad because Francis** has had horrid operation and can't get over David dying. much love Ma

27 Bishop's Road, N6
Tuesday [August 1989]

Dearest Tina,

I could hardly believe that you'd taken the time to write me a letter and such a nice long one. I loved hearing about the house – I still have your letters describing Milène's family, and Uncle Georges in the cellars, and this one is even better. I'm so glad you went to Brittany as

* E. H. Shepard.
** Francis King, novelist.

the weather is so wonderful you've got every possible advantage, and a
proper garden and fruit and grass instead of a square of paving and 2
geraniums in pots and an unclimbable carob tree. I, too, wondered if
P.* might be thrown out, and am so glad he isn't, I can imagine him
climbing and singing and Jemima <u>running</u> – how she ran on the beach
at St Audries – and Luke, I can see, quite invaluable, bless him, fancy
producing his French at 2 o'clock in the morning. No-one will ever
have grandchildren like mine, you know.

It is lovely here having all my meals in the garden if only it wasn't for
these dreary reviews and this pesky novel, but I must try and finish it
now, I daresay Collins (soon to move to Hammersmith as part of
Murdoch's economies) would let me put it off but I can't bear it dragging
on, though I feel myself getting stupider all the time. I felt quite grand
flying to Edinburgh** and eating the executive breakfast – orange juice,
fruit salad, bacon and egg and hash-brown potatoes, roll butter and
marmalade and a bran and raisin scone. Presumably to prevent
constipation. Hermione Lee was very kind, although she clearly thinks
I am hopeless about feminism, and says this is the generation gap – and
Marina Warner not bad, she admits I taught her at the Westminster
Tutors but says I made up her mind for her to give up her faith and she
went straight to Westm: Cath. to make her last confession – I'm sure I
<u>didn't</u>. B.P. (patrons) gave us all a vast lunch at some hotel. The festival
was in gaily striped tents and marquees which took up the whole of
Charlotte Sq. – and Edinburgh did look nice in the sun and wind
because they've had rain up there. I made the P.R. girl come on a bus
trip round the city afterwards so we had to get quite a late flight. And
now all the shuttle services are on strike because one of the hostesses has
been accused of selling the free executive champagne to the tourist-class,
of course they do! – Thursday I go down to the BBC to start these
recordings but I don't have to interview Anne Thwaite till next week.

All this must sound more than dull when you are on the plage (do
you remember the dear old French O-level papers with pictures?).
Meanwhile I want to wish you a happy homecoming but won't send

---

*   Paschal.
** To the Festival.

you a YOUR NEW HOME card as the bungalow isn't exactly that, but 10000 welcomes back, all my love to all of you –

xxxxx Ma.

You're quite right about Sarah. You <u>always</u> make nice friends – the wild craftswoman-hairdresser at Weston was nice – but Sarah was someone in particular, and my word how she'll miss you. I wonder what will happen to the Methodist Hall playgroup? But new times now and new places.

Mary had an X-ray because of her constipation but as far as I can make out there is nothing to worry about. Must keep her off diets. There's a new one, Bio-lite, which you take for a week and feel much lighter, – it's been shown to consist of 95 per cent tapwater.

[postcard: Millais' 'The Boyhood of Raleigh']
9 November [1989]

Thought Lukey might like this, though Raleigh of course inferior to Drake. Went yesterday to help unveil plaque to Burne-Jones on grim flats built on site of his gracious home. Fish-paste sandwiches and white wine in local library, where mayor asks us to drink toast to Pre-Raphaelites remembering that they were all good socialists. Kind lady gets me cup of tea, but John Christian sportingly drinks toast. Off to Kirkby L. to-morrow, back Tuesday, Wednesday Iris arrives in London. Longing to see you all but M. tells me you've started <u>teaching</u> again, how can you manage and what would you like for Xmas

will ring all my love Ma

27a Bishop's Road
London, N6
Sunday [1990]

Dearest Tina,

I was so cheered up when you rang, but felt furious with myself afterwards because (as always) I kept talking about all these unimportant problems of mine which aren't really even problems, as they will solve themselves – but I didn't like to ring back – however I really wanted to know about Kelly, and about your classes, and Luke's (not Lukey's, he was quite definite about that) school – as you left it, you were saying to me that it was most certainly something to remember all his life – a playground with the moors stretching away to the horizon in every direction – and he was getting on fine, but you wondered if there were any children there anywhere near his standard – and I wondered if that mattered to a child who was going to be outstanding anywhere, like Luke.

Poor R. Dahl died (what of?) and there were TV pix of the Giant Peach, wh: made me think of Luke's room, and his picture, with the teacher's comments, which I've lain and looked at so often in the early morning.

I also wanted to ask how dear P. was getting on, and whether Jemima still approved of the place wh: is privileged to look after her. But I never said anything about any of these things, nor do I expect you to answer them, but perhaps some time, at Christmas or after Christmas.

Willie gave me such a beautiful picture of you (she tore it out of her album) taken when we went up to Yorkshire – you were younger than Jemima is now, but Thomas thought it <u>was</u> Jemima, and the expression is exactly the same – serious, but immensely hopeful –

so much love to you all

Ma

[1990]

[incomplete]

. . . hasn't sold any of the tickets at all, which is scarcely surprising considering he's charging £37.50 for them. He says there are lavish refreshments, but who wants to go and eat lavish refreshments at Channings. Meanwhile I'm bracing myself up to tell Jeannie I'll do some weeding (I'm never allowed to spray) as I'd much rather do that than go and sit in a hide on the reservoir waiting for spoonbills. When they were working they never used to do anything on their days off because they were so tired, and I think that that really suited me better.

I've been listening to a sermon on the radio about preparation for dying, wh: he called the Last and Most Dreadful Journey of All, this is true of course but I do find it more than a bit depressing. Afterwards there was a Handel concerto, such a relief as he sounded as if he hadn't a worry in the world, though I believe he had plenty.

Kindly letter from Nan Talese at Doubleday saying that they are not doing too badly with the Gate of A. in spite of total ruin in the publishing industry and she would like to make arrangements about the next novel but alas there *is* no next novel.

It was a treat for me to see Paschal's school. I did not stare at him as that would not have done, but sitting at the other table I could see what he was doing and he worked so well and industriously and was enjoying it so much and enjoying doing it right, as of course children of that age do. It was quite hard work for them I thought but I suppose there are more recreations after lunch – much love to all Ma

[postcard]
[1990]

Please let me prune the rose again this spring. Fertiliser also needed of course although honeysuckles never seem to need anything.

27a Bishop's Road
London, N6 4HP
Wednesday [*c.*1990/91]

Dearest Tina –

I love Hope Cottage, the green, the elms, the rooks, the view, the new cooker and everything about it, and had a wonderful 2 days and it was such a treat to be collected from Sheepwash,* and to have Luke show me round Castle Drogo. How amazing he is Tina. I'd give so much to know

* The Arvon Foundation in Devon, where PMF had been teaching.

what is in store for him. You and Terry were so patient during the difficult time* and as a result he's growing up with all his self-confidence intact and the move has done him no harm, quite the contrary.

You said to me 'Paschal will talk'** and of course he <u>will</u>, I never doubted it, but the way you said it was very heartening, and I daresay when Jemima starts to talk they will understand each other better than anybody. P. manages very well considering his intelligence is so very much all there but doesn't get the supplies (yet) that other children do and he has to rely to a great extent on his own inner world.

The escalator up to the Archway Road is back! Smiling operative says You better ride up and down on it, lady, before they shut it again – but I can only hope it lasts till you all come. – John has taken a day off to mend large numbers of things including my bath taps, which suddenly wouldn't turn off. – I thought your plans were all admirable – the lean-to in particular, though I suppose the kittens will all move in – 'all' if they increase, as they might do at any moment since you say you can't tell their age. – Please don't think I was criticising the Great Hamper, I can assure you I didn't mean to. Dressing-up things are of vital importance and last their whole childhood and the Hamper is just what you needed. New York Times rings up again to say they are putting in 'a few sentences' about Van Gogh (wh: they pronounce Van Go': is that right?) and Cézanne as these are the only artists the readers have heard of, it seems. Article ruined in consequence but no matter.

Valpy rings up to say Red Cross and U.N.O. are sending him to Cambodia for a month, the President of Cambodia read some of his articles and asked him to advise, I can't help worrying as Khmer Rouge invasion in full swing and shall be so glad when he's back, poor old Angie must feel rather desperate. No post in and out of Cambodia. I rang up Rawle to ask him how dangerous it was and Rawle himself I'm afraid is very poorly as his back is so painful he can hardly walk, doc has taken x-rays – I know it's really bad as Helen came onto the line stammering frightfully. – But oh what a nice time I had at Milton

---

*   Her grandson Luke hardly slept until primary school age.
**   Paschal has Asperger's, and only learnt to speak when he was seven. He is now a graduate.

Abbot. – I hope Terry had a good journey back, at least – wind seems
to have dropped – much love Ma

Have been asked to judge next year's Arts Council £5000 bursaries for
novelists – 32 novels to read, but might be able to get something for some
crony. – I am going to ring up soon to ask what you want for Xmas!
Gloom and despair! But you did say you had a number of things in mind.

[1991]

Dearest Tina-

Not sure of price of Just What I Wanted as I know you kindly got it
from another catalogue, so enclose £20, tell me if it's not enough or if
it doesn't cover postage won't you. Thankyou so much, I'd given up all
hope. Of course if you should see a small armchair . . .

I see Maura* is appearing at the Islington Literary Festival to-night –
it says her recent Explaining Magnetism 'was hailed by the Literary
Review', wh: I don't see – but if I come to Marshville again – if I'm
asked, I mean – please do let me read the poems as I'm hopelessly
behind.

John off to Singapore to inspect the risks, I think, but may well be
wrong.

I foolishly went to PEN who are getting impossible and want to buy
a grand new writers' house (Cath. Cookson sportingly says she'll give
£100,000) and was nabbed by I. Quigley and asked to write a 'serious
article' in a New Tablet series, but what about? I thought of the
difficulties of teachers, but I don't know where to get the material. The
Tablet of course never pays anything. They call this an 'honorarium'.

I wonder if sedum would do well in your garden. It is tough and
flowers quite late. I'm sure you have too many suggestions.

So glad you had that marvellous weather on Saturday.

Haven't seen Sense and S. yet, but think it absurd that Edward
should be a painter –

* Maura Dooley, Terence Dooley's sister.

27a Bishop's Road
London, N6
[1995]

Just a note on one of my superior <u>cards</u> – deeply impressed by your
having <u>headed writing paper</u> already – I enclose the £600 wh. I hope
will help a bit, I think you've done marvels on the move and can
hardly believe you're welcoming visitors already but I know that's your
way – will post this now – I've told them at Dartington (where
organiser writes that 'the parched landscape looks more like Provence
than Devon') that you'll come and take me away some time on Friday,
1 Sept – I'm afraid it's farther than I thought but I look forward to it
very much
    love, Ma

                                        23 November [1995]
Dearest Tina –
    Am sending labels and cheque now as I don't know when you'll
have time for another raid on Plymouth and must get some wrapping
paper when I know what is to be wrapped. I thought Terence might
like the all-in-one life of Ivy Compton B, but otherwise I suppose the
familiar old book token.
    Poor Mary is in rather a state because 'the darkies' are preventing
her from looking after Monica. I think the trouble is that Monica
is really quite ill. It's a pity because the art teacher, though terrifyingly
bright, is really encouraging Mary a lot and the genial chiropodist
(whatever makes anyone take up chiropody?) was giving everyone
treatment and trying to raise a smile with little jests. Janet writes
that she has given a party for 100 in the village she lives in near Pau.
How can she be so energetic, or rather how can I have got so decrepit?
And Nancy tells me she is getting up a dramatisation of The Pillars
of the House for the new Charlotte M Yonge Fellowship (which is
causing great rage and anguish to the superior and ladylike Charlotte
M Yonge Society – restricted to 24 members)

Marina Warner came to lecture at the Highgate Institute on
Tues. – embarrassing as the members had made a clean sweep of all
the sandwiches and canapés by the time she got into the reading room.
It might have been an Oxfam distribution.

If Luke has an end of term photograph please let me have one –
much love to everyone Ma

Monday [*c.*1996]

Dearest Tina – This card is not at all nice enough for P.,* but even at
Muswell Hill they haven't anything such as I should wish, and the
thing is for it to arrive in time. And I'd be very grateful if you could get
one of the things on his list (not too well understood by me) –
meanwhile I have to think seriously about what Luke would like.

Alfie's eye seems much better now, but Ria has a kind of flu-like
feeling, which I'm sure comes of doing so many things at once. <u>Many</u>
costumes have been made for the play, which seem to me to need much
more work than anyone could fairly ask of the mothers. – you have to
tear up materials (gaily variegated) into strips and attach them at the
neck [illustration] – but Thomas seems quite pleased at taking part, and
like all his friends he's very bored with this last term at primary. Michael
has a large part (but his father now seems rather worryingly ill).

Joan (Theo's mother) died last week, I think simply worn out with
dragging up and down to St John's Wood to look after Theo – I can't
think how he'll manage without her. I heard from Desmond (who
lived in the basement) at Christmas, but he is determined never to go
and live in the house again.

Wednesday is the dreaded day when I have to get down to the
Gargoyle to have lunch and judge the poets – now that everyone
knows how very old I am I expect not to be asked to judge anything
again, but this doesn't distress me as I'm finding it more and more
difficult. – (There was <u>one</u> poem I liked very much, but I don't know

* Paschal.

whether I've still got the energy to fight for it and I expect I shall be
trodden underfoot.)

V. interested in news of your garden – the things that are making
headway are all practically wild and I'm sure that's the important
thing – the clematis Montana will do so much for you in spring and all
it asks is to be left alone.

Looking forward so much to seeing all of you –
Much love from Ma

27a Bp's Road
[1997]

Dearest Tina,

I meant to send this at once and got it ready and didn't send it,
more evidence that my mind is weakening. I hope it's not too late for
you to get something – I used to get presents for the dons, but I realised
from what you said that their day is done. Try not to indulge melancholy
thoughts about this.

The Guardian rang up (they never ring me up usually) to ask for
Five Wishes for the World for 1998. I couldn't think of <u>anything</u>, except
to abolish off-road motoring, and have those little packets of salt in
crisps again. Of course they meant serious thoughts about world
affairs, but the truth is, my horizons are shrinking.

We had snow here, and Eddie seems unwilling to go outside at all.
On Sunday I have to go to Jane Hodge's 80th birthday, in <u>Wimbledon</u>,
I ask you. She said 'no presents' because she doesn't want to carry them
back with her to Lewes by train. Of course, I should have sent something
by post, but I've only just thought of this –

much love to you all
Ma

27a Bishop's Road
N6 4HP
Tuesday [1998]

Dearest Tina,

This is just for when you're able to eat again,* and to say how worried I am about you. It's been such a long time, but you don't need me to tell you that.

<u>Alice in Wonderland</u> went off well at St Michael's – Sophie was one of the playing cards painting the rose-tree, and Ria recalled having taken the same part, but where could it have been? Parents loyally served wine and sandwiches, and collected large sums for the lighting, which eccentric Mr Williams, advancing from the stage, says is on the blink. – Valpy came to lunch on Monday – John did <u>swordfish</u> with lemon, and baked apples with raspberry coulis – Valpo looked well, but is not at all doing what the doctor ordered, just back from Washington. He says he has a high cholesterol level, but Ria bracingly says that doctors admit now they can't measure it accurately. His job lasts till next February, and after that he has to <u>find</u> commissions, but he doesn't seem worried by this. Of course, Angie is going to teach, but this won't improve things financially as V. has been claiming her as an administrative assistant against tax all these years. Laurence on the other hand is giving up the designer shoe-shop, and is going to teach English at some of Oxford's numerous schools for foreign students. Surely this is a step up. Greg has already been asked to lecture on his subject, wh: turns out to be thermal physics, at some Italian university, although he still hasn't finished his never-ending course. He has no plans to marry Lidia and Valpy says, perhaps as a joke, that she may be getting anxious, and Greg must remember that her brother is a guardia civil.

I enclose a piece from the Guardian about Stuart,** unpleasant in tone like all their interviews. (Why is it that when I'm talking to Ria, but at <u>no</u> other time, I always call it the Manchester Guardian, which makes her understandably scornful?)

---

* Tina had had pneumonia.
** Stuart Proffitt, PMF's editor at HarperCollins, who had recently left the company.

I've at last finished my intro to <u>Emma</u> and the OUP says it's all right.

All my love and good wishes,
dearest Tina, from Ma

[1999]

Dearest Tina,

I enclose the cheque feeling guilty as always at leaving everything to you to do. Do you wake every morning and check through a list of things that <u>must</u> be done before you go to bed again – mine is very trifling – must get one thing, or even one page or one paragraph written, something in the house cleaned (<u>never</u> a good turn-out, that's beyond me now), one person rung up (but I often don't do this) &c &c. I have at the moment 2 pieces for the LRB to do (but have written to get out of one of them), an intro. for the Folio Society for Middlemarch, an intro. for J. L. Carr's A Month in the Country for Stuart,* a serious piece for the New York Times on Vol. 2 of Richard Holmes's Coleridge and a vexatious piece which I'm also trying to get out of, for the New York Times magazine on the Best Idea of the Past Millennium, an absurd subject. I feel they want things like toast-racks and telephones – well, you may say, a few days' work but I am so <u>slow</u> and spend <u>far too much time</u> thinking about my ailments, and then going to the shops has its problems – the drink shop has been taken over by new proprietors who have installed a <u>very stiff door</u> wh: I can't manage – a good thing too, you'll say – and the grocer next-door urges things on me which he says he's got in for me specially, and it's true I <u>have</u> enquired about them, really by way of making conversation, which I've never been good at in shops – and one way or another I am terribly behind – terribly. And then I think of all you have to do –

Poor Paschal, poor Luke – but his fingers <u>aren't</u> thin, they are slender and distinguished, like yours. But of what use to tell him that? It's funny I remember Valpy used to worry so dreadfully about being thin.

* Proffitt, now at Penguin Books.

I think it's going to rain, but Ria has given me her new umbrella, it really is good of her, I used to nip down to Kings Cross to get them, but can't do it now. Getting old is not to be recommended, but it's so wonderful to have kind daughters – wonderful.

all my love your dithering old ma

27a Bishop's Road
N6 4HP
[c.1999]

Dearest Tina – I was so stupid when you rang up – as I explained to you, or tried to, I got home and just closed my eyes for a while, so didn't really take in what you were saying. – I'm <u>so</u> relieved to have this splendid present for Ria chosen for me. I did want something special and was trying to screw up my courage to go down to Oxford Street, but even then I didn't know what I was looking for, and, Tina, it was <u>really unselfish</u> of you to allocate some of your precious time and your present-finding capacity to helping me out. Yes, it truly was.

John is back, says Frankfurt is hideously cold. Lyn has had another boy, called Louis (rather unexpectedly). Feel another generation is knocking at the door.

I did enjoy the week-end, and both the concerts, and sitting by the sea in the winter sunshine (I'm not sure that Maria believed this). You were so kind, and it was <u>wonderful</u> being cooked for and looked after like that.

Much love
Ma

Embarrassing letter from the American Womens' Club, hoping I'm not tired out by giving them 'words of wisdom'. But I know they always go on like that.

Your children are a great comfort.

[c.1999]

Dearest Tina – Am sending this at once, as arranged. Feel ashamed to have complained about so many things whereas you are looking forward to double the amount of work, and dear Luke enjoys things in such a heart-warming way. I do hope he always will.

Have written to David Godwin* pretending not to understand exactly and hope that will keep him at bay. After all I'm very old, and can't be expected to grasp things properly.

Eddie scorns me. While I'm fiddling about trying to find my keys he stands on his hind legs and puts his paw on the keyhole in case I don't know where <u>that</u> is.

love to all Ma

27a Bishop's Road
[1999]

Dearest Tina,

I'm afraid I've asked you this so very often, as I feel very worried at the idea of carrying down 10 Easter Eggs and I shall have to ask you if you could get some, perhaps in Bude before the end of term. I will send some labels, but the important thing is the £££ I think.

Sophie is off to her Activities but John tells me they have <u>no</u> arrangements for anything to do indoors, surely they must have? It's fine to-day, but dreadfully cold.

I'm so <u>sick</u> of being ill, and now my foot's gone wrong again and I've lost my travel pass! I rang up Help the Aged but they tell me I must go to Wood Green or Crouch End and there are no buses. I think I must have dropped it while I was paying the taxi back from the Café Royal. I wish now I hadn't brought it with me.

My back feels as though it is under a bacon-slicer. Complain! Complain! But it's been like this since we took the trip to Oxford, which I enjoyed so much.

---

* The literary agent.

Trying to conceal an absolute conviction that Salman Rushdie's new novel* is a load of codswallop, in spite of his newly narrowed eyes.

How can they manage this new selective teaching system? Won't they need many more specialist teachers? Or will it just sink under a load of abandoned schemes?

Still I have my Golden Pen. And I do so want to come and see you all at Easter.

much love to all Ma

27a Bishop's Road
[1999]

Dearest Tina – I expect you've seen these pix** in some version or another but sent them just in case. The ones who seem to me to have <u>changed</u> are Mark and Martha, but we've all changed I expect. Film had good reviews, but I alas haven't seen it. Perhaps I'll have a chance one day, as I should love the lavish backgrounds. Stayed in all yesterday but man did not arrive to see to The Boiler. Really this could not matter less but it poisons one's whole life for the time being –

All my love Ma

10 July (I think) [1999]

Dearest Tina,

Luke here, such a pleasure to see him. Yes, he has grown a foot at least.

This is not a proper letter, but just an enclosure for Paschal's birthday. Ria is getting him the Right Kind of Lego, but I do not know which is the right kind.

I think I'll <u>have</u> to resign from the Royal Soc Lit committee, as Maggie Gee is due to come on to it.

---

* *The Ground Beneath Her Feet*, but she liked *Haroun*.
** Of the Fiennes family. Martha had directed *Eugene Onegin* starring Ralph.

Expeditions to the shops getting rather painful and I always drop some money and feel people are laughing at me –
much love to you and Terence – Ma

[1999]

Dearest Tina,

This is just to say, at the risk of always thinking of myself, which Ria does warn me about, that I do very much want to go on holiday, but I can now only <u>just</u> get down to the shops. But can you think of anywhere?

So glad Luke has arrived so successfully in Seville. It's rather a strange feeling to have him growing up like this – not painful, that would be quite off the mark, but it is a 'stage in life', even for his granny. all my love Ma

[1999]

Dearest Tina,

So much love and many thanks for arranging holiday – you mustn't think me ungrateful, I'm just a bit <u>creaky</u> – Ma

27a Bps Rd
Highgate, N6
[1999]

Will stagger out to the post with this – if I collapse on the way, take it as a sign that I did very much want to go to Oxford.

Independent have just rung up to ask about my education – I can't remember any thing about it. A haze is descending – all my love Ma

Maria Fitzgerald*

185 Poynders Gardens
London, sw4
18 April [1965]

Dearest Maria,

Just a short note as, of course, I've really got nothing to say! After seeing your train out of the station I went to the Charing X Road, and after some difficulty got the Lara music from Dr Z. for the piano – no guitar setting I'm afraid but at least the notes are there! Then I went for a walk through Soho to smell the cheese and wine and pretend to myself I was having a foreign holiday. Very racy outside the Spanish and Italian shops in Old Compton Street. I note you can get 'catering' sizes of all these Spanish things, olives and so on, so Angie would always be able to get them cheap that way.

Have had a bit of a tidy in your room. I bought myself Mozart's Kleine Nachtmusik, while I was in the music district, it has a terrible cover with a sultry blonde on it (<u>why</u>?) but it sounds nice while I'm dusting and polishing.

Sudden thunderstorm so I must take the things off the line. Sheets of rain, and the cringing inhabitants are driven indoors from the playground. Not like the lovely view through the arch out of the yard at Terry Bank – I love that view, and I hope it stays sunny for you.

Please give my love to everyone and tell Auntie Willie I feel very melancholy at not having come and am now going to the kitchen to have a glass of something – <u>it helps</u> –

Send me a line some time –

much love, dear

Mum

* PMF's younger daughter. The letters date from her first absences from home through to her time at Oxford. Thereafter she and her mother lived in London, and there was no further need for letters.

St Deiniol's Library, Hawarden
[postcard]
14 July [1965]

Can't show my room because it overlooks the graveyard at the back! Wanted to say that I found another card of red buttons and they're in the button basket, if you want them. Hope all is well and you aren't worn out with school and housekeeping.

(X for Daddy) Love Ma X

15 July [1965]

Dearest Ria – just in case you're too busy to think of these things – if frig: is giving up could you turn dial (inside back) to 6 or 7 till the heat-wave is over? Don't forget sunglasses and colour-film! I expect you've thought of all these things! Lovely here under an oak-tree by the stream in Mr Gladstone's grounds. (Guess who this is on the statue!). I'm so lucky to have this weather here. Please offer Daddy my sympathy in his thick clothes! XX Love Ma

Many more clerics now – we're quite full up.

Poynders Garden, sw4
14 July [1968]

Dearest Ria,

We're missing you <u>very</u> much and wondering how you're getting on cooking your first dins, but by the time you get this you will of course be an experienced old hand; perhaps your first postcard will come soon.

Tina is walking about restlessly packing and spraying things onto her shoes, only <u>one</u> sandal can be found. Yesterday they went out shopping and Terry bought some wet-look half-boots, and an orange top at <u>Miss Selfridge's</u> – <u>I am saying nothing about this</u>. We're all going to <u>The Idiot</u> at the Old Vic this evening, it's very nice of them to let me go with them – I don't know <u>how</u> often I've seen it by now so must guard against saying It's Not Like The Book.

I have now been to fetch my new specs from Mr Miranda, the genial oculist, they are very small and mean looking, like toy spectacles, with thin frames, and give me a stingy, cruel expression, and Tina laughs every time she sees me – but they <u>do</u> enable me to see the A to Z.

I went up to Grove Cottage, all the tiles are off the roof and lying about the garden, with ladders, battens &c. – Grandpa stood at the door looking at it all gloomily and then said: 'On the whole I think the garden looks <u>better</u> like this.' Mary showed me some of the old 17th century tile-pegs they found in the roof – they were made of birch-wood.

I've got so many books on my table I haven't read that there's a sort of barrier all round me, and nobody can see the T.V.

Beautiful weather, raspberries cheaper, clematis still flowering. The Devil Rides Out is on at the Balham Odeon, and Daddy wants to go, and says If Ria was here she would come with me, but I wonder.

When Tina goes to the Major tomorrow I shall have to start clearing up, but I shall be sad. She says it's the dullest little house possible, and she and the major will have to sit opposite each other at the tiny dining-table over the macaroni cheese, and give him a shopping list each day so he can fetch the things in his car. But perhaps it won't be too bad, and they go to Aldeburgh later. Anyway, no temptation to spend money. – Tina says she hates <u>all</u> the things she's got and all must be altered! – Wondering so much how you are getting on, you'll have to be patient and tell me every one of your adventures –

much love Mum

*Chez Mrs Parsons**

1 August [1969]

Dearest Ria,

Thankyou so much for your nice letters – I do hope Jenny is better now – I'm sure you'll cheer her up, as you've often done to me when

---

* Where Tina was nannying.

I've felt low and depressed. I feel I haven't much interesting to say, compared with gorgeous doings in Malta, but I'll write anyway!

Tina is giving me a course in <u>modern</u> baby care, which I am sure will prove <u>useful in the future</u> – things have not changed v. much I find since you were in your Moses basket – not nearly as much as they did between my times and Grannie's – but I didn't know the new way of folding the nappies, and how to put on the new 'Babygrow' rompers. Tina gets a bit impatient with me sometimes but I hope I'm helping her a little! The Parsons are back this week-end, driving back through sun-drenched France, as Mrs Parsons puts it, and staying in hotels chosen from the Guide Michelin – but England is also sun-drenched, a bit too much for poor Daddy who's still flogging down to the office in his fusty suit, and still doing those fearful tickets!

I feel much better for my stay at St Deiniol's and had some very nice beaux – Dr Buckley, in his neat orange wig, sometimes came and had a tiny glass of sherry with me and my favourite was called Mr Snodgrass, believe it or not, he was a curate from Liverpool with a real Liverpool voice – unfortunately he went for a day out to North Wales and the friends he went to call on were out so he went for a cup of coffee and a roll 'at a modest café' and his front tooth <u>broke</u> on the roll so that he had to talk all the rest of his time at St Deiniol's with his hand over his mouth! We had lovely weather all the time and I was very happy relaxing among the cows, buttercups and oak-trees. I've also done nearly all my work for next term.

Thankyou very much for looking after Daddy &c. while I was away. Things were getting a bit dusty when I returned and many eggs had been cracked over the stove, but all is straight now.

Tina is going up to Oxford next Tuesday to settle Francesca into her new flat and hang all the pictures and fixtures before Suza gets to it!

We have now received an invite to William and Mary Jane's wedding on the 6th September – unluckily the day that Tina and Linda are going to Málaga, but I've accepted for you (it's a Saturday), and I do hope this is all right as I regard you as my great supporter at weddings! (I'm sorry, it strikes me I said this in my last letter; forgive me. You see how little news there is.)

I went to return my (over-due) books at Chelsea and couldn't imagine how the Kings Road inhabitants could endure the heat in long velvet gowns sweeping the pavement. However, some thundery rain now which will be good for my plants. (The weather – discussion of the weather). I got V and A* an African violet for their first wedding anniversary. Daddy says they really did bloom in the wadis, but the flower was over in the same day: he can't understand why ours goes on blooming.

Mrs Pereira is still very smart, but for some reason she has purchased a large bucket of small white stones, which the sturdy baby throws about the landing, causing everyone to slip up.

I'm keeping your 'Petticoats' carefully. The owner of the newspaper shop is now keeping it himself, having come in one morning and found the ridiculous manager fast asleep in bed – he never used to get up and sort out the papers so they were never ready for the children to deliver, and that's why they were always so late.

Much love darling. I wonder what colour your shorts are? Have you been to see where St Paul landed – love to everyone and to Alison – x Ma

Poynders Giardino
5 August [1969]

Dearest Ria,

Thankyou so much for lovely letter, boat trip to the islands sounds truly wonderful. So sorry Ellie is seasick (I do remember Mrs Packer I think calling her Ellie before?) When you say sailing boat, I suppose it has an inboard engine? If you get any chance of sailing and actually holding the little ropes, do try – don't laugh at me – as any chance to learn these rich sports should be taken, opportunities aren't so many, and it's amazing how useful it comes in afterwards! You were too little to try sailing at Blackshore.

Very hot here and Tina quite exhausted with the twins – she went up for her day off to Oxford to help Francesca with the new flat and

---

* Valpy and Angelines.

Mrs Parsons told her: <u>Of course I had to have a proper breakfast and a stiff drink after my heavy day looking after them by myself</u> – Tina never has either! She's coming home this week-end for a flop.

I too went up to Oxford (not the same day) to try and see Uncle Rawle, but just missed him, very irritating, William's flat was empty except for boxes of old shoes and torn up engagement books from which (spy, spy) I managed to find out their next telephone number. On the way back one of my shoes fell off just as I was getting into the train – it fell right under the train – but just before we started a kindly man managed to hook it up with his umbrella – I was so grateful – but his wife, in a white plastic hat, seemed rather annoyed. How could I have arrived in London with only one shoe?

Thankyou very much for the photos, which have just arrived but we haven't had time yet to study them as they deserve.

I will write again and give you details of your train to Cornwall &c. I quite agree it's better to find out these things in advance! (and arrive at the station one and a half hours early!)

I got 2 bathtowels at the Sales but the clothes are hopelessly expensive – I'll have to go on dressmaking! No lace for me, dear, thankyou – it was granny you know who liked lace, not me!

much love

Ma X

[Poynders Gardens]

10 August [1969]

Dearest Ria,

I think your best train to Rachel's* will be to Saltash which is 9 miles away. There are many more trains to Plymouth which is 14 miles away but this seems rather far to ask her to fetch you. The Saltash train leaves Paddington at 12.30 p.m. and you get in at 16.55 (cost 62 shillings each way). There are earlier ones but it might be a strain catching them! Tina will still be in London – is going down to Jinnie's later.

* Rachel Hichens, a friend.

I will write to Rachel and tell her you are coming on this train and I'm sure all will be well as after all Liz can meet the train if Rachel is busy.

<u>Very</u> hot here. Tina and Francesca were here on Saturday and we just lay about in heaps. There is a little air on the terrazzo, where our geraniums are now growing strongly. Hippies have invaded the centre of London and are sleeping out in Piccadilly Circus, stealing milk off the doorsteps. The sky is a sort of leaden pink.

Just been up to Grove Cottage – Grandpa very frail in his white linen suit and says he can just about manage to walk 50 yards a day – no more. It turns out William and Mary Jane are going to get married <u>twice</u> – once in a Catholic church and once in a C. of E. church. Surely we shan't go to <u>both</u> ceremonies?

Rawle is much better and is writing a book.

I'm still altering my summer dresses for the holiday – the blue one with daisies (which I don't suppose you remember) fitted quite well in the end – I took Daddy to the C and A and he got a decent pair of khaki trousers. Unluckily he bought a pair of hippy Chinese pyjamas with three-quarter legs (you couldn't tell this from the packet) and Tina and I had great difficulty in making him take them back.

Thankyou again for the lovely letters – they're all by my bedside. It seems ages since I saw you but I'm so glad it's all such fun – much love Mum

[postcard from Istanbul]
19 August [1969]

Hope you had a good journey home and are comfortable in most unglamorous Clapham! We've forgotten the strings of the li-lo! This came of my losing my list, but otherwise all is well, a lovely breeze and temp: of 100 on the beach (less than Cordoba though!) sitting under fig-trees and acacias – Daddy in new M & S finery.

All our love Mum X

Beach Hotel
Attakoy
Thursday [1969]

Dearest Ria,

I think it is really better to write to you at the flat as I am not sure how long you are at Rachel's and the post is hopeless here. I'm going to try and put different things from my letter to Tina if I can. Note I'm using the lines supplied by my 'Winfield' air-mail paper, like Valpy, so as to write really nicely!

Very hot here but nice breeze from the sea – fish-laden near fish-market – we are sightseeing keenly, but not in luxury as you did – we have been to Hagia Sophia which is huge inside, I don't know how these buildings with domes, mosques and Byzantine churches, were built so high, much higher than cathedrals and yet they're strong, because you go up to the galleries up a ramp inside the walls, broad enough to drive a horse and cart, and the floors of the gallery are solid marble, very cool if you take your shoes off, wonderful carving, but the rotten Turks have broken a lot of the crosses off. Marvellous mosaics in gold and colours, with John the Baptist's beard waving in 7 shades of brown. And Ria the Bazaars are so wonderful but Daddy's not keen on them, naturally, and I've no money and I suppose we couldn't get the stuff home anyway, but there are piles and piles of Roman antiques, embroidered kaftans, sheepskin coats – but alas the prices have gone up – still low by Kings Road standards, but too much for me – they are wistfully fingered by hippies of whom there are large numbers in the smelly picturesque old quarters. They try and sit on the edge of the cobbled streets, but are either knocked off by beggars who want to sit down themselves or knocked sideways by lorries and donkeys.

We're doing quite well about cafés because of course they don't sell glog, but real lemonade, which is nice, and Turkish coffee in those little brass things, and large hot rolls with fried eggs in them. We get stale rolls of course at the Beach Hotel, but there is very good bread baked in ovens in the street. Daddy walks about in thick socks and shoes as this is what they did in the army! He's very good with the map though.

The Poly-Lunns are nice and superior, but not too pleased as they daren't risk the Turkish transport and are stuck in the Beach Hotel, except for costly expeditions. However to-night they're going on a Night Life tour, with a <u>cocktail</u> at the Istanbul Hilton!

Much Love, longing to see you and hear all news X Ma.

(At last I've heard a muezzin calling to prayer!)

[postcard addressed to the Misses Fitzgerald]
26 August [1969]

Thought you might like this peacock. We're looking forward so much to seeing you Tues: though as I have to go straight to work I'm a bit worried as to how Daddy will get back with all the luggage – I'm afraid he'll collapse on arrival! Went to a yoghurt parlour and pilgrimage mosque yesterday – on to Izmir to-night. (Travel description ends here) much love Ma

The Abbey
Iona
Friday [1970]

Dearest Maria,

This is my last day in this lovely place – am sitting looking at the sea which is a kind of silvery colour, locked in by islands, with 2 white doves and a sheep staring at me from about a yard away: I'm sitting on a bench on the seaward side of the Abbey – I ought to be at meditation, but am writing to you instead. Tomorrow I have to catch the ferry – an open boat to Mull, and then the ferry to Oban, a lovely crossing among the Inner Hebrides, a bus across Scotland to Edinburgh and then the night train to Clapham – I shall arrive before the underground opens I fear.

Letter from Daddy says that you are charging across Yugoslavia and having a wonderful time, and I don't suppose I shall ever hear one half of your adventures.

We went on a pilgrimage all round the island on Wednesday, singing hymns on the beaches, in the old marble quarry (lovely pale green marble of which the altar in the abbey is made, but the quarry is not worked now) and on the hill-tops. The sheep and highland cattle gazed at us. Great variety of dress, including full ski-ing outfits and Alpine boots, and one American pastor in jungle survival kit and a tartan bonnet marked Commonwealth Games 1970. (I could see his children were embarrassed by this.) A young Finnish pastor, with a pipe and blond beard, went barefooted but wearing a knitted white hat. I always look at myself as a sedentary timid kind of person but on these occasions I realise we really are quite used to walking and it's such a relief not to be carrying anything that the rocks and hills seemed to be nothing!

I am sharing a room with a kindly grey-haired lady and we get on very nicely. I am on lunch duty, as we all have to help with the work here, but I don't mind that: I'm in charge of the washing-up. In spite of long walks and sea-air, am getting very stout on porridge, bacon and eggs, scones, Scotch pancakes and gingerbread. Fruit only comes over once a week on the boat from the mainland.

The communion service here isn't a bit like ours – the bread (a delicious loaf baked in the abbey) and the wine are consecrated at the altar and then brought down by deacons and passed along the pews, and you break off a bit of bread and pass the loaf along – I thought I'd hate it, but I rather liked it in the end: a Scottish minister here told me that in some Scottish churches everybody has separate glasses for the wine! The Presbyterians, too, don't kneel, so if you're in the row behind them there's not much room to put your arms, but one shouldn't be worried by these little things.

A new group of American ministers have arrived – they sailed across from America as a yacht crew!

I am doing a lot of pebbling on the beaches, which are lovely, with pinkish-white sand and light and dark green marble pebbles.

much love darling and always thinking of you all x ma

185 Poynders Gardens
London, sw4
Friday [*c.*January 1972]

Dearest Ria,

Thinking of you very much and wondering if the snow has begun to fall, and when your first letter will arrive.

I'm back at Queens Gate, which has been transformed with more white-painted fire doors so that it's impossible to get from one part of the school to the other. The Russian teacher – typical in every way, with beard, elderly, scented, and one of those turban like hats – came back into the staff-room saying 'Where is now the class? I cannot reach because there is no doors in the walls.' Fortunately my very worst pupil has been asked discreetly to leave the school so I shan't see any more of her.

I watched the ski championships on TV with some alarm – lorryloads of snow were being poured on the <u>piste</u> and everyone was falling down and making 'marvellous recoveries'. C & A are still selling the dreaded ski jackets, but they are not so nice with yellow linings.

I have bought some Irish tweed in the sales, dark orange and brown, to make a skirt, as those in the C & A aren't long enough for me – I do hope I can cut it out right, as it is herringbone and must all go the same way, and round the waist the other way – it's what the patterns mysteriously describe as 'with nap'! I'll report to you how the old sewing machine goes as I expect you'll eventually want to make some summer things, incredible though that seems – that is (it's just occurred to me) if you come home and not to the problematical flat.

<u>Very</u> short letter from Valpy, who is staying at Downside while Angie is at the wedding in Córdoba, getting up at 6 and wearing his habit. I suppose they ring a large bell. I do hope he'll get into the way of writing longer letters when he gets to Guatemala.

Trying to clean up a bit, but I <u>can't</u> repaint the bathroom because it means going without a bath for 3–4 days <u>twice</u>, while the two coats dry, and I'm wedded to my bath. It does look awful, though.

Mrs Sée's memorial service yesterday – lovely singing, absurd and tactless remarks by the vicar –

X much love mum

Miss Freeston's
[Westminster Tutors]
6 January [1972]

Dearest Ria,

I'm writing this at Miss Freeston's, although I expect to see you at supper-time, because I wanted you to get a letter soon after your arrival, just to wish you luck! No pupil just at the moment (it turns out that Miss Freeston didn't like the first timetable and the 2nd was actually chewed up by Topsy, who is dirty, blind and smelly beyond words) and I'm sitting here in my carefully brushed fringe and new M & S blouse and nothing to do. I've resolved not to go into the Army & Navy as I simply mustn't spend any more money, and the only way to avoid this is to sit still on someone else's premises.

I realise that you must have been feeling sad this week and John* looks very sad and his beard very long and dispirited looking, but I'm glad that this is a decision you've taken entirely yourself and I hope and think it'll be something you'll enjoy; if it's not, of course Daddy must bring you back at once and we shall think of something to tell the Speisses.

I shall be very lonely without you and without your encouragement in my depression, but I shall and must get used to it, and I've been fortunate in that, having 3 children, it's been spaced out over the years and you get accustomed to it as you do to everything else – nature is remarkably self-healing in this as in other respects, but it's a great wrench, there's no denying.

Now don't forget to eat well and be in the fresh air as much as possible, because your health has not been so very good after the extremely hard work for the exam. (The trouble is I think that it gets dark at 4 and then one starts eating cakes, but they're wholesome too.)

Best Love and we are all thinking of you – X Ma

* John Lake, Ria's boyfriend, now her husband.

185 Poynders G.
Saturday [10 January 1972]

Dearest Ria,

John called back looking very depressed and beard more drooping than ever with the car-key, and told me you had had to start from Birmingham! A most unwelcome extra trip up the M1. I'm afraid and I can't think <u>when</u> you'll get into the Mayrhofen! Longing to hear how everything is.

Meanwhile I'll tell you about the poor way I've been managing so far! I started down to the British Museum, but fell asleep there over my books, and had to be awakened by a kindly American scholar sitting next to me! So I thought I'd go home, but then felt wide awake. Then I thought I'd do some sepia drawing with my Rotring, I'd been saving this up, as I love drawing and it calms me down, but it wouldn't work AT ALL and when I unscrewed it it poured dark brown ink all over me and my drawing and my notebook and the library book kindly got out for me by Auntie Mary! And when I re-screwed it up and tried to draw the nib just scratched, and when I pressed a bit harder the nib <u>broke</u>! I'm so miserable as it was my Christmas present and I'm sure would be lovely to draw with and now it's ruined! I don't understand the instructions at all, and fear I shall have to wait for months until you come back again!

I've taken the rest of the evening trying to mop up the ink, water &c. and repair the ruined things.

However the glove is going quite well, and now I'm working out my own pattern and shall write it down and throw away the dreadful glove booklet.

I'm thinking so much about you, I think it's most courageous to launch out into this formidable world of ski hotels and ski instructresses with flashing smiles, but I'm sure you'll get the measure of them – after all you managed very well with the postmen.

The bathroom basin is stopped up <u>again</u> but I think that's one more little thing Daddy must do when he returns.

Do hope your nose is not getting too cold.

Much love always X Ma

Poyndersgarten
16 January [1972]

Dearest Maria,

So distressed to hear about your loneliness which I understand perfectly, and though I hope perhaps things may get a bit better, <u>you must not worry for Daddy will fetch you back after a month if you feel you can't go on</u>. It might be awkward for him but <u>if</u> you feel the whole thing really won't do, you know we should never let you go on being unhappy. Daddy is putting through a call to the office tomorrow and I do hope he will be able to speak to you direct and then we shall know exactly what you think.

It's always awful at first – Tina rang and said that even Lynne felt like walking out of Harrods after 3 days, because nobody spoke to her in the tea-break! <u>But if it goes on and on, that's different</u>. (Needless to say, Oxford must be quite different, as your friends must be in various colleges anyway and you'll have to work in some kind of team in the labs I expect.)

Sunday afternoon and Daddy has just woken up and is making himself a large cup of tea! He's annoyed because I didn't call him earlier and says he's lost 3 hours of his life! But I meant well in letting him snore on!

I have cut out my Irish tweed skirt but daren't look at the pieces in case I've cut them out the wrong way up. Several vital pieces of the pattern are missing anyway. Have also finished the bootees for Miss Singh's illegitimate baby, but can't find any baby ribbon.

I'm turning out the kitchen cupboard bit by bit, and washing the drawing-room carpet section by section (this doesn't appear to make a bit of difference) as everything makes me so stiff these days. I can still touch my toes though.

I don't remember whether I told you that I lost one of the precious Fair Isle gloves on the 45 bus, and the heart just seemed to go out of me, so I've given up – but not entirely! I've unpicked the famous red gloves and am knitting them up again for you!

This letter seems to be all about handiwork, but I'm thinking so much about you dearest – love Ma X

185 Poyndersgarten
23 January [1972]

This is not a proper letter but just to send you these forms, as they should be sent <u>to the school</u> (Godolphin) by Jan 31 and I can't fill in some details about your exams – also am not sure about date of your <u>leaving</u> school – shouldn't you technically be there till March? As you see I've got Daddy to sign it so it can go straight to the school secretary.

I'm waiting now for Daddy to ring you up tomorrow and see how things are and what you feel about staying.

I went to Oxford on Sat – Tina stunning in sage-green trousers and Francesca getting avocados ready for little supper for Pole. Tina now thinking (vaguely) of year in West Indies at some point: she MIGHT ask Francesca's brother, the blind headmaster, about it, however, her finals are obviously the main thing at the moment. We both had a good worry about you!

John came round this morning and kindly helped with collapsed tyre and total non starting of car: I asked him to lunch next Sunday but he is all booked up with many engagements! Also very busily preparing these lectures, surely it's very good that he's been asked to do them? Beard much the same length. He tells me Mrs Packer thinking of coming to Austria for week-end, but I've rather ignored this and sent Alison the cost of 7 days holiday in case she could manage this.

I've sent the part of your form that has to go to the <u>college</u> straight to Lady Margaret Hall.

Had lunch with Auntie Mary and went to see Grandpa's headstone in the churchyard* – I know this sounds gloomy! But it looks very nice – green slate with lavender rosemary and roses planted in front of it.

Thinking of you so much and waiting anxiously for another letter. The reports here don't say there's any snow! –

much love always

Ma X.

---

* At St Mary's, Hampstead, where PMF is also buried.

185 Poyndersgarten
29 January [1972]

Dearest Ria,

Your last letter which came this morning actually made me laugh (I mean about breaking the skis) which none of the others have, as you can imagine. So glad you can be outside more, instead of inside with the willing infants – one of the great points was to get a few weeks fresh air – I expect fresher but scarcely colder than it is here, for all the things on the line are freezing.

I've had such a horrid Saturday morning – I was looking forward to it so much at the end of a long hard week! I got all dressed up to go down to see 3 art galleries which were said by the Times to be showing pictures by you-know-who, and one gallery was shut, in one the director hadn't turned up and the tottering uniformed assistant didn't dare open the safe to take out the Burne-Jones, and in the third the B/J turned out not to be by the Master's hand at all! When I went to Marks & S. to cheer myself up by getting a petticoat for Louisa (she's about three quarters finished) I was told sharply that little girls don't wear petticoats now! And when I got home I found I'd lost my quite new umbrella! (not the broken one – the best one). And when I started distempering the kitchen ceiling I slipped again and broke Daddy's large bottle of Pear Brandy which was presented to him at Mayrhofen and which he values highly! I haven't been able to tell him this yet as he's working to-day. I feel really low, and I do love a free Saturday – I thought I was really going to get things done: Yesterday evening however I went to see some early English watercolours at Agnews with Mme. De B., and they were very nice: but she's getting rather tottery – mislaying her bag, &c. – too!

Tina has been so good, frequently ringing up at her own expense for a chat, so I don't feel so lonely. She seems to have had a tremendous feed on her birthday, but her digestion is perhaps a bit better now.

I shd. love to see your red skilehrer's jersey.

much love always Ma X

Poyndersgarten
12 February [1972]

Dearest Maria,

So glad to get another cheerful letter, and about the jam pancakes. But I wonder why there's no snow, when it seems to fall in the other valleys?

Electrical blackouts are now in full swing and very boring, as I can't sew, and everybody talks about them the whole time. I'm hardened to them because of the not-to-be-mentioned Blitz and the frequent crises of the houseboat, but had a very macabre tea-party with Miss Chamot and her Russian companion, Lulette – many samovars, ikon-lamps and silver candlesticks were produced, and <u>many</u> references to the old days. But Miss Chamot was so kind to me and lent me her precious Burne-Jones notebook to look at properly. Yes, his sacred handwriting is now beneath this humble roof! But the lights keep going out!

I am colouring some book plates I've drawn for the Peter Norton baby, to stick in the 5 Beatrix Potters I've bought as a christening present, to make them look a bit more individual – but anyway they're rather expensive now, and I shall leave the prices in! It's the thought that counts!

Letter from Liz to say can she come and see us soon, and she's taken on Guide Camp as well as the lunatics' outings, crippled classes &c. She really deserves some reward because she's a good girl. I always feel an absolute swine when I hear what she's been doing.

V. hard work at Queens Gate as many staff absent and I feel I'm getting very nasty to the girls, I said something nasty yesterday. I must check this,

Best love always. X Ma

Miss Freeston's
17 February [1972]

Dearest Ria,

Daddy says some schnee has fallen so I hope there's enough cover to please the Lunn Poly's.

The christening on Sunday was most strange, 6 families at once in freezing all-glass modern church – fathers were young dockers with moustaches and purple velvet shirts with matching ties, the grannies with pale blue and pink hair and orange velvet trouser suits: it was very good that they'd come to church at all, but the vicar was clearly acting as a kind of missionary and referred to the Our Father as 'a little prayer we often say'. I was so sorry for Peter and Stella when the lights went out during the christening tea and the children began to howl while others stumbled over the plates of ham and tongue, tea, trifles, whisky, coconut cakes and Guinness. The baby was sweet, but Canvey Island itself is a nightmare, all brand new houses in little squares of earth standing in pools of water, for it's all practically below sea level, and unmade roads to the 'estates'. Of course Peter has worked away fitting up cupboards &c. with wood removed from half-built 'homes' on other estates. Incidentally the Gaskaren Road houses now look nice, with neat black tiles, but these have been fixed onto damp wooden packing-cases!

My candle is burning low and Miss F. allowed only one each. I have 'got' that you want to head home on the 26th, though, and if more snow falls, and if Daddy can take me out in March, it would be lovely to be out there together, however I expect you have made arrangements of your own with John and needless to say it would be lovely to see you at any time.

Lady Hardinge on Sunday (she's turned off all light and heat to help the country's economy) and Tenants' Association meeting tonight –
much love Ma

[postcard from St Deiniol's, Hawarden]
[14 July 1972]

Dearest Ria, All well here but they have locked the gate in the park which led to the dogs' cemetery: however I climb over it. Have got wool from Latchie shop, where tea-cosies well understood. Hawarden choir have won at the Eisteddfod and this is the main topic of conversation.
much love Ma

Sunday 18 July [1972]

Dearest Ria,

By the time you get this you'll be in Teheran – so I can safely
congratulate you on your tremendous undertaking. But at the moment
I calculate you're sitting in St Mark's square with the pigeons, while
I'm turning out the flat, also with the pigeons outside, but there the
resemblance ends,

I am giving your walls another coat of good quality olive as can't
afford more undercoat, but taking down the posters that were stuck up
with glue large portions of the wall came away and the posters also tore,
some of them – I'm so sorry but my only consolation is that you spoke
of changing everything and I expect you will have acquired many
fairings from the bazaars and souks of the mysterious mid-orient.

Tina is getting on all right with the Major – he is very nice it seems
and says 'Excellent, what ho!' no matter what she cooks. Awkward
moments though when the dotty wife comes back and tells Tina about
her tensions: however I'm sure Tina has told you all this.

I have at last got a lustre Sunderland plate, with THE LORD WILL
PROVIDE – like I used to have. I went into a shop where I've been
before, to talk to the nice queer man about them, and I asked if he had
any cracked ones for £1 or £2, and he said 'Yes, you can have this' – and
it's hardly cracked at all, and was marked £10 in the window! I thought
these things only happened in TV serials!

much love always Ma

[Poynders Gardens]
23 July [1972]

Dearest Maria,

Sitting on the sofa peering through my small, eccentric looking
spectacles (I don't have to sit near the light now and it's a much better
olive – if only I could leave the 4th wall you'd see the difference!) I've
just been dragging the furniture about and I think I have broken my
leg, but I'll tell you whether I have or not in my next letter: in any case
I am stained indelibly olive green. It won't come off my legs at all, and
makes me look like something from a horror movie.

Really I haven't any news at all except the story of Tina, the Major and his mad wife, and this I am sure she is telling you in her letters: whereas you must have so many things to tell you won't know where to start. I'm longing to hear about the Yugoslav – Turkish border and the Turkey – Teheran part – holiday snaps! Holiday stories! At the moment I imagine Nigel and Jan drifting in a gondola 'neath the Adriatic stars and him recklessly using the whole 30 shillings a day standing her a cassata, but perhaps it wasn't like this.

Eddie, the slobby Irishman, is back – I heard him saying to a lady in the yard 'aren't you glad to see me again?' but she did not reply. Next door they've bought a budgie, which stands outside moulting in a very common-looking cage. The little girls take no notice of her whatever. I wish they'd go away on holiday.

I must now start getting ready for my trip to Iona – I have given Daddy the money, but he has not given me the tickets, so I am rather anxious. I've been watching the Commonwealth Games on TV and see that there is a high wind and rain and that Keino, the gold-medal miler, says the weather is fit for ships, not men, so I suppose a thick jersey and mac? I expect you've forgotten such things exist!

There's a national dock strike here which saves a lot of trouble, as there is nothing in the shops and I can't afford what there is.

much love always. how is Hettie? not lost I trust? X
Ma

[postcard of Abbey Church of St Mary, Iona]
26 July [1972]

Just to show you what the abbey is like. – Had a lovely bus trip across Scotland, with a stop for hot scones, then a boat to Mull and a fishing-boat to Iona.

Lovely weather with just a silver haze, large sheep and tiny cattle. – Hope all goes well –

much love – miss you so much! Ma

5 August [1972]

Dearest Ria,

   Feeling rather low, as I've just rung up Valpy and he was rather grand and said I'm afraid I can't talk to you now we have dinner guests; and Mrs Packer (now reconciled with Mr P. and off for a motoring holiday through bonnie Scotland) who tells me that James left long ago because of indigestion, and the girls went on at him so, and that Nigel actually had a crash near Venice, now all this is happily over but I think you might have told me! I expect you didn't want me to fuss, but I do that anyway. I felt such a fool talking to Mrs P.

   Tina came up to London yesterday. I met her at Waterloo and we went on a shoe-buying expedition – very tiring but we got 2 smart pairs, one black and one brown – but Tina already declares she'll never wear them! Also a nice pair of hoop ear-rings with a small gold ball in them. She seems a bit tired, it's an exhausting job, but truly worthwhile as the poor major is helpless without her. I expect she told you how Mrs Dooley went on strike in the new semi-detached at Bristol about the stereo recorder and the new noise-making attachment bought by the boys – it seems it had great effect as she's never screamed at them like that before! She simply said she couldn't stand it another moment!

   I'm going down to Suffolk tomorrow to see Rawle and Helen – but now they're queerly miffed because I don't want to spend the night – I want to come <u>back</u> and climb into my own familiar bed where I know I shall sleep soundly! Signs of old age! I expect you sleep like a top on a few stones on a Greek beach – but I had poor nights in my bunk at the Abbey at Iona – apart from the fact that there are only 3 hours darkness in the Hebrides in the summer.

   Thankyou so much for your letter and I'm glad you liked the camels – I was also struck with the horses in Turkey, some of them were so fine looking, with small feet. Longing to hear about Persia (as I call it). Valpy off to Karachi on Thursday, with grand new tropical tailor-made suit: that's why I want to see him and Angie off to Don Rafael and the Señora for 2 months. They're so rich and grand now, and to think I used to cut down my things to make his dungarees! I remember taking him for his first haircut! Yes, I'm in a bad way! Perhaps I'd better have a glass of sherry!

Much love dearest M

185 *Poynders Gardens, sw4*
13 October [1972]

Dearest Ria,

Still worried about your evident weakness, and your poor delicate thin neck coming out of your newly-made red pinafore, but I hope you'll be able to get good regular meals and put back your strength. The final blow to our scheme of a Mediterranean holiday which would set you up for the winter!

John seemed quite enthusiastic about Wolfson North 2, and drew a diagram (which of course I couldn't follow) of exactly where it was, and I was impressed with the 2 armchairs and 2 razor-points, it does seem you've been fortunate, although of course I don't know the LMH rooms at all – I'm looking forward to having a peek at them. It was kind of him to call in and tell me, as I was more than anxious about you. Tina rang up, too.

I can't pretend that much has happened! I could not face going to Miss Bell's choral reading of The Waste Land this evening, and fighting my way back in the underground – but she was very hurt and said she had made the exact number of sausage-rolls – I feel terrible and I also feel that I'm getting too feeble to go out at all and I shall become quite inhuman – I feel so tired at the end of the day I can't think what to do.

Daddy has started clipping those tickets again! He says everything is in chaos and all the staff have left. He never did drill the holes in that chest, and now Peter wants the drill back again, so there was not much point dragging it up and down! However I've impressed on him that other things being equal we'll come to Oxford next Sat: but you must let us know about your matriculation –

much love dear

your Ma

P.S. You've now rung up and I've said all these things: but I might as well send it.

Tina says matric: takes <u>either</u> all morning <u>or</u> all afternoon, but you must let us know if you think there'd be no point in our coming. Daddy has now fixed the key plate on the chest, and it looks nice: it's the first time he'd used a Black & Decker and he was thrilled. I wish I had one, I could sand and polish everything

Queens Gate, sw7
26 October [1972]

Dearest Ria,

I feel I'm definitely getting past it as I look forward to the end of the day so much! When I'm asked out to various dreary festivities I can't face them, I'm longing to creep home to a bath and cup of tea! But then I've always been amazed at your energy in going out. I <u>must</u> go to Mme. De B's club next Monday to have tea with her (I dread the club because I think the superior attendant in the Ladies' cloaks always takes my coat with distaste: but I could wear my new suit perhaps) – I <u>want</u> to see my old friend but I already dread not being able to go straight home! On Tuesday I went to the Old Vic with some of the girls to see Olivier in Long Day's Journey into Night and we went in a coach and had a chicken dinner first, but even so I could hardly keep awake! It was wonderfully acted, but Olivier got <u>very</u> red and I was afraid he would collapse. Tina told me that she also dozed off during the last act. I'm so glad the student has now come to MacEntee and will take some of her classes and give her a breathing space so that she'll be less tired – she has put so much into it and done so well that I'm afraid she'll be reduced to a skeleton.

I am doing a bit of cleaning and decorating at the flat every evening – half-an-hour before I start correcting – at the moment all Tina's old books are in the hall but hard work will get it straight. I am longing to get on with my little bit of writing but you can't do it after work, your brain is so empty, so I get on with other things and shall have a good go in the holidays.

I did enjoy the visit so much and am looking forward to the 4th. Auntie Mary would love to come, so it will be a real family outing, rather a strain for you but I'm sure your courage is equal to it!

Needless to say I have got some Viyella and baby wool but they are so expensive I have modified my ideas of making an extensive layette – I'm sure Angie doesn't want it anyway, as grannie's ideas are always hopeless. But I must just make one or 2 things. Oh dear, I wish Baby wasn't going to Peru for 2 years, I shall miss so many Stages of Development.

I can't stand the new French lady, she is covered in hair and talks ceaselessly of what she said to her husband, who, she claims, constantly begs her to lie down and rest, but she won't do so even if he has tears in his eyes, because she knows that everything at home depends on her.

Longing to hear about all you're doing and what your work is like – much love, dear
Ma.

Could we 4 have lunch in Hall on Saturday. I will pay you back of course for lunch tickets.

Miss Freeston's
21 November [1972]

Dearest Ria,

My candidates are all ready now to sit for Ox: and Camb: tomorrow – including Charlotte, I suppose, though I haven't seen her lately – they are quite green, and cannot sleep – pity them!

Feel much better for the trip to Paris except my feet – quite worn out with the tramping round Les Halles &c, and the Louvre of course, but we were careful not to look at too much. Seine embankment not quite built over yet, so we were able to walk about in the nice clear sunlight and we negotiated the metro very creditably.

We had a queer cheap hotel with a worn staircarpet and shutters and a courtyard and 6 floors of tall rooms, but lovely bread and coffee for breakfast and a proper table and chairs so we could eat the supplies I brought from homely Sainsbury's – just one dinner out in a student restaurant but we felt it didn't matter going in as there were many families with children there, and it was delicious.

Mrs Cassavetti received us very kindly in a lovely flat in the Rue St Jacques near the Sorbonne and all the bookshops – she doesn't seem to have tea, only vodka, and wears sleeveless dresses all the time – trendy long-haired children come in from various lycées – terrible painting done by the eldest boy of himself as he <u>would</u> look in a film he would <u>like</u> to make of Edgar Allan Poe – well, you can imagine it. Unfortunately Daddy mistook a shaggy-looking teen-ager, brought in by the 14-year old daughter, for Mrs Cassavetti's son, and kept addressing him as such, although he didn't know a word of English, but I hope this didn't notice too much. It was impossible to make him understand by signs.

John rang up last night and said he'd be seeing you – I don't know whether to ask him round, but of course he knows I'm pretty well always there! He said he'd thought up another half of a theorem which seemed good news.

I'm reading for my bedtime book Eliz: Wordsworth's account of how she founded LMH – worried about the view over the men's tennis courts which was quite undesirable. I'm sure she was a great woman, however.

Hope so much that you, your work and your bike are going well and that you got the £££ safely –

much love always

Ma

185 Poynders Gardens, sw4
25 November [1972]

Dearest Ria,

Nothing to say really, just to wish you well and hope you have your heating on! Tina as I expect she told you got half frozen to death on the Teachers' Protest March and when I met her at the Polytechnic she was quite blue – I think only the cold had kept her awake! She says she'll get a warmer jacket for the winter.

I've laid out all the surplus Xmas presents and feel quite helpless as I can remember <u>nothing</u> – in particular who had sauna soap last year. I've got two nice shopping lists, but there again I believe I sent away quite a few of these last year, who wants one anyway? But that of course isn't the point at all. I notice that Heals and Liberty's although they're nicely got up have in fact brought out a lot of last year's stock again, and I sympathise with them.

Daddy has had another tooth out and is in bed feeling poorly. Mr Robinson threatens still more extractions just before Christmas! But as I tell him it's just like my specs: once he's got his snappers in he will get used to them and I'm sure he'll find it much easier to manage, he'll be able to eat with slight graceful movements! I've actually laid out the money to get a radio, so he's got that in his room with him and can listen to many newses. The music sounds quite nice, but of course after stereo <u>all</u> music reproduction sounds funny. I'd so much like one, a record player I mean, but Valpy and A. (who are definitely coming to Mary for Christmas by the way) spend £5 a fortnight (I think) on records and I could never do that. They haven't got the Messiaen Et Expecto, the one I like, but they played me some Elgar. I haven't heard myself from Valpy so hope baby Gregory is going along all right. But Tina thinks it will be a girl. It'll be awful when physiologists are able to tell you which it is – it will take all the anticipation out of life.

Nearly all the shops in Balham High St are shut and ruined – large holes in the side streets. Woollies has been done over with terrible fluorescent lights like an interrogation chamber and crude colours, and all the nice pins and needles and screws and things have been taken away so you can't get anything you want – racks of orange nylon nighties. The supervisor tells me it's given her a headache and 'she's in the hands of the doctor'.

much love darling
Mum.

185 Poynders Gardens
London, sw4
30 November [1972]

Dearest Ria –

A lovely day off, while they take their entrance exams, and though I seem to have spent all of it running round in circles (with a nice spell of sunshine in the Agnes Riley), I thought I'd at least make sure to write my letters! And thankyou so much for yours.

The car is said by the scoundrelly mechanic at Chiswick to be getting on all right – I hope it is: then of course it's got to be retested, but they said that would be all right if the minor repairs were done – though they thought this year wd. be its last and I fear it will.

We went to 'Patience' on Tues. at the Coliseum – it was really nice and they had wonderful 'aesthetic' costumes and art nouveau settings, and the singing was good. On Fri: we have to go to the John Arden King Arthur at the Aldwych – it starts at 6.45 so we have to take sandwiches – it seems that John Arden is picketing the theatre as his play is being misinterpreted – I wonder if we'll be the only people in the theatre? Anyway Patience was very full, which was nice. I shan't forget your heroism in accompanying me to the 'Kabuki.'

It was rather terrible because Mrs Slack, the Chemistry teacher at Q. Gate, whom I like very much, had left her husband at home with a bit of a cold and when she got back he'd got up and was sitting in the kitchen having a cup of tea and when she went up to him he was dead – a horrible shock and she insists on coming back next week, you know the way people are.

I quite understand about the work and if the upstairs neighbours are very noisy which I fear they are as they've now grown larger and fiercer, I'll gladly pay your fares to the Science Museum library every day if you'd like to work there – or anywhere quiet you'd like to go.

The lino-cutting things are all ready for your Xmas card! I'm meeting Tina on Saturday a.m. to contribute my Xmas present towards a winter coat – 10 o'clock to join the battle at Peter Robinson's – hope to emerge unscathed –

much love always Ma. X

                                                   [postcard]
                                                   3 December [1972]

Just to thank you for letter – they do cheer me up – and to say that the Chiswick man has not yet got all spare parts tho' he says by end of next week but I cannot rely on this. So if you could manage up by train – let us know and Daddy will meet anyway and carry bags: sorry about record player but you can have my new radio in your room as fixture during vac: looking forward to seeing my favourite postwoman –

Love Ma

185 Poynders Gardens
London, sw4
20 January [1973]

Dearest Ria,

The place certainly seems empty without you, but I should be grateful I know, because if you have 3 children and they leave home gradually you at least have a chance to get used to it. I am just tidying up and hoovering, and have put all loose papers, letters &c into a folder for you to check over when you come back. I have thrown away the apple cores, and also the berries in the milk bottle as the water was fermenting. The cactus is struggling along.

We have just been to the annual meeting of the Clapham Antiquarian society – Daddy said I got just as excited as a child at a birthday party, but I reminded him I hardly get any outings, but usually have to go out by myself as I did to Lord Hardinge's. There was an enormous tea provided by the ladies, with sandwiches and angel cakes, and Mrs Billington gave a talk with holiday snaps which actually ended 'and so farewell to exotic Istanbul' with a sunset postcard. My nice friend from the old Russian classes was there. It was all v. exhausting for Daddy but he has been home 3 days now and says pottering about has given him a distended stomach – and in fact it's just like a baby's, quite full of air – I do hope he's all right. I think he has had a really nasty time with these teeth but by Sunday he should be better as he's kept quiet and warm.

I also had a nice tea-party with old Mary Chamot, who has now been entrusted with buying drawings by the New Zealand National Art Gallery, and she has been getting some Renaissance drawings for them on appro: which she showed us. Unfortunately all the little patisseries and things she gets are rather stale, as she never eats them herself. She's now got a lodger, a young scientist from London University. She charges him £6 for his room and all heating and breakfast and supper when he wants, which is not bad, but I wonder how he likes it. I heard him creeping about in the kitchen and longed to see him but he understandably didn't come in to tea.

Tina rang up to know what colour the earthing wire was on a plug as she has decided to use her spare fire, I'm so glad as it looks like snow. She says she has bought a new pair of trousers (green) to go to a party, I can't keep up with all the trousers you've got between you.

I feel very achy and elderly this evening and am beginning to see how useless it is to worry, as everyone does what they want anyway and it is best not to care so much. So much pain is caused by the illusions and dreams you can't help making for yourself – no-one can – when your children are tiny and just sit on your lap and can't speak and tell you that they'll soon be individuals with quite other ideas.

I shall get my draft next week and will send you some £££ in a leaflet for safety so don't throw away any leaflets! Thinking of you and glad your collection is over by now and your room is nice and warm. I expect you're already swept up into everything.

much love X Mum

I can't get on with Mrs Smith the new English teacher. She is Warm and Generous and Splendid and has blonde hair, sometimes in a pigtail though she isn't much younger than I am, and calls Kuala Lumpur 'old K.L.' and says she misses the cocktail parties. I wonder why she left?

185 Poynders Gardens
London, sw4
2 February [1973]

Dearest Ria,

Here are the pix – the negatives are here as I did want one or 2 for my never stuck-in album! When I look through my Memories I despair of ever getting albums large enough to put them in, I shall just have to bequeath them to you, but they're all safe. – I think some of the pix are really rather good, and get the feeling of coldness, and that sort of golden light of the very short afternoon.

When Tina comes back she will tell me about Easter, but if you are coming back for Easter I shall CERTAINLY be here, though T and T will be in the caravan.

I went down to Bristol yesterday for Mrs Fisher's* funeral – of course took the wrong train and arrived at a station 10 miles out of Bristol, but got there somehow in time, with my woolly hat askew, and my flowers dreadfully crushed. Afterward we had a family lunch at Christopher's house in Bath which I rather enjoyed though I got a pain from eating some pâté. Saw many relatives I haven't seen for years – we were all immensely old – but they'd all got so stout, I felt quite thin! Except Edmund's** new wife who is 27, over 6 foot, and as thin as a bean-pole. Promise me to spare yourself and knock off work sometimes and have a cup of tea and a nice think. Would Feb 22 be any good to come and see you?

much love X Ma

Queens Gate
13 February [1973]

Dearest Ria,

I enclose one of the driving test forms, but Daddy is going ahead independently and is trying to get them to send you another card, which I could keep for you in the well-known black bag. I also enclose £40, I hope you can manage through somehow until this arrives, and apologise for the delay.

I was very lucky to get a cold sunny day at Oxford, my favourite weather, and very glad indeed to see you, it seemed rather a long time, but then it always begins to be the moment you go out of the door! But I'm not getting depressed, don't think that. I'm happy with my pebble-polisher and picture books in the evening of life, and much cheered by seeing you.

I still have hacking cough, although I felt better after our seaside expedition to Deal on Sunday. The wind on the beach was amazing,

* The mother of her friend, Jean Fisher.
** Edmund Fisher, managing director of Michael Joseph, who published PMF's biography of Edward Burne-Jones.

but not too strong to prevent me staggering about and picking up pebbles. Your grey one came out very nicely by the way. I like Deal – it's full of mouldering houses and pubs with gilt lettering and has a general decayed air that suits me.

Venice is all right so far – Tina says they'd like to come too but the trouble is that we can only get 2 double rooms, and I'm sure she wouldn't like to leave Terry for the wk: end, otherwise you and she could go in together of course but I don't know that she means it seriously.

Ria, I know you'll consider it open-mindedly if I ask you – would it be possible to have your party in John's room if he's still in it? – it's not the money – I wd: contribute to it gladly, indeed I'd like to, because it ought to be a nice party – but I've been at such pains to quiet the neighbours and have at last managed to get them to be quiet some of the time, and I feel very much that even one party would give them an excuse to start again, and I feel the flat isn't suitable a bit for a party where everyone comes in and brings drink, whereas as John is leaving the room anyway he mightn't mind: I would write to him myself but I thought it would certainly not be the right thing to do without consulting you first.

Please be indulgent about this and believe that I love you very much,

Love X always X Ma.

185 Poynders Gardens
London, sw4
17 February [1973]

Dearest Ria,

How lovely to have so many valentines – I had only one! A large blue one with very red roses – you can guess who from, but I was very lucky to get even that at my age. I also received 2 bottles of sno-pak to eliminate typing errors.

On Wednesday we ladies went in a flock (me, Mme. de Baissac, Susie Svoboda our German art historian, Mary Chamot and another lady) to Lord David Cecil's lecture at the R.A. on Rossetti, it was abysmal and even he seemed to feel there was something wrong with it as he shuffled his feet and kept consulting his watch: however I enjoyed the girlish outing, and afterwards we all went to Charing Cross station, so that everyone could catch their trains, and sat looking like bedraggled hens on our smart white stools. Mary Chamot mysteriously produced a wonderful fur hat and coat which she got in Moscow before the First World War and wears in cold weather, and this lent distinction to our queer party.

Tina tells me she has a dreadful cold and a red nose, but quite a lot of gas as they're on the North Sea. Valpy has I suppose a bit more leisure, as I see the Economics research graduates have refused to teach the undergraduates any more until their complaints are dealt with. Anyway I had a p.c. from Angie saying she liked the pink jacket (my last effort) and that baby was already in position and she thought it would come early, but one always does think that, and you got into position and out again 6 times (Yes! It's impossible now to stop me telling these morbid anecdotes, but I shan't mention them to Angie.)

Very exhausted after long session with Mr Bunting our local tenant association organiser. He is a communist as I thought and those 'students' he sent around to make that enquiry, and I wouldn't answer one of their questions, were communists as I thought: I wouldn't have minded if they'd been honest enough to say so. He's mad, and wants the council to rail off Poynders Rd. with a steel fence. I advised him to read St Matthew, so lucky that Daddy was snoozing, and couldn't come.

X love Mum

In Bed!
Sunday 20 [February 1973]

Dearest Ria,

Unfortunately I have a queer go of flu, and a feeling in my lungs (I feel it in my chest but I suppose it's lungs) like broken glass – I'm very anxious to go into work on Monday as I'm fighting a battle with Mrs Odescalchi, who says she has too much correcting to do and wants to reorganise things in such a way that she does even less – so

I must miss Mary's lunch party and stay in bed – only I think I'll have to get up a bit while Daddy's out because he hasn't cleaned anything.

I felt all right yesterday p.m., it just came on in the evening: the night before I kept getting up and trying to open my stone-polishing tumbler, because it was stuck, and so didn't sleep, so perhaps that brought it on. Enough of my symptoms, you'll say.

The Annual General meeting of the Clapham Antiquarians passed off quite well except when I went down to the Church hall kitchen to help Mrs Smith (the treasurer's wife, in a green hat and cardigan) to get the tea (for 47 famished members) she was having a crise de nerfs, she told me she'd been worrying the whole of the week about the tea for the meeting, and, do what I could, I couldn't get her to put on more than one kettle, so the tea could only be made in small relays and the Antiquarians, who'd already sat down and eaten all the cakes, were getting quite riotous. I brought some sausage rolls but as soon as Daddy started handing them round they disappeared, everyone said they fancied something savoury. Unfortunately I dropped off to sleep during the talk with lantern slides, so missed many interesting facts about Clapham, I've always wanted to know about 'Rosemead' but I'll never know now whether Mr Smith said anything about it or not.

Tina and I got a lovely pair of shoes at Ravels, and a pair of pyjamas with Swiss embroidery at Marks for Valpy. I have your gifts of course to give to Tina next Sunday. Tina much exercised about their holiday. She thinks of swapping flats with Austrian teachers, or cottage, but all these mean shopping, cooking and cleaning and she agreed that she ought to stop doing that for a fortnight. These mortgages certainly do make a lot of financial wear and tear, though well worth it to get a nice place.

John dropped in with the keys looking rather tired, but I was so glad you could go back by car after all and the gears certainly work better now.

I'm very annoyed with myself that I can't manage to do more in the evening. All this dropping off must cease. After all I hardly ever go out so I should be able to get more done. One must justify one's existence.

It was lovely having you back for the vac: and needless to say we miss you immensely, but I mustn't give way to this feeling too much – Let me know how everything is.

much love always dear

I can't find the bike keys anywhere – not behind the bed, I've had that out –

> *Miss Freeston's*
> 27 February [1973]
> (how time flies!)

Dearest Ria,

Thankyou so much for your lovely letter this morning – I did enjoy your account of the formal dinner party. I mailed the £££ on Saturday, so hope that it has arrived by this time.

I have been in a nervous state as I made a mistake and thought that Baby Gregory was due on 27 February, but this is wrong, and it is still March. But Valpy is still insisting on putting it in a series of Sainsbury's boxes. Tina says that she saw a nice wicker basket in a shop window at Bound's Green, from the bus, for only £1.50, can this be possible, she v. kindly says she will get off the bus next time and see – and perhaps it could be dispatched to Cambridge by British Rail – which was the way you sent your bicycle in the end?

We had a lovely day on the Downs on Saturday – I was very upset at first and left my purse in the train, but got calmer later – it was wonderful up on the ridge walks, windy and sunny, and we came down by Rodmell and saw Virginia Woolf's old house (very much in need of paint) and walked down to the river, the same walk which she took when she drowned herself (morbid) and then saw the 2 Norman churches, one tower like this [drawing of a roofed tower] and one like this [drawing of a castellated tower] and then got a train at Southease Halt, where there's just a signal box with a man in it making tea and working the signals. He also gives you a ticket. I was also very worried he wouldn't work the signals when the time for our train came, but Daddy (who had been visiting the Man's outside loo, covered with green creepers) said it would be all right, and it was.

Distressed that my old beau Douglas Clarke has died, he was asst. editor of the Sunday Express. We are all beginning to drop off the perch I suppose. They gave him a nice obituary in the <u>Times</u>, but he'd hoped to live to retire and write political books and it does seem hard.

Off to the Academy to the Victorian Society Wine Party where Mary has promised to meet us. Must be there at the beginning or the Victorian maniacs will drink all the wine, which will be a great disappointment for Daddy! Hope you are keeping warm, dear.

The car went well on Sunday and we just went to Battersea and back without accident.

much love always M

185 Poynders Gardens
London, sw4
Saturday 10 March [1973]

Dearest Ria,

Just a month till your birthday – 20 years of a much improved world! I've got £5 put by (now worth about 5 shillings) but I expect you'd like to choose something yourself.

Daddy has painted the tail-light – with red nail-polish! – as we're having difficulty replacing the antiquated glass. The Chiswick man suggested this, but Daddy was quite familiar with it having had to stop the men putting nail-polish on their boots instead of polishing them during the war.

On Thurs: when I went down to work Miss Freeston (who was outside in the sun, wrapped in many shawls) said she hadn't been able to take Topsy to the lamp-post because there was a large bomb outside St James's station – we'd had to turn out of the tube at Victoria, but I'd thought nothing of it – I rushed up to Mrs Black and told her that Miss F. was really slipping and we'd better get the doctor – but of course she was right, there was a bomb outside New Scotland Yard – a large crowd of men in blue suits who shd: have been in their offices waiting to see it taken away.

Tina's cold much better and still energetically trying to get a cradle – I don't like her to have to put herself out like this, it is very good of her,

I myself am swamped with exams to correct – I shd: like to go out into the 'Riley' and do some of them but the cruel council has taken all the benches away.

We now have 1800 Embassy coupons but I can't decide what we ought to have next. – I've sent for large numbers of carpet samples but none are dark green! However, they've provided a large number of small rugs for the dolls house – do you think they would look nice?

You'll let us know what you want about next Saturday, won't you? I mean how you are getting back to London and what you want us to do?

Upstairs neighbours still singing and dancing – we've made an official complaint, but I dare say it will be of little use. The Tenant Association and The Poynders Sport and Social, respectively communist and labour, are now at hopeless loggerheads.

We went to the Misanthrope on Wednesday, it's fun and not too long, and we sat in the slips, as in the old days and had pie and a half bottle of wine and queer Americans sat next to us. This evening to the Elgar with Mary, I hope she doesn't give me too much to eat as I find it hard to keep awake even during plays and music in the evening, even when I really love them, as I certainly do the Dream of Gerontius. I thought perhaps I might wear my new skirt I made, as a try-out, to see if it falls to pieces! Also a concert is a good test of whether it crumps or not.

Very touched by the dissection of the tortoise – and most sincerely glad that you like your course

much love and looking forward to seeing you – X Mum.

Haus Schmid
Hauptstrasse
Westendorf
Austria
8 April [c.1973]

Dearest Maria,

No shops open and no stamps but I have borrowed one (her last) from Eileen (the rep whom we've met already in Turkey: full of complaints and packing to leave on Wednesday, but nice and kind, with dozens of neat trouser suits) so as to write to you in the hope that it will bring you my best birthday wishes in time.

We had rather a bumpy flight but didn't have to have smallpox immunisation after all, so were able to get the right plane, whereas the unfortunate passengers for Palma had to join an endless queue to get their jab in a small office with 2 harassed doctors in it. Most of the (few) passengers were going to Mayrhofen and we heard a wealthy South Kensington lady (mad: she said 'I've been having a severe illness and my husband thought it would be best for me to take the two kids for a holiday') saying that she'd heard it was such a wonderful children's skischule at Mayrhofe and she feels quite sure the kids would be looked after all day. Clearly she intended to spend all her time in the bar.

We have been given a room in this nice gemütlich Haus Schmid, with a lovely sunny balcony overlooking the mountain Alpenrose (the Hohe Salve, which we climbed last year, is on the other side) and large duvets, and gorgeous hot water. We really should have a room mit bad but that would mean being in that unfinished (yes it really is!) Hotel Mesnerwirt where we have our meals – (nice, but lots of dumplings in the soup and chicken and chips and I feel the precious inch I've lost through worrying (which I notice when I do up my skirt and trousers, the surest way of measuring) is rapidly being put on again) – anyway, instead of having our bathroom, we're allowed a daily bath in the family bathroom, which is clean and new but all the ironing is done in there and all the postman uniforms are hung up (Herr Schmid is the local postman which seems to be a position of honour and certainly it must be a job getting through the snow to some of the outlying farms). Last night I got locked into the bathroom and couldn't open it so tonight I thought just to put a chair against the door, perhaps weighed down with the postman's uniform, what do you think?

There is much more snow than last year, but the primroses (very tiny ones) are coming out on the south slopes and the horses are being let out of the farm opposite. This morning I worked on the balcony, Daddy snoozed inside and read The Eustace Diamonds, a very long and rather soporific novel by Trollope which I've brought for him: in the afternoon it is really pretty, with a church painted lemon yellow and up and down paved streets – even the bed of the stream is

paved – and a lovely open view towards the Wilde Kaiser. We took a
little train back, what weakness. Dinner is at 6.30! but we're quite glad
of it. – Thinking so much about you and your party and again many
many happy returns dear –

love Ma X

185 Poynders Gardens, sw4
28 April [1973]

Dearest Ria,

Thankyou for the Green Shield stamps! We now after what seems
years of collecting have nearly 2 books – and I suppose about 8 are
needed for a coffee-grinder – but I can't lay hands on my catalogue.
They used to have them at the dairy at the crescent, but now it is
all boarded up with cardboard and has nothing. There's an agitation
in the local papers to buy up all the disused dairy depots and put up
low-cost housing, but nothing will be done.

John kindly came in and said you had got up safely and straight
down to work. But at least this particular exam will be over by the time
you get this, I do wish you the best of luck, dear.

We miss you so much and your room looks queerly tidy and
empty.

I should be so grateful if you could manage to find out 2 things
for me.

1. If you see Charlotte Knox at the Ruskin I do wish you'd find out
where Oliver is living in Italy and what he's doing – is he writing a
book? – I believe he did once think of it.

2. If you pass No. 33 High St could you see if it is a shop or what, as
it is supposed to have a room on the first floor decorated by Burne-
Jones and Morris in 1856, scribbling on the walls I'd call it, I wonder if
it is possible to see this?

Terrible din here – the only boy who hasn't got a squeaker on his
bike has been issued with a large dinner bell! They all climbed up into
the balcony of the disused flat and the porter had to climb after them

and fell and nearly killed himself. I'm glad to say he picked himself up and managed to hit a few of them. (Free creative play.)

Tina is coming to lunch, it's good of her to come on her last free Sat: Perhaps she would like to go out somewhere this p.m. in the poor old car.

Oh dear these jobless people, Daddy and John both, we must pray that they soon get something.

I can't decide whether to colour my pix. of Valpy and Baby Gregory, or whether to try pen and wash, or what – and I can't think what to do about my holiday – I do like to look forward to it for a <u>long time</u>.

I haven't forgotten about your £25 and will send it as soon as I can. Do write when you've a moment as it's lovely hearing all about what you're doing.

much love Ma.

                                              Queens Gate, sw7
                                              2 May [1973]

Dearest Ria,

Do hope the exam was not impossible: how hateful they are. John came by to pick up Hetty (I was so glad as I thought she wasn't going up this term) and I took the opportunity to send some £££ as it would be quicker, will send the rest as soon as I can. I <u>must</u> pay first instalment on our fine new gas heater, which does work quite well after all.

Aunt Mary has been taken ill with a terrible pain and rang up sounding really dopey – she'd been given an injection – she had to go away from the telephone to be sick – the ambulance took her to New End Hospital – I don't know yet if they'll operate, but could you send a get-well card to her home address 7a, 97 Frognal as they might let her out in a week, and I'm sure she'd like a funny one? She's so upset about her bazaar on Saturday and on the fact that she'd promised to go and look after old Mrs: Moors twice a week – I keep telling her this doesn't matter and she must think of herself, for once.

I got a day off for Mayday but poor Tina didn't – says she already feels exhausted but think of the money! But I shall have to make up all my lessons some other time.

I have been completely poisoned by having a rich dinner with Diana Ladas in amusing mews flat lent her by typical woman barrister who has decided to become a nun – it was the shrimp soup which poisoned me – she was <u>very</u> wild and said we must lock up the drinks (of which it struck me she'd already had several) because her husband's alcoholic mistress was staying in the flat – Diana had tried to get rid of her by sending her for 3 weeks in Butlins – why do rich people always have these complications – I advised her to marry her ex-husband again. I'm sure it would be the best course.

Hoping to go to the Messaien Et Expecto at Westminster Cathedral on Thurs: if I can go up and down to the hospital in time after work. My favourite artist, Patrick Caulfield, is exhibiting some illustrations too. I should so much like to go and see them – they are illustrations to Laforgue, but when I asked about it they told me it cost £200 a copy! I would so much like to do a bit of painting and printing and messing about, but you can't indulge yourself once the term begins. I ought to have done it during the holidays –

much love dear

Mum

Nice and sunny so imagine you on green lawns.

I'm told that the Japanese logic man at Sussex is fed up with his job and wants to leave. Couldn't John write to him and suggest taking over? I do think one has to arrange things a <u>little</u>.

Queens Gate
14 May [1973]

Dearest Ria,

I put off writing this till after the baby's 'naming' – by the way I must tell you that V. and A. had expected you to come although I'd thought it most unlikely, but you didn't send a p.c. to let them know, although you <u>did</u> write and send a lovely p.c. to Mary, who was delighted – so now if you could send <u>another</u> p.c. to Cambridge – but the cost of p.c's is heavy I know.

Tina met us at Liverpool Street – she'd got to bed at quarter to 4 after a dinner party at Islington: but she staggered on gallantly. We went to Fisher House after a cup of coffee at the station to restore us – unluckily we'd been seen at the station and they were worried we took so long coming – anyway we got to Fisher House and there was Valpy in his brown suit and Angie thinner but not thin yet, but she's got a kilt that expands with one of those safety pins (Scotch House) and Baby Gregory had a bit of a rash (they always do) but was very good and didn't cry – he's got a sucker, just like you used to – and we had a rather strange service, the sermon by a breezy visiting Canadian chaplain, more suitable for a beach service really, asking us to prayer meetings later in the week, and then a trendy mass where you drink from the chalice yourself and the priest's prayers were in a spring folder – but it was nice – the kind that makes Mme. de Baissac's French relations say that they attend mass 'sans plaisir – c'est comme un bistro' – then we walked back (Tina with her long legs like a sleepwalker) and after a long wait (Valpy was very naughty and kept picking Gregory up, saying: I'm never allowed to see my son) we had some of Valpy's soup, with which you're familiar, and cold salmon – and raspberry slop, and then it was time to go back. Valpy says my drawing of him and baby was not like him, but like Solzhenitsyn, but I still think it wasn't a bad likeness. They seem very happy and baby is a dear and the doctorate has been sent in.

On Wednesday Tina and I got Mary out of hospital and walked her back home – I hope it was all right to do this – carrying her suitcases, and they're x-raying again on Tuesday and the doctor will see her again the following week: it's all so slow, and she still has <u>twinges</u>, but they <u>won't</u> say exactly what it is. They think perhaps they won't operate, but still don't say for sure. She insists on going back to work, but when Daddy and I went up on Saturday, she had tottered out to Lindy's to get some of those dreadful cakes, oh dear –

If John is coming next week-end, we won't come, as it is too much for you to entertain all this generation gap, I hope the Open University was reasonably satisfactory – what a business it all is. Daddy is definitely starting at Times Lithographic in June, so no more sunny holidays! But I'm truly thankful that he has <u>got</u> a job – that is what

matters – and he'll get a benefit from Thompsons I think and it will be
<u>something</u>.

much love Ma

P.S. This letter is a disgrace (on scraps): I met John on the tube this
morning going to work and he says he's not sure whether he'd like the
Open University job anyway! Suppose we came on May 26 – Would
that be any good? You may well be occupied but could you send me a
p.c.? Enc. £5 love Ma

185 Poynders Gardens
London, sw4
10 June [1973]

Dearest Ria,

Just to say that I have had a nice picture postcard from John
Christian (trendy B/J expert in Christ Church) to say could I see him
next Saturday a.m. So if we came up to Oxford that day (16th) would
you be free at all? I know it's short notice and you are working hard
but I hoped perhaps you could do lunch or tea, and anyway, could we
come to L.M.H., where we could sit on the lawn if you were out or
busy?

We went to Cambridge yesterday – Baby Gregory weighs 13 lb. now
and is very long – eyes still dark blue – healthy and thriving. Valpo has
taken this university appointment as Assistant Director of Overseas
Studies, which is quite good, £3000 p.a. and he hopes also to get a
Fellowship at some nice college, which would give him a room there
and the right to eat dinner in Hall and the university are very good
and give you a very easy mortgage on a house, so they are going to
have a fortnight in Cordoba (Don Rafael has bought flats for everyone
but the house in the sierra has still not gone up, though he's planted a
hedge round the site to keep the donkeys out) and then start house-
hunting: but there seem to be plenty of houses in Cambridge, not like
Oxford. Well as I say Baby Greg is Very Well but otherwise things are
going to pieces a bit as there was nothing but fried eggs for lunch, I
didn't mind truly but Daddy was a little disappointed, however a baby

is a great disruption and they are so happy with him. Unfortunately when I was giving him his bottle (he's on the <u>bottle</u> now as it seems Angie hasn't enough milk, strange as she's still pretty large round the bust though she's reduced elsewhere) he quietly sicked it all up but I had a nappy handy and was able to mop it up rapidly without being noticed. He's a dear little creature and knows how much he needs. – Daddy has kindly offered to get the supper and is crashing about in the kitchen, but I don't like to go and see what he's doing. – Tina seems so happy but has not had time to go shopping for her <u>dress</u> yet – however the holidays are approaching. Very difficult to stop Mary suggesting turning out of the flat all together so as to make it easier for the wedding, but I keep telling her monotonously that we'd rather have her and no flat than the other way round, and she is being most good and generous and has sent Tina £30 and asked what else she'd like as a special present: I thought one of her drawings might be an idea, but that is for Tina to say of course. The flat seems to be going through well and all seems set fair.

Now you'll think – what about the most important matter of my 3rd kiddie – thankyou so much for your letter, it was lovely to hear what you were doing, and it was very kind of you to be patient with me when I'm dreading the correcting which starts next Thursday: also I feel that Valpy is so grand now, lecturing only to graduates, that I must seem absurd teaching the VI form – though of course he hasn't said this or I expect even thought about it! – By the way he thinks his doctorate must be all right because they've just sent him some books to review and the letter was addressed to Doctor Fitzgerald!

I do hope it will be all right to see you for a bit on Saturday dearest as there are so many things I'd like to talk about – don't think I'm going to pieces though! I should be correcting, but am going to take the day off as an undeserved treat.

You don't mention anything about the Pathology, or how you got on with the Principal.

Don't think I've forgotten <u>your</u> exams, far from it. One must keep one's head clear and think of one thing at a time. I'm so glad your

Italian plans are going on well anyway, there are so many lovely things to see.

much love always Mum. X

Try and send me a p.c. but if we don't hear we will come along to L.M.H. about 12 or so and hope to find you. X

185 *Poynders Gardens*
London, sw4
23 June [1973]

Dearest Ria – Just a line as I hate not writing to you, though the exam: correction position is truly frightful, and you must also be feeling the pressure – still the agonising decision whether to go out into the grounds or not.

Yesterday was the Grand Fête at Poynders Gardens but we missed it as we had to go to Brompton Cemetery to look for the grave of Burne-Jones's aunt (yes!) – it's so lovely and shady and atmospheric there, like a Turkish graveyard, and then on to Keats House where I've rashly agreed to take the girls next Wed: (of course it's all under scaffolding and of course as it's a post-exam course half of them won't come) and then on to see Mary, who is well but terribly fussed about Tina's cake which I'm sure will be lovely, ordered from a costly Patisserie, but she wants it just right) – Tina is in Bristol so can't be consulted. I'm putting off thinking about arrangements until I can consult you, and until all these exams: are over.

Lovely sun on the balcony and my clematis and geranium are out giving a lovely range of hideously clashing colours, but Daddy is in his little back room with the light on smoking furiously with all the papers!

What a bad year for hay fever, all are sneezing. I have studied various peoples' symptoms seriously, and it seems really true that, all remedies and anti-histamines apart, the symptoms disappear with eating something substantial and for about 30–60 minutes afterwards – now there must be a good medical reason for this, and I seriously wish you would think about it some day and see if a remedy (not a cure) for allergies couldn't lie along those lines – asthma is a different matter – but hay fever is bad enough –

much love dear and wishing you all luck for next Friday
X Ma

P.S. I've been getting up at a quarter to 5 each morning to do the papers, but am not sure it was a good system.

[postcard of Palermo*]
16 August [1973]

Have lost your schedule temporarily but want to send love to all. Very hot here, but so it was in Clapham, after all – and all the wine tastes of volcano. Have had many bathes, Marks costume standing up to it well and getting larger rather than smaller, but I wish I'd taken out the 'armature'. The hotel is huge and absurd but food is nice and we are setting out to-morrow to see all but to-day we only walked to two villages which is mere weakness, can't afford 'expeditions' so shall take buses.

Best wishes for all your expeditions Much love Ma.

185 Poynders Gardens
London, sw4
11 October [1973]

Dearest Ria,

I am sitting here terribly sleepy but determined to write a word to say how much I miss you, and how nice it was to have you here for the vac.

John came in with the car-keys but would not have coffee, tea, or even water. He said you approved of your room, that it was slightly smaller but a very good position, and the green-painted drain pipe was in place. – We

* Desmond was now working again in the travel business.

went to the 50th anniversary of the Clapham Antiquarian Society and received a glass of sherry each (Daddy said they ought to pour out more, but it was all at poor Mr Smith's expense) and cut a large cake, bearing the arms of Clapham and the Atkins family in blue and yellow icing, and (as it turned out) heavy as lead. The lady in charge of cutting it was very inefficient, particularly as before starting she felt it necessary to demonstrate how she had made a cake the year before exactly like the Tower of London, with a bridge that went down and up. Then came a lecture on 'Clapham as I know it' and we crept quietly away and had dinner and watched the horse show. Very harassed with much work, and can't get anything duplicated as they've pulled everything down around Victoria Street – the work of unscrupulous speculators. Mary's party seems to be getting completely out of hand and she keeps sending me biographical notes of the various people who are coming so that I can talk to them; I don't suppose that they will want to talk to me. – I note by the way that you did not take the ivy from the balcony so you must let me know if you want it and we will bring it when we come. – Quite cold now and a clear moon, I shall go to bed with a hot water bottle. – Just a scrawl to send you my affectionate regards –

much love always Ma. X

Daddy refuses to have his attention drawn to the St Bede's lottery tickets.

Queens Gate, SW7
24 October [1973]

Dearest Ria –

John just dropped in last night to fetch a book and kindly stayed to chat a little though I was distraught having just had heavy day and dreaded dentist (youthful Mr Gregorio – took some x-rays with uncertain hand and will let me know results later, but I WON'T have anything out). He says (after experiences in Wandsworth Comprehensive) that teaching is NOT to be his career! I hope all goes well with doctorate – but he mentions giving up his room at Xmas, where will he go then, I wonder?

We went to Cambridge on Sat: for Valpy's doctorate – a solid impressive figure in hired crimson-lapel gown – I felt very proud and was allowd to hold baby Greg on my knee, extinguished by a large woollen cap, he looked such a sight, chewing my umbrella handle. The house in Humberstone Rd. is going along very well and the kitchen fitted up beautifully and 2 nice chests of drawers (already stripped!) have arrived, and many things ordered, but V. mysteriously seems to have plenty of money, he was very genial and Mary enjoyed it I think.

Mary madly insists on selling out £1000 of stocks to print 1000 hardback copies of grandpa's poems, she has told the bank manager that she <u>will</u> do this, so I suppose it's the best thing – they're to be done by Holywell Press, but how can they be distributed?

I'm just drinking an unpalatable cup of tea at Q. Gate – I notice that Mr Morris, the weedy new guitar teacher, is 'ill' again, he daren't face the girls, do you remember those awful 'Guitar Archives'.

The G.L.C. now say that owing to the change in mortgage rate they can only lend £7000 on our present so-called incomes – though this too depends on my continuing working at my present rate – and then we still have the £1000 to deposit – but I begin to despair of finding anything – still less somewhere quiet with a bit of garden which is my dream. Whatever happens I mustn't land us in real financial straits again.

Daddy still ensconced with his 'girls' and the ever-ready coffee-pot – in the evening to the tavern with Peter – don't know when he'll go to Paris on this famous inspection trip but I believe I'd be better advised not to go – in a <u>nice</u> way – I can't be doing with these reps, and couriers and he has to go to 5 hotels – What do you think?

John says you've started <u>new</u> crafts at Oxford – don't forget the all-important business of the Xmas cards! I'd so much like to know how to do lino-cuts with wax resist to block out certain parts – but I expect it would be messy.

Are you expecting us on the 3 Nov? I'm not quite sure? I don't seem to have seen you for such a long time –

much love always

Ma. X

185 Poynders Gardens
London, sw4
Sunday [late 1973]

Dearest Ria,

It really cheered me up to see you yesterday as you have the art of putting my worries into proportion! I have a roof over my head after all and a separate loo and bathroom and enough to eat and can (more or less) pay my way, but it's not in human nature to be satisfied.

I got back in good time (20 minutes early at Oxford station I admit) and Daddy was at the launderette when I got back so I was able to fix his dinner. I also found a letter from Auntie Willie asking me to come to Madeira for Xmas with them all expenses paid! Granny had persuaded them to go there as the winter is too much for her, then at the last moment she said she didn't want to leave her cosy home – however needless to say I've no intention of going.

To-day we went down on the foreshore at Battersea (the mud still smells just the same) to see if we could find some large flat pebbles but there seem to be large flat everything else <u>but</u> pebbles. I took a fancy to a very large filthy brick from the old Battersea bricks, Daddy made quite a fuss carrying it back, I can't think why, nor can I exactly explain what I want it for. It's most annoying that I can't find a source of pebbles.

Willie's letter also mentioned that the 'livingroom' (trendy warehouse on the way down to the station) also belongs to Jay, and he also has 2 other trendy furniture businesses in Oxford, he's living at Wolvercote, just the other side of Port Meadow.

Prompt me not to get further involved with the master tapestry embroiderer as I feel he's most sinister; I agree the old French designs are lovely, though.

Monday to-morrow, my worst day, really hard.

I enclose Valpy's telephone number and the test card.

Much love Ma X

I like your new trousers – I truly do

Miss Freeston's
Thurs evening [1 March 1974]

Dearest Ria

This is my shopping evening and I rather dread going back with my heavy load in the rush-hour. I've brought my umbrella, but of course when you have 2 bags you can't put it up.

Daddy and I went and voted this morning – we discovered we had a Liberal candidate (there's also a White Residents' you notice) – but all this will be very out of date by the time you get this. The voting was at the Bonneville – the ladies on duty were all smiling and eager when we went, they'll be tired out by this evening – to my disgust the Conservative lady outside snatched away my card, saying – I'm only taking <u>ours</u>, dear – I didn't like to say I was Liberal for fear of hurting her feelings – she had put a nice green hat on and everything – I often see her in church.

We only have a fortnight's holiday from Miss Freeston – April 4–22 – it's really not enough, but I can't argue. We still don't know what's happening* – the man from the Ancient Buildings Dept. of the G.L.C. came – I didn't know there was such a thing. He said the building is a fine example of Victoriana, and the Albert Public House over the way has been saved, so there's hope yet. It would be lovely if Tina were to come here,** but I really don't know if the place is good enough, and then one gets used to having all one's paper, ink &c supplied, nothing like that here. The stapler has gone wrong, such a nuisance. I can't mend it.

I am sure John's seminar was excellent. I've read through both his papers as I thought it would be good for me, whether I followed them or not.

I've been to the National Book Sale – rather disappointing really – but I got a rather nice book on 'Letter and Image' which you might like to look at. Mary is giving a tea party for all her cook-book assistants

---

* The block in Victoria Street which housed Miss Freeston's Westminster Tutors was under threat of demolition.
** To teach.

(not me) and it really seems nearly printed.* Such a business as it's all
been, we've quite forgotten the original purpose. – Nora** has fallen
<u>again</u> – over the dog this time

    much love Ma X

185 Poynders Gardens
&c. &c.
[6 March 1974]

Dearest Ria,

How horrible for you to have been having flu – Tina told me, and I
felt a beast not having known you were ill. – I would like to send you a
bottle of tonic wine – Hall's Tonic Wine Mike and Willie used to drink –
but I don't know how to send it through the post, so I send you a small
contribution, hoping you can get a bottle. You do need something to
pick you up or the depression gets unbearable.

I have filled my 'Pentel' with brown Rotring ink as I've given up
trying to make my Rotring work – I find you can refill these pens
perfectly well if you get off the top with a spike or something.

I have been taking a day off to sort out my Little Bit of Writing† –
the end is in sight you'll be glad to hear, although I have a lot of indexing
to do before I can give everyone back their books! We had a really nice
day at Rottingdean and had our lunch on a bench in the sun on the
green, just a few pebbles from the beach for my polisher, and a good
walk on the downs, you can get so quickly out of sight of houses and
the air does me good I think.

It <u>is</u> very good of Tina about the party, you kindly say it is nice to
have a 2nd home but I wonder if you feel you have a 1st one! But we
love you very much and that must count for something. Will check on
car's M.O.T. but it's not too bad as we had that new clutch you remember.
Have you written to the <u>Middlesex</u> Hospital? It's a teaching hospital
and I thought might be a possibility?

---

  * *The Mary Poppins Cookbook.*
** Mary Knox's father Ernest Shepard's second wife.
  † PMF's biography of Burne-Jones.

I realise exam: is on 19th – I have to go to Tunbridge Wells on Sat: 17th when Daddy goes to Paris for weekend – when are you due back?
much love X mum

185 Poynders Gardens
London, sw4
Sunday [6 May 1974]

Dearest Ria – Thankyou so much for your nice funny letter. I have told Valpy, several times, exactly what you're doing.

Unfortunately I have a dreadful cold, or flu or something, anyway a temperature. Yesterday I had to visit a magnificent mouldy Victorian Gothic castle at Stanmore (William Morris Society) but unluckily this meant taking the underground through Wembley Park with the Cup crowds and I got quite a kick on the leg and, when they started fighting in the carriage, really thought my ribs were going to break, which I've never thought before. I wouldn't have gone on, only, having got onto Oxford Circus platform, I couldn't get off again! It was a very long walk up Stanmore Hill to the mansion, and icy cold in there as it was quite disused, with lovely Morris mosaic floor in 'Daisy' pattern, though, luckily, I'd brought my little thermos, as no provisions were made for tea. But I do feel rather poorly to-day – but I must go in, it is only the 2nd week of the term and it looks as if I'm shirking – I haven't even seen some of my classes yet.

I can see poor Daddy is appalled at the idea of my giving up work – he says he would have to earn double the salary. But I'm getting so old I feel I must give up Queen's Gate some time. I have tried dyeing my hair with a tea-bag, but it did not make much difference.

John popped round for the alarm clock. I wonder how many times he's done that walk along Cavendish Road? It's very good of him to search for a nice district – Stanmore is not bad by the way, but looks expensive – there are delicatessen.

Rawle doing many articles in the Spectator which is good in a way, but he sounds very depressed and says the hopelessness of it reminded him of being a Prisoner of War.

Money very difficult – the crippled typing agency man will want about £40 and the Post Office people have taken my book <u>again</u>, they say they have to compare my signature – with what? I used to have such trust in the Post Office, but it's no use since it moved to Glasgow.

It's raining in Venice ha! ha! so we were lucky to get the sunshine. Must take some more white tablets and try to get my temperature down. Looking forward to seeing you next Saturday. I'll bring a small picnic and some soup to hot up –

much love dear, Ma X

185 Poynders Gardens
London, sw4
12 May [1974]

Dearest Ria,

Lovely sunny windy day here and I am truly glad you are in the country. I can't get rid of my queer cold either, so that I should only have been a menace if I had come. I am doing the index for my everlasting book, and we are also doing a bit of spring-cleaning, repainting the filthy drawing-room ceiling and we are going to take the looking-glass in the hall out of the frame and buy a new piece of good glass, as it's a handy shape but the glass is deteriorating more and more. John also very active – called round for a saw and hammer to fix up his record player.

Conversation between me and the red-haired little boy:

INFANT What are you doing?
ME I'm going to open the door with this key and go into the house.
INFANT Where's your mum?
ME I haven't got a mum. I <u>am</u> a mum.
INFANT You can't be a mum, you're a lady.

This depresses me very much.

Tina has had toothache but has an appt: with the syndicate of demon dentists next week: she says it's better now. Daddy has your letter with curr. vitae and will do all he can. This is just a note as I must go up to lunch with Mary (many manias to which I contribute).

Much love dear Ma X

185 Poyndersgarten
London, sw4
12 June [1974]

Dearest Ria,

No dreaded Black Water, but crippling indigestion so I daresay I have failed to assimilate the iron – I am obviously an unsatisfactory subject! So nice to see you, and Mary very struck with gardens and with ginger cake, which she seems not to have had before: I'd forgotten how nice it was, but yes! You look pale – I do wish you didn't have to work in the vac: – I'm so sick of being poor!

Cousin Oliver asks me to dinner next Thurs – they've been rebuilding a quaint palazzo in Urbino and live there all winter and in quaint stonebuilt house in Ireland all summer and write and paint and never <u>have</u> to work at all. Would that be nice? Well, yes, it would be, but I suppose it has its worries.

Faced by piles and piles of foul A level scripts I have a sensation of wasting my life, but it's too late to worry about this anyway.

Mary seems pleased about the book and I must say the printer couldn't have been nicer or more patient: I think he'll do his best to make the book <u>look</u> nice and that in a way is half the battle.

Do look after yourself my dear,
much love always Ma

best of luck with house-hunting

185 Poynders Gardens
London, sw4
Sunday night [June 1974]

Dearest Ria,

Just a note to say how glad I am that it was such a glorious week-end, exactly right for bathing in mill-streams. I felt terrible because after all at the last moment the old lady we were going to see was whisked away to the Radcliffe (where as Tina pointed out you may well be putting electrodes into her) and so we didn't need the car, but we couldn't of course possibly have told this. So I sat here on my balcony getting on with this dreadful ticking, the never-ending pile of inky scripts.

Uncle Rawle and Auntie Helen are now coming over to stay with Mary on the 28th, I find all this very confusing and so does Mary – we shall just have to take things as they come.

I've just looked at myself at the glass and I see a decrepit sight: must try dyeing my hair with stronger tea-bags, like <u>Death in Venice</u>. Daddy says I mustn't say anything more than 3 times: he is very severe to-day –

Much love darling

Ma

(I wonder how the dress is going)

P.S. Daddy thrilled with Da's day card. – Anne Gallagher has bought a car! Says please come and see her as soon as you return

St Deiniols
Hawarden
Flintshire
27 August [1974]

Dearest Ria,

Here we are with Daddy having his 12th cup of tea of the day and reading a tec yarn and you may be doing exactly the same, but here it is sunny and windy with large white clouds and the grounds of Hawarden are full of bracken and falling leaves and large pheasants and you will be getting exceedingly brown. Well, I imagine you in your crystal-blue bay and send you all best wishes, you worked so hard for it and it's worth it. – We rang up Tina who said she had the screaming Habdabs packing everything to go to Paris.

No screaming Habdabs here, it is very quiet, which is suiting us both, it really is. No-one else seems to want to play croquet so we have the lawns to ourselves with a lovely view over to the horizon, and the rabbits come out. We went to see Hawarden castle, an excellent ruin approved of by Daddy, and I got the key from old Major Sharpley the potty caretaker and there is a little chapel right in the thickness of the wall which is still used for services, it's been there ever since the castle was built and fortunately wasn't destroyed in various wars.

We are now gathering strength to walk up Moel Fammal – not quite as high as Delphi I think! Still it takes 2 hours.

I'm longing to know all about Camping Hellas, the cooking arrangements, loo &c. – these things interest me strangely.

No luck about my uncle Dillwyn and his secret work* – no-one will help me – but I shan't give up.

We feel much better, but dreading going back to work and seeing Mrs Odescalchi. I mustn't be ungrateful. Some nice letters from the girls –

Much love to you and John

X Ma X

I hope there is good water for John's glasses – or do you switch to wine in foreign parts (– – – I think – I've forgotten even almost how to write the letters!)

185 Poynders Gardens
London, sw4
6 October [1974]

Dearest Ria,

Thankyou for your note, and it was lovely to see you. I wd: have liked to say a few words in the morning, but you were so fast asleep.

---

* At Bletchley Park, as described in *The Knox Brothers*.

Tina also was sorry to miss the party, but is now much better after
2 days in bed: she didn't want to miss her classes at Godolphin anyway,
so early in the term.

I had a nice sunny day at Rye and a nice talk with Dr Alec Vidler,*
who lives in an amazing 14th C. house, with lovely things in it and a
view over the marshes to the sea, but also an electric fire with a log
and cauldron over it and some frightful pix: mixed up with lovely
old prints. He had a small Jack Russell terrier called Zadok, which
sits on your lap and trembles. He was very kind and helpful about
Uncle Wilfred and all my difficulties but gave me a frightful 'light
luncheon' which nearly finished me off, comprising a home-made
cold soup which was completely <u>stiff</u>, Cornish pasties, heavy as lead,
from <u>Simon the Pieman</u> (where you got the fudge) and <u>then</u> an
apple pie 'which I've also purchased from Simon the Pieman'. This
was also heavy as lead. Later came a surrealist tea-party with 3
people who'd come for the week-end (a trendy cleric, his dull wife, a
long-skirted daughter, going up to read English at Hertford, who
evidently hadn't wanted to come, and Henry James's manservant
(still living in Rye, but with a deaf-aid which had to be plugged into
the skirting) who couldn't really bear to sit down and have tea, but
kept springing up and trying to wait on people, with the result that
he tripped over the cable – and contributing in a loud, shrill voice
remarks like 'Mr Henry was a heavy man – nearly 16 stone – it was a
job for him to push his bicycle uphill' – in the middle of all the
other conversation wh: he couldn't hear. At 4 p.m. the Muggs arrived,
and Dr Vidler rushed out of the kitchen with two kettles and some
flapjacks (from Simon the Pieman) which were so heavy that they
almost cracked the plate: no-one could eat them except Dr Vidler
himself, who looked very flourishing, and the ex-manservant.
Malcolm Muggeridge was very nice and kind, and entered
enthusiastically into the idea of my book, so that I feel encouraged;
apparently he was converted by Uncle Wilfred at Cambridge, as
everyone seems to have been, though Uncle W. certainly never <u>tried</u>

* Theologian, left-wing cleric, former Dean of King's, Cambridge, who helped PMF with
research for *The Knox Brothers*.

to convert anyone. Mrs Muggeridge frail-looking and ethereal, but I didn't have a chance to speak to her as I had to run for my train.

I am writing to Mrs Batey* to suggest we come on <u>Sunday 10th</u> Nov, and I hoped we could stay on <u>Sat night, 9th,</u> or if not room for both of us Daddy says he will go to a pub (!), I do hope this will suit you, anyway let me know what you think.

Keenly interested to know how it all goes, and how you find it about going to the labs: &c. Best of luck with everything,

much love always,

Ma, X

*185 Poynders Gardens
London, sw4*
20 October [1974]

Dearest Ria,

Thankyou so much for your letter. It was a great pleasure to me to hear that the house was going so well, and that you've got a respectable sixth inmate. How will he be about cleaning the kitchen floor, I wonder?

We are quite all right – Daddy going to the doc: again on Wednesday to know result of test: I can't help feeling there must be some sort of microbe. I'm on at him, as they say, again to come straight home from work more often, partly for his own sake, partly for mine, because I had an obscene telephone call the other night and felt rather lonely – it's strange because our number is not in the book.

Tina tells me there's a lectureship in Logic and Maths going at Birkbeck, but I'm sure John knows this. – Tina and I were working together yesterday in the Brit. Museum, and putting our 2ps into the coffee machine. Terry came along having bought yet more books – Tina says the only hope is to open a second hand book shop! She seems so well, and really likes Godolphin, where she has of course great credit as she's almost the only one who's ever taught in a comprehensive: the ILEA keep writing and saying do you realise your staff at Godolphin are quite unsuitable for the new go-ahead

* Mavis Batey, Dillwyn Knox's assistant, code-breaker at Bletchley Park during the war.

non-stream education &c. But where would they get a better teacher than Miss Rowe?

As to Miss Freeston, I went in early the other day and waited for her, to ask her about these vile schemes of the Freshwater Company to pull us down – the planning order at the moment only looks like they must leave the façade – she still looked a formidable figure as she came stumping along from Ashley Gardens with her stick and black hat – no Topsy now of course – and she was very clear-headed and took in all that I said – but she's determined to fight it out – the solicitor above, a wily old bird, has 16 years of lease to run and he's <u>her</u> solicitor too – so I shall try to fight it with her.

Well, that's quite enough about education, you'll say – otherwise, I'm struggling along – I cannot read the cipher in Dilly's tin box, so I've sent it to little Mr Kahn, who I hope will help me. And I've bought a <u>new vest</u>! in M & S (not a cherub, unfortunately). Tina encouraged me to do this, and got a tweed skirt in the C & A. Next Sat: we go down to Cambridge to hear the news, and see how much Greg: (and Valpy!) have grown. Angie must be so happy to have them all together again. I must hear all about Peru before they set off for The Hague!

Although I know I must be cautious, I was delighted to hear you're a bit more hopeful about the job research situation: I know your next year is on your mind, and feel useless that I cannot be of any help.

Mrs Batey sends another kind letter – looking forward very much to seeing you Nov: 9–10 love always Ma X

[postcard]
28 October [1974]

Just to say (though I expect you know already) that Francesca's little girl, <u>Helen</u>, was born on Saturday and she's in Radcliffe till Thursday (I think weight 7 lbs). Also the Westminster library are threatening us about a book on <u>sleep</u> – I can't find it in your room – have you got it at Oxford? Much love, see you Sat after next, Ma X

185 Poynders Gardens
London, sw4
5 November [1974]

Dearest Ria,

Lovely to see you and you were a most kind hostess to large family party. I hope you don't think I was complaining about the lunch, I thought it very good – 2 green veg: is not bad, is it? – but I just took too much! I enjoyed the ceremony and so did Mary, but I agree with you Barbara Craig* is getting beyond anything – it was absurd that she said nothing at all to Mary – but I don't think she's at all well.

Poynders G. is now blackened like a battlefield with discarded fireworks. Let's hope the dogs eat some of them and that this reduces the dog population.

Daddy got the car down to Chiswick all right, and will go down there on Monday morning and discuss about repairs, but I believe it will pass the test all right for this next year.

I have been spring-cleaning your room and in the process have turned it all white. I do hope you won't be displeased at this – it does look a lot cleaner, and more like a physiologist's retreat! Am washing the coverlet and curtains. If there are really bad strikes this winter, the candle mould may yet be used! But I've bought a hurricane lamp. I enclose the 'lunch money'. Hope to come again tho' your term is so short I think you'll find it rushes by. Must design Xmas card –

much love dear Ma.

185 Poynders Gardens
London, sw4
11 November [1974]

Dearest Ria,

We were so very sorry to go, it is so cosy and welcoming in your house. We didn't feel at all like ancient intruders, and it cheered me up

* The principal of Somerville College.

to see all the housekeeping &c. going so well. I can't imagine where you put everything – I never seem to have room, even now – but everything gets stowed away somewhere. Of course the spacious dining-room (which I suppose was formerly an outside w.c. and shed) makes a great difference.

It was a shame about the moped, and I was disappointed not to see you in action, but it may come back from the garage better than in the first place; my typewriter did.

I ought to have brought this form down with me, as it <u>does</u> require a signature as you see. Your passport number is —— but I can fill in all that if you wd: sign and get 3 awful photos and sign them up the left-hand front border – I feel the sooner we get all this done the better, and then we'll be on our way, so to speak.

Mary is taking the last week in Nov: for her <u>only</u> holiday in the year, to distribute <u>In My Old Days</u>.* I do hope there are plenty of orders by then.

much love and many thanks darling
X Ma

185 Poynders Gardens
London, sw4
23 November [1974]

Dearest Ria,

Just to begin with a request before I forget it – did I leave a book called <u>Meditation and Mental Prayer</u> by W. L. Knox in Tessa's room? I value it highly, but can't find it. If found, it's <u>not</u> Joe's – not his kind of meditation at all! – The library book about <u>sleep</u> I did find – down the side of the bed, I can't think why I didn't look there before – the other library book I haven't found yet.

Very exhausted as Des the neighbour has been having an all-night party and is still going on (9.30 on Sunday morning!) I'm afraid the new baby is deemed old enough not to mind parties now. Let's hope it's the last one for a while, but I don't know how it will be over Xmas!

---

* Mary Knox's memorial selection of her husband's poetry.

Tina kindly came to tea with me in the pale green stuffy gilt-edged Army and Navy Club (waitresses in caps and aprons) to say good-bye to Marielle de Baissac who I'm afraid really is going to distant Malmesbury. I shall miss her so much, she was so sympathetic to all my absurd literary projects &c., and it was so nice to go to a house with a real wood fire. This made Tina very late for her evening class, and gave her indigestion from the toast, but she gallantly said it didn't matter.

In My Old Days has been held up! As poor Mr Burroughs (gallant printer at Holywell Press) couldn't get the cloth of the peculiar shade of blue Mary wanted, and there is much worry and distress – but he's now promised it by Dec: 1st and I do pray he can manage it – it means so much to Mary. I've persuaded her to let him bind it in any colour he has on hand, and I wish we'd done this in the first place.

Belinda is recovering well from the terrible car accident – she must be 6 weeks in traction for the pelvis, but the stitches (on her forehead and chin) have healed very well and won't leave a bad scar, and of course she has many visitors, the officers &c, but it's a wretched business, and coming just after the one to Jay's wife (of course Willie is down in Oxford looking after Jay and the 3-year old, who's in a state of shock) while the baby is still in hospital being operated on – I didn't know babies' bones could break. Makes me worried at the idea of anyone going on 4 wheels at all, but I know you are very steady on your 2 wheels and as careful as you can humanly be – but you can't guard against other people's carelessness.

Meanwhile Rawle, Helen and Belinda can't stand it at Prehen and must move again, but I don't know yet where to: it's been too much for poor Auntie Helen and she is recuperating in Dublin.

Petrol to go up to 75p a gallon, but I feel at the moment we must keep the car going – it is a priority. My long-term serious plan is that somehow or other I must be near either you or Tina, when either of you 'settle down' – not to call in every moment and brood, but just so as to have a human link – I know it would be asking too much to hope to be near both of you. Of course I do not know if T. and T. will stay for ever in their maisonette, nice as it is, if Terry gives up his present school, which is such a dreadfully long journey.

How is your household, which impressed me so much. – Mary's vicar (bossy, spiritual and bearded) annoyed me by leaning forward and saying intensely, ah your daughter lives in a commune. And how are you, and when may we hope to see you?

much love always X Ma

185 Poynders Gardens
London, sw4
(which at least is still £7 a week only!
Let us be grateful for that!)
20 January [1975]

Dearest Ria –

Lovely to get a letter from you and know all is well in the house, as I think that you told me the diplomat was rather out of harmony at one time, but now all is well, which must make it much easier to work. Tina says she's heard about this lunar month thing before, and I suppose it can't be helped, but she should have made it clear at the beginning.

Tina's dreadful cold now much better, but really she has not been well this winter, I'm so glad that one evening class has been given up, too.

I'm still digesting everything I saw in Russia. They really did make a very deep impression on me – those Northern capitals, with all those buildings under snow and those quiet drab people shouldering each other about and that terribly dead Lenin, and those golden palaces and theatres. When I shut my eyes at night I see everything again. It's odd to think that all the time we were there Brezhnev was ill and they were scheming in the Kremlin as to who should have the power next.

Did I tell you that Miss Ashbee (art teacher) was on the Thompson's trip that I <u>should</u> have been on, the one before: she thinks it's all very odd, and keeps questioning me closely! I told her we went to Moscow first, and so must have missed her – she appears to believe this. She asked how I liked the New Year in Russia? I said 'Oh, we were met by maskers and buffoons' – which is what it said in the pamphlet. I think she thinks I'm cracked.

Daddy is having his weekly Bath, and is going to boil me an egg
when he comes out. He says, would you and I like to come to Vienna
with him for the Easter week-end? I can't recollect what you said about
Easter – would you like to come, or would you be too busy? I know
you're staying in Oxford to work – don't think I've forgotten
everything!

John collected your hottie and alarm clock – but your flannel is still
there – do you want it?

I have got a new skirt in the Sales – perhaps I could wear it when I
come to Oxford, Feb 8th or whenever, I don't think it's embarrassing. It
is orange tweed again, but longer. Marks and Spencer's blouses are over
£5 now, it's dreadful. But I should be past caring about clothes. However,
I <u>must</u> have another longer skirt for summer, plaid cotton perhaps.

I should love to see Neil's exam paper – I wonder if he has a copy –
much love always Ma X

Could you keep the £28 in your account against next term?

> 185 Poynders Gardens
> London, sw4
> 25 January [1975]

Dearest Ria,

John came in to fetch one or 2 things, and said you did not need your
'flannel' any longer – it was to be discarded – but this seems reckless.

I am sorry Oxford didn't come up, but he takes it philosophically
as always. I suppose if he did decide on the Bank of England he'd be
eligible for the mortgage loan at 2½%, which would be something! But
not <u>everything</u>.

To-morrow is of course Sissy's birthday and I am anxiously making
an apfel strudel, as I know she likes them and they are too much trouble
to make ordinarily. I have NOT lost your mysterious parcel wrapped in
red tissue paper. We went on Thurs. night to get her a new pair of
shoes, which I thought would be quite fun, but none of the shoes were
really what she wanted, all very heavy, or very high [drawings], and not
what she wanted, to wear with a dress – we did get something in the

end, but not really right I fear. I also got a book of the <u>Impressionists in the Louvre</u> as I know they liked them in Paris.

Tina is madly buying a hoover 'as like a trundler as possible' and another bookcase, as the books are overflowing again! (Q. – as Terry genuinely wants a quiet dull job, to save energy for writing and poetry, wouldn't he be happy in a bookshop?) But then, one doesn't make any money there.

My old crony Mme. de Baissac, is definitely going to Malmesbury – has rushed up there with all the carpet, tiring herself out – and really seems to be getting dreadfully wandering and confused – I hope she'll be better when the move is over. I shall have to save up to go to Malmesbury on a day ticket – not that it's on the railway. – And Lord Clwyd (another crony) has fallen out of an apple tree, and has to creep about slowly – yes, we're all getting very old! (the Clwyds somewhat older than me). He kindly sent an original watercolour by Beatrix Potter to the staff-room for me to look at.

Daddy has been to fetch his new suit – pepper and salt with a waistcoat and narrow trousers – it suits him, and now he can go to the S. of France in it next week-end.

Oliver writes that his novel is coming out on June 9 – it is to be called <u>The Italian Delusion</u> and Charlotte has done the jacket – you could have done <u>my</u> jacket, if I'd been allowed any say in it, but they never asked me!

The Russian snaps will be ready next week and I'll send them, or Tina or John could bring them.

much love always Ma X

Let me know about Vienna at Easter won't you? I'd thought John would be at Gomshall, but perhaps he's not!

Queen's Gate
Monday [11 February 1975]

Dearest Ria,

Thankyou for your letter. I look forward to getting them. I hope you'll always write!

I think I'd better go to Vienna for Easter. As T and T will be away in the caravan (I hope the weather will be good and nothing indigestible is served) and I shall be ready to tuck you up with a cup of tea for a good rest when you do come back. Some rest you <u>must</u> have, and the fairy-like disappearance of The Mushroom has made <u>some</u> difference to the noise, although the ice-cream men, driven insane by the cold weather and reduced sales because of the high prices of Freez-ee whip, seem to call even more often.

Mary is not taking the job with the Diplomatists' magazine, she's been very spirited about this, as they refused to make a proper arrangement about the £££, and she is staying at home for 2 months to do the Mary Poppins cook-book – Pamela Travers writes daily from the U.S.A. to make new suggestions, and to ask why the rolling-pin is not floating on the ceiling &c. Mary has to do 10 full page pix and the book jacket. She says it feels odd not going down to work every day, and so it always does at first.

Daddy had a very nice time at Nice, I think – he went in his new suit and it was carnival time so he had plenty to watch from his balcony. General Bertrand* was an ancien militaire of the most correct type and his wife anxiously looks after him, like Mary did for Grandpa, and kept drawing Daddy aside and begging him not to let the General go upstairs to fetch more souvenirs de la guerre as he might never totter down again. The General's stomach has been ruined by drinking vodka in the war in order to encourage Polish secret agents, so that he can now take nothing but water, but he offered Daddy red and white wine, good thing I wasn't there to frown pointedly! Oh course Daddy couldn't eat all they ordered in the restaurant at Theoules, where the General was mayor for 18 years, so you can guess how excited the proprietor was, and no justice at all could be done to the immense chocolate cake. The whole subject of Enigma is getting so complicated, but I won't burden you with all this.

On Sunday we dropped off the largest tin box with Christopher** and Joanna, so at least I've got rid of that out of the flat. We were

* General Bertrand wrote the first book, in French, on the cracking of the Enigma code, in which Dilly Knox played a key part, at Bletchley Park.
** Christopher Knox, Dilly's son, cousin to PMF.

greeted by the geese, who certainly guard the cottage very well
(do you remember Clancy?) and are a tactful idea of Joanna's, as
Xtopher is rather afraid of dogs. I had a sudden idea how nice it
would be to live in a cottage, with geese, but Daddy said nonsense.
The air smelled so nice and fresh. Then we went on to Bletchley to
take photographs (Peter's camera, not well understood by us, so
many bits and pieces) and as we had some time left over we went
on to Woburn Abbey, wh: Daddy had never seen, of course there
weren't many people there, being February, and it was lovely in the
thin sunshine. We looked at all the pix and had a cup of tea. (8p –
I ask you) in the Flying Duchess cafeteria named after the eccentric
countess who disappeared in her single-seater aircraft at the age of 70.
Some of the rooms are really lovely, but the Flying Duchess had hers
hung with paintings of dogs and kittens from floor to ceiling, and
her skating boots were there – of enormous size. You can see the
pond from the window, just filmed over with ice.

Daddy is still trying to take a good snap of me as the publisher has
to have one, but I'm not a good subject.

I had dinner with Jeannie and enjoyed it very much (indigestion
though from the rich food) but couldn't help smiling after din: when
the guests all (except me) discussed whether it wasn't a good idea to
strew £5 notes about the room when you left the house to divert
burglars from the valuables. They were all very nice though.

Tina's headache is better and she is definitely giving up evening
classes (Terry to take them till the end of term) and has promised to go
to Miss Dean and say she can't teach in every lunch hour. I'm sure
Miss Dean will be sympathetic. Tina is doing so well and has 2 people
who want to do Oxford entrance. It's all overwork, I'm sure, not
organic.

Love X Ma

Stop Press: Valpy and Angie's new baby due in 3rd week of August!
They thought we knew this, but we didn't!!

185 Poynders Gardens
London, sw4
Sunday 24 February [1975]

Dearest Ria,

Lovely to see you, and am now sitting on the Terrazzo among my
daffs and washing, hoping you enjoyed the Odessa File. I really had
a lovely day yesterday (in spite of your thinness!), the picnic was
so funny, and since it was a bit of a failure when we went down to
Cambridge it was particularly nice to see Valpy being his normal self.
I perhaps should apologise about the dreaded anorak. Valpy did ask
me why I had come in combat dress. But it is warm as you know and
I've felt rather queer lately and dread getting ill again as I had to give
flu as an excuse for my Russian holiday and was much embarrassed
by everyone's sympathy.

Looking through my Advance Proof I find that many of the lines
are out of order so that it makes no sense at all. Do you think they're
always like that? Perhaps it's an improvement really. Anyway, looking
through a pile of mouldering mss I've decided my book is dull and
unintelligible anyway. I had to cut out so many intervening sentences
that I can't make head or tail of the incidents. (This was at 2 a.m.
however.) Then I overslept and was late for church. There is a moral in
all this. –

Tessa and Neil were most kind and welcoming when we arrived, it
was much appreciated.

I shall ring up Tina about the cheese dish this p.m. – After lunch
to-day I have to go and see a potty lady (less potty than myself, however)
the secretary of the Lytton Strachey trust, about some papers. Going to
Blackwell's sale had a sobering effect, however, so many potty ladies, so
many biographies. Clearly it comes over one. Meanwhile, the flat is
filthy, and all Daddy's clothes in rags!
much love darling –
Ma X

185 Poynders Gardens
London, sw4
3 May [1975]

Dearest Ria,

Just back from Tina's, and Monday to-morrow, Ugh! They come round so quickly, but perhaps you don't find that yet.

Tina's very disappointed, as I expect she's written to you, that the oculist says glasses would not help her strange double vision and headaches, although it's comforting to think that he said her eyesight was so good, the best pair of eyes he'd ever tested, he said. But he wanted her to go to hospital to see an ophthalmic surgeon in case it might be some kind of nervous thing, because after all an oculist is only an oculist. It does seem to get much better when she isn't tired, but then all these eye things do. Everyone seems tired – I don't know what age it begins at.

We went over to Walthamstow (still no cottages for sale!) to see the new arrangement of the William Morris Galleries, which seems to me to consist of lowering the lights and removing a lot of the things, I can't think where they've all got to. They used to have quite an interesting bit showing how Morris did indigo printing, bleaching out the white parts of the pattern, and how he glazed his tiles, and there was the enormous breakfast cup Morris had, because the doctor told him only to take one cup of tea – all gone, heaven knows where. It's very artily arranged, but there's so little to look at.

All the photographs of me make me look hideous beyond measure, so that I feel quite frightened to go out into the street and show my face, if I really look like that, and what to do about the publicity lady I don't know: perhaps they don't really need one.

Next weekend down to Cambridge. I am making Little White Dresses, but, like all white sewing, it is beginning to look exceedingly soiled. I often drop asleep over it.

We are watching some dreary music by Michael Tippett and Daddy keeps saying 'When does the shooting start?'

Weighed down with frightful exam papers to correct: I keep counting them to see if they'll get any less –

much love, darling

Ma. X

[postcard]
[March 1975]

Sunday, Dearest Ria – You'll forgive p.c. this week as the exams and reports have set in with dreadful force. I feel a bit overwhelmed, and find it very difficult to teach anyone anything: The Songs for Europe are on too, and I haven't the energy to switch off, and they're horrible. To Cambridge yesterday where A. is better, we drove out to a pub in Fen Ditton where unfortunately she felt faint but all was well, little Greg in great form and now a keen footballer and gardener, pulling up all the plants. V. just back from The Hague* – £200 for a week's lectures so he's having the fence mended. Tina also very tired and you too I'm sure, my dear. Looking forward to seeing you.

    X Ma

185 Poynders Gardens
London, SW4
5 April [1975]

Dearest Ria,

    Lovely to see you in snow-bound Oxford on Thurs: And so that is the Nose Bag, which I've heard about so often! It was very nice, but what <u>hard work</u> someone is doing, to home-cook all that food – it really does taste home-cooked, though.

    I had to take shelter in Littlewoods in the end, it was so cold – I've never been glad to be in Littlewoods before, I had to pretend to examine some cardigans, like a store detective. But I arrived at the Lobels at exactly the right time – they were very kind (though Prof. Lobel** is a mere boy of 85 so I must have made a mistake about the date of his publication). He was out having his constitutional, so Mrs Lobel showed me some marvellous maps she is getting ready

---

  * Where Valpy later became Professor of Economics.
 ** Greek scholar who assisted PMF with research on Dilly Knox's classical scholarship.

for publication, they show the mediaeval plan imposed in colours on the present map, I don't like that sort of thing usually but I couldn't help liking these. Presently the Professor's wavering step was heard on the uncarpeted stairs (the whole beautiful little house was <u>freezing</u> except for a small coal fire in the drawing-room, but I'm used to this) and Mrs Lobel said: 'I hope Edgar will talk to you as he is <u>very eccentric</u> and sometimes takes dislikes,' however, I got on rather <u>too</u> well with the Prof as he spent nearly all the time telling me about his emendations to Aeschylus ('You will of course be familiar with the first two lines') but he was very nice. There were some of those frightful cakes made of chocolate and cornflakes, in fluted paper cups, Mrs Lobel had bought them <u>specially</u>, and the Prof had never seen them before and examined his critically, but neither of them could eat them, so I <u>had</u> to have one.

I am just watching the National – T and T have got a colour TV now! So they'll be able to see it in colour. All my children are going up in the world: I suppose the black-and-white is beginning to look rather dowdy.

I got Daddy's savings book back just in time before it all went! He never did transfer the £50 from the other book but drew all that out, and then he started cashing the deposit and took out over £300! I don't know what he did with it and nor does he! It seems he had a dreaded Barclay card too at one time, I should <u>never</u> have let him lay his hands on these things.

Tina and T. have a week by themselves in the caravan at Whitsun, which sounds very nice – but I suppose you won't really be able to give yourself a break until after the Finals, but then . . . I must say I should like some sea air myself. (We were going to Brighton to-day, but poor Daddy is ill again and retired in a heap under the bedclothes.)

It is Friday 19th evening you're coming, isn't it? I'm looking forward so much to seeing you –

much love always –

Ma X

Queen's Gate, sw7
(Ugh!)
Wednesday [April 1975]

Dearest Ria,

I really mean it when I say it was lovely to see you. It cheered us all up and it was <u>good</u> for Mary (as she subsequently said to me) <u>not</u> to have a serious business talk but to hear about the (equally serious if not more so) things that you're doing and hoping to do. (Anyway, Nora, Kipper's wife, has declared that she doesn't want Mary helping there in the house on any account – so polite! – and I think Mary's pride ought to tell her not to go on offering – much better just to call there from time to time, and see how her father is).

You looked remarkably well considering all things. I do think of you <u>such</u> a lot, and how hard you are working, but I thought I wouldn't say too much about that, as you had come for a break.

Tina and T. and Daddy and I went to (sorry about red ink) see Nureyev in the Sleeping Beauty last night at the Coliseum, which I enjoyed immensely, although Daddy opened his eyes suddenly and said he really didn't like male dancing except Fred Astaire! But even he relented a bit in the last act. Nureyev had a spotlight on him the whole time, even when he was sitting down and surreptitiously having his hair-ribbon put back by an assistant! But why not, I expect he <u>has</u> to be vain. The settings were rather gorgeous, like the Russian children's book fairy-tale illustrations – very rich colour, no-one wore white, only gold and cream and brown.

What do you think, we (at Q.Gate) have just been told that we can't eat lunch in the staffroom, because someone left a banana skin last term! They regulate the teachers, but not the pupils it seems. I shall have to lock myself into the loo with my sausage roll.

It's so awful, I've lost my glasses! Not the case, just the glasses, they must have slipped out of my hand in the Tube, but I can't think how it happened. I had to go to Mr Miranda, who said Ah! How the years slip away! And our eyes I fear do not improve! And I don't know how long he'll take to make new ones: and I've borrowed Daddy's, as I can just about see through the reading bit, (they're bifocals) so poor Daddy is quite cross-eyed – but he always <u>says</u> that he doesn't need them for reading, and I don't know how to get on without them, and it's dreadful with these large classes.

I have to meet Mme. de Baissac after work at Her Club, I'm so tired I'd really rather not, and it's always so awkward avoiding tea, if she orders it, it costs £1 a head! But I must see her as I really think her wits are beginning to turn, over the question of the house. Doubtless my wits are turning too.

Michael Joseph say they don't want the biography of 4 brothers (grandpa and my 3 uncles) together, but only one at a time – this is quite useless and I shall have to find a new publisher. I think I'd better get an agent?

T. and T. going to Oxford for christening on Sunday and T. buying a new dress on Saturday for the occasion.

much love dear Ma X

                                            185 Poynders Gardens
                                            London, sw4
                                            12 April [1975]

Dearest Ria,

It looks to me as though you must have had a lovely weekend at the mill, and we all thought of you very much on your Birthday.

Yesterday T. and T. and I went to Ightham Mote – you remember John and you went, and I think hitch-hiked back, and I've still got the booklet you brought back, and always wanted to go – we walked there from Sevenoaks, but the fields were deep in mud and the farmers had ploughed everything up and it was <u>very</u> hard going, however we staggered on gallantly, and thought the house was lovely – but you won't be surprised to hear that we got a bus back to Sevenoaks in order to be in time for scones and tea at the Copper Kettle.

I could not think what was wrong with me this holidays, but I finally realised that this was the first time for I daren't think how many years that I haven't had some one home for a holiday (<u>please</u> don't think this is a criticism, how could it be? – and it's lovely to have you back for 2 weekends anyway) – and of course I must and shall get used to this, but I suppose it needs adjusting to like other things.

Tina has no more trouble from her eyes now, so I needn't have fussed about this! I'm afraid Miss Freeston's has been rather dull, and of course ill-paid, but I hope it has been a rest for her, after MacEntees.

They say The Gambler is very good (though not the Dostoevsky story, it seems) but I don't think I could bear to watch him dribble away the money like that.

Mary is being wonderfully energetic going round bookshops selling In My Old Days. It was well received in the Times Lit. Supp: this week. She says she doesn't want a job now, she is too busy, which is a good thing really, because after grandpa died she told me she couldn't face life without some dull, hard, everyday work – and now it's clear that she can manage without this, which means that the feeling of loss has healed to some extent, as it ought to do.

I've started at Miss Freeston's now of course, but I mustn't complain, after all I'm earning on those days instead of spending, and one or 2 of my pupils are paying for themselves, and are keen and quite interesting.

I am sorting out the Black Bag, and putting all your certificates &c into an envelope of your own. Such a lot of rubbish there is – going back to the Earls Court days.

I am so glad you got a break, dear – I don't forget how hard you are working, looking forward to seeing you. Love, Ma X

> *185 Poynders Gardens*
> *London, sw4*
> 10 May [1975]

Dearest Ria,

Just a bit of a letter, as I want you to know we're all thinking of you as you bend over your automatic reflexes. I know the work seems endless, and I hope you have arranged breaks for yourself, and cups of tea at frequent intervals.

Yesterday we went down to Hampton Court to see the Mantegnas – they've been cleaning them for 16 years, and I never remember seeing them properly, but now they're hung by themselves in an old coach-house painted pink, and they are lovely I think. The flowers in the garden were lovely – there was such a scent of yellow wallflowers that I felt quite drunk. Daddy went into the cafeteria and had coffee as he always feels cold, being thin, and I sat on a bench and finished my last nightie for Baby Flora. Daddy is a little bit better, I think, since he had another 2 teeth out, but I'm still worried about his health. He is going to get his cards away from the dreaded Dr Magonet (not so easy as he's never in) and go to Dr Blair, at the top of Balham Hill – you know, the ones who built their own house.

To-day we had lunch at Mary's and Tina wore her new almond-green over-dress, which suits her so well, and the Usbornes were there, who are looking after Fenton House, I can't help feeling envious as they get such a lovely flat, but it must be a nuisance opening it every day and taking the money for the tickets. They were playing the harpsichords and spinets in the various rooms, and I always think it sounds lovely, going from room to room, but Tina said it gave her a headache.

I am very pleased because I got a letter from Jonathan Cape's saying that I was a finalist (though NOT a winner, like Neil) in the Times ghost story competition,* so it will come out in their Ghost book in November. They say they'll send me £50, which is better than a slap in the face with a wet fish! But I haven't got a publisher, yet for my book about my uncles &c. – please keep your fingers crossed.

Tina tells me that you have more or less definitely decided to work at London Univ: on the mechanism of pain next year, I was very interested, naturally, and when you have time I hope you'll tell us all about it. I expect you feel it's enough to get through the next few weeks.

Well, I suppose I must get down to my indexing, reports &c. It's very slow work. And no cups of tea in the evening, because my ankles have started swelling again. (complain, complain)

Bless you darling and don't get too thin –

much love Ma

---

* With the story 'The Axe'.

185 Poynders Gardens
London, sw4
18 May [1975]

Dearest Ria,

No! No! I was <u>not</u> squashing about your holiday, or if it seemed that
I was then I must have said things wrong as I so often do – you've
often told me that I'm an old bag, who says nothing will turn out well
(viz: the moulded Anglo-Saxon chess set, which came out beautifully)
but I certainly didn't mean to do it this time, I was only afraid to
disappoint you about Ian Price's magic carpet as he only does very
commonplace trips, the Costas and Majorca, but I have sent off the
Darmead envelope which I hope has reached you, and don't forget that
you can book through Daddy and get 10% reduction.

<u>Of course</u> you're thinking about your holiday, it's an absolute
necessity after a very hard spell of work, and rest assured that I am all
on your side and I <u>like</u> Malaga – I liked it when we were there, and
even if a car was too expensive to have all the time, there are those
2 stations, the big marble one with trains to Ronda (and Cordoba, 108
grados) and the little one to Fuengirola and Torremolinos, and buses
to Nerja &c the other way, and the harbour, and the archaeological
walk with the peacocks – if I really seemed to think it was a bad idea, I
must have been raving, but that is quite possible, as I have felt a bit
overworked too, though you may permit yourself a quiet smile at that.

I have just finished the proof-reading and indexing, or as much as I
can do – I think I had better send it away, as every time I look at it I see
further errors, and it has to be in by the 19th: it was a terrible job, and I
really need weeks more to do it properly. – Daddy has had another
tooth out and is a <u>little</u> better, but still very rotten inside, and I have
persuaded him to try a new doctor, so he went to get his cards, but Dr
Magonet was very angry, and shouted at him that he didn't want him
as a patient anyway as he was always complaining, though Daddy has
only seen him 3 times in 10 years. But Daddy told him he was unfit for
general practice, and I'm glad someone has told him so at last. He
hasn't hardly any patients left anyway.

We have just had a letter from the G.L.C. offering a 3-room flat in
Battersea, they say I must come and see it on Tuesday morning, but I

can't go in the middle of the week just before the exams, when all are revising and working furiously. We must ask to see it later, but I won't let it go, of course it is smaller and still on an estate and I fear will have bathroom and loo together which is so difficult with Daddy but I suppose I'll have to face this sometime. Anyway I will let you know what it's like. Oh, what I wouldn't give for a little house and garden, and an attic to put things in. But they are a great luxury nowadays.

Tina and Terry off to Bristol for the weekend, with the almond-green dress back from the cleaners, and then to the caravan next week, as they have a week off, and the forecast is for good weather. But Daddy hasn't got next Saturday off, so I'm not sure that we can go away.

Well, here I am rambling on about my affairs. Really I am thinking of you darling, I promise you, and your enormous work-load – I wish I could learn it for you, but I should never be able.

much love always dear bless you Ma X

185 *Poynders Gardens*
London, sw4
Friday [30 May 1975]

Dearest Ria –

Another wretched letter written in a hurry, early in the morning just before I get up to get the tea. (If I get up before 5 a.m. I allow myself an extra bit of bread-and-butter; if later, not).

It's just that Daddy has to go into St George's, Tooting, on Sunday June 8th for an operation for a nasty ulcer in the back passage – you remember Dr Magonet said there was nothing wrong – he said this in a letter – but the new doctor discovered it at once and said he must be hospitalised as soon as possible. Thank God we are clear of Dr Magonet.

If they have to cut through his sphincter muscle poor old Da: will have to manage with a plastic bottle for the rest of his days, but this may be avoidable. Pray it won't happen, won't you darling, and if it does, well this is just one more difficulty to face and we have already faced many.

He really has been rather ill and has not booked for Malaga <u>yet</u>, but I have written to John about this and am sure we can fix all and you can still get 10% reduction – also I shall have to ask John to look after the MOT test for the car – I am sure you understand.

I am telling you all this NOT TO WORRY YOU – <u>No</u> reason to worry – but because you are Ria and I tell you everything –

all my love Ma

Not a good week – poor Tina lost her bag with £30, her cheque book, key, Barclay card, theatre tickets, everything – you know the feeling! You have to build up everything again, like a limpet losing its shell.

Miss Freeston's

3 June [1975]

Dearest Ria,

Lovely to see you on Sunday, and Daddy much cheered up. John called round on Monday and will take the little car away on Thurs: morning. It is very good of him. As Rail strikes are threatened for the summer it will be absolutely necessary to keep the car going, even if it costs more than the original £130 to repair it! Then I'll get the insurance and licence. It's a great relief that he'll take charge, as everything is getting too much for Daddy. But Daddy will see to the Darmead booking, that will be quite all right. I am <u>very enthusiastic</u> about the Malaga scheme and remember the peacocks' tails streaming over the Roman ruins at this very moment.

Have had to spend a long time with the police this morning about Tina's bag – but they won't find anything, he interviewed the caretaker (who is deaf) and the caretaker's wife (who is simple) and suggested that one of the girls might have taken it 'for a prank' – at that moment an elegant pupil aged 36 came in – he said 'oh, I see you have more mature pupils'. However it's as well that the caretaker should know we've had the police in.

I am thinking of telling Miss Freeston I shall have to have a bit more money as the fares make it hardly worth coming down here, but I know I am lucky to have a job at all.

Tina is coming to have tea at 4.15 as our Lyons is shutting down, as indeed they are all over London, and we thought we ought to consecrate it with a last cup of watery tea. If she has any houses nearby on her list we might go and see them. She has found a very nice one in St John's Hill, she says, rather like Valpy's, but it backs on the railway, and you do hear the trains go by. Or there is a flat in Grafton Square, which Terry fancies, but that might be too small – that is £10,000.

Daddy goes in to have his x-rays on Friday (no liquids) and I am taking him to the theatre on Thursday night (preview of the Gay Lord Quex) as I thought it might cheer him up. I have got seats at the end of the row, I thought this very tactful, as he can slip out, but the man was very surprised and kept saying, I can do you two nice ones in the middle of the row, dearie, you'd see much better.

Otherwise it is just a question of sticking it out till Sunday, because he is evidently worse but I just don't know what to do about it, but they will know in St George's.

My A level candidates know <u>nothing</u>. They are 'learning quotations'.

Best of love, dear. I think of you all the time. Marvellous how you keep going, because I know what the work is like. I hope you can get out into the garden and sample a lettuce – like the Flopsy Bunnies – X Ma.

185 Poynders Gardens, sw4
12 June [1975]

Dearest Ria,

Just to tell you that Daddy is safe back in Belgrade Ward after the op: I don't know exactly what had to be done, but he wouldn't be back in the ward if he wasn't all right, he'd be in the post-op, so I shall go to bed in peace. I will go round and try and find a doctor or staff sister to-morrow.

I enclose a letter from the Town Hall about your little stall – just put it by, till you have time to write.

I have the cheque for the car now, but could not get through to the Poly all day – <u>at last</u> they answered at 4.30 in the Maths dept but John of course wasn't there – I should be so grateful if he could fetch the car – I know I keep asking him to do things but he is most kind –

T and T have many offers (at £8950) for their flat so will get their deposit for the house quite soon I do believe – it will be very exciting when they can go in, and Tina says I may prune the roses, which I should love to do. Everything seems to move so quickly, and all you children are suddenly householders.

This is not my good-luck card – I shall send that in a day or two. Back to my foul correcting now, and 1000 good wishes to you and your revision,

much love,

Ma

[Good-luck card]
[June 1975]

And very best wishes for your exams from your loving

Ma

John is fetching the car to-morrow and will be down to get your things, and Daddy is mending slowly: Tina thinking about carpets for her new house, and I'm ticking at my scripts and we're thinking of you as hard as we can.

X

Maryllis Conder ('Willie')*

25 Almeric Road
London, SW11
16 October [1976]

Dearest Willie – Excuse this dirty piece of paper and a short letter –
I know you will. I did value your letter so much, as you understand
these things. I was told a year ago after his op. that Desmond couldn't
live, but didn't really prepare myself as I should have done, and I do
feel it as a dreadful blow, only I really oughtn't to complain as I'm so
lucky being here, with Tina and Terry upstairs, and their bicycles in
the hall, and someone to talk to whenever I need to; the truth is I
was spoilt, as with all our ups and downs Desmond always thought
everything I did was right – I sympathise so much with what you say
about your aunt.

I'm so glad we were able to get the move over so that Desmond died
at home, and not in hospital; the district nurse was there that morning,
such a kindly person, not much of a nurse but a very good woman, and
she helped me to see him out of this world and read a Bible chapter,
absolutely naturally, as only a West Indian could do, and I have to be
glad the suffering is over, but I do miss him.

Everyone (<u>not</u> you) says work will take your mind off it, but I don't
find this at all, I feel much worse at Queen's Gate with the classes, and
very tired at the end of the day: so I think I'll retire in summer and just
do a bit of coaching at the Westminster Tutors, after all I'll be an O.A.P.
and can get reduced bus tickets – so I shall become one of the shabby,
talkative, penniless and opinionated Old Friends dreaded by Mike and

* PMF's best friend from Wycombe Abbey days. The surviving letters cover the years of
Penelope's widowhood and remember the annual holidays she spent at 'Terry Bank', the
beautiful Jacobean house, built by a Conder, near Kirkby Lonsdale.

shall come and see you – I do want to so much. I haven't been to the
Channel Islands since I was 12!

much love –

Mops.

25 *Almeric Road*
London, sw11
5 January [1977]

Dearest Willie,

Thankyou very much indeed for the headscarf. It's so pretty – I
<u>thought</u> it was myself, and then I <u>knew</u> it was when Maria, who was
opening the parcels, said 'I wouldn't mind having that'. That was high
praise.

When you said you ordered most of your presents (from the
National Trust &c.) I had a mental picture of you sitting in sort of a
lighthouse (as I always imagine the Alderney house with glass on all
sides and birds peering in through the windows – waiting for parcels to
be rowed across, through spray and storm – but then as you know I still
can't quite make out where you <u>are</u> living, so to speak, permanently –
by the way, I remember you told me that the lighthouse was pretty
always full up during the summer with family, relations, dependants
&c., but if there is any time left in August when I could come and see
you there, will you let me know?

Christmas wasn't as depressing as I expected, as the children made
big efforts, & Valpy, Angelines, the 2 little boys and Angie's brother
and his new little wife (no English at all and very worried at the idea
of setting fire to the pudding, but later on took to it rather and tried
to set fire to the mince pies) all came to stay, and chatting to Gregory
(now 3) took my mind off things. I really don't see how one can do
without a family. But why one makes quite so many efforts I don't
know – Jeannie writes to say she had dishes of burning raisins
(snapdragon?) &c. which I'm sure were lovely – but I think we
middle-class ladies are really driving ourselves mad by doing all the
things that were formerly done by a 'staff' and keeping up our
cultural interests as well, – tho' there you are, we can't help it. But

when I lived in the council flat I noticed the other ladies seemed to have time to stand on their doorsteps and talk to each other all day, and I thought they managed better than I did.

Valpy is finishing his book on the economy of Peru and I think transferring his field of interest to Mexico, as the regime in Peru has changed and now they have to accept loans from the U.S., which apparently means that their economy won't be worth studying. Maria has another year to go for her physiology MSC. She had to do electronics as well, to design her own apparatus – she describes this as quite good fun, but then everything seems fun to Maria. And as you know I'm occupying the ground floor of Tina and Terry's house so I can always consult her about things.

Mary's father Ernest Shepard died this year (90) and we have been quite busy with various exhibitions – there's going to be one at The Hague now – as there appears to be a kind of mania about Winnie the Pooh at the moment. He left a quarter of his royalties every year to Mary and this has made her reasonably well off for her lifetime, which is a great relief.

I have delivered my tattered, ink-tea-and-tear-stained MS of book about my uncles to Macmillans, and now await a telephone call to say it's all got to be altered, and that there is not enough sex in it, although I've told them that there is none to put. However in any case that won't be out till next autumn. The index comes next, but I rather like doing that.

Dear Willie, you will send me your Christmas letter, won't you – I don't mind waiting 2 or 3 months for it.

Best of New Year Wishes to everyone – I hope Mike is very well – I thought of his marvellous kitchen garden this summer as I proudly cultivated my tomatoes in the back-yard – much love Mops.

25 Almeric Road
London, sw11
27 July [c.1977]

Dearest Willie,

Am keeping to <u>plan</u> of writing to Terry Bank as all continue to complain about the post and I want to be sure you get this which is just to thank you so very much, what a wonderful holiday, the weather, I suppose, was good luck but everything else was care, kindness and hospitality – I went over the whole week in my head before I dropped off to sleep and apart from the whole glorious impression I thought of so many little things, such as the moment when all the puffins dived, and our bathe, and the heroic row over the bar, and the wonderful view every morning from the top of the fort, and the gannets, and my biscuit.

I feel enormously much better, and what's more Maria and John are still here and say they'll come round this evening so I shall be able to drone on, and show them my sun-tan.

Garden now a jungle of marigolds and shasta daisies, shall have to get down to it and cut everything down. Tomatoes gleaming fitfully through the greenery. Froggies, exhausted by sight seeing, present me with seven bottles of milk, & say they never take it in coffee or tea, as it is malsain. Certainly it is poor stuff, compared to the Alderney milk, but I feel vaguely offended as Tina had told the Express to leave it for them. The Froggies go to Marks & Spencer every day. They brought very little luggage so as to carry back vast quantities of M & S.

Maria says they are Bananas.

I'm sending Anne a little birthday present separately as I was vexed at not knowing the important date. It was lovely to see her, she was so friendly and welcoming and with such an original viewpoint on life, or in process of arriving at one. We must hope that she'll never cut the honey-coloured hair.

Thankyou and Mike again, truly it was the perfect seaside summer holiday. I'm emptying the sand out of my suitcase with the greatest reluctance –

love to everyone –

Mops.

25 Almeric Road
London, SW11
5 January [1979]

Dearest Willie,

Thankyou so much for your Xmas letters, you know how I look forward to them – though that's ungrateful, because I've had several this year. – Ria who's proudly bought a car out of her salary as a physiologist with Professor Pat, took me to the midnight service at Southwark Cathedral, and everyone started trooping out at the end without listening to the (lovely) organ voluntary and I thought of you so much then, you remember how your teacher told you to fire away at the end as you'd be able to please yourself then. Valpy and Angelines and the 2 little boys (cowboy hats, I've shot you, you're dead) came for Christmas – for some reason I'd forgotten how much they all ate, and had to get up in the small hours to make bread. But it passed off well and it was wonderful to see them. It's Valpy's sabbatical next year and he's hesitating between Mexico, Texas, and Aix-en-Provence (which however is part of Marseilles 2 which isn't a proper university) and Sussex, I don't know which it will be.

Of course. Please don't give another thought to The Blotter – there was something Amiss this Xmas I think with the National Trust supplies – they have a large shop at the old Bluecoat School just behind where I work and I went in there several times and they had practically nothing but soap – disappointments of the ladies (both staff and customers, who are very hard to tell apart incidentally), it was a really kind thought, and I appreciate it. Some publisher's photographer came in the summer and said – please sit at your work place in a Natural Attitude – now that's when The Blotter would have come in handy.

I am so sorry about gallant Sue, if only the children could really find the right person and be happy, one begins to think one wouldn't mind anything else, but he <u>wasn't</u> right, was he? did you ever think so? Jay is so strong-minded, like his father in that way , but I wonder if he needs quite such a strong-minded female, he likes to lecture a bit, and tell people what to do, in the kindest possible way – and some girls love to be told.

I loved the story of the tenant and the church decorations – but am worried about the lampshades constructed out of lollipop sticks. I consider the scheme madness. I know some people who construct dolls' rocking-chairs entirely out of split clothes-pegs, and they are going mad. It's the snow, you'll emerge at the end of winter like the woodcutters of the Tyrol having carved and fashioned many things but gibbering and staring wildly at each other. Think of Sicily! That's really something to look forward to, it will be glorious.

Long melodrama at Duckworths which I feel I'm much too old for, so now I have to find yet another publisher! However I quite enjoy it, it's like weaving, I suppose, it keeps you busy. I am trying to write a novel about the houseboats on Battersea Reach, where we used to live. Thankyou so much for being so kind and supporting my efforts. It was good of Mike to write, I hope he's not doing too much and trying to lift many hundredweights of snow singlehanded –

much love alway, & best wishes for 1979

Mops.

Westminster Tutors
27 May [early 1980s]

Dearest Willie,

I feel broken-hearted not to say good-bye to you properly after so much kindness and such a lovely weekend, but I was disconcerted by seeing so many brightly-coloured people on the train at Oxenholme. I did enjoy it so much, and there was no question of having specially nice feeds on the first and last occasion: all were specially nice. I feel ashamed to have dragged you round the woolshops and the ill-organised festival, please don't think I take all these things for granted, they make life just about bearable. – That looks like a complaint but wasn't meant to be.

I was so glad to see both your daughters – Anne always gives me such a friendly welcome, and doesn't hold it against me that I let my attention wander during the Demon Patience. (Greg points out that I can't even really keep my mind on Beggar My Neighbour which I suppose is the simplest of all card games) and so does Sue, in her quiet way, which makes me feel there's more in her than may ever come to the surface.

You'll forgive me if I lamented over the <u>barn</u>, I see I'm completely ignorant about such things anyway, it was only a momentary pang for such a wonderfully large empty space. I felt the same about Les Halles in Paris, and Covent Garden, and it's a sign that I'm going to pieces.

I managed to get a seat on the train and a 77 which goes all the way to Battersea Rise from Euston, so no trouble there. The Froggies had all arrived and were sitting in Tina's kitchen making themselves nauseous tisane, with all the central heating on. I switched it off with an intimidating smile, no good letting foreigners carry on just as they like. Fortunately they're out all day, wearing themselves out at the Tour de Londres &c.

One of them turned out to be male, he is crushed by the others and has to sleep in the passage.

I can't remember whether you said you liked Barbara Pym, but am sending <u>Quartet in Autumn</u> in case you haven't got it, otherwise it can go to Mothers' Union Xmas sale. I <u>do</u> like her very much, the incidents look so trivial that there's nothing in them and then you suddenly realise how much she's said. When she died last year she left one more novel, <u>A Few Green Leaves</u>, which I'm hoping to review.

My desk (i.e. kitchen table) is in such a mess I haven't the heart to clear it up. Every now and then a vital document rises to the top, but I must send this off before it disappears, to tell you how much better I feel for my visit, a few wheezes here and there are of no importance –

So much love to you and Mike –

Mops.

27a Bishop's Road
Highgate
13 November [*c.*1990]

Dearest Willie and Mike,

Please note the stamp, which clearly represents father and son stealing a sapling from the nearest plantation.

Thankyou so much for such a wonderful holiday. Don't think I've forgotten Mike's old Chinese saying – 'fish and guests should never be kept in the house for more than 3 days' – I felt this had been <u>quite</u> <u>overlooked</u>, and as always it was so good of you to take me to these beautiful places and look at them almost as if you'd never been there before. We used to laugh about the Autumn Tints, and indeed there was a moment when you and Helen began a very serious discussion between maize and pale yellow – but all I can say is the autumn trees were beautiful. And it was a treat to see Helen, and you two are so wonderful together. It amazes me that she seems to know everyone for many miles around, and of course sympathises with all their catastrophes – I know she lived in Old Terry Bank for several months at one point, but all the same – what a gift it is to care (not to make yourself care, that's quite different) for so many people.

I don't know how often Helen comes, but you must think sometimes about the distance – I know we do, with Tina in Devonshire. Ria says Somerset was one thing, but Devonshire is just over the top. Having said that, I feel – as so often – ungrateful. After all, Tina might have been living in Australia, or Canada perhaps and the children would have been interested in nothing but ice-hockey.

My train to Euston was late, which was very satisfactory, as I <u>did</u> miss the rush-hour, and the vintage marmalade came through intact. The children loved the vulgar postcard of teddy-bears back-packing through Lakeland, which Sophie, I'm afraid, takes for the real thing. The only little disaster has been that, while I was away, the American bookseller came to lunch on the wrong Thursday, with a bunch of flowers which he seems to have given to the nanny, and I haven't got his telephone number and I don't know whether he'll come with another bunch of flowers <u>this</u> Thursday as well. One shouldn't allow oneself to be upset by such things.

I'm so pleased with my photograph of the Troutbeck window* and one of the infant Tina wh. reminds me of High Dalby and the moors and Mrs. Payne (wasn't it?) as well as Tina herself in the smocked Dayella dress. Do you remember Dayella?

I had a feeling of your being distressed over the Christmas arrangements. But mightn't it be that the break just for one year from the immensely labour-intensive meals &c might be a good thing in the end, mightn't you worry less and sleep-walk less, in fact not at all? And then next year there would be Old Terry Bank to contain them all,

---

*   The stained-glass window in Jesus Church in Troutbeck, near Windermere, by Burne-Jones.

which would make all the difference. You must promise, however, not to pine in Edinburgh.

It's easy to give good advice to others. – I must remember the prayer, and indeed I took it to heart.

Meanwhile I don't think I said enough in appreciation of the fine cookery at Terry Bank and all your kindness, so I say it now,

Much love and many thanks –

Mops

I enclose a flower of the field from Jerusalem, <u>not</u> a recognisable species I'm afraid.

27a Bishop's Road
Highgate
Friday [1991]

Dearest Willie,

It was so good of you and Mike and Helen to sit it out with me in the admittedly newly done-up and award-winning Oxenholme waiting-room which, all the same, has something of the feeling of a 'custody suite' in an enlightened new police station, people sitting rather apprehensively under the bright lights, and it was marvellous to have the tea, and be able to talk to you until the last moment. The poor train, when it arrived, was full of very discontented passengers – two carriages had had to be taken off at Carlisle because 'the windows had been broken by vandals' and as a result there had been a 'rearrangement of accommodation' (i.e. people sitting on the floor), and then they'd had to stop because BR was re-laying the track. But we got into Euston only 2 hours late and I had a seat, although I felt rather mean, but I kept telling myself I was very old. (We actually made an 'unscheduled stop' at Nuneaton, which was very exciting, although no-one got in or out because of course they hadn't known it was going to happen.)

I was very lucky to come when Helen, Anna and Joseph were all there – somehow it was 'like Christmas', as Sophie says. Really I had a lovely time, so many indulgent little sit downs and helpful hospitable strong drinks, as well as expeditions and what I enjoy so much, stories of old times and distant relatives, although new ones appeared this time (Cousin John, for instance) that I hadn't a grip on. Helen's memory is amazing, she seems to know who <u>everyone</u> is within a wide area of Kirkby Lonsdale, as well, of course, as Burwash. (I remember when they thought Paschal was seriously deaf I thought of Helen, I thought, my word, she managed all right!)

The birthday party was superb, Willie, I honestly think it was the best salmon recipe I've ever had, (so I suppose, if it came from next door, I shall have to overlook the incident of the clothes-line, or rather let it fade from memory). Who'd have believed, during that terribly anxious operation time, that Mike's next birthday party would be like that? I don't mean that you don't have any anxiety – I know very well you have – but it was a pretty good birthday party.

I slept so soundly at Terry Bank that I feel I don't need any sleep for a bit – like Joseph and his dinner – at least I tell myself I don't. At T.B. I always turn off the light and imagine what the hill opposite will look like when I wake up in the morning – and I'm almost always wrong.

I've hung up my new pink jersey from Jumpers in the wardrobe (so-called) and look forward to its first outing – Carol Walsh from Sydney has rung up (<u>again</u>) saying she hopes I'm only going to bring <u>light clothing</u>, so I suppose it won't do for Oz.* Perhaps when I get back.– It's terrible, Willie, I'm always giving myself little <u>rewards</u> and <u>prohibitions</u>, as if I were 3 years old, and I suppose, in fact, it's a sign of second childhood. Now I'm telling myself that the pink jersey (from Jumpers) will be something to think about and keep me going while I'm giving dreary talks at Mietta's restaurant and on Hobart waterfront. It's a disgrace.

I had a wonderful time and this is to send you best love and many thanks –

Mops. –

P.S. It was very good of Anne to give us lunch on her marvellous round table. –

* PMF was to attend the Hobart Literary Festival.

27a Bishop's Road
Highgate
29 December 1994

Dearest Willie,

I'm so sorry that you should have rung up and I should have seemed to be out, but I think I must really have been next door, that is to say in Ria's house – I can scarcely call it helping, but <u>trying</u> to help. I might mention here that Mary (my stepmother) who we fetched out for the day from her Residential Nursing Home was <u>sick</u> halfway through lunch – we had to find some of my clothes that fitted her and carry on regardless with lighting the pudding, Poor Mary, she's getting rather <u>vague.</u> Ria made the pudding herself, but frankly bought the (3) stuffings and the brandy butter from Waitrose and very good they were, so I can't pretend in any case there was a great deal to do. But I certainly wasn't out anywhere (though we did go to see the Nutcracker, very well done by the old Sadlers Wells company down from Birmingham) – because unfortunately I just can't get rid of this tiresome irregular heartbeat and breathlessness and general inability to walk anywhere much, it's been going on since <u>September</u> as I'm sure I've told you only too often, was very tiresome at the Cheltenham Festival and if anything is worse now. The doctor says it's asthma but in my opinion it's <u>not</u> and I <u>do</u> feel that I know a little bit about asthma. Well, there it is, but I feel properly stuck and have to cancel all the immediate things I promised to do, as I was sure I'd be better by this time.

But your (admirably word-processed) letter cheered me up when I read that Mike felt better than he had done for the last 3 years – more power to him, I say – and you know he's always said what a treat it would be to have a quiet Christmas – and I don't think he ever says what he doesn't mean – and you actually succeeded in having one! Only I understand absolutely what you mean about the house standing ready and looking beautiful for Christmas and yet not expecting any one – (although they'll all be there by the time you get this) – it seems, as you say, <u>weird</u>, as though the house had forgotten what it was really for. And Anne's cottage must be rather the same – only I can't help feeling she will come back one day.

Meanwhile I don't know who the Bayleys are. I'm sure that wasn't the name of the people with the boat-house and the gardens? Bayley?

Valpy seems settled down at Oxford – except that he has to keep going to Mexico, Madrid and the Hague to make ends meet, and nothing, not even the Forest Bark, will keep the ground-elder down – and he is pruning the apple trees, I think, rather too wildly and Laurence (his 2nd son, who now tells us we must call him Larry) is working at a nightclub at the other end of Oxford and not persevering with any form of secondary education, except becoming a waiter – Greg has managed to pass his exams so far at the Oxford Polytechnic (now called Brookes College) after failing to do so at Imperial College and Durham – he is now 22, pig-tailed and quite delightful, – his girl-friend is a dental technician in Cordoba, at least she has a respectable job. Little (9 years old) Camilo has gone to St. Frideswide's Junior School and may well turn out to be the least trouble of the 3.

Tina and family have just left, after a visit largely occupied with a Star Trek game, played with a video of Klingon, whose brain, composed of electric circuits, is outside his skull. He kept pointing and laughing fiendishly and I thought Jemima was rather frightened. Poor Tina and Terry still haven't managed to sell their cottage, although plenty of people have been to see it, and it's in a nice village on the edge of the moor, and has roses and honeysuckle round the door. But I do have trust that the right purchaser will come along.

I have finished another book,* only a short one and not quite a novel, and we are now looking for a really good jacket design, I always used to have Old Masters of some kind on the cover but the sales department say that they are now hopelessly out of date.

How nice that the silent security man has turned out so helpful to Anne – he must, of course, have become much less silent – and what a blessing that Leo has got into this practical mechanics course because that surely was what he wanted to do before all these disasters happened.

---

* The Blue Flower.

I don't quite know what to do – whether to cancel the things I'm supposed to be doing for the <u>whole</u> of the year, or hope for the best, (which isn't ordinarily something I ever do).

This year I'm the last of my family, that is since Rawle died in June. But oh dear, I daren't read this letter through again, it's so disconnected, and I still haven't thanked you for not <u>one</u> but <u>two</u> most generous presents – a beautiful hot water bottle with a close coat of fur the colour of a golden retriever and the 18th century lovers – everything for an evening on the sofa, thankyou so very much, you can guess how I appreciate these truly nice things. – All my love and best wishes for 1995 from Mops

27a Bishop's Road
Highgate
30 March [1995]

Dearest Willie,

Thankyou so much for your letter and your kind reference to My Symptoms, which Ria would feel a bit of an indulgence, I'm so <u>sick</u> of them, Willie. All I want them to do is go away. But I suppose sooner or later you get to the illness which is going to finish you off, or as my dear Burne-Jones calls it 'the pale face that looks in at the door one day' and then you're obliged to recognise it. Don't think I'm becoming morbid though. I'm looking forward so much to seeing you and am very lucky that you can manage May 11th.

I'm afraid I don't take the <u>Times</u> and haven't got Edmund's obituary – but if Jeannie liked it, that's all that matters. Meanwhile it <u>does</u> seem that they've found the right treatment for Mike, but she of course must watch him very very carefully and I'm afraid there'll be no question of her coming with me to decrepit old Somerville, where they're giving a lunch (not really <u>giving</u> it) for our year in June.

I'm so glad the M.U. still sing <u>There is a Green Hill</u> – nothing like that here – all rhythm and blues so I only dare to go to the dear old 8 o'clock which I expect will soon be given up. – And I'm not surprised you were a little off balance after your marathon birthday treat – I'm so glad you had a look at 34 Well Walk – it was sold about three years ago and the owner, who I knew, asked if I would like to come up one last time and just see the whole place and my old room – I thought it was really kind of her considering she was sitting there with all the carpets gone and her luggage packed – and do you know it was hardly altered at all, although I believe now it's tremendously smartened up – the rent in our day was £40 a year. – My mother didn't die there, but when we'd moved to the horrid grand house in Regents Park, which they felt they <u>ought</u> to get when Daddy became editor. – I think the garden you sat in must have been Bush House, which is now a kind of arts and music centre and intensely respectable restaurant.

Mike and Elizabeth are miraculous. Who worked the miracle?

I just crawl out in the evenings, feeling it's feeble not to – not every evening by any manner of means. I went to the Merchant Taylors Hall (or was it the Fishmongers) to hear a lovely Purcell concert got up by the British Council – but they're going to send it around the world to celebrate something or other and I can't help wondering whether in Russia, The Bermudas &c they're really going to appreciate so much countertenor, theorbo, lute &c or whether they won't think it all sounds scatty and wouldn't prefer a brass band selection, or the pipes and drums.

But it was very melancholy and soothing.

I wonder how Anne's singer, that she used to accompany, will get on without her? Not at all, I suppose, as Anne seemed to be supplying all the go and spirit. But I hope you'll find time to tell me all about everything in May –

With much love,
Mops.

27a Bishop's Road
Highgate
17 May [1995]

Dearest Willie and Mike,

Back in Highgate, and although I haven't really got a proper stretch of gravel for the dear little Siberian violets, I've planted them and put a little gravel round them to try and fool them. As though one could ever fool a plant.

Such a wonderful holiday I had at Terry Bank, one treat after another. Because I have such a bad memory for the names of places, and I can't say it's getting any better – and you're always wonderfully patient about it – you mustn't think I don't look at them or appreciate being taken to them or that I don't remember them in my own way.

When I got back I looked up the date in Dorothy Wordsworth's Grasmere Journals, wh. start on May 14th – rather surprised that she's transplanting radishes and hoeing peas, and it made me sad (for the 100th time) that she would so much have liked a 'Book of Botany' to make out which wild flower was which and she hadn't anything <u>at all</u> and now there are so many. – I also read a bit about Four Gables – I see that Webb <u>did</u> choose Morris wallpapers originally and sent for sampleboards so that the local painters could match the colours <u>exactly</u> – can you imagine them at it – and also that the house was supposed to rise straight out of the grass, 'in the Pele tradition'; which it doesn't do now, does it, they've got a flower-bed, I suppose that's a lot easier for the mowing, though.

But the best thing was seeing you both looking so well and undertaking so much and so many responsibilities – (this made me rather ashamed of myself as I have so few now – I feel weighed down even by looking after the goldfish when the children are away) – without seeming to find anything too difficult – it's a miracle, really.

I was very lucky to see the garden in May and had so many treats – one of them being able to come down in the early morning and just lean against the beautifully warm Aga while the kettle boiled – I don't mean that I was cold, of course I wasn't – but oh, I <u>do</u> hope Tina gets her house with an Aga one of these days – and then going upstairs again there was a glimpse of the blue poppy from the landing window.

Don't forget to let me know, will you, if you come in June. I see I'm supposed to be going to a lunch on the 15th and the so-called specialist at the Whittington on the 16th but could EASILY cancel these things, specially the hospital, so do remember –

with many thanks and much love Mops

P.S. Talking about Pickering &c made me think so much about Jay as a little boy. I'm so glad that everything is turning out right for him –

27a Bishop's Road
Highgate
18 July [*c.*1995]

Dear Mike,

Lovely to hear from you, and I hope you've also made a note of it in your letter book, which has always impressed me a good deal.

What wonderful news that Diana (I think that's what she was called) has gone to live in Wycombe, though I wonder what she's going to do with her brother? He'd better not get in the way, though. I know you and Willie have always been very kind and generous about her, but I've never been able to forgive her for moving her clothesline into the vegetable garden and pretending her own had blown down. She was ruthlessness personified.

I'm not surprised Old Terry Bank needs putting back into order, but you mustn't think of doing it yourself. You must put an ad. in the Cumbrian Gazette for a handyman.

Perhaps your Man Saturday could suggest someone – by the way, I thought you had 2 youths, who moved all those shrubs on the lawn below the assault course?

Your garden sounds wonderful, and it's a pity, in a way, that you stopped asking the Mothers' Union to come in for tea and admire it. I agree that it's been a good rose year, though we haven't got any Rugosa (I love Frü Dagnar, but is she really a Rugosa?), but our garden, I don't mind telling you, is in a sorry state – like most of Highgate it's really in the middle of a wood, and reverts at the slightest opportunity – the magnolia and climbing hydrangea were overwhelmed and didn't flower. The mallows grew 8 foot high, and the sparrows and thrushes have been driven away by rampant jays, magpie and blackbirds. In front, the (ill-named) climbing rose Compassion has grown enormous thorns which have impaled the postie, who doesn't like delivering my letters – I must say it smells very sweet, but this doesn't impress the postie – and, another thing, the Siberian violets are <u>still</u> flowering and they've been at it since the spring.

I'm so glad Joseph isn't going to have a reception in the house! But you and Willie will have to <u>dress up</u>. Have you thought about that?

I'm horrified to hear that Willie has been carrying buckets of peat. Believe me, no nasturtium is worth that. I'm still gridlocked by arthritis, and it has just struck me that it isn't going to get better and go away, as infirmities always have done in the past. However, you've set me a good example, Mike, so who knows?

All my love to both of you

Mops

P.S. Just a word about the Blue Poppy. You say specialists are at work improving it, but that, of course, will make it something different. Left to itself I don't think it does more than 2 years in captivity. It was you, wasn't it, who told me that it should always be seen from below, which means a hill garden, like yours. –

27a Bishops Road
Highgate
22 October [*c.*1995]

Dearest Willie, You're quite right, I was relieved to get your postscript – it isn't that I wasn't worrying about Mike, who could help it, but that the 10 stone is a most comforting figure – only Willie, surely he doesn't <u>like</u> being weighed? I can't think how you persuade him to it. What a relief that he's able to eat, so it's worthwhile going into Kirkby Lonsdale and getting something really nice. It's so terribly difficult to keep one's mind on a high level when it's consumed with worry,

Ria and family have gone off for the half-term to the farmhouse they've bought in Wales. I haven't seen it yet, I'm waiting for the new wood-stove to be installed, and when I <u>do</u> get there I shan't be able to struggle up and down the hills – but I'll have a go when spring comes. John was up so early, attaching the children's bikes to the bike rack and balancing the lawn-mower, in its special waterproof bag, on the roof. I beg him to get a gardener in from the village, and also a carpenter to put up bookshelves, that's what the locals will expect as they clearly regard him as a harmless millionaire sent to provide them with employment. – He works so hard and it does my heart good to see how happy he is at the idea of fiddling about with the window-catches and damp-courses, and Doing Something About the Barn. He also loves the instructions for the wood-stove – but it hasn't got one of those nice round lids in the top which you take off with a little iron thing, and then you forget where you've put it.

Very exhausted by the Chinese exhibition at the BM although it was much smaller than I expected. Perhaps it's time to give up culture. I told you I'm sure about my evening as a poetry judge at the Groucho when my leg bled all over the floor. Safer at home.

I loved Anne's poem and hope it's always going to be true, I mean I hope she's always going to have happy days and thankful evenings. I'm glad Carl(o?) has been given his dismissal – he's had plenty of time to become a fine man, if he was going to be one. But what a good girl she is, looking after her aunt Helen, I am sure she wants to, but how many daughters are there like Anne?

Delighted that Helen's op went off so satisfactorily.

Laurence (Valpy's 2nd) has now taken up with an older woman who runs a hair-dressing salon and thinks of starting a new life in Brighton. – Valpy says he's given up commenting on what his children do (though this is not quite true).

All my love to both of you,
Mops.

27a Bishop's Road
Highgate
15 June [1997]

Dearest Willie,

Thankyou so much for your p.c. – you must count it as an <u>answer</u> to this – I know you haven't time to write. – I think it's very clever of you to find a place where you can have <u>some</u> nursing if you want it – Bet there are some fairly ridiculous people among the guests, though. – But wonderful that Mike feels well enough to make the trip.

I'm just watching the Queen's guests who were married the same year she was, and to my dismay I found tears in my eyes! Really, this won't do. But one woman said how she'd opened the envelope with the invitation in terribly carefully for fear of getting it torn, and I wondered if the British Public had changed at all, in all the many many years I've known it.

I'm glad to tell you that I don't have hay fever any more – I'm <u>too old</u> – I do have my old enemies, My Back and My Heart and they're a proper nuisance particularly when it comes to walking uphill – and this Welsh farmhouse which Ria and John have bought is lovely, but it's poised on the side of a hill, and quite near the top, and I feel I'm a bit of a nuisance there, though nobody has said so. Actually I'd be quite happy just to sit there and look at the view out of the windows and the sheep and ponies on the hill.

I've had a mild success in America with <u>The Blue Flower</u> and in consequence an alarming photographer lady called, dressed in silk and linen – she came from New York, and in a car from Brown's Hotel, which she left outside, (including the poor driver) from 10 a.m. till 3 – she wouldn't have coffee or tea, and I felt fit to drop – she specializes, so she says, in informal author portraits, and kept pulling the furniture about (I'd stuffed a lot of things behind the bed) and springing on top of things to take interesting angles, I always look dreadful in photos and these will be no exception. And a <u>dreadful</u> drawing of me in the New York Review of Books, done from photos I suppose, but the U.S. publisher says I ought to be grateful as it's a famous artist, even more famous than the photographer.

Very good news of my Siberian violets that Mike gave me and which I thought weren't going to survive the late frost last winter – they're now multiplying furiously, even though I've no gravel to give them. So I must survive until next spring to see them in flower again.

Willie, you don't tell me about your eye operation – I did say don't answer, but do let me know about that – just a word –

Much love to you all – Mops

27a Bishop's Road
Highgate
[1997]

Dearest Willie,

I didn't know your eye op. was to be so soon – nor did you, I
suppose – and I think it's hard you couldn't spend what sounds to me
like a pretty hard day thinking entirely, or even a little bit, of yourself,
and being indulged every minute, or at least for a few minutes, but I
know you wouldn't see it that way. With those formidable women
doctors you have to think, well, they probably had every kind of
discouragement, and feel that they have to demonstrate their authority
&c at every moment, but all the same, it would be nice if they were
gentler and kinder.

It was <u>mad</u>, dear Willie, to have a large party (<u>16</u> staying in your
house, even though it's a mansion – you must have had people sleeping
in the log-basket) just a few days before the op. but, mad as it was,
it was obviously a stroke of genius, and it must have made up for
everything when Leo gave you the Great Hug. (You don't tell me,
though, what you think of his girlfriend? Bournemouth is such a long
way from York.) But I didn't know Joseph had been ill – I thought he
was training to be a solicitor – I don't even know what Crohn's disease
<u>is</u> – and poor Jay – but they're better, thank heavens, you say.

I'm not quite sure whether Jeannie's op was a cataract. But I do
know that telling you to keep still <u>wasn't</u> nonsense, and you must
absolutely avoid doing Useful Things.

You kindly ask me what I'm working on – well, <u>nothing</u> at the
moment, I had taken a quarter of an advance (they pay it in quarters
to keep the tax down) on a new novel, but hadn't done anything, or
even had an idea of anything, when Chris Carduff* (lovely name) – he
was the one who called his kitten 'Charlotte Mew' – got a job with the
best publishers in Boston – I think I told you this, but you know how it
is, Willie, one's memory isn't perhaps one's strongest point – well,
Carduff, who I only know from talking to him over the telephone

---

* PMF's American editor at Addison-Wesley, Houghton Mifflin and Counterpoint.

about his wife, his children, and his beliefs, has always been a kind supporter and has now bought in all my titles and arranged about advertising them on the internet &c – and so I don't actually <u>need</u> to write anything more, and I think the best thing to do is to keep the Harper Collins advance apart from everything else so that if I can't think of a new novel, or don't want to, I can send it back just as it is.

I've now been elected to the council of Royal Society of Literature and I go to their meetings because they're at 4, and I've more or less given up going out in the evening. Tea is served at these meetings and I'm amazed at the amount the male writers <u>eat</u>. Perhaps they have nothing else all day, but whole cakes, and plates of sandwiches, are soon reduced to crumbs. Luckily there is a very competent secretary, otherwise we should get nothing done, and, if I've followed things correctly, we've just inherited a large sum and are negotiating to buy a new building. I do wish, though, that I'd been born a more efficient committee member. I truly think they're born, not made.

so much love and very best wishes to you and Mike – Mops

27a Bishop's Road
Highgate
30 August [1997]

Dearest Willie,

I don't think I've made it clear how much I appreciate your cards, particularly of Brantwood perhaps, but no, I loved all of them and they made a kind of traveller's diary. You say you're 'idle' during the mornings, but this seems to me frankly ridiculous. You know you always have too much to do.

I'm glad the bank is so good this year. Maria had a great fit of energy and hacked down the <u>R. Ponticum</u>. She just couldn't bear the way it infringed on its more delicate neighbours. This was when they came back from their farmhouse in Wales, where I also went for a few days this August. You remember it's their holiday house, and they made a giant move, having bought 6 starter sets from IKEA, each with one knife, one fork, one glass, one bed, one chair &c, a wood-burning stove and a ping-pong table, but they've done a tremendous amount since, and transformed the barn, or one of the barns, into a sort of visitors wing. It's all on a tremendous slope, so that I have to walk quite cautiously about the garden to avoid falling and breaking something, which would make me more of a nuisance than ever. But it's a lovely place.

I wrote the above on Saturday evening and was going to finish it on Sunday morning but then Ria came in early to tell me about Princess Di. It upset us immensely and made us feel unreasonably sad and guilty, and yet we couldn't exactly say why.

Children of course fed up, as all their favourite TV programmes cancelled.

Tina's house in Cornwall is now repaired and very much improved, all the old kitchen lino gone and the old slates uncovered, new snowy-white frig and gas cooker, new carpeting on the stairs and new bathroom and TV. She feels like a lottery winner. But <u>no</u> wistaria – even the clematis montana won't take – only things with stiff, gnarled branches, and thorn-bushes. Perhaps I've told you all this before, if so forgive me.

Another good thing is that The Blue Flower did unexpectedly well in America (none of the others did). And <u>another</u> good thing is that Anne could be with you during the early summer. What a <u>brick</u> she is – a very old-fashioned term, but it's the one I want.

All my love to you and Mike. I'm so glad to hear he's correcting your driving. It's like old times – Mops.

27a Bishop's Road
Highgate
Scarcely any berries on
the holly down south.
27 December [1997]

Dearest Willie,

What beautiful black gloves you sent me, emphatically for best, and I shall keep them for best. Turning out what I think of as my glove drawer I found lots of terrible odds and ends and got rid of them to make room for the new ones, an immense improvement.

And thankyou for the mysterious and beautiful pendant for my birthday.

I hate Christmas being over, all the more because (quite unlike you) I do scarcely anything whereas Ria is indefatigable, making mincemeat, adjusting the children's computer &c – both she and John are white with fatigue (Ria has got a new office in Great Ormond Street, to work in conjunction with the Children's Hospital, as well as her office at the university, and John is sorting out heaven knows what about the Korean financial crisis), and John's parents have arrived for 3 days stay, with bags and umbrellas.

All the traditional disasters happened – the cat got into the cellar where the turkey was waiting on a nice cold shelf and it was only just rescued in time, Alfie appeared quite well, but mysteriously ran a temperature as soon as he was put to bed and was only restored to health by being brought downstairs, and I was laid low by backache, so I can't quite explain why we all enjoyed ourselves so much. There's just the pantomime this afternoon, then reality again. For me that means starting on next year's Booker Prize, as I've agreed to be one of the judges this year. I can't think why as I feel much too old and feeble-minded to be anything of the sort. I suspect they're finding it difficult to get <u>anyone</u> to do it.

This is a very selfish letter – please remember I'm thinking particularly about Mike and you this Christmas – and I did so like Mike's specifications for Jay's speech – not more than four minutes, and nothing low.

all my love and best Christmas wishes
Mops

27a Bishop's Road
Highgate
11 January [*c*.1998]

Dearest Willie,

So glad to hear from you that Mike is so much better and Jay has this good job. You did sound so depressed (I don't mean you

complained) and now, such a miracle, you don't. The only thing I feel
doubtful about is the sticks – of course they must help or you wouldn't
use them, but personally I find that when I'm going out I'm always
carrying something, and that often takes up both hands or at least only
leaves one, which I feel I may need to grab hold of something. And so I
stagger on without one.

John and Ria's farmhouse in Wales is getting quite grand, with three
bathrooms and a ping-pong table for the (frequent) wet days. John is
undoubtedly a house person. He looks really radiant when there's any
need to go up on the roof and check the flues, or put up the fences
(blown down by the wind) again, but he says he won't stay much longer
as Head of Group Risk Management at the Deutsche Bank – it's just
too exhausting – he has to go to Frankfurt or Utrecht every week or so,
and he says he's getting too old for it.

Tina has been without electricity or telephone for days – it's just
been put back and she ventured about into the garden and found
snowdrops in flower – we haven't got any this year. But the Siberian
(Alpine?) violets you gave me have come up gallantly. Luke, Tina's
eldest) has just reached the moody stage, playing stormy chords on the
piano, or lying on his bed muttering 'What is the use of life?', the
younger two are still cheerful.

Willie, I could never do all the cooking you do, and I can't imagine
how you get it done. I'm just going to drag myself into my little
kitchen to peel a single potato (perhaps two) for dinner. Just think of
all the people you've fed in your lifetime! Convey my very real
congratulations to Mike.

Ria is back from California – she says there was an entire village in
Swiss chocolate in the shopping mall of her hotel – and Valpy back
from Bangkok, where he's been on a conference about heaven knows
what. I am reluctantly facing the things which I put off to think about
after Christmas – the worst one is that I really don't think I can write
another novel, I am too decrepit, so I must break my contract with my
publishers, and it will be such a nuisance, and a cause of reproach, and
of their behaving honourably and decently, or perhaps they'll behave
indecently, I don't know which will be worse.

We had a splendid Christmas here except the pudding managed to boil dry – but Ria kept her head and served up the middle part, which was still more or less all right, wreathed in flames, and no-one noticed. I'm sure your 'quiet Christmas' turned out to be nothing of the sort, by the way, it never does, but I do so hope it left you both feeling well. I've just remembered another of Mike's sayings – the unaccountable feeling of satisfaction when you finish a packet or a jar of anything and throw the empty packet into the bin: you feel you've achieved something – he's absolutely right about this –

all my love and best wishes to you both, and indeed to any of the family who happen to be in the house Mops

27a Bishop's Road
Highgate
1 April [1998]

Dearest Willie,

How lovely to hear from you, only I'm sorry Mike has these ups and downs. You say he didn't feel up to the outing to meet Michael Harker – was that the man you once took me to lunch with – but where <u>was</u> it – it was a house he'd lived in when he was a boy, but he seemed to take that so calmly and have no regrets – honestly Willie you sometimes complain about your memory, but mine has become abysmal, and to my dismay I can clearly remember (as you're always supposed to) things that happened in childhood, and everything after that is increasingly hazy. I can't even repeat Keats' Ode to a Nightingale to myself right through, which used to have such a good calming effect when I was having the babies.

But in a way I don't care – I'm a very old woman now and feel I must be borne with.

I felt really cheered by your description of Jay's visit and so relieved that he finds the directors civilised. – I think for the very first time, isn't it – it looks as though this was going to be the long-sought-after right job.

I was staggered by getting the U.S. Critics' Book Award, Chris did ring and tell me I was on the shortlist and I was pleased about <u>that</u>, he said could you send me a few words by way of a Speech of Acceptance, I said I wouldn't dream of it as it would make me feel such a fool. So <u>he</u> wrote a few words of acceptance and went to New York with them and lo and behold he actually had to get onto the platform and deliver them, just like the Oscars. It's the first year they've allowed non-Americans to be considered, so I feel proud, yes I do.

Meantime my dearly-loved English publisher, Stuart, has left HarperCollins on a point of principle, as he had got Chris Patten's Memoirs ready for press and then Rupert Murdoch said it must be cancelled as it might get in the way of his deals with the Chinese. I see Stuart has been awarded 'a six-figure sum' as compensation for constructive dismissal, but I feel I must leave HarperCollins and go wherever he goes. What a nuisance, I don't like these upsets, I like everything to go on just the same from day today. <u>My</u> cup of tea at 7.30, <u>my</u> little walk to the shop to get the Evening Standard – it's dreadful really, but Willie, we're survivors, so we might as well revel in it.

Ria and John do far too much, but they <u>love</u> their farmhouse in Wales – 3 bathrooms and a lawnmower like a small car, specially for hill-mowing – and swallows in summer –

much love to you all from Mops

27a Bishop's Road
Highgate
7 May [1998]

Dearest Willie,

I don't think reminiscing <u>is</u> senile. It gives you your time over twice, and some of them were such good times. Leaving Wycombe Abbey, Bucks. was one of them. I can hear Auntie now, up on the dais praying for 'those who go forth from this school', I couldn't believe I wouldn't ever have to go back to it again. And yet some of them were really nice. Rachel was. We couldn't believe it when she, courageously, told the house that she was engaged, and yet I suppose she was only between 35 and 40.

And your p.c. of Alderney brought that back to me – the house on the rocks and that strange museum full of mouldy stuffed birds, and your stalwart rowing to get over the 'bar' – and you were so small, and the boat was so large.

I certainly wish I hadn't taken on the Booker judging this year. I thought it would be a nice sedentary occupation, and after all I have done it before, but I've definitely gone downhill since then and I think books have got longer – I've only done 35 so far (I keep counting them) so 100 more to come, and already there's hardly any floor space left in my little room. Also, I drop off to sleep almost immediately when I start to read them – it's becoming an automatic reaction.

It's so good of you to ask me to come and stay when you have so much to do, but the trouble is I have attacks of arthritis (My Back which I now dignify by the name of my Degenerative Arthritis), not all the time, thank heavens, but I never know when it will come, and when it does I have to stay put and ask John to get my oranges, potatoes, and all important alcohol with the household shopping. Do you think I could write again, as it's rather bad at the moment? I don't mind whether the weather is cold or not – not a bit – and I should love to see you.

Maria and John getting on very well with their Welsh hill property. They went up there at lambing-time. John bought an amazing new mower to take up there – I told him it reminded me of a Baby Austin in the old days and he said it was built on the same principle.

Must now go to a Royal Society of Literature committee. I hate committees, and can never think of anything to say, and there is a woman called Selina Hastings who is always making me feel small –
all my love to you and Mike – Mops

27a Bishop's Road
Highgate
12 July [1998]

Dearest Willie,

To start with, I do appreciate your re-reading my books. Really, it makes it worthwhile having written them.

I agree Charlotte Mew's short stories do take some getting through, but I think her short pieces, like An Old Servant, have a certain something. I was very glad to have been given her candlesticks, just plain brass, and I don't use them – and a drawing by Burne-Jones, not signed, just a sketch for a portrait, but it's wonderful to have something you can touch, and I also managed to go and see people who had known or at least spoken to B-J and had known Charlotte Mew quite well.

I want to explain about your kind invitation, more than kind, considering all you've got to do – but that involves talking about My Health – and I seem always to be talking to people who say My Aunt is wonderful – she is Eighty, but she might be Any Age and She Never Complains – well, I mightn't be any other age and I do complain – my real trouble is this arthritis, which didn't, so to speak, come naturally, but as a result of the various drugs I'm given to keep my heart ticking (not warfarin as I've always refused to take it) – however, you know all about these – the doctor says (more or less) that if I stop taking these nasty pills my heart will stop altogether – I don't really feel outraged by this, and I remember Mike did, rather I feel sorry for my heart which has made such an effort for so long, (rather like the horse that comes in last on the Saturday afternoon racing on TV, which I sometimes watch, and we're told 'the distance was too much for poor old _____'. I was supposed to be going on a tour of Europe, Germany, Belgium and France – (a dismal prospect anyway, you'll say) – for the British Council, but have had to say I can't go. – I can just about walk down to the shops and back, or to the top of the hill where I can get a bus to go and see Mary (who is still in her nursing home and gives me a great welcome but alas! doesn't know who I am at all). The upshot of all this is, that because this arthritis has got worse at the moment I don't really feel up to a long journey, but I do so much want to see you and Mike – indeed, I was caught myself sitting and thinking, shall I ever see Mike and Willie again in this life? but then told myself that this sort of thing wouldn't do.

Do you think I could ask you again in the autumn – Sept–Oct? – surely I must be better by then – I've been all wrong since last Christmas. (I even have trouble getting out of a taxi, my knees don't bend properly, it would be better if they bent the other way, like a horse's). It wouldn't matter a bit if the weather was bad. We could just sit still and I would try to pitch my voice up, it's usually all right if you sit straight opposite the person you're talking to, I find. Anyway, it's often lovely in autumn.

All this is in answer to your PPS How is Your Back? But there is also a PPPS about the garden and how it's been a wonderful flowering season – you say in <u>M</u>'s garden – so I take it you mean the rhodos which I regard particularly as his – that must be lovely, and I hope you weren't tempted to ask the Mothers' Union in to see them, as I think you used to do.

Ria took the whole of her department over to Berlin for a conference – how could she? – they went over to East Berlin for their meals and sat in the mitteleuropean sun. Tina laid low by some pneumonia-ish thing, she has lost her voice and can't eat anything, it seems, but cream crackers. These young women work too hard in my opinion. They are both <u>very</u> thin – Tina and Maria. Valpy is expected to lunch today, but will probably be late. He has just been to Washington – to discuss the apparent lack of money in the Far East – But what can he do about that? – I am feebly turning over the immense pile of Booker books – which, fortunately, I can do lying down – but then there's a temptation to close one's eyes –

all my love to both of you – mops

27a Bishop's Road
Highgate
27 December [*c.*1998]

Dearest Willie,

What a delightful surprise – Mike is absolutely right about the whisky-taking moment in the day, although I usually don't have whisky itself (unless I'm staying at Terry Bank) – but <u>now I shall</u>.

It does <u>help</u> so! A. E. Housman was so right to write

Ten thousand times I've done my best
And all's to do again –

I can't help feeling this every morning, although it passes off with a cup of tea, to some extent, but when 7 o'clock comes I have an illusion that I've <u>earned</u> a rest, actually <u>earned</u> it, even though I haven't got anything to show for it, and now I shall be able to have a nip of whisky, and think of kind friends.

Oh the blessed peace and quiet, it seems unbelievable. – Let's just hope that your trailing geranium is spared.

As to writing a book, things are not very satisfactory – as I only have myself to cook for and have allowed mind-your-own-business to grow between the shrubs in my little bit of garden, so I don't have any weeding to do. I really ought to have got down to it, and with that in mind I signed up a contract for a new novel, but meanwhile I had this good luck in America and The Blue Flower sold so well that I actually have a bit of money and now don't feel impelled to write any thing at all. – This is with Houghton Mifflin, the Boston publisher, where my editor is so nice and has called his cat Charlotte Mew and rings up to tell me how his children are getting on in school and what he's growing in his yard. They are now bringing out The Bookshop as well, although it will seem very old-fashioned by now. Historical, let's hope. I enclose a paperback of Burne-Jones, which now has a few colour plates, in case you'd like it, if not it will do for the next Kirkby L. coffee morning sale.

Mary is still in the Goldhurst nursing-home and, although she always gives me a great welcome, she is deafer than ever and I don't feel she really knows who I am – but on the other hand she doesn't worry about things as she used to do, in fact she doesn't seem to worry at all. It's so sad when people change so much, that it hardly bears thinking about.

All well otherwise – the siberian violet you gave me has at last got going and I have great hopes of it next spring –

All my love to you and Mike –

Mops

27a Bishop's Road
Highgate
March 28 [*c.*1999]

Dearest Willie,

How lovely to get your letter but I was APPALLED to hear of your fall in the kitchen, just like Alan Bennett's <u>Talking Heads</u> and I <u>hate</u> to think of how painful it must have been. Also I don't quite understand (but I must have got this wrong) – I thought you'd made the grand move downstairs, installed a downstairs bathroom &c – but here you are still <u>up</u>stairs, counting your sheep and lambs – and Willie, the divan in M's dressing-room must, surely, be uncomfortable in the extreme. And the steroids too, and to think of the complaints I'm always making about My Back.

I'll tell you one thing, though, Willie, and that's about Jay and his move north – I take it he could do his new job from there, but the reason you feel Beatriz is in duty bound to go with him is because he's your son – if it was Carlos moving you wouldn't feel that Anne ought to give up everything and accompany him, because she's your daughter.

But I'm glad they're all doing so well. The Silent Man is obviously going to continue thinking about nothing but security until his dying day. You remember the first Christmas he came up to Terry Bank he was left with Mike while you all went to church – What did they talk about?: Security.

This is the first Palm Sunday since we came to Highgate that I haven't been to early morning service. I've got all my Palm Sunday crosses stuck behind a picture. I could get up to church all right, but I dread not being able to get up from a kneeling position – just think of it, Willie, the embarrassment, the vicar kindly putting out a helping hand &c. I shall be down in Cornwall with Tina on Easter Sunday, and perhaps I shan't be able to manage it then.

However, at least I have a <u>golden pen</u> – only gold-plated, I fear, but anyway it was awarded to me at the Café Royal on International Writers Day, for my (alleged) services to literature – Willie, the Café Royal is getting so tarnished and worn-out looking – statues chipped, curtains coming off their hooks, and a horrible lunch with <u>hard</u> roast chicken which you could scarcely bite into – however all the writers turned up and I just about managed to get up and down from the platform without collapsing in a heap.

My Siberian violets are out: But I expect yours have been out for weeks.

Dear Willie and Mike, do look after yourselves – all my love and best wishes –

Mops

P.S. I <u>loved</u> the prayer. But what possessed you to show it to Diana?

> *27a Bishop's Road*
> *Highgate*
> Monday 17 May [1999]

Dearest Willie,

Thankyou for the lovely de Morgan tile. It's quite true, we used to find them, or bits of them, washed up with the tide at Battersea. Of course it's all been smartened up now.

You'll notice that my writing's gone to pieces, another result of this cursed rheumatism, or arthritis, or whatever it is. But I feel ashamed (really, deeply ashamed) of making these complaints when I have no real responsibilities and even at the moment I'm lying warm in bed – which is the best place, you know, Willie, after all – and you have these many worries and anxieties. – I thought steroids were drugs that disqualified you from the Olympics – I'm not surprised they make you feel odd. But as for loss of short term, or indeed long term memory, or what you call general dottiness, you mustn't let that worry you, that is just the mind resting itself. It will be perfectly all right when it's done that. I've now got to a stage when I not only don't remember people's names and faces but read through the instructions (let's say) on a packet of Tikka Masala, throw the packet away, then find I've clean forgotten them and have to go all through the rubbish to get the packet back again. – I've just had a letter thanking me for agreeing to judge the Marsh Biography Prize and referring to some dinner or other where it's going to be awarded. But I can't remember anything about the Marsh Biography Prize – not a single thing – my mind is a total blank.

So you see. But the headaches are something else again. <u>Anything</u> is better than pain, I sometimes think.

How does Mike keep going? Well, I know the answer to that – it's because you are there to look after him. But he's wonderful, he really is. Oh dear, it does seem a long time – it <u>is</u> a long time, since we were driving past High Street and he said 'Well, I shall never walk along High Street again.' But he doesn't dwell on things – if they can't be helped, he just accepts them.

Luke is just about to take his G.C.S.E.s – they have a 'leavers' party at his school (sorry, his community centre) – much anxiety as a <u>suit</u> has to be hired and he is too thin for all the suits in Plymouth and Exeter – he just gets taller and thinner. Poor Jemima has broken her arm – can't play basketball, can't play the piano – she feels it's a tragedy, whereas I can remember how relieved I was at my horrible prep school when I broke my arm and didn't have to 'join in' with anything, particularly the dreaded Chocolate Box Dance. – As for Greg's wedding, I really don't think I <u>can</u> get to Cordoba at the end of August. It will be so dreadfully hot, and he cheerfully says we shall all be expected to dance until dawn. And then they (i.e. Greg and Lidia) are going to Australia, bushwhacking or roo-trapping or whatever for 3 months and then coming back to Oxford with nothing to live on, Valpy says they really can't live with him.

It's awful how you don't want to do things any more! I've been asked to do a speaking tour of Italy, staying in nice places, but the very <u>thought</u> of it! Yet I suppose even ten years ago I should have been quite glad to go.

I must tell you that the Siberian violets are ignoring the fact that they're planted in heavy clay and have taken over more or less completely. And it's such a good year for the Wisteria. Everyone who walks past the house stops to look up at it, and it'll be out again in the autumn, so there's that to look forward to – (I have to prevent myself from smiling at them out of the window – a kindly old lady gibbering at complete strangers)

All my love to you both,
Mops.

27a Bishop's Road
Highgate
13 January 2000

Dearest Willie,

Once again this is not at all a letter that needs answering, it's really just to tell you that I've spent your kind Christmas present on 1: superior olive oil which is one of my great treats – it doesn't really fry well at all but it is wonderful in salads and the smell of it brings up a wonderful Mediterranean moment, 2: a new African violet, as I'd been raising cuttings from the old one for so long that the underside of the leaves was plain green – not purple any longer and so half the beauty of the plant was lost and 3: a new pair of sharp scissors – nail scissors really: Now these things constitute a splendid Christmas present.

Christmas in this house was almost entirely electronic – Ria had a new lap-top and Tom some contraption or other (not a new e-mail, he had that some time ago), and Alfie had an electronic chess set, which at least stopped him offering everyone a game of the dreaded Pokeimon, a Japanese card game – the name I understand is short for Pocket Monsters – anyway, all of them sat clicking, whirring and emitting those short bursts of irritating music – it was quite a relief when the time came to play murders in which I always do my very best even though I'm still secretly very much relieved when the lights are turned on again.

I'm <u>still</u> lame and have decided never to go out in the evening unless I'm driven from door to door. Still we did manage the pantomime at Richmond which meant driving past the Dome to which Maria is gamely going to take the children – she tried to book tickets on the internet, but apparently they're not selling them for February yet. We saw the fireworks from Kenwood, quite a good viewpoint – we didn't walk down to the river as Alfie is only seven and was already pale with exhaustion. Lidia and Greg (Valpy's oldest) came, having got married two months ago. She was a sweet girl and gets along like a house on fire with Angelines (Valpy's wife), an old-fashioned Spanish mother-and-daughter-in-law relationship. Eddie (the cat) took great exception to all the celebrations and will only just deign to eat out of his bowl. But it was lovely to have all 3 children together (children! Valpy is 51) – I hardly ever do.

Very best wishes for your health and Mike's and all my love,

Mops.

Rachel Hichens and Elizabeth Barnett*

185 Poynders Gardens
London, sw4
17 April [*c.*1966]

My dear Rachel,

   It was such a lovely holiday (the weather didn't matter a bit, people were sweeping piles of dirty snow off their doorsteps in London) and your vicarage is a wonderful place where you make people really feel at home and not a bit in the way in spite of the large numbers.

   We feel much better for the visit, Zennor is beautiful, (much more beautiful than Fowey which was the last bit of Cornwall I visited surely) and apart from that it was such fun to see you again and I feel very proud of my god-daughter – when I think that I've got to go back on Tuesday to my pupils (one turns up in an old postman's uniform with a fore and aft cap and another in a plastic leopard-skin shift, and all need black coffee before they can start work) and think how pretty and cheerful Elizabeth is and how she's clearly well able to take on the whole household, I wonder how you could possibly worry about her even slightly, but I suppose if it's true that 'God sends the love with the child' he also sends the worry with the parents!

   Maria tells me that she did go up to Zennor Head when she went for a ride, so she <u>did</u> send it after all, and I'm pleased about this – she tells me that she's writing a letter, but it's to Liz, and to her school, apparently.

   Thankyou again for letting us come down to see you, and love to Tom, and to everyone –

   Mops

I hope the leaking church roof is all right, and you get your little bookcase at the auction.

---

* PMF and Rachel had known each other since childhood, in Hampstead, meeting through their mothers' friendship. They saw each other at intervals throughout their lives. Her daughter, Elizabeth, was Penelope's god-daughter.

I'm just opening this because I've had a letter from Mary – thanking you 1000 times for the kind offer of having them to stay or letting them stay in the cottage, it was so very kind of you to say 'yes' like that at once – but she now thinks that Daddy oughtn't after all, to take any kind of a long journey this year – she thought perhaps next year – though I'd have thought that <u>more</u> uncertain, but she always knows best about him and I'm glad to accept her judgement – I don't want you to think that Daddy is a total wreck, but he's simply old, and fragile – not ill – it was he who said how much he'd like to come down to Cornwall once again, but as I say Mary now feels she ought to keep him in Hampstead though I know she needs a holiday very much herself. – Please forgive this muddle. – love Mops

> *Theale Post Office Stores*
> *Wedmore*
> *Somerset:*
> (most weekends)
> [1981]

And this really is my home, as Tina and Terry are running after the baby and keeping the tiny shop and post office there. Don't forget if you're coming through the West Country!

Very sorry to hear from Liz that Tom hasn't been very well, but I hope and trust that he's better now.

The wedding must have been a wonderful occasion, not many people can say they've been married on a rock cut off by the sea* and it's so nice that he's a farmer, a lovely country life ahead for the grandchildren,

Love and Xmas wishes and best of good things for 1982 –

Mops

---

* Rachel's daughter Celia was married at the Church of St Michael, St Michael's Mount, where Tom, Rachel's husband, was chaplain.

[Christmas card of Theale P.O. drawn by PMF]
[1983]

Lovely to see Liz, but I thought she was staying much longer, or perhaps might decide not to go back!* But I do admire her. – Best wishes for Christmas and 1983 to you and all your family and much love to you both

This is Tina and Terry's post office and village stores at Theale.

[postcard]
15 May 1985

Dear Liz – Thankyou so much for letter – unfortunately I shall be down at Theale during week of June 8 – I've got time off from school as Terry has to be away and so I'm going to help Tina with Luke and with another baby she takes in during the day (as well as a disabled one on Wednesdays). Very best luck with your talk in West Hendon, I know you're well used to giving them however. And please let me know, won't you, if you've got another day. Hope you survive all these late nights!
    love
    Mops

[c.1985/6]

A little Theale lavender though I'm sure you have plenty! So nice to see Liz this summer, but I wonder where she's going next. Many congratulations on new grandbaby – with best Christmas wishes from Mops –

---

* To India where she worked for the Mission for Lepers.

27a Bishop's Road
Highgate
London, N6
2 October [1991]

My dear Rachel,

Just a note to say how delighted I was at Liz's news, she sounded so happy, as though after travelling all over the world she'd really 'come home' – surely it's the right thing happening to the right person and you and Tom must be very happy for her too

love and best wishes

Mops

27a Bishop's Road
London, N6
2 October [1991]

My dear Liz –

I'm told this paper is for writing letters of congratulations* and there couldn't be a better occasion – I know that one shouldn't congratulate the she, only the he, but whatever one should or shouldn't do I want to tell you how happy I am about your happiness, and, my word, Liz, if anyone knows how to manage a parish and parishioners, it must be you. In every way he's a lucky man, but I could tell from the way you talked about him that you consider yourself lucky also. What could be better?

This is just a note, which I wanted to write at once.

love and all possible best wishes –

Mops

---

* Liz had announced her engagement.

27a Bishop's Road
Highgate
London, N6
8 November [1991]

My dear Rachel,

Thankyou so very much for the invitation to Liz's wedding on
the 7th of December – I should so very much have liked to come,
particularly as it would have meant seeing you and Tom again after all
these years, but most unfortunately for me I'm due to fly back from
Australia on that day – (this trip to Tasmania has been nothing but a
nuisance) – I wish her every possible happiness and at least I shall
be able to think of you on the 7th. – If you could manage to send a
photograph among all the thousand and one other things you have to
do, I'd be most grateful. A photograph, of course, with you and Tom in
it, if you ever have a moment – with many regrets and much love,
Mops

You'll forgive me for sending this unseasonable Christmas card as
well – I've had to do everything early, but I feel you'll understand this –

Milton Abbott
Devon
16 April [1993]

Dear Tom and Rachel,

I'm sure no-one else but you would have asked anyone to stay, or
<u>allowed</u> anyone to stay, so soon after such a serious operation – no
matter how many carers, gardeners, milkmen &c had been recruited
to help – and I did appreciate that, and do appreciate it, but can't
regret it, because it was such a treat to see you after so long, and
honestly, Rachel, you were getting the better of it all so bravely and
perseveringly that I couldn't feel depressed. And what a chance to
see Richard and Lis – Maria has always remembered (although I
daresay <u>he</u> won't) how he showed her round Exeter Cathedral – I
can't think when this can have been, but Exeter, not Truro – and she
says it's the one cathedral she's always felt she knows properly. –
He's a person of great kindness and efficiency. And you could <u>see</u>

how happy dear Lis was – she seems to have sailed into exactly the right harbour and I'm so glad for her.

The taximan tells me he'll always remember Perch Cottage in future, so I've added a little to humanity's store of knowledge. – Tina and family were all at Plymouth, where we went to have a picnic on the Hoe in a stiff breeze. They're going to move to a bigger house in Launceston, if they can find one, but I think they'll always miss the elms, and the rooks, and the church green at Milton Abbott. You've moved such a lot of times, you'll know exactly the feeling.

Lamorna was looking marvellous, with so many violets on the path round the head, that they were almost in layers. It will be a great day when Rachel takes her first walk beyond the garden – with many thanks for all your hospitality and much love – Mops.

27a Bishop's Road
Highgate, N6
18 September [1993]

My dear Rachel,

(Why did your mother use to call you 'Racon', I wonder – was it because that's the way you pronounced the name yourself?) – I was very distressed to get Liz's letter telling me that you were in hospital again, although you'd been so much better that you were <u>driving</u> – I felt that you had been through quite enough and more than enough, and so gallantly, (if you don't mind my saying so), and that it hardly seemed right for you to have to bear any more pain – abdominal pain, Liz said, although she also speaks of thrombosis of the spine – but perhaps it's of no use to explain things to anyone as mentally ignorant as I am. I can only say how sorry I am and wish you the hell out of the place as soon as it's at all possible. I <u>did</u> think that you had some remarkably helpful and friendly people to lend a hand at Perch Cottage, and Lis said she had found someone to housekeep for Tom.

I don't know whether you want to hear my bits of news when you have so many other things to think about – but here goes – Valpy, as

I think I told you, has come back to Oxford from the Hague, although
he still has a contract with the Mexican government (whatever that is)
and has to go over there every so often, and they've bought a house
some way up the Woodstock road with plenty of cupboards and fruit
bushes and a fruit cage – not near any shops, but I think they'll like it –
Valpy's eldest at Durham, reading Physics, which entre nous I think is
too difficult for him – Tina and Terry still teaching (at Bude and
Launceston) and the handicapped 2nd child is making immense
progress – I must say Devon and Cornwall are both very good in this
department – and here in Highgate the baby, Alfie, is walking, and John,
Ria's husband, has to go to Frankfurt 3 times a week at the moment –
That's what comes of knowing about money. Of Rawle I haven't such
good news, I am afraid he definitely has Parkinsons, but although it is
progressive they can slow it down much better than they used to. –
Don't think about that, think about getting better – I enclose some
wishing dolls!!! and my best wishes and love to you and Tom – Mops

> *27a Bishop's Road*
> *Highgate, N6*
> [1995]

My dear Rachel – This isn't a letter that needs answering, and it's one I
should have written weeks ago, to say how glad I was that James* had
been given the kind of job which I am sure he wants, I mean one with
more scope and Euro-importance – but now I'm making him sound
like a character out of Trollope, which isn't what I meant at all, as I'm
sure you realise – but I felt that he was quite rightly looking for
something out of the ordinary, and with Liz to help him, Liz who has
been to so many places and coped with so many far-out situations, and
takes them all so calmly, well, there's no end to what they'll be able
to do.

* Liz's husband; he'd taken a job in Strasbourg.

You won't be able to help missing her, but it's not so far, and what a mercy that Richard is there – he might have gone to Australia or the U.S. – I always dreaded that with Valpy, it's a relief that he's got back to Oxford.

Tina, Terry, Luke, Paschal and Jemima have now crossed the border into Cornwall – they sold their roses and honeysuckle cottage at last (it was impossibly much too small for them) and have bought a house called Marshville – not a reassuring name, and there are ditches cut in the garden to carry away the water – at Tresparrett Posts – not really a village, but there's plenty of room, and an enormous garden which won't need a lot of doing because it doesn't grow anything but rough gorse and blackthorn and it's quite near both Tina's job at Bude and Terry's at Launceston – they're <u>waiting</u> to move in at the moment and living in a converted barn, but it should all be through by the end of next week and then in theory we all go off on holiday to Provence, though I'm beginning to wonder if we shall ever manage it.

I am feeling a bit decrepit as my heart (presumably as a result of old age) doesn't work as well as it should and I have to take a lot of nasty pills – the registrar at the Whittington hospital (I'm supposed to see a specialist but he never seems to be there) – the registrar, a harassed little Sri Lankan, rejects my complaints and says 'you are elderly and must take these substances'. But I don't need to tell you anything about the tedious subject of doctors and treatments. I do so hope that you yourself are defying the doctors.

Love and best wishes to you all –
Mops.

27a Bishop's Road
London, N6
17 May [1996]

Dear Lis –
Thankyou so much for your letter, and I'm not surprised to hear that you are housekeeping in Strasbourg just as efficiently as you did in India, where if I remember rightly you had to have a new kitchen and even a new house built. Tina and I had to go to the supermarché

in Provence last summer and were aghast at having to weigh everything
for ourselves, but perhaps you don't have to do that.

I'm sure Tom would congratulate you on your fruit garden. I
remember so well his efforts to grow parsley, which wouldn't take at
all at first in Lamorna, but then he got it going on a ridge he dug for
it – only to find that Rachel didn't really want it, as she had laid in
quantities of dried parsley from a W.I. shop. He was a marvellous
gardener and I expect you inherit it – I remember your rhubarb too,
in Truro.

Lovely that you were all able to be there for Rachel's 80th birthday. –
It's quite true that I'm not as well as I should like, because my heart
doesn't tick properly, and although the specialist at the Whittington
has given me large quantities of pills in different colours, all of which
make me feel ill in different ways, none of them seem to make my
heart any better. I feel rather sorry for it, as it's worked excellently for
so many years and obviously needs a rest. – However, Tina is able to
meet me at Exeter, although it's a long drive to Tresparett Posts. They're
on the north coast, just five minutes away from the sea at Crackington
Haven, splendid for the children even if it's three miles to the nearest
shop. (It's near Camelford, where you used to be, didn't you?)

John and Maria have just bought a holiday house in Wales, on the
road from Welshpool to Barmouth, or rather <u>off</u> the road, on a sheep-
covered hillside. John loves everything to do with DIY and converting
houses and there seem to be a lot of barns and sheds and a main
building with a good slate roof and sanded floors and they have
bought quantities of Swedish furniture, and are starting from there.
Thomas (now 11) wants to get a billiard table, in case it rains, which
of course it will in Wales.

Meanwhile, all the blossom is out in Highgate and I sit here
surrounded with books which I'm supposed to be reviewing –

love to you and James,

Mops

27a Bishop's Road, N6
15 October [1996]

My dear Lis,

It really was good of you to let me know about Tom – you say that
Rachel is being amazing and I'm quite sure she <u>is</u>, but you must have a
terrible lot to do and arrange as well as giving support and comfort,
and I did appreciate getting your letter.

Even when I last saw him I could see that he was growing frailer
and, sadly, a bit cut off from the world into which he'd fitted so well,
first as a farmer, then as a parish priest – I can guess what a tremendous
loss he must be to you, it's like losing a bit of your own life.

I'm so glad now that you made the decision to come home from the
East when you did and that James is there now to be your right hand
(and I expect you're his) and to take the service at Zennor. All my
prayers and much love, Mops

27a Bishop's Road
Highgate
London, N6
18 June [1997]

My dear Rachel,

This is just to welcome you to your new home – it will be strange
to think of Cornwall without you, but it's lovely round Winchester,
(which is where Belinda, Rawle's daughter, and her husband live. He
commutes up to London every day, and seems to find it no trouble).
Moving is such a complicated business, but then you've undertaken it,
with so much courage and spirit, so many times, and I hope this time
it will take some of the day-to-day worries off your back. I wonder if
Richard will go to live at Perch Cottage, and write his operas there?

I don't mean this in any way to be a sad letter, really it's to
congratulate on a new beginning, but I do want to send you all my
thoughts and prayers –

love, Mops

What fun it was going over to St. Michael's Mount! I'll always remember that day –

27a Bishop's Road
Highgate
London, N6
4 October [1997]

Dearest Rachel,

So glad you've successfully moved and acquired such a good secretary. But you don't say anything about yourself, Rachel! I do hope you're going along all right. I know that nothing daunts you.

Thankyou for the news of the family. I'm still living in a small flat, which suits me very well, in the corner of John and Ria's Highgate house. Tom is now 12 and goes across to Hampstead, to U.C.S., every morning. Sophie, who is 9, and Alfie, who is 5, go to St. Michael's, the church school at the top of the hill. I'm not sure that they learn very much, but there's plenty of time, and meanwhile they're very happy, which is what matters most. – Tina and Terry and family are still at Tresparrett Posts, just 5 minutes from Crackington Haven. Luke (their eldest) is at Launceston College, now called Launceston Community Centre (I think) and was immensely excited at taking part in the school production of <u>Lorna Doone</u> (as a musical) at the Minnock (not sure how to spell it, but I first went there with you, and I remember your being very firm about taking plenty of rugs and blankets). It was on for a week, and they stayed in the Youth Hostel and had a high old time. Tina's house is more or less straight at last – the insurance paid for more or less everything, including re-tuning the piano, and the kitchen lino has been cleared away revealing nice old-fashioned slates. –

Valpy and <u>his</u> family are still in Oxford – Greg (his eldest, now 24) has I think at last finished his Physics degree and I suppose is thinking about marrying his Lidia, who has still never been out of Córdoba, but they've been faithful and true to each other, I must say. Valpy is still a great gardener – it's hit him late in life, and it's hit him hard. Unfortunately they go away to Spain for the whole summer and so they always miss the raspberries.

Liz must be terribly busy! But she's used to that, she was always a great 'doer' and ready to try anything new. I hope her garden is growing well – best wishes and love

Mops

27a Bishop's Road
Highgate
London, N6
27 December [1997]

My dear Lis,

You and James dash about so much that I can never be quite sure what country you're in, but I calculate you're back for the Christmas services, so I can thank you for the European Social Charter Calendar (very cheerful and not at all what I should have expected) and the nice soap from the Holy Land.

I liked your description of the giant lunch party. But, I'm sure, Liz, it wouldn't daunt you – you've been used to them, I imagine, ever since you can remember. If I shut my eyes, I can imagine Rachel making dozens of small Yorkshire puddings – it must have been for some large gathering. She served them with golden syrup – it's a long time since I saw a tin of <u>that</u> – after the beef, not with it.

We're all quite well here, Ria just back from California, and Valpy (still living at Oxford) just back from Bangkok. I have taken to staying put, as I am getting very old and slow, but I'm surviving –

with love and best wishes to you both –

Mops

21 August [late 1990s]

Thankyou so much for your card. I'm amazed at all the things you undertake – African philosophy, Tolstoy (<u>Master and Man</u>, I hope, that's one of my favourites) theology, archaeology, and now a visitation of 500 pilgrims, some of them probably quite tiresome. You'll have to have a giant holy tea-party, but, Lis, I know you're up to it, after all you've been through in foreign parts! And to think I'm driven distracted just by a few books, which seem to be all over the place.

We're all all right, but both Tina and Maria have had pneumonia and took some time to recover. Luke playing in St Genny's Silver Band – love to you and James – Mops

> *27a Bishop's Road*
> *Highgate*
> *London, N6*
> [*c*.1998]

Dear Lis –

Many many thanks for the embroidered spec. case – I can't believe you can have time to make it yourself, but perhaps you did, I know you're used to an extremely busy life.

I can see that it was a good thing, in fact essential, for Rachel to move, but it seems strange to think of Perch Cottage without any of you there. And time passes at such a rate. I went down to Cornwall to hear Luke (Tina's eldest) sing what I suppose will be his last solo as a treble in the church at Bude. He is now almost as tall as Tina.

Hardly any berries on the holly this Christmas. I've forgotten whether that means a hard winter or (what seems more logical) a hot summer last year. – with love and best wishes to you and James

from Mops.

> *27a Bishop's Road*
> *Highgate*
> *London, N6*
> 29 December [*c*.1998]

Dearest Rachel,

Thankyou for remembering me at Christmas and thankyou for sending me the zip-up purse, the kind I used to take on foreign travels.

I imagine you surrounded with grandchildren, as I am myself at the moment – Tina has brought her 3 to stay and Maria's 3 are all in the house – but I can't pretend that I've even done so much as to peel a brussels-sprout – everyone else does things so much quicker than I do.

Mary is quite well at her Residential Home but I have to admit that I'm not sure she always recognises me, though she gives me a great welcome. She still enjoys the weekly art classes, though it's sad to see how she has lost her own skill. But that doesn't worry <u>her</u>, and she is looked after by very kind nurses. I don't protest against time any longer, just let it pass –

with love and very best wishes for the New Year from Mops

27a Bishop's Road
Highgate
London, N6
30 December [1999]

My dear Rachel,

Thankyou so very much for your delightful presents, the case and the handkerchief, which were just like Christmas presents used to be – don't misunderstand me, I mean this as a very genuine compliment.

Lis told me about your very well-thought out means of transport, which I think must have been particularly useful at Christmas. Meanwhile, Maria has courageously asked sixteen of the family to stay for the Millennium. John asks her if she's sure it won't be too much, but Ria tells him it's only once in a thousand years. (John himself won't be there as he has to stay at the international bank where he works till 3 a.m., to make sure the whole computer system isn't breaking down).

Terence and Tina and their family are already staying with Ria. Terence is still teaching French and Spanish at Launceston School (or Launceston Community Centre as they insist on calling it) and all three children go there now, but Tina is still teaching at Bude. Her school burned down recently – no-one hurt, but all the classrooms destroyed except, by great good luck, Tina's. Everyone else has to carry on in draughty mobile classrooms which were hastily towed to the spot. Apparently the fire started in the kitchens,

Love and all best wishes for the New Year, and the new century (I suppose I should add) – Mops

Mary Knox*

Queen Mary's Home
13 April [1953]

Dearest Daddy and Mary,

Thankyou so very much for the letters and the lovely flowers, I do wish I could see you but they are difficult about the visitors, in spite of the fact that old Q.M. apparently planned this place to be just like home, no hospital atmosphere, so we have dainty traycloths and screens that fall down on top of us, and the staff are very kind, but I shall be so glad to be home again. Maria is a dear little baby and so far has dark blue eyes, but I don't know whether they will last. She is on the greedy side, rather like Tina. It was such a relief when she was born and they held her up and I was able to count her toes and see they were all correct. I was getting quite worried with all the messing about. The surgeon who gave me the induction is a frightful old show-off and stopped at the last moment to say 'Where are my students? Why are no students watching me?' He sounded like Beerbohm Tree.

I do hope the children will approve of Maria, Valpy wanted a brother, of course, but I think she will be convenient for dollies' tea-parties and fit in quite well.

Thankyou again and best love from us both
from Mops

25 Almeric Road
London, sw11
Sunday [February/March 1976]

Dearest Mary,

I started down to Cambridge yesterday and found there was a strike at Liverpool Street and I couldn't get a train! So instead I went down

---

* PMF's stepmother. As Mary Shepard, she illustrated the *Mary Poppins* books. Though they met frequently, they often wrote to each other. Sadly only these few letters survive.

to the Garden Centre again, very nearly lost my head completely (as most people seemed to be doing – they were buying large trees and huge sacks of earth and cramming them into small cars) and only got some monbretias, as I notice they seem to grow anywhere, and a stout looking fuchsia, and a white jasmine, said to be hardy, but I don't know how it will like Battersea. Have nearly finished my terrazzo, and Tina actually sat on one of them, and it didn't collapse.

I think the St Leonard's idea is good – you won't, I'm sure, want me to say this, but it truly is good of you to undertake it and nothing could be more worthwhile, particularly in early summer when I dare say they find it hard to get proper helpers, and it could be rather nice by the sea then, and having a modest half-pint with the other social workers in the evening, as for giving you other jobs, I should imagine they'd jump at you. I may go away for a week before Easter (this sounds downright selfish compared with your enterprise) because Desmond's friend Peter Norton, who works in the same office, and is married to a trained nurse, and lives down in Canvey Island in a little house with a vegetable patch and 2 children, one named after me, has asked him if he'd like to stay for a week, and he'd be comfortable there and Stella (the nurse) knows all about his op: and so I should not be worried: I might take a week therefore, after D. comes out of the Royal Marsden for the 2nd dose of this nauseating (literally) drug, and if he takes it well this time, but I don't know where I'll go. – Tina and Terry are taking a school party to France for Easter, it's really very good because they haven't got to take charge all the time, the children live with French families, some in the town and some in the country (agriculteur: milieu très simple) and they only have to be there to sort out any difficulties – they have their own flat, and an allowance for food, vin rouge &c – so I think they will enjoy this very much. Tina has a nasty sore throat at the moment, but is recovering, I'm glad to say.

I shall venture down next Sat: to Cambridge, as they go off to Cordoba in a couple of weeks. Valpy hopes to go to Cuba and Mexico as well as Peru, but perhaps I told you this!

Thankyou so much for the invaluable list of letters, Mary. Looking forward to March 19th, pottery party –

much love always

Mops

I want my 10p back that I offered to the Donatello plate. I've decided that I don't really like the plate anyway. –

Theale Post Office Stores
Sunday [October 1983]

Dearest Mary,

Thankyou so much for your very kind letter and offer to come, just like you! and very distressed to hear about your own fall – no, I won't say 'fall' it sounds like an old lady, but your difference of opinion with the landing steps, which must have been horrid and painful, and somehow it seems so horrid and treacherous for them to let you down suddenly, the ladder was quite different as I never ought to have gone up it at all, but it's the only ladder we have and perhaps one gets reckless. I fell out of the (ground-floor) window at Almeric Rd. once when trying to clean it, but landed in a bush, and was quite all right, but one can't always be lucky. If only I hadn't 2 black eyes! I feel they don't look at all right for a teacher. And the garden is terrible, Mary, lawn grown very long, geraniums need potting up and taking into the greenhouse, vegetables need digging up and bed got ready for next year, the winter lettuce needs spacing out – I can see it all from the window but am quite helpless! But the district nurse is going to take out my numerous stitches on Monday and I expect I'll feel better then. It does hurt to <u>cough</u>, though. I can't see why one needs to cough all the time.

Complain! complain! Of course Tina <u>mustn't</u> do any lifting and little Luke is only six weeks, and it was terrible to give her this extra work, but I am quite able to crawl about and open tins and wash up for myself now, but she has done endless telephoning for me and been an angel. And if this hadn't happened I could have come and looked after <u>you</u> a bit, which I'd have been so glad to do.

I was just thinking about Rawle – if only he'd been well enough to stay at Boughton! He was really in charge there, and organising it all so well, and v. interested in the house and its fine pictures and furniture and the flat, though not as nice as Ashe Cottage, was pretty good – but there you are, they really asked too much of him and it couldn't be managed.

[incomplete]

76 Clifton Hill
Sat: morning [1986]

Dearest Mary,

Thankyou so much for lovely p.c. – yes I'd love to come and see Belinda's pix, and to lunch in Winchester, though can't quite make out if the private view is Fri or Sat, but will ring you. Just off for the long trek down to Theale. Longing to see them, but oh that endless bus journey round by Radstock and Midsomer Norton. Still, I'm lucky to have a bus at all. They're introducing small yellow buses now – Small Badger lines, much like Hoppas.

Another photographer yesterday, very slender and wonderful looking, and called Tara Heinemann – clearly better if <u>she</u> was photographed – lives in a 15th century stone-walled thatched cottage near Banbury with her husband – and that's the last of them I do hope, for the American publishers who are due to bring out <u>Innocence</u> next spring, though I'm afraid it's not quite the sort of thing they read in America.

Joan is digging an enormous hole in the garden with a spade larger than herself, to put in peat. What energy – then she's off to Ireland. – I went to dinner with Susie Svoboda who tells me that she always works till past midnight, as it ensures sleep.

I don't think it was hard work that made you ill, though, Mary, (though you do work hard, of course), I think it was <u>worry</u>, old worries and unhappiness that came up into the forefront of the mind, as such things will. But they're all gone now, and I think you're managing so well, knocking off the prescription slowly and getting really better at your own pace. Glad Mrs R so helpful about the exhibition (I mean the finger food!)

much love Mops

76 Clifton Hill, NW8
30 November [1986]

Dearest Mary – So sorry I couldn't find you at Waterloo yesterday till the last minute, I was stupidly looking all over what BR call the concourse – no matter, we made it! I enjoyed it very much, the house was so welcoming and full of children of all shapes and sizes – it was a <u>party</u>, as your exhibition was too. – I'm just writing to thank Belinda, and have told her something which isn't quite true, viz: that you got one box for me, but please don't think it <u>is</u> for me, it's just that I didn't quite see my way to buying anything – that sounds horrid, but isn't meant to be – clearly the whole exhibition was a great success and many more orders will follow. – Nicolette's book is a different matter, you're right, and I must make an effort and get one – you have to go the publishers (Kentish Town) or to the Shepard home in Limerton St., both rather an effort. How lazy I'm getting! – But I <u>did</u> enjoy yesterday, and William's children are as nice as they could possibly be, William stays so calm amid all the coming and going!

Needless to say, Mary, I didn't want you, partic. with all these farewell parties, services &c, to bother about my Women Artists, it's just if you should happen to think of anything – I shall have to do my best, and 'fudge it, Madam, fudge it' as I believe Bird's Nest Hunt used to say – Of course one shouldn't undertake to write about things one doesn't know about, but there it is.

Lovely to see you anyway love Mops

<u>Innocence</u> was mentioned in the <u>Spectator</u>'s best books of 1986 – only once! And by one person – still once is better than nothing and Collins are pathetically pleased.

76 Clifton Hill
Thursday

Dearest Mary – just a note, although it ought to be <u>much more</u>, to thank you for the lovely dinner, and then on coming back I found your birthday card, so Theale-like and comforting with all the livestock at peace for once: and your most kind present, which mustn't be and won't be spent without thought – but I do really <u>need</u> a new little radio as mine is just worn out, new batteries don't help – so I think it will go towards that, it's hard to work without a little music.

Thankyou 10000 times – I've got to go down to the Arts Council now for yet another meeting and Julian* has just rung up quite madly from Ireland, I can't make out what he's talking about – very <u>ill</u>, as usual, but, I think, really perfectly well.

Much love and many thanks
Mops.

Really it's a great treat to have a card drawn exclusively for you – and I won't say you <u>shouldn't</u> have sent the £££ because I appreciate it so much.–

27 Bishop's Road, N6
3 August [1995]

Dearest Mary,

I am so sorry that I'm laid low by something, possibly to do with the heat, and so are poor Thomas and Alfie – and on Saturday I am supposed to be going to Provence with Tina and family, so am trying to get better, so as not to be too much of a nuisance! We've rented a house at Grasse, just for 2 weeks, as Tina was suddenly taken by a fancy to smell the lavender and roses. I hope they'll all be out! We're going to fly to Nice, and hire a car there to drive up to Grasse.

Meantime I thought I'd send you what news I have. Bryony, William's eldest, has done very well <u>indeed</u> in her metal-work and

* Knox.

sculpture course and won an important prize (£1000) awarded by the
Worshipful Company of Goldsmiths for the best exhibits in the art
colleges, for a Gryphon in copper or silver (I think), she has real talent
and I'm sure will do great things. Ben and Rowan are both in Sri
Lanka, staying with William and Jenny [passage obliterated by
water stain]

Tina and Terence have moved into the new house. It's called
Marshville, which sounds like a penitentiary, but they're not going to
change the name, because everyone round there knows it. It's only
10 minutes from the sea, a lovely beach at Crackington Haven, and
although of course the move was a terrible business, as moves always
are – and Tina even brought her little toolshed with her – and nothing
is straight yet, – but it's wonderful for them to have a proper room
each, and 3 living rooms counting the kitchen, which is nice and large
so they can have all their meals there – they couldn't even all sit down
together in Milton Abbot – and a <u>huge</u> garden where they won't have
to do a lot of work, except mowing the grass, as it is so close to the sea
that only fuchsias and blackthorns and things like that will grow. At
first the children were doubtful about going to the bottom of the
garden, it was so far away, but then Tina organised a picnic under an
apple-tree at the very end and they began to realise what a wonderful
place they'd got to play in. There just wasn't room for them in the
cottage – they <u>had</u> to move, and I'm so glad that at last they've found
someone to buy the cottage, although I shall miss Milton Abbot, it was
lovely with its rooks and elm-trees and the view of Dartmoor. But it
will be much easier for Tina at Marshville, and a shorter drive for her,
too, to work at Bude.

They have bought a brand new petrol-mower, which I'm sure was a
good idea – it's no use getting a 2nd hand one, they always go wrong.

My geraniums just love this weather and are flowering away like
mad, and the roses too but they seem to die away so soon.

Please don't think I've forgotten about your poor shoulder, I certainly
<u>haven't</u>, and hope it's not giving you too much trouble –

All our love, dearest Mary – Mops

Helen Knox*

27a Bishop's Road, N6

23 February [1998]

Dearest Helen,

I did so much appreciate your asking me down yesterday and the ceremony, if that's not too grand a word for it, was so absolutely right, and so were the words on the memorial stone – 'writer, humanist and friend' – I'd expected to find the beautiful spring sunshine rather saddening but in the end I <u>didn't</u> – I think none of us did – and the curate (I think she was a curate), without knowing Rawle at all, said exactly the right thing.

Belinda and Robert were so kind, picking me up at Reading, which seemed to me to be miles out of their way, and Ben saw me into my tube at King's Cross, what a very kind boy he is, refusing to be bored by his elderly relatives.

They're all doing so well – (it will be a treat to see what Bryony designs for the Worshipful Company of Ironmongers –) and Rawle would have been so very proud, even if he only expressed it in a very few words.

And it was lovely to see you all – I'm only sorry that I was in such poor condition, although much restored by the delicious lunch, which made me feel that perhaps I'll soon be getting better – about time!

with many thanks and much love

Mops

---

* PMF's sister-in-law; wife of Rawle.

II.

WRITING

Richard Garnett*

25 Almeric Road
London, sw11
18 June [1976]

Dear Mr Garnett,

Thankyou very much for your letter about the Knox brothers' book –
I <u>am</u> getting on, and am relying on the summer vacation to get most
of it done, and I haven't lost heart, although we're now threatened with
<u>another</u> book on Enigma, this time translated from the Polish, I think.

Looking through my file I find the names of numerous people who
say they 'would like to see the draft before there's any question of
anything being printed', but as they're mostly eminent professors &c.
who are likely to make criticisms from habit, I think it would be best
to ignore this, and hope that they've forgotten all about it?

I would like to ask you one thing, as a Kingsman – I've had it
suggested to me several times by now that Frank Birch was the real
'Third Man' who was in touch, presumably, with the USSR and got
Burgess and Philby away. But Mrs: Birch, his widow, is still alive, so I
suppose I'd better not hint at this? (Frank Birch, I should add, was a
great friend of Dillwyn Knox and was with him in the
Communications dept. in both world wars) –

yours sincerely,
Penelope Fitzgerald

25 Almeric Road
London, sw11
7 August [1976]

Dear Mr: Garnett,

Thankyou very much for your letter of 3 August about the Coward
McCann contract. Needless to say I <u>do</u> think it should go ahead, and I

---

* PMF's editor for *The Knox Brothers*, published in 1977 by Macmillan.

am most grateful to you, and rather amazed that the subject should be interesting to Americans, or thought to be interesting, but I'll do the best I can to make it readable, and, meanwhile, thankyou once again,

yours sincerely,

Penelope Fitzgerald

25 *Almeric Road*
London, sw11
4 November [1976]

Dear Mr: Garnett,

I'm afraid I have another problem, and once again have to ask you for help.

I enclose about 1000 words from my draft about the 4 brothers: it's about Lytton Strachey's mild attempt to seduce my uncle, and I want to keep it in because so much of the book has to be about Xtian doctrine, Bible translation &c, and I hoped this incident would act as light relief.

The problem is this – the quotations are from unpublished letters from Strachey to Duncan Grant: I am sure Duncan Grant wouldn't object as he has lent (or sold) them to the British Museum, and they are on open deposit, filed as ADD. MS. 58120: but as they are unpublished, I have to get copyright permission from the Strachey Trust.

Unfortunately, the Trust itself can do nothing: all permission has to come from Michael Holroyd (who is always away) and Paul Levy.

Paul Levy (whom I've never met) lives in various Oxford farmhouses, one after another, taking with him most of Lytton Strachey's correspondence. He's been sorting it out for several years and won't let one (or me, at any rate) consult it. The Strachey trust 'hoped' that all the letters would be deposited in the BM last year, but they hoped in vain.

They describe Mr Levy as 'not altogether an easy person to deal with'.

Meanwhile I have written to him to ask permission to use the letters to Grant, which as I've said are luckily not down at the farm-house but in the MS room of the British Library. I enclose a copy of his reply.

I don't know why he is going through my Burne-Jones book, (which was checked by the top Burne-Jones expert) but that is perhaps not the point. Nor do I understand what he means by my notes – the notes I've taken <u>are</u> from the original mss, there's nowhere else to get them from. But it's clear that he has taken against me.

I wondered therefore whether you would write and ask for permission to use these extracts from ADD MS 58120? I know it's all a great fuss about very little, but all writers are more or less intimidated by all publishers (and I think Paul Levy <u>is</u> a writer, although he doesn't seem to write anything). I hoped that if you wrote he might simply agree without any more fuss.

I also realise that it's my business, really, to get the permissions, but in this case I'm daunted. I've never had this trouble before –

yours sincerely
Penelope Fitzgerald

25 *Almeric Road*
London, SW11
14 November [1976]

Dear Mr Garnett,

I enclose the references to the passages from the Lytton Strachey/ Duncan Grant letters and should be more than grateful if you would write to Mr Levy, as I am sure he will give consent at once in that case. I'm afraid my mistake was in asking to see his papers at all – I've just been looking through some of his old letters and I see that he told me I could come and see them in June 74, but nothing ever came of this. They were not catalogued then – I don't know if they are now.

I would also like to apologise for appearing so harassed but it's the time of year when the university entrance exams come up and teachers get unnaturally agitated. It's all a very small matter – I do know that –

yours sincerely
Penelope Fitzgerald

P.S. I'm also sorry that I sent you an uncorrected copy, but the one I enclose is corrected. My whole life is spent in apologising to someone or other, I'm afraid.

[postcard]
[1976]

I'm sorry I said quadratic instead of simultaneous equations when trying to explain the routine work on Enigma – I don't wonder that as a mathematician you shrink away in disgust – my only excuse is that I'd been trying most of the rest of the day to explain the difference between irony and satire to my VI form – I'll get down to work now and try to send you a readable typescript – PMF

25 *Almeric Road*
London, sw11
5 February 1977

Dear Richard,

Thankyou for your letter and for the photocopy. Looking blankly at it I notice some mistakes (mine, of course) which I've attached to this letter, and would be very grateful if you could correct them. I also attach the <u>acknowledgements</u> which I hope are all right. My persecutor Paul Levy can't go in there, he'll have to go in the <u>permissions</u>, which I'm afraid I can't finish till I hear from the Kipling estate about the R. K. letter I've quoted. I've written to them, however. (There's also an unpublished Maynard Keynes letter on p. 172, but it is quite trivial, and I don't want to ask permission as Lord Kahn is so unpleasant and refuses everything on principle.)

The names and dates are:

EDMUND (Evoe)   1880–1971
DILLWYN   1883–1943
WILFRED   1886–1950
RONALD   1888–1957

I think they could have their ordinary christian names? It's a puzzle, I admit.

I enclose the best photograph I have of all 4 of them together – it's dark, I know, but has a period charm, particularly as the Bishop appears to be holding a Bible.

I've also done a family tree, which I enclose, though I'm not really sure how to do them – I couldn't type it, my typing is not up to it, so if it is of any use do you think you could get one of your operatives to type it? The original family tree was lost by Evelyn Waugh, but I daresay it was largely imaginary.

If you'll allow me to say so, I feel terribly depressed at the idea of the million machines &c. Wouldn't it sound like Blue Peter, or the old Would you believe it columns? I think the figure, whether yours or the Faculty of Economics, will make a good impression on its own?

On the other hand, I do apologise for suggesting that the order of the Enigma keyboard had nothing to do with the order of the contacts on the rotors, to which it was wired, because it did. If the keyboard is in alphabetical order, A is wired to the first contact, B to the 2nd, &c. and this means that the decipherer can ignore the keyboard altogether when he is working out the displacements – it doesn't add to the complexity at all. But if the machine has the typewriter keyboard, Q will be wired to the first contact and (assuming that the rotor starts at setting A) this will be a displacement of 10, and W E R T &c. will all produce unknown displacements. This I AM SURE YOU WILL AGREE makes a simple simultaneous equation impossible. (Dilly's solution of the keyboard really was important – all my informants were certain about this – and I thought I was lucky to have found one complete solution which could be explained, because I'm sure most of his work would be quite unintelligible.)

I'm afraid I do need a bibliography, I can't get everything into the acknowledgements, but I'll make it as short as I can and send it in a day or so. Will that be all right? – best wishes Penelope

P.S. I still think the BBC TV programme on Wed: night may explain everything much better than I can. I'll try and watch it anyway.

P.P.S. I'll ask the BM for a photo of the Herodas papyrus in case that might be useful.

25 *Almeric Road*
London, SW11
11 February 1977

Dear Richard,

Thankyou for your letter and in particular for offering to tackle Lord Kahn, the scourge of King's – it's not so much that he could possibly object to this harmless note from Maynard Keynes, but that he objects to everything on principle – (I wd: have liked to use the Keynes/Grant letters in the British Museum but didn't dare ask, perhaps just as well as they're so disagreeable) – but I expect if you ask him he'd say yes.

The photograph* reads

(top row) Wilfred (apparently making communist salute) arm in arm with Dilly, Winnie, Eddie.
(bottom row) Ethel, Bishop, Ronnie.

This is taken at Bishopscourt, Manchester, in 1904 I should think.

I enclose a bibliography if there's room for it, as I don't think these books are properly acknowledged otherwise.

As for the million monkeys typing the whole of Shakespeare, I must put them in if you like them, but I'm less able to work this out than the sum. I like the noughts, and think they're impressive, but I do notice that everything written about Enigma gives quite different figures.

I think a printable drawing of the wiring from the keyboard to the contact is necessary, as otherwise the explanation, never very successful, will be quite unintelligible. I didn't think the BBC programme very helpful, as it didn't distinguish between the solution of the setting and the solution of the displacements, and evidently they couldn't persuade many people to appear, so that Peter Calvocoressi was shown, as usual, as the sole inhabitant of Bletchley.

The BM say they can produce a photograph of the Herodas papyrus in about 5 weeks, do you want this?

I also, while conscious of being a nuisance about this, would like to ask for 2 more corrections

---

* Eventually to be used on the cover of *The Knox Brothers*.

p.177 8 lines down. Owen Seaman was given his baronetcy in 1933

p. 198 4 lines down. My informants now tell me that the F.O. didn't provide an Enigma so I shall have to correct 'The Foreign Office . . . no more than that' to 'from the commercial machines already on the market, they could study the general system, but no more than that'. I apologise for making these tiresome changes, but at least they come from the people who worked on <u>Enigma</u>, and that is something.

Thankyou once again –

Penelope

> 25 Almeric Road
> London, SW11
> 2 April 1977

Dear Mrs Burgess,*

Thankyou very much for the proof of the jacket for the <u>Knox Brothers</u> – personally I think it is just right and like it very much, particularly the expanded lettering, and I think it was a brilliant idea to put the excerpts on the back as they suggest that one <u>ought</u> to know who these people were, and surely that's just what is wanted.

There is one thing that worries me, and that is that <u>E.V. Knox</u> (top name on the spine) was <u>born in 1881</u> not <u>1880</u> – I know exactly what Richard will say to this – 'doesn't the wretched woman even know when her own father was born?' – Well, I <u>do</u> know and have no excuse or even explanation so I can't offer any. This mistake of mine also appears on <u>p. 12 of the text</u> and I think on the <u>title-page</u>–

In spite of this I venture to say once again how much I like the jacket –

Yours sincerely,

Penelope Fitzgerald

---

* Probably Richard Garnett's assistant.

25 *Almeric Road*
London, sw11
[*c.*April 1977]

About the <u>Russian</u> names in the index, I am feeling wretched about all
the inaccuracies and having looked at my notes in the cellar here I've
decided I don't honestly know what their Xtian names are, and in any
case they look silly without their patronymics, so can they appear just
as <u>Khinchuk, Meler, Zudyakov</u>? Meler strikes me as an assumed name
anyway. They're not in the Soviet Biographical Dictionary because
they made such a failure of their mission and in the ARCOS
publications they're just Tovarich, without initials. – I don't think
there are any more A's – Mrs (Bp.) Knox died in <u>August 1892</u> (that
really is right) – Penelope

25 *Almeric Road,* sw11
16 September 1977

Dear Richard,

Thankyou so much for your letter – I was just wondering a bit
whether there were any advance copies, as I have had mysterious
messages from the reviewers and I'm not sure where they got <u>their</u>
copies* from, all a failure as usual, the <u>Spectator</u> person, in spite of, or
possibly because of, being plied with drink by Oliver, says the whole
book was quite beyond him, and as for the <u>TLS</u>, I asked Dick Usborne
if he'd go and extract it from the heap as he is always amiable and
would have put anything he was asked but unfortunately it had already
been asked for by M. Muggeridge, I can only hope he's in sunny mood.

I did write this mystery story,** largely to get rid of my annoyance:
1. about the Tutankhamen Exhib: as I'm certain everything in it was a
forgery, and: 2. about someone who struck me as particularly
unpleasant when I was obliged to go a lot to museums &c. to find out
about Burne-Jones, I'd very much have liked to show it you, (the story

* Of *The Knox Brothers.*
** *The Golden Child.*

I mean), but it had a cipher in it, and I thought if I produce any more ciphers I shall get thrown out into Little Essex St – I thought quite well of the book at first but it's now almost unintelligible, it was probably an improvement that the last chapters got lost, but then 4 characters and 1000s of words had to be cut to save paper, then the artwork got lost (by the printer this time) so we had to use my roughs and it looks pretty bad, but there you are, it doesn't matter, and no-one will notice, and Colin* works so hard, I wouldn't be surprised to find him, sitting in the Old Piano Factory with a bottle of whisky doing all the packing and despatch himself, so everyone has to do the best they can.

It worried me terribly when you told me I was only an amateur writer and I asked myself, how many books do you have to write and how many semi-colons do you have to discard before you lose amateur status?

I shouldn't write such a long letter as I know that reading can't be a recreation for you, but it was so nice to have a letter that didn't enclose a bread recipe, particularly as bread-making is one of the things I can do and be sure it'll turn out right, unlike my attempts to get good notices. – I'm just taking an Oxford entrance class and the wretched children are trying to work out – of which of the following can it be said that it has a right and a left? A person, a street, a boat, a pair of scissors, a tree, – a cat? I know they're confident I'll be able to answer this – best wishes Penelope

> 25 Almeric Road
> London, sw11
> 1 October [1977]

This is a <u>short</u> p.c. to thank you for the 6 copies of the <u>Knox B</u> – incidentally, taking them home feels exactly like bringing a new baby from hospital, so who can say that life's experiences don't recur? – I always liked the jacket, but now I see that you've got them to darken the green and I think this is a great improvement – best wishes
P.M.F

* Colin Haycraft of Duckworth who were to publish PMF's first novel *The Golden Child*.

25 *Almeric Road*
London, sw11
31 December 1977

Dear Richard,

Thankyou very much for the photocopies – as a matter of fact I never really saw any notices after the first 2 because as soon as you sent the money I took the opportunity to go to China, as I've wanted all my life to see the Great Wall under snow, however this is of no importance.

The dubious American Knox Center which traces your relationship to the (notional) Knox family, for 5 dollars, tell me that the book will appear in the U.S. at the end of March. I expect they're trading in on the family tree you did for me, you ought to charge a commission.

Since I see you're now looking after a different division, could I please ask you 1 thing, that is, if I have any other ideas (NOT about China) shall I try sending them to you or not?

Best wishes for 1978,
Penelope

25 *Almeric Road*
London, sw11.
25 February 1978

Dear Richard,

I'm sorry about the Creighton mistake, I don't know how I could make it as I've read his memorial stone ('He tried to tell the truth') so often in Peterborough Cathedral – but Dr Vidler, who was the first of many to point out the error, wrote to me 'he spelt it Creighton, perhaps because he knew no better' – I don't see how you can put it more nicely than that. – I'm afraid that there are other errors, I recall that my heart sank when you said 'I have the right to expect accuracy'. – No-one questioned 25 factorial however –

best wishes,
Penelope

P.S. The Oratory of the Good Shepherd want to reprint some passages, I said I'm sure this would be all right, if the publishers are acknowledged –

25 Almeric Road
London, sw11.
11 March 1978

Dear Richard – Thankyou for letting me know about the Readers' Union – I think it's wonderful that you've got them to take a book which, after all, is about church history, cryptology and theology, <u>not</u> the top ten subjects I'm afraid.

My correspondents now say that <u>it is impossible for a magpie to nest in a chimney and they've never been known to do so</u>. I wish I'd asked you about this before, as I've just been reading my literary diaries, (which have depressed me intensely) and I see that you know a lot about birds – a magpie <u>did</u> fall down our chimney, however –

best wishes,
Penelope

25 Almeric Road
London, sw11
8 May 1978

Dear Richard,

Perhaps you remember saying that I might write to you about any further literary troubles, or ideas, they're the same as far as I'm concerned really, so I'm taking the opportunity to ask your advice and will try to be as short as possible, I'm trying to work (in the middle of other seemingly endless duties such as sorting through (literally) thousands of E. H. Shepard drawings) on the Monros, Harold and Alida, and the Poetry Bookshop, the material is good, a very sympathetic human story I think, but I can only use it as it stands, I can't quote from it directly, not because there are any living relatives whose feelings might be hurt, but because the executors are an Edwardian couple who live surrounded with piles of old papers and photographs, illusions, delusions &c., in a way they have been hard done by, – about 10 years ago they asked Patric Dickinson to do something but it is all hopeless and Patric tells me he is at a standstill and I'd better go ahead.

Among the Poetry Bookshop poets I would include <u>not</u> Masefield or de la Mare whose biographies have been respectively 5 and 15 years in preparation, but T. S. Eliot (who told me that the Poetry Bookshop staircase made an appearance in <u>Ash Wednesday</u>) as far as he comes in; Ralph Hodgson (how pleasant to know) and a number of others, but particularly Robert Frost, Edward Thomas, Anna Wickham and Charlotte Mew. There is terrible in-fighting over the last 2, the poetesses, but I try to find my way round it.

I remember being taken to the Poetry Bookshop as a little girl quite well and the Monros too, this was a time when writing and reading poetry was a natural activity, and at Oxford I thought I'd ask Edmund Blunden and Lascelles Abercrombie to teach me, and since it turned out that Lascelles didn't believe in education, and was dying anyway, poor soul, he spent all the time talking about his golden days before 1914 with Frost and E. Thomas in Gloucestershire.

Who was Lascelles Abercrombie? you may say, and why am I not being offered a decent typed treatment on 2 pages, but before doing that, as it is so difficult to do, I hoped you wouldn't mind if I consulted you –

best wishes
Penelope

As research, it is not altogether easy – I'm told I must interview the only person who can remember being picked up by Harold Monro as a young policeman on the beat, but I do not know how to open the conversation.

25 Almeric Road
London, sw11
20 June 1978

Dear Richard,

I'm sending you 4 (I'm afraid) sides about this Poetry Bookshop project, for which, however, I can't think of a name, also one of their lists, as you asked me how many <u>Georgian Poets</u> were ever sold? And perhaps you wouldn't mind looking at the 2 letters from the Luttrells and Patric Dickinson. (The Royalties on Monro's published work <u>don't</u> belong to the Luttrells, but were left to the joint executor, with the poodles, any toothless ones to be put down).

Patric has got very gloomy and has thrown away <u>all</u> his letters except one from Walter de la M., to my ill-concealed annoyance, and says that (nothing) can be done about poetry, and all biography is a mistake. I don't agree –

best wishes –
Penelope

25 Almeric Road
London, sw11
4 July 1978

Dear Richard,

I just wanted to thank you for writing to your EG biographer, who kindly replied and told me about ET/EG* – and thankyou for letting me know about the PB book, however I feel depressed about this, I think perhaps it's too difficult to go on with, Patric has now retreated to an addressless cottage in Westmorland as he finds Rye intolerably noisy and his letters are partly in Greek.

Halfway through my examining I thought I might go out just once and as a result I was instantly poisoned, a Ministry of Health inspector took away the food and I feel worse than ever,

yours ever,
Penelope

---

* Edward Thomas and Edward Garnett.

25 Almeric Road
London, sw11
11 August 1978

Dear Richard,

Thankyou so much for your letter about the Poetry Bookshop &c. –
I still feel attached to this book and believe it will turn out well in the
end, but I quite realise it won't do for you, and perhaps I shouldn't
ever have suggested it while it was in such a hazy condition, but I
thought it might be worth trying.

Thankyou for all your help in the past –
best wishes,
Penelope

25 Almeric Road
London, sw11
20 October 1978

Dear Richard – I wonder if you'd be kind enough to help me with one
more thing – The Poetry Bookshop Rhymesheets are suddenly being
collected, advertised for in the TLS, &c, so that it's increasingly difficult to
get hold and I'm still not allowed to photograph the BM collection – but
I'm still working on them as hard as ever – well, no 7 of the Rhyme Sheet
2nd series (Jane and Ann Taylor's <u>The Vulgar Little Lady</u>) was illustrated
by your mother and she may have done others as there seem to be no
complete lists – if you've got copies of these, and I do recall that you keep
your family papers in cupboards, do you think I could photograph them?
best wishes,
Penelope

25 Almeric Road
London, sw11
28 October 1978

Dear Richard,

Thankyou for <u>The Vulgar Little Lady</u>, I appreciate your lending it to
me very much. Please believe I'll look after it very carefully and return

it in the same packing, only may I keep it until I can get down to the BL and compare it with the rhymesheet? I can also give you the correct Add Mss no. then.

I think it's lovely – the rhyme sheet, (which is a broadsheet really, only one side) is reduced and very inferior. I wonder how Monro got hold of it? Mrs Rooke might know, though she may be rather sick of me after so many B/J enquiries. – The trouble with the permissions is that I can't reproduce from the actual collection, and no-one else seems to have copies – they've all perished, like mine.

I know you didn't think too much of this Poetry Bookshop book, and that weighed with me as I do respect your opinion, however I still think it could turn out nicely, only it'll need an Arts Council grant to reproduce these rhymesheets &c properly, it has to be either properly done or not at all. Wish me luck! I'll send you a p.c. if I ever get anywhere.

Yours,
Penelope

25 Almeric Road
London, sw11
2 February 1979

Dear Richard,

Thankyou very much for the photographs, I'm glad to have them as they're much better than the originals. – I'm amazed to hear that there is room for any more books about Enigma (of course there's still the official history to come), but if this man wants to reproduce the original Gilbert Spencer portrait of Dilly, then it would be best for him to write to Oliver Knox. It's Christopher (his elder brother) who actually has the original, but he's rather queer in the head, poor soul, so it's best to ask Oliver.

On the other hand, when Dilly had to stop work he gave good photographs of the portrait to his staff, and one person who has one is Mrs Mavis Batey. Jozef G. ought to be in touch with Mavis anyway as she was Dilly's brightest assistant at Bletchley and she is always kind and helpful, (though I feel she's letting the Dilly persona get a little out of hand in a recent article where she describes him as <u>often</u> stuffing sandwiches into his pipe, surely nobody would do this <u>often</u>?) However I'm sure if she was asked nicely she would have a copy made of her photograph –

best wishes

Penelope`

[postcard]

10 February 1979

I'm so sorry you've been put to so much trouble over these errors in <u>The Knox Brothers</u> – couldn't you recommend this Bambridge man, to whom I think you're being rather too kind, to a job with Paul Levy? I'm sure they'd get on splendidly?

Incidentally, Molotov-Pyry is the French spelling, which Gen. Bertrand used himself, but what's the use. People can always find more mistakes – my son is attacked in Cambridge by the Theological Book Club and this Xmas I was sent <u>more</u> samples of brandy butter from both universities – but I feel ashamed because you are such a good book editor and deserve better from the writers – Penelope

25 Almeric Road

London, sw11

25 February 1980

Dear Richard – I do wish I'd kept <u>The Vulgar Little Lady</u> I had on the wall of my nursery, but it's long since disappeared alas – there <u>is</u> a copy of this broadsheet in the BL Manuscript Room, in the Poetry Bookshop envelopes Add Mss 57758 and 57759, I'm afraid I don't know which of these 2 it's in but it's certainly there. – I'm going to Nyork at Easter and hope to see one or two maddened collectors and if there's a copy on offer I will let you know.

I've managed to trace all the titles but 3 and I am almost sure that this is the only illustration your mother did for this series.

Best wishes with your list –

Penelope

Harold Macmillan*

25 Almeric Road
London, SW11
19 November 1977

Dear Mr Macmillan,

Thankyou very much for your kind letter about <u>The Knox Brothers</u>. I <u>did</u> find it difficult to write about them, although, or perhaps because, I loved them so much, and I can't say how much it means to me that you should have approved of my book,

Yours sincerely,

Penelope Fitzgerald

[Macmillan had written to Penelope:

'I have just finished reading "The Knox Brothers" and I feel I must write to send you my warmest congratulations on the remarkable skill which you have shown in keeping these four lives separate yet strangely conjoined. It must have become extremely delicate and difficult to do and in addition I think you have brought out marvellously well the characteristics of these remarkable men. Naturally the one I knew best was Ronnie with whom I had a deep friendship for many years. Dillwyn I knew fairly well and also Wilfred at one time. You have made it all so living and, to me, in my old age deeply moving.']

* The politician and former prime minister. He appears in *The Knox Brothers* as Ronnie's pupil.

Mavis Batey*

25 Almeric Road
London, sw11
25 July 1980

My dear Mavis –

Thankyou so very much for <u>Alice's Adventures in Oxford</u> – I was feeling deeply depressed as I always do in the middle of summer and am now quite cheered up – the cover is so ingenious in the first place, the water-colour tones on the front match so well, and then on the back the little door opening into the garden give exactly the right idea of not knowing where fact ends and imagination begins, just like L. C.'s preface to <u>Sylvie and Bruno</u>. As for your book, well, I've been longing to read the rest of it ever since you let me see the bit of it about the frog footman at the Chapter House door, and <u>what</u> a good book it's turned out to be – my only complaint is that I'd have liked it to be 10 times longer and perhaps it <u>will</u> be, as I'm not certain whether this is the only version. What struck me was the immense amount of research work, ingenuity and care that must have gone into these delightful stories and resemblances and references. Of course, you don't really want all this hard work to show, but I wish there was a way of making people notice it more. – I think the talking fish and the chestnut tree in the Deanery garden are my two favourites – for detective work, I mean, if you can call it that – but the whole book is as interesting as it can be and puts <u>Alice</u> in a new light and a very endearing one, I think. What's more they've got it up well and laid out the illustrations in the right places and it's not too easy to get printers to do that in these days.

---

* She and PMF became friends when she helped research *The Knox Brothers*. A Germanist, she had assisted Dillwyn Knox with his code-breaking work at Bletchley Park. Later, she became a biographer, and a well-known garden designer.

I notice you're listed with Charles, Prince of Our Time, and the Life of Christ, as a Treasure of Britain, Mavis – that looks like a good start! Very best wishes for the success of the book – love Penelope

I love the bit about the decanters 'finding their way back to the Common Room'.

27a Bishop's Road
London, N6
19 November [1990]

Dear Mavis,

Thankyou so much for your letter and for your kind words about my books. <u>The Knox Brothers</u> will (at last) be out in paperback some time next year, and I must try and get this idiotic mistake of mine about Dilly's birth-date put right, although I'm supposed to have finished doing the corrections. You put it so tactfully – 'the trouble with the date 1883 having been given previously' – <u>I</u> did the 'giving previously', and you've been put to all the trouble of finding out the right date. Not for the first time, the solution has been left to you. I'm so sorry, Mavis, and at the same time grateful to you for putting things straight. – I'm afraid 1883 has been repeated wrongly in a number of places, but from now on they will have to go by the DNB.

I'll let Oliver know – he has a grandson called Edmund now – whether he'll turn out to be like my father, who can tell? None of my 8 are like him at all.

I agree with you – too many fifth men – but Frank Birch is still never mentioned.

best wishes and many thanks –
love
Penelope

27a Bishop's Road
Highgate
London, N6
4 September

Dear Mavis,

Thankyou for the letter from Ralph Erskine – I must say I shall be very interested to see what he has to say in his entry on Frank Birch. It <u>could</u> be a great deal, certainly more than I ever found out. – Thankyou too for the copy of your letter to Sir Philip Duncombe and his reply. You've gone to the point and so admirably – (I must admit I'd never quite realised that you never actually <u>saw</u> the double-cross machine until they made Station X –) but the most important point for this particular letter was the cottage and the possibility of restoring it while Peter Twinn and you are still ready and able to help. Really you have been 'valiant for truth' in the whole business, Mavis – the truth would have disappeared without you.

I wrote 'restoring', but in fact you write the rooms were just as you remembered them – it's a question of what to put in them. I went to Christopher's* funeral and couldn't help feeling that there was very little of Dilly left at Courns' Wood Cottage, but then I could hardly have expected that there would be.

love,
Penelope

27a Bishop's Road
Highgate
London, N6
22 June [c.mid-1990s]

Dear Mavis,

Thankyou so much for your letter and for sending me what you call a few notes, but is actually a more interesting account of Ultra. You're quite right, the word seems to have insinuated itself, I suppose because it's showy. What would Humpty Dumpty have thought of it?

---

* Christopher Knox.

I've been trying very hard to remember the name of the man who came to talk to the Highgate Lit. and Sci. Institute. I was asked to meet him at dinner too, and was disconcerted when he wouldn't talk about Dilly at all. I <u>think</u> he was in charge at Bletchley – but this would have been quite three years ago. The trouble is that the Institute is not exactly closed, but dormant for the summer, so I'll have to wait to find out from the secretary.

Do please give my address to anyone who might help. I do so much appreciate what you're doing.

with best wishes to you and to your family –

Penelope

27a Bishop's Road
Highgate
London, N6
20 February '99

Dear Mavis –

Thankyou for your letter and, although Dilly didn't (after all) appear in the Abwehr programme, I must take the opportunity to say that if you hadn't told the world about him so faithfully and accurately I honestly think his work would have been forgotten, or almost – so many other names and colourful and talkative people appeared, and then there have been dramatisations, like that play, <u>The Code-Breakers</u> – so that altogether, Mavis, we feel truly grateful to you.

I don't know what you thought of Claire Tomalin's <u>Jane Austen</u>. She's a very fine writer (Claire, I mean) but even she can't find out anything more about the Austens. You got as far as anyone can, I think.

Please do send me the details about the future of Bletchley if you have a moment –

love and best wishes

Penelope

Malcolm Muggeridge*

25 *Almeric Road*
London, SW11
30 October 1977

Dear Mr Muggeridge,

Please may I thankyou for your kind notice of <u>The Knox Brothers</u> (as a matter of fact you advised against this title as you said it would sound like a circus, but Macmillans' wouldn't listen to me) – and particularly for your remarks about the four of them. It meant a great deal to me to read what you said about Uncle Wilfred. – Thankyou so much –

Yours sincerely
Penelope Fitzgerald

* The writer, television personality and religious controversialist. PMF had consulted him while writing *The Knox Brothers*.

Colin Haycraft*

25 Almeric Road
London, sw11
11 April 1978

Dear Colin,

Thankyou very much for your letter and the contract for <u>The Bookshop</u>. I'm returning the carbon. I'm so glad that you and Anna thought it was all right.

Please may I ask one thing, where there are lines dropped, could they stay dropped, I know copy editors can't bear the sight of this and always close them up, but I did want them there.

As to the biography of Leslie Hartley, it was you who asked for it, so if it ever got into manageable form I should always ask you first whether you would like to see it. But so far although I've got some way, I haven't got family permission to go ahead (therefore you really don't need to read the rest of this letter). – Your cousin was very kind and as helpful as he could possibly be, he seems to know everyone, and to be a kind of general literary election manager.

I did succeed in getting invited to LPH's childhood home, unchanged since 1900, with the old brass electric light fittings and baths &c, and by talking to his sister I got the psychological key to his novels, every novelist has one, I suppose, the situation his mind goes back to when he's alone – and I also discovered that his manservant was trying to poison him with veronal and that was why his bank-manager locked him up and forced him to make a will, not in the manservant's favour – I was surprised when Francis** commented on this, that surely anyone would prefer to be murdered by someone they loved, rather than have them leave and blackmail you – these seemed to him the

---

* Managing director of Duckworth. He published PMF's first two works of fiction, *The Golden Child* and *The Bookshop*. The earlier part of this correspondence does not appear to have survived.
** Francis King.

only alternatives, but I can think of so many other duller ones. Anyway, the result of our efforts is that Leslie Hartley's sister and Lord David have started 'going through' his papers, which are all stuffed into old toy-cupboards &c – this is a pity, as Francis says he's had <u>his</u> letters back, but many are now missing, not surprisingly I suppose. I would say that I have covered the ground fairly well, but the permission simply depends on who drops dead first. There is a Quest for Corvo atmosphere about the whole undertaking I'm afraid –

best wishes
Penelope

25 Almeric Road
London, sw11
23 April [1978]

Dear Colin,

Thankyou for the money, and here's the typescript of the <u>Bookshop</u> and the notes you asked for, I'm not much good at these I'm afraid.

I regret the jacket, but have to leave that to you of course.

I'm getting on as well as I can with LPH and am going up to Derby when I can manage it to interview the brother of the murderous manservant, but I can't sign on to write anything because I don't know whether I'll ever be able to deliver. I can't even press too hard for permission because then I should have to write under the supervision of the family and Lord D. –

best wishes
Penelope

25 Almeric Road
London, sw11
14 August [1978]

Dear Colin,

I wonder would you be kind enough just to let me know what is happening about Charlotte Mew? On this subject I'm told: 1. Duckworths are bringing out a new edition with a new introduction (<u>Editor of Four</u>

<u>Decades of Poetry</u>) 2. Duckworths are not bringing out a trade edition, but Carcanet are printing the Complete Poems with Alida Monro's introduction (<u>Val Warner</u>, but this was two months ago and I had to meet her for half an hour only in a pizza bar on Victoria station) 3. Duckworths are reprinting the old edition (<u>Arts Council</u>). It's very hard to get an answer from Val, she asked me (on Victoria station) to find out who Charlotte Mew was in love with, which I did, as it's hard for her to research in Swansea, but what's happening I can't tell. (This is all relevant to my interest in Georgian poets &c I shd: explain.) best wishes Penelope

25 Almeric Road
London, sw11
12 October [1978]

Dear Colin,

Thankyou so much for the advance copies of <u>The Bookshop</u>. I like it very much, and what's more the jacket gives a very good idea of Southwold common looking towards the Blyth. I should also like to thank you for a cutting you sent me from the Dutch Library Review. That was really nice. I put it in my scrapbook.

I asked for information about Leslie Hartley in the TLS and got a number of replies, some referring discreetly to the drink problem – one of my difficulties however is that the only person I can find who was actually at Harrow with Leslie (in 1910) is Paul Bloomfield, who is at the same time much too easy and much too difficult to deal with, and also I wonder how much longer he'll last?

best wishes to you and Anna,
Penelope

25 Almeric Road
London, sw11
21 October [1978]

Dear Colin,

Thankyou so much for your letter. I was staggered as I had to write <u>The Bookshop</u> in rather a few weeks and I remember even the place-names weren't spelled correctly and had to be put right, but I was so pleased, particularly as to be shortlisted* makes me more typical of The Old Piano Factory.**

I'll make sure my son goes over to Cambridge to vote for John Sparrow – I'm ashamed to say that none of the rest of us have ever had the money at the right time to take our MA degrees –

best wishes

Penelope

I am in hopeless trouble (as usual) with all my Georgian permissions. Except for yourself, everyone who has to deal with them becomes maniacal, secretive, suspicious, very old or very ill. I'd no idea there would be such trouble.

25 Almeric Road
London, sw11
1 November [1978]

Dear Colin,

Could I just ask you one or two things, first of all I am very sorry not to be able to come on the 8th, I hadn't realised it was a Wednesday and so my day off, and I'm due to go to Cambridge and am not sure when I'll get back that night. 2. About the tickets, (or whatever they are) for the dinner† on the 22nd, my elder daughter would very much like to come, but you said that wouldn't matter as you would be able to get another invitation (or whatever it is) – evidently there's much more point in you being there than me – is that all right? 3. If I could ask for a word of advice: do you think it would be a good idea to write another novel or not, as I'm never likely to do much better than this?††

Thankyou very much for the cheque [incomplete]

---

* PMF's first shortlisting for the Booker Prize. She won the prize in 1979 with *Offshore*, and was shortlisted again – twice – after that.
** Duckworth's premises in north London.
† The Booker Prize dinner.
†† An unwise question that had an unwiser answer.

[postcard]
6 December [*c.*1978]

I do like your satire* as I was brought up to take Latin very seriously. I must tell you that I think you ought to have kept <u>Catulli</u> as a line ending, it sounded right – Wouldn't <u>illacrimabiles omnes</u> have done for the runners-up – also doesn't <u>Jones</u> usually translate as <u>Junius</u>, I think that's what Milton did? – thankyou very much for the chocolates.

Penelope

25 Almeric Road
London, sw11
19 January [1979]

Dear Colin – Thankyou very much for the notices of the <u>Bookshop</u>. – I'd just like to say, having taken the advice, not to say instructions, you gave me to find another publisher for these novels, that I'm very grateful for the start which you and Anna gave me. – I'm sure you were right in saying no-one else would have taken them, and I was happy at Duckworths and very much admired the firm for its spirited conduct of the war on every front. – Best wishes and I hope you and Anna have nothing but happy years ahead – Penelope

25 Almeric Road
London, sw11
24 January [1979]

Dear Colin,
    I'm terribly distressed at having done the wrong thing and caused trouble when I meant to remove it. That is, I'd thought the most helpful thing to do would be to take myself off without making a fuss.

---

* This may refer to Colin Haycroft's satire in defence of the short novel, published in the *TLS*.

You did tell me, you know, that if I went on writing novels you didn't want it blamed on you and that Anna thought I should do detective stories and also, by the way, that you had too many short novels with sad endings on your hands, and I thought, well, he's getting rid of me, but in a very nice way. I don't at all expect you to remember everything you say to 32 authors, but the trouble is we take all these remarks seriously and ourselves too seriously as well, I expect.

I would have liked to stay, because I'm not the sort of person who ever has any money anyway, and I admire the firm so much and then you were always so clever and funny that everyone else seemed exceedingly slow by comparison. However having made this mistake, and I'd rather be taken for an idiot than a liar, I'll be careful to make it clear that it <u>was</u> my mistake, which is what you want, I think.

I told Collins that I wouldn't give them an option on non-fiction just in case you were still interested in the LPH biography, – by the time I get the necessary permissions for that I expect you'll have forgotten my various errors and misunderstandings so it would be worth asking you again –

best wishes
Penelope

25 Almeric Road
London, sw11
16 February [1979]

Dear Colin,

Thankyou for your letter, it's quite true that I've been going on doggedly with L.P. Hartley, and got quite a long way with it, but still with the same difficulty, that 1. permission to quote letters &c has to come from his sister, who by the way I've come to think is really more interesting than Leslie 2. she'd never give it if she saw the draft 3. I expect her to outlive me by far as she is only 78 and the Hartleys are indestructible, LPH only drank himself to death with the greatest difficulty. If the permissions ever come right, then I'll see if by any chance you are still interested in it.

best wishes
Penelope

Thankyou very much for the copy of <u>The Bookshop</u> –

> *25 Almeric Road*
> *London, SW11*
> 16 May [1979]

Dear Colin,

Thankyou very much for letting me know about the German translation of <u>The Bookshop</u> – it was a nice piece of news for me – as to the royalty statement &c, you didn't in fact enclose it, but perhaps one day.

best wishes
Penelope

> *25 Almeric Road*
> *London, SW11*
> 5 September [1979]

Dear Colin – Thankyou so much for writing, I value your good wishes a great deal,* as you can imagine.

Please may I congratulate you on your American expansion, I had to go to Dallas and Austin earlier in the year and looked up at the buildings and wondered how Duckworths in Dallas was getting on –

best wishes
Penelope

* On *Offshore* being shortlisted for the Booker Prize.

[postcard]
29 October [1979]

Thankyou so very much for your congratulations* – One of the first
pieces of advice you ever gave me was to write short novels because
you didn't believe people really wanted to read long ones, and I'm very
glad I took it –
  best wishes Penelope

25 *Almeric Road, sw11*
[postcard]
3 December [1979]

Please, are you thinking of reprinting The Bookshop?
  best wishes Penelope

* On *Offshore* winning the Booker Prize.

Francis King*

[postcard]
28 January [1978]

– I'm just in Bath tracking down one of LPH's secretaries – it is more like the <u>Aspern Papers</u> all the time – I wanted to thank you very much for interceding with Norah,** as it must be a result of your letter (although she doesn't say so) that she now writes to me to apologise for her delay (18 months) in answering – but she had found great difficulty in finding a <u>kennelmaid</u>. If I was a true biographer I suppose I should offer to take the job, I like dogs from the point of view of character but couldn't (as it seems Norah does) prepare them for Crufts – anyway she tells me to come and see her – meanwhile Lord David writes to the <u>Radio Times</u> to point out that only he can interpret &c. Well, that's my progress report – Penelope

Thankyou also for your kind words about my biography – I expect my uncles <u>were</u> dislikeable, but I loved them and got used to them.

25 Almeric Road
London, SW11
29 January [1978]

Dear Francis King,

Thankyou very much for letting me see Norah's letter, which I'm returning as soon as possible, as it seems to me you've suffered from being so generous in these matters. It was very good of you to write, as I think otherwise nothing would have happened at all – Norah is a nice

---

* Novelist, critic and valued friend, PMF worked with him at PEN International. He encouraged her to undertake the biography of L.P. Hartley, and provided the necessary introductions to his circle.
** L. P. Hartley's sister.

person, and good, and brave, what more can one want? But she is also rather forgetful I gather. Anyway I'll go to see her in February and if you want I could always ask again about the C. B. Kitchin papers.

I feel very much encouraged, because as you know I'm not a professional writer but only very anxious to write one or 2 things which interest me, and if Norah doesn't want anything published I should still like to get all the material together as far as possible – I could always leave it to you in my will! A primary biography by people who know the subject and are really fond of him or her is a protection, I think. Perhaps artists should be judged by their work, but it's only too evident that they <u>aren't</u>.

I <u>can't</u> understand why Norah's solicitors haven't settled the Dreda-Owen case by now, as all the evidence must have been deposed long ago – I think it <u>must</u> be a matter of settling out of court. But I discovered at Bath that the bank actually locked Leslie in a room and made him sign a will, as they were dreadfully worried that he'd be made to sign his property away and would then be murdered. That was why the will was so short. Someone said that Leslie must be looking down on us all and dictating the plot himself as it goes along – which I think you also suggested. But I don't know that the eventual sum <u>was</u> as large as all that, as a lot was made over to a relation who couldn't make his farm pay. – Many examples of generosity, and apparently he always paid a third of the expenses at Fletton Tower anyway, and offered several people (besides myself!) money so they wouldn't have to work too hard, but no-one accepted it (or no-one I've met) because it would be a destructive thing from the point of view of friendship – I now have to write to an ex-professor at Bristol, August Closs (surely no-one would dare use this name in <u>any</u> novel) – who was one of the people Norah asked to go to Avondale after LPH died and choose something from his possessions – he's said to be very difficult, but has many LPH letters which he's always intending to sort through – however I refuse to be put off by these ups and downs – I'm afraid you'll be getting tired of all of this, and should like to thank you once again – best wishes Penelope

(I expect you saw the Michael Joseph <u>Lady Ottoline's Album</u>, and I think the photograph on p. 76 of David Cecil and LPH says volumes – poor Leslie would never take off his shoes on the lawn of Garsington but Lord D. <u>has</u> –)

[postcard]
3 February [1978]

Thankyou so much for your letter. I'd love to come to dinner on Feb 8th and shall look forward to that.

Almost giving up, as I hear (completely unreliably) that the spirit of L.P.H. appeared at a séance and said he would wish to abide by Lord D's opinion. But if you would give me Mary Wellesley's address (I was told she lived in London) I should be most grateful – Penelope

25 Almeric Road
London, sw11
12 February [1978]

Dear Francis,

Thankyou so much, I did enjoy Friday evening. I feel in a certain sense I was there under false pretences as the quest for LPH is proving a bit beyond me, but I shall go a little farther with it anyway, and meanwhile it was really kind of you to invite me.

I can't find the red setter results in the paragraphs about Crufts, and they too are sensational, with references to poisoning and dognapping. Where will it all end?

At this moment I'm frustrated in every direction, as I can't persuade your PEN doyenne, Mrs Watts, to part with information about the PEN early days (which I need for something else I'm doing) as it's the most important chapter of <u>her</u> book about her mother, Mrs Dawson Scott, and she still (I think after 20 years) can't find a publisher. (Mrs Dawson Scott also used to receive spirit messages, I remember, but this doesn't help me much.)

I can't think why I go on doing these things, but in any case I'd like to say once again how much I enjoyed myself –

Yours sincerely –

Penelope

25 *Almeric Road*
London, sw11
25 February [1978]

Dear Francis,

I went up to Peterborough yesterday and hope you won't mind my writing to tell you how things went at Fletton Tower. Norah (who went to St Hilda's by the way, not at all like Eustace's Barbara) was wonderfully kind, and every now and then quite unpredictable. Like her brother, she is a magnificent person. – She still has a very slight Northamptonshire accent, which LPH eliminated, as it would not have done for Lord David.

Fletton Tower was built I should say about 1850, but the Hartleys went there in 1900, and everything, down to the tablecloth-presses and brass light-fittings and glass shades, and all the baths &c, are as they were, unchanged. It seems to me that you as a connoisseur of atmosphere have a duty to go there, particularly as Norah was very fond of CBK, and thought him one of the most interesting people she'd ever met. (Incidentally LPH's cellar was full of Burgundy when he died because CBK kept sending it to him although he knew LPH only liked claret. Why?) – Also you would be much better than me with the dogs – I rather like dogs, but these are deerhounds (NOT setters) – 6 foot high when they stand on their hind legs, as they frequently do – other older ones are in large baskets indoors, where they appear to be dying – but all go out to the kennels (the old stables) at night and then Norah is alone in vast Fletton Tower. She's lived there all her life (since 1902) and keeps her files where she once kept her toys.

On the other hand there is a large staff during the day, and I see now that I was quite wrong in thinking that LPH's idea of a household was assimilated to Henry James's great good place or the Cecils – though I still think they played some part – at Fletton there is a gardener,

chauffeur, cook and parlourmaid who wears a <u>cap and apron</u> in the
evening – their <u>average</u> length of service is <u>50</u> years – the woman who
comes in to clean has been there a mere 15 years – Norah is fanatical
on the naturalness of the master/servant relationship and read me a
long address by old Mr Hartley on this subject. So although it seems
LPH didn't like Fletton as a house, he never really escaped it.

The gondolier (Pietro Busette, now dead, you remember the oil
portrait) actually came to stay at Fletton, although he didn't know one
word of English, and had to make signs (what signs?). However, I
mustn't go on and on as I made notes of everything (in P'borough
waiting-room) but thought you might possibly like one or 2 points –
there was an unsigned will in the 1950s, simply appointing Walter
Allen as lit. executor and leaving him all mss – so Norah followed these
wishes in 1972 – but asks me 'is Walter Allen dead?' All mss eventually
went to Cyril Connolly, as Christie's adviser on 20th century mss, and
he deposited them at Christie's, where they still are, but can't be sold
yet because of death duties (I don't understand this) – when they are,
Christie's thinks they'll go straight to Texas. The law case is no further
forward, I didn't like to press for details, but nothing was said about
illegitimate daughters, indeed Norah kept saying that the only
descendants were Cousin Maurice and family, and she says the
plaintiffs are really the same as the man who tried to murder Leslie
with veronal, causing his collapse in 1971. She thinks the bank is slow,
but I believe that they're waiting, knowing very well that these people
were relying on getting a settlement quickly, and will collapse if the
proceedings drag on. – She also told me a lot about LPH's childhood
and I was able to get a clear picture – no Miss Fothergill, though, they
each had an equal amount of money, held in trust. – She said that LPH
hadn't really needed her during his middle successful years, but she
now says how lonely he had been at the end, and wished she had gone
up to London more. (I don't believe Lord David went at all after LPH
began to drink so heavily). I said that you <u>had</u> continued to see him,
and she said she felt very grateful to you. – She asked him whether he
really ought not to get rid of the murderous manservant, and he gave
the inimitable LPH smile and said 'my dear, he's no worse than the
others.'

There are thousands of letters, albums and photographs and I do not know what will become of them. Lord David presides over all. Norah didn't even ask me to promise not to write anything, which I appreciated because it's nice to be trusted. But she <u>does</u> agree that it would be a good idea to collect all the possible material and she told me to try the Radfords (the last Avondale couple) and Princess Clary (hopeless, I can't get to Venice and I daresay she wouldn't 'receive' me), but apparently she is the only one, apart from Lord D., who could describe the Venetian period. (She's about 80). So that, if you could let me know the addresses of Mary Wellesley and the doctor, I would be very grateful – I haven't forgotten that I've asked you a lot of things already.

When I saw LPH's desk and the cyclamen transplanted from Avondale in one of the flowerbeds opposite the stables, I felt like crying, he was such a good friend. – The temptation to make it into a novel, if biographers are not allowed, is very strong, but I shan't do what I've undertaken not to. – And really he did destroy himself, and it turned out to be right when he told me (and many others I expect) that <u>Eustace and Hilda</u> was 'meant to be my own tragedy'.

This is quite enough, you'll say –

best wishes

Penelope

Norah tells me that she hardly ever gives permission to use <u>any</u> unpublished letters – wouldn't let any LPH/Ottoline Morrell letters be printed, for example, so it perhaps doesn't matter so much that mine are all at the bottom of the Thames.

[postcard]
10 March [c.1978]

This is just to thank you for putting me up for PEN. Lettice suggested I might join and I know one can't go wrong in following Lettice's advice, she is splendid – it was very kind of you – best wishes Penelope

25 Almeric Road
London, sw11
12 April [*c.*1978]

Dear Francis,

Thankyou so very much for the photocopies of your letters. I knew you were a good friend of LPH's, but not how <u>much</u> you did for him. I don't know how you managed it, because some of his books seem to me irredeemably bad, in a quite distinctive way, and yet they've always got something readable about them. I see also how tactful you were, and that was necessary, because he minded intensely about them.

By the way, wouldn't you agree that the worst thing about the opening of <u>Howards End</u> isn't so much the letter itself (as a method) as the 'One may as well begin with'. It makes me feel resentful. Why begin at all, if that's how he feels about it.

Anyway, apart from the interest of your letters, they encouraged me, as I felt at a loss, being checkmated by the doctor and Mary W., although I've now had another letter from her saying she remembers meeting me in <u>1952</u> (the time dimension is getting alarming but I think she must keep diaries) – as a matter of fact I <u>do</u> remember the occasion as it was a little dinner for Augustus John, then very ancient, and he collapsed completely and John Russell and I had to drag him out to the pantry to revive him, I can't think this is a particularly sympathetic incident but it's more friendly than her other letter. She says 'no need to answer this because you must get on with whatever you are writing at the moment' and I'm not too sure what she means by this.

I have written now to Roger's brother Colin, and to Lady Aberconway, who I'm sure won't answer, but who is said to be thinking of depositing her LPH letters in the British Library (probably on reserve for the next 50 years). As to Venice and Compton Bassett, the background of <u>The Boat</u>, I'm stuck at the moment, Colin (Haycraft, not Radford) writes to say How Is It All Getting On and I find it hard to explain how difficult it is. And yet I feel there's the story of a whole era there, and LPH was so much nicer than Forster.

Meanwhile I daresay Lord David has tottered up to Fletton Tower to tear up the rest of the letters, just as the last daffodils come out. – I suppose there might be some at Hamish Hamiltons but I don't like to ask again, as Raleigh Trevelyan was so discouraging, though I'm sure he never means to be.

I'm afraid this letter is very disjointed, but I must just say one thing about the <u>Harness Room</u> – LPH told me and I'm sure many others, and actually wrote to Peter Bien, that he wanted to persevere with his central idea (which he believed was also the central idea of <u>Wuthering Heights</u>) that it is the supreme experiences which make life worthwhile, but they are <u>always</u> destructive, whether they are what is usually called moral or not; (that's why Hamish Hamilton should have let Timothy go down with his boat) but he <u>didn't</u> want to express this idea in a specifically homosexual novel because it would raise totally different and irrelevant issues – as it always does. That, I'm sure, was part of his uncertainty over the <u>Harness Room</u>, and why he felt on surer ground with the <u>Hireling.</u>

No-one who is brought up an evangelical can quite learn to trust earthly happiness, it must destroy you somehow.

Well, thankyou again, and I'm sure you won't mind if I write to tell you any further progress – best wishes Penelope

I will keep an eye out for May Sinclair. There are some letters of hers in the Berg NY collection aren't there?

25 Almeric Road
London, sw11
2 June [*c.*1978]

Dear Francis,

This is really to say how much I liked your Bernard Leach review, partly as a long-term potter (we're going to have a raku firing here in Battersea which I daresay will blow us all up and end our troubles in this world) and also as an ex-pupil of Edmund Blunden, – I did like your reference to him.

I never give up about LPH, and went to Derby last week-end to see the Radfords, who told me a lot of things I didn't know before, but the difficulties get greater and greater and some of them are, so to speak,

'not fair' e.g. this Sitwell biography which is coming out, and which
Sacheverell S. says is going to send him down with gray hairs to the
grave &c is I am sure going to upset Norah very much and cause more
wholesale destruction of letters &c. Well, – 'publishing scoundrels!'
   best wishes,
   Penelope

It must be terrible for poor Colin* and I don't see how he can keep
going – I mean the euphoria, the confidence, the cigars &c, on top of
so much wretchedness.

25 Almeric Rd
London, sw11
[postcard of motor buses at junction
of Northcote Road and Battersea
Rise *c.*1913]
9 June [1978]

It would be so nice if you came to dinner one day – this part of Battersea
is seedy, but not so very far from Kensington really – I <u>assume</u> that
you're very busy but would 19 or 20 June be any good? – Thankyou for
your letter, it made me rather sad though –
   Penelope

25 Almeric Road
London, sw11
13 June [1978]

Dear Francis,
   Yes, please do come on the 30th – if I'd known, or paused to reflect,
on what it really means to be a theatre critic, I wouldn't have had the
courage to ask you, so I'm glad I <u>didn't</u> – I do remember now that

---

* A reference to death in an accident of the Haycrafts' son, Joshua.

Mrs Trewin told me they frequently had to take a helicopter from
Battersea, to get there in time – but if the 30th is free, that would be
very nice, and I'll send you a card later to say how to get here, it's not
too bad really.

I feel I ought not to worry you any further about LPH matters,
which get worse and worse, (e.g. it turns out that Paul Bloomfield, an
essential witness as he can recall LPH at Harrow and Balliol, has had
(like many others I'm afraid) a wounding quarrel with poor Colin,
perhaps all these differences may be made up now). But please could
you tell me some time how to write to a Principesa (this is the Principesa
Clary) <u>no-one</u> knows how to start the letter – the Italian Institute
doesn't know – the only guide I have is Dylan Thomas's letters to
Marguerite Caetani and they are not a very safe one I feel – and it's
easy to annoy people, however nice they are –

But in any case, please put down the 30th –
Yours
Penelope

Colin writes that he's composing a Latin epitaph for Joshua – I don't
know whether that would make him feel better or worse –

25 *Almeric Road, sw11*
22 June [1978]

This is just about Friday. We're looking forward so much to seeing you,
it is just my daughter and son-in-law who wd. so much like to meet
you – you won't mind this I know – the 49 is <u>still</u> the bus and overleaf
<u>is</u> the place but not as recognisable as I should like – the 49 stops at
Arding and Hobbs, the Mecca of South London, and if you could get
out at the next request stop, quite soon after, in St John's Rd, and walk
on a bit, then turn <u>left</u> up Battersea Rise, and Almeric Road is first on
right – at the bottom is a notice board of the Tulipean Brethren, a
religious sect – <u>don't</u> go in there – we are <u>25</u> with a laurel hedge – P

25 Almeric Road
London, sw11
21 October [1978]

Dear Francis,

This is just to tell you, as the university entrance exams come in sight, what a marvellous help your book has been to the Forster specialists – I know you didn't write it for their sake but it is just right for these bright students, they like something summed up with the expert touch. – I can assure you that it's appreciated.

Joy Vines told me that she'd been to see you, but I wonder if Val Warner did – but she's a poet and there's no way of reckoning her comings and goings.

I put an ad. in the TLS for information about LPH, more to clear the ground than anything else, and was rather surprised at the number of replies I got. Drink was naturally referred to, but tactfully.

<u>No</u> answer to this needed – it was really just to congratulate on the Forster (see above) –

best wishes,
Penelope

25 Almeric Road
London, sw11
3 November 1978

Dear Francis,

Thankyou so much for your kind letter, which I found very encouraging. How you manage to keep so cheerful, and also so generous to other writers, after so much experience in the literary world, I don't know, as after 3 years of it I find it most harassing and puzzling. I was very pleased about the shortlist,* but couldn't really believe it, and I thought Colin must have made a mistake, only it's not the sort of mistake he makes. He tells me the winner doesn't need the money (though it's hard for me to imagine anyone who doesn't need

* For the Booker Prize, with *The Bookshop*.

£10,000) and he'd asked whether all the runners up couldn't have something, like the Miss World contest (£200 and a package holiday in Bulgaria &c) but the organisers were adamant. However I can honestly say I don't mind this at all, and am delighted to be there with such a simple story.

I'm going along very slowly with LPH, and saving up to go to Venice to see Princess Clary (Aspern Papers again!) – Norah writes to say she had 3 champions this year from one litter, which doesn't help me, but she is so nice. – I am sure Mary Wellesley is misty and forgetful rather than anything else: she wouldn't see me because she said I was her 'rival', which is absurd, but she wrote again later, and if ever I get to the starting point I'm going to see if she won't write something for me on LPH and the river, because she went out in the various boats more than anyone else.

Joy Vines came round the other day – she was full of energy, had written to Robert Liddell, was going to see the publican who served E. Taylor* with her gin and lime every day &c (I may have got the details wrong). On the whole, I think biographers are madder than novelists.

I do hope you're better now. Illnesses contracted in Spain or even Catalonia are worse than any others and last longer, so you have to leave plenty of time for recovery,
    best wishes,
    Penelope

                                                    [postcard]
                                                    24 November [1978]

You were quite right about the Booker dinner of course only I enjoyed it because I hardly ever go to such things – we had to file up just like the school prize-giving – Colin gave his ticket to Anna and couldn't get another one and was sadly missed – I couldn't cheer

---

* Robert Liddell and Elizabeth Taylor the novelists.

Anna up, Caroline Blackwood also sunk in gloom, no wonder of
course – I really wrote to say (what you certainly know already) that
it was nice to hear the applause when <u>The Trial</u> was mentioned –
best wishes

    Penelope

29 December [1978]

Please may I keep the LPH book a little longer? I expect you've been
too busy to remember about it, but anyway, may I?

    For some reason I don't much like the idea of 1979 and expect worries
of all kinds, but very best wishes and I hope you somehow get your
necessary 6 months peace – Penelope

25 Almeric Road
London, sw11
19 January [*c.*1979]

Dear Francis,

    Thankyou so much for lending me this, and once again apologies
for keeping it so long. It is very worthy and painstaking, though it's a
bit disconcerting to find Leslie's novels all treated exactly the same, like
Judgment Day – but Jones is a 'theme' man, I suppose, and that's how
he does it. And I <u>can't</u> get used to U.S. academic language, I just <u>can't</u> –
it seems to get more and more distant from English – and yet he's
employed at the National Endowment for the Humanities and is a
'frequent discussant for theatrical productions' (as you are too, in a
way, I suppose).

    I did just write to him to point out that <u>The Hireling</u> couldn't
possibly be about Charlie, who died 2 years later, not earlier, than
Leadbitter – the original was the proprietor of Jack's Car Hire in
Brixton, I think.

    I keep getting more material, and strange suggestions – I've just had
a letter from Haifa to tell me that old Mr Hartley's name was 'really'

Hertz, but he changed it. Supposing it <u>was</u>? I'll have to ask Paul Bloomfield, he is kind and I hope won't be offended.

I've followed the advice you kindly gave me (after all it's not much use asking for advice if you don't take it) and changed publishers, I went to Collins who were very welcoming but said they'd have to have a T/S by mid-January to get it on the autumn list, so I had to sit down and write a novel and, worse still, type it although all the family type-writers are out of alignment after heavy duty on physiology theses &c. – and this is the real reason why I've taken so long reading your L. P. Hartley. I'm sure Colin will be glad to get rid of me, I'm only causing embarrassment there, for some reason.

Please may I say how much I enjoy your theatre column, when I can get it, it's a real guide to what is worth seeing – I thought you were a little hard on Michael Bryant, I was struck by the way he held the whole theatre silent in <u>Double Dealer</u> although he was speaking in lower than mezza voce – 'But that's not it' – Still I'm sure all your correspondents want to alter <u>something</u> you've said, we can't help it – best wishes Penelope

25 Almeric Road
London, sw11
2 March [*c.*1979]

Dear Francis,

I'm afraid it's another LPH enquiry, but I'm hoping that you'll help me once again – my LPH situation has got better and worse, (in a way) as Anthony Powell, whom I went to see, rang up Lord David, out of pure kindness of heart, and told him to come off it, as Leslie's biography was sure to be written some time. Now Lord D. writes to say he has 'withdrawn his objections' and is at my disposal, as he puts it, meaning that <u>I'm</u> at <u>his</u>, as I'll have to write what he says, and how to get round this I can't think – meanwhile I haven't heard from Norah for a while, and I fear she may be distressed by the frightful accusations of

[incomplete]

25 *Almeric Road*
London, sw11
13 April [*c*.1979]

Dear Francis –

Thankyou so much for giving me the Bewleys' address. David B.
very kindly told me that he had sold the letters through Bertram Rota,
& I'm trying to trace where they went to, as Rex L. is a valuable
witness, having been at Oxford with Leslie. I'm sorry he didn't think
life worth going on with.

It was very kind of you, too, to say a word for me to the BBC, and
although I can see from the producer's suggestion of 'coming to have a
talk with you' that he has no intention of paying <u>anything</u> – (I used to
work at BH and I remember the desperation of getting to the end of
the month and having to produce programmes without any money)
still it's a great help to me to be identified as the LPH biographer and it
was very good of you.

He added that <u>Bookshelf</u> was 'for the kind of audience that is likely
to be at home on Saturday afternoons' – my heart bled for him. He
also asked me where he could find 'memorabilia' of Leslie. I thought
silently of the poor Radfords and their cherished bathmat 'which
Mr Hartley stepped on so often'. Apparently they're going to ask Norah
if they can go and look at the 'memorabilia' at Fletton Tower but I
refuse to be responsible for this.

I've had a delightful, but cautious letter from Frank Magro at
Montegufoni about his recollections of Leslie. I didn't realise that he
(LPH) was Osbert Sitwell's trustee – trustee for what? – I didn't know
he had so much business sense, but I suppose he must have done or he
couldn't have managed all those PEN committees – Magro tells me
that he had to be quite sure there was a bible at Leslie's bedside
'whenever he was Sir Osbert's guest' – his tone is half way between a
steward and a naval petty officer – he's a very interesting person.

I miss Colin* very much, he was so clever, and always knew what
you were going to say before you said it, so it wasn't necessary to finish
the sentence – a family characteristic, perhaps? – he was also so

* Haycraft.

persuasive that after half an hour on the telephone I was almost persuaded I had been in the wrong – e pur si muove – or rather he certainly <u>did</u> tell <u>me</u> to move on, and I was somewhat disappointed as I thought I could write a rather better novel next time – but I suppose everyone always thinks this! However, he's quite certainly forgotten about the whole matter by now, he has a most enviable ability to do this, necessary, as he told me, if you're an optimist married to a pessimist. – If I really get anywhere near finishing LPH I shall have to ask him if he still wants the book, and brace myself for a possible cutting reply, or none at all. – I still have to see a number of people, including Derek Hill, who flits about rather, and Ralph Ricketts, who tells me he has another 100 letters, not to speak of Lord D.

I can't imagine why I'm going to Texas, I hate hot weather and it is just getting so nice here, and my grape-fruit tree has come into flower –

I can't agree about the <u>Tempest</u> but I was very interested in your notice of <u>Pericles</u> – and yet I don't know that it <u>ought</u> to be done on a bare stage – surely it was a great relief for Sh. to have stage effects, trick scenery &c, <u>at last</u> in the late plays – you can't grudge him those at the end of such a career –

best wishes

Penelope

I hope that you'll do what you say and start a new novel, no matter what.

25 Almeric Road
London, sw11
29 April [c.1979]

Dear Francis,

Thankyou very much for your letter – it was nice to hear your voice on <u>Bookshelf</u> which the children put on tape for me. Frank Delaney is a real Tipperary boy, of a good catholic family as he didn't need to tell me, and I'm sure will get on well in life and cause much pride at home, but as to his devotion to Anglo-Irish novelists – well, I can't feel that he really understands <u>The Real Charlotte</u>. – I couldn't approve of the way he cut the programme (but then of course no-one ever does) leaving in scarcely anything about the novels themselves and <u>nothing</u> about Leslie's sympathy and kindness, that nice story you told in the <u>RadioT.</u>, for instance, about the carpet-slippers – however I've had a letter from Norah since, offering to take me to see Leslie's mysterious farming cousin, that he lent the money to, and she made no complaints, and indeed didn't mention the programme at all – someone who <u>did</u> was Ralph Ricketts, who was at Leslie's deathbed, but I've written to him diplomatically (I hope). I felt you talked so well and gave the programme authority.

If you go to Italy this year I am sure Frank Magro would be <u>delighted</u> if you called, his one ambition is to talk to literary people, to have the opportunity to 'converse on many matters' as he calls it – I understand that he is not popular in the village and must lead a lonely life in the castello.

What a business it all is, I feel on the verge of giving up on LPH and starting on Shakespeare – there's something to do there, the Stratford man obviously being the wrong one. – Lord David writes, too, that his memory is failing him, and Hamish Hamilton that his correspondence is in a dusty warehouse, but they'll both have to make an effort, in the cause of literature. I'm looking forward very much to your lecture, and I certainly <u>shan't</u> ask any questions –

best wishes

Penelope

I really enjoyed myself in Texas, and what a collection! Vast reserves of everything – even Constantine Fitzgibbons' telephone bills are there.

17 June [1979]

Dear Francis –

This is just to congratulate you on what must surely be a recognition* not only of your public career, so to speak, as a poet,

---

* He had been awarded the OBE.

novelist, organiser and president, but of all the groundwork you must have done, things people say must and ought to be done, but are strangely unwilling to undertake themselves. – I don't suppose there are any honours for listening and giving good advice, otherwise they might be added in too.

Congratulations and best wishes for your Brazilian tour – Penelope

25 Almeric Road
London, sw11
29 October [1979]

My dear Francis –

I was just going to write to you anyway, on the subject of the continuing saga of LPH, which you've so kindly listened to through the years, but first of all thankyou <u>very</u> much for your congratulations,* I do value them. In the stories I used to read when I was a little girl cab-horses used to win the National and everyone seemed to cheer, but you can't expect this in real life, and I know I was an outsider – however Asa Briggs explained to me that they'd ruled out novels evidently written with one eye on the film rights as they'd been looking for <u>le roman pur</u>, and I (naturally) agreed with him. – When I got to the Book Programme, soaking wet because I'd had to be photographed on a bale of rope on the Embankment, R. Robinson** was in a very bad temper and complained to his programme executive 'who are these people, you promised me they were going to be the losers'. – I couldn't help enjoying the dinner, though the Evening Standard man told me frankly that they'd all written their pieces about Naipaul and felt they were free to get drunk, wh: he certainly was; I <u>did</u> notice the <u>Spectator</u> man, but thought he was perhaps dead. Even so I had a lot of happy moments, and the best was when the editor of the Financial Times, who was at my table, looked at the cheque and said to the Booker McC Chairman 'Hmph, I see you've changed your chief cashier.' Both their faces were alight with interest. – I'm afraid Booker McC rather wish

---

* On *Offshore* winning the Booker Prize.
** Robert Robinson, the broadcaster.

they'd decided to patronise show-jumping, or snooker – the novelists are so difficult and odd, not appreciating their surprise announcements and little treats.

I worked really hard this year on LPH, but I'm going forward and backward at the same time, as I know I'll never be allowed to publish – Norah has now won her law case against the mysterious claimant, is in splendid form and has celebrated by extending the kennels and breeding numerous more setters, also by writing fierce letters to Frank Delaney (the Bookshelf man, who's now reappeared as literary critic of the Universe; he tells me I deserved to win because my book was free of objectionable matter and suitable for family reading). She's also offered to drive me across the fens to see Leslie's paralysed cousin; who lives in a lonely farmhouse – the one Leslie lent the money to. But I know she won't at all like what I want to say, even though I did love Leslie, and am suitable for family reading.

It's the shades of snobbery and affection that interest me. Jimmy Smith (at tea on his lawn in Cadogan Lane) said 'but you can't mean that Leslie was a snob – why, he was accepted immediately'. He doesn't seem to see the force of that word 'accepted', nice as he is. And then Lord D. insists that Leslie's life was completely happy. He added that his life was completely happy, and that he can't remember ever being unhappy. I asked him whether LPH wasn't heartbroken when he got married and he said, well he did seem upset, but I asked him to be best man – as though that made up for it! But he'd never seen Leslie unhappy, he repeated. I said, has it struck you that Leslie was happy when you were there, and not when you weren't, like sunshine and shadow? Lord D. looked rather taken aback. I don't know how he can sit there under his portraits by Aug. John, &c, of himself as a pastorally handsome young man. – I couldn't get a look at his letters, he kept putting them back in the desk. 'nothing, just literary matters'. As a matter of fact, they quite likely were, I think. LPH certainly wanted to marry Lord D's cousin Mollie Berwick, that does seem clear, but what a time it all takes.

The Cecils were the only people I've ever known who have toast at tea in a toast-rack. Perhaps aristocratic.

You'll be relieved that I've got to the end of this piece of paper. – Thankyou so much for telling me about Anne Wignall, indeed I'd love to meet her. But I expect to go down to the grave without bringing this book out. It's just a kind of feeble obstinacy that keeps me going on. 'Call it going, call it on' as Beckett says. Meanwhile Collins declare that they must have another novel and it ought to be longer, although I was trained at Duckworths to write short ones. But I deeply believe that 'less is more'. I like <u>Daisy Miller</u> better than <u>Wings of a Dove</u> and even <u>Master and Man</u> better than <u>War and Peace</u>. Now I really have got to the end – best wishes Penelope

I just must add one more thing – I managed at last to get into Hamish Hamiltons – HH of course was very suave and charming but I also went through Leslie's files, and couldn't resist having a look at one or two other ones and when I saw what publishers <u>really</u> think about their authors, and their staff memos, I wondered if it was really worth going on.

25 Almeric Road
London, sw11
2 February 1980

My dear Francis – Thankyou so much for forwarding Anne Wignall's letter, and indeed for continuing to help me with the LPH biography, which seems to go on forever, and in a sense gets more difficult, because even after walking all over the Brickfields with Norah (and with a curious feeling of how easy it would be to shove somebody or be shoved into one of the ruined furnaces, now all overgrown with brushwood, and never be heard of again) I still can't tell how much she knows or guesses about Leslie – and I'm so fond of her. – But it would be a great relief, apart from any thing else, to get back to the general list, I don't think I'm tough enough to make a novelist really. – I have written to Anne Wignall of course and hope to go down there in the spring, bearing in mind your warnings. The trouble is that I've got no grand connections at all; Hamish Hamilton kept saying 'You'll be related to the Knight of Kerry' and even 'surely you <u>must</u> be related to the Knight of Kerry' but I'm <u>not</u> –

best wishes,
Penelope

25 *Almeric Road*
London, sw11
29 September 1980

Dear Francis,

Thankyou very much for your kind words and also for your good advice, (which I'll try to take only I'm not sure if I have the capacity) in the <u>Spectator</u>. I rather wish I didn't have to be Miss Fitzgerald as it seems to discount my husband, of whom I was very fond, not to speak of 3 children and 2 and a half grandchildren, but I suppose that's an occupational hazard of writing short, powdery novels.

Anyway, I do truly want to thank you. –

Just a few faithful at PEN. – Jasper Ridley walking about with a piece of paper with the obituary you'd written on it – he said I hate reading aloud and after I have had a glass of wine I can't read at all – I asked him if he had had a glass and he said yes, but it all went off very well in fact.

very best wishes for your opening,
Penelope

Anne W. and loved one now coming to live in Battersea – just round the corner, in fact

25 *Almeric Road*
London, sw11
10 January [*c.*1981]

The U.S. edition of this just arrived so I thought I'd send you one – <u>not</u> because I expect you to read it but because I haven't anything else to send and wanted to thank you for giving me so much time and advice –

    best wishes
    Penelope

I still feel puzzled about LPH but less so. I suppose he <u>was</u> just selfish, and I hadn't the wits to recognise it.

> *76 Clifton Hill,* nw8
> 22 February [1983]

Just to congratulate you on the 'Why do we write' speech – Lettice tells me she thinks it was the best talk she ever heard at PEN – we were both touched by what you said about the actual necessity of writing, and the threat of shortening time, (although we agreed that it would be many years before you'd need to worry about that) –

    love, Penelope

> [postcard of The British Library]
> 23 May [1983]

Back at work in this place, though I'm getting so peculiar that if I don't manage to get seat H5 my whole day is ruined. – I did enjoy the visit to Padua so much, partic. Petrarch's villa – <u>none</u> of my assorted crockery is broken and I'm keeping the glass boots as a perpetual souvenir – thankyou again for tireless organisation and protection which meant such a lot – love Penelope

> *76 Clifton Hill,* nw8
> 1 April 1984

Dear Francis,

    Please forgive this paper, I'm down at the post office in Somerset and can't find anything better, and I just wanted to write you a note about the PEN grant, or rather the disappearance of it.

I don't know who decided this, but it certainly was never discussed by the literature department's (alleged) consultative panel. So I suppose the literature department (Charles, his dog, Josephine, Kate and a secretary) settled it themselves, or perhaps Finance did. The regions were given a list of organisations and asked which ones they'd like devolved to (or is it onto?) them, and PEN was on that list. They all said they didn't want PEN, but the question was absurd in the first place.

I asked whether anyone from PEN had been asked to come and make a case before the cut was decided? At each of the literary panel meetings one or more 'clients' usually appear (e.g. John Calder, Alan Ross, the National Book League in force, the alarming Federation of Worker Writers &c) and say what they're doing, and why they ought to be given money, but no-one from PEN ever came, or was asked to come. I was told that the grant was made solely on account of PEN's work in receiving international writers &c, and yet something could have been said about the archives. (I mean the tape recording of interviews and personal reminiscences) or the encouragement of English writers, or the recent proposal to invite VI forms from the schools to the meetings (which I admit hasn't got far as yet, still it might do). The whole case went by default because no-one was ever asked to put it.

I expect you know all this, but having now attended my last meeting, very exhausting with Jonathan Miller conducting his alternative meeting next door, I thought I would just send you a word about it. I know, of course, that everyone thinks they've been unfairly treated –

love, Penelope

31 July [1984]

Thankyou very much indeed for kind words about Charlotte Mew, (and incidentally for the reference to Mrs Dawson Scott, wh. fitted

in rather well with what Valls said, that he owed his release to
International PEN).

On seaside holiday – but I'm sure alas that I could once make better
sand-castles than I do now love Penelope

76 Clifton Hill, NW8
[*c.*1984]

My dear Francis,

Thankyou so much for your kind letter – I don't know what Collins
are doing, except that Christopher Maclehose and his sweet but
ominously named apprentice have now suddenly become the Harvill
Press, but I'm glad they sent you poor Charlotte M. and very much
appreciate your taking the trouble to write to me about it.

I say 'poor Charlotte Mew' because she seems to have been so
unfortunate even in those who liked her and those who didn't, and
now she is coming out at one of the worst times in the publishing year,
owing to difficulties (so they say) at the printers. No matter, at least
she's out, only just in time, as Marjorie seems to have got a publisher at
last, which I'm glad about really. At least Collins produced a very nice
glossy enlargement of the picture of herself and her mother, so I've
sent that to her in case she wd. like to use it as an illustration.

I <u>do</u> remember <u>The Romantic</u> – I think the heroine is called
Charlotte Redhew – May Sinclair being very reckless about names. I
went to see an old lady who remembered her (i.e. May) quite well –
but at the end of her life, of course. It didn't seem to her anything very
remarkable that Miss Sinclair had 'lost her mind', and I could see that
she thought of it as a likely fate for writers and 'artistic people'.

Since my visit to Leslie's Avondale, now transformed into the Misty
Waters Grade 2 Hotel and canoeing centre, I feel I can't write any more
biography, as in Leslie's case he always seemed to get one jump ahead,
so to speak, of anything I could write. They were running his big
greenhouse as a nursery garden and <u>of course</u> it suddenly fell down
one day, as though by magic.

I've got the right things here for making redcurrant jelly and
strawberry jam and looking after the baby, but no <u>paper</u> except endless

post office forms (one of them gives the <u>scale</u> of rewards for resisting
armed intruders) – there <u>must</u> be some paper somewhere, but
meantime I thought I'd write this –
    love
    Penelope

> *76 Clifton Hill,* NW8
> [To Francis King CBE]
> 2 July [1985]

So very many congratulations, which I would have sent before, only
news gets so slowly down to the depths of Somerset –
    Penelope

> [postcard]
> 30 August [1986]

Dear Francis, Thankyou so much for your kind p.c. – you'll hardly
remember, having been to so many other places since, that you told me
the story of the Italian family and their dwarfs yourself, for which I
also have to thank you.
    I hope everything went well in India – love Penelope

> *27a Bishop's Road*
> *Highgate,* N6
> 25 November 1988

Dear Francis – (This is not the right sort of paper, but I ought to be
writing something else, only I thought I would very much like to write
to you first) – I hoped perhaps I might see you at Raleigh's party last
night, but Josephine explained that you hadn't much felt like a lot of
noise, and there <u>was</u> a lot of noise – she also told me that you'd had a
good report from the doctors, and that's the point of this letter, simply

to say how glad I was. I count on you to defeat time and nature, just as you've got the better of so many other things.

I hope you don't miss the theatre – it seems to me that one expects to miss things, and then doesn't, or not as much as expected – I don't miss teaching as I thought I would. But I admit that I do miss you as president of the PEN English Centre, when I make my way down there from the northern heights.

This, of course, is a letter that doesn't need answering, it's only to send my sympathy for everything that's been painful and tedious and my best wishes.

love

Penelope

I'm just sorting out, not my letters but various notebooks, drafts and backs of envelopes which seem to me of very little interest, for sale to Texas (I shan't let anything to do with Leslie Hartley go). I'm weighing them on the bathroom scales, and I suppose selling your papers is a ritual stage in a writer's life – a very late one.

[15 October 1993]

Many congratulations on your speech at The E. Standard lunch – I know you've made a good many speeches in your life and I've heard only a few of them, but I thought it was particularly successful, specially the change of tone at the end, which gave me some idea of the book – love P

27a Bishop's Road
London, N6
19 December [*c.*1996]

Dear Francis,

Thankyou so very much for the copy of <u>The Buried Spring</u>. It's an ambiguous title, like others of yours, but I don't find it depressing, because springs are buried (like the Twill mill-stream) only until they reappear again.

One good thing about having flu, which seems to be, and indeed <u>is</u>, lasting for weeks, is that I've been able to read things slowly, as they deserve. But they're sad poems, Francis! I've read an immense amount of poetry this year for the Forward Prize and stuck to it that John Fuller ought to win, (as he did), because of elegy on his father – 'and this is what it is to grieve'. I thought that in <u>The Buried Spring</u> there might be an elegy for your mother, but I was quite wrong and I should have known that it's not my business to look for a poet's subjects, but to try to understand them when they come.

So much of your distress seems to be on other peoples' account –

How could I even if I choose
Now let another swimmer drown?

This seems to go against what you wrote in your autobiography – 'why could one not be brave for one's own sake?' but I think it isn't difficult to sympathise with you in both cases. – What makes me sad is that (like Housman) you sometimes seem to write as though life was a kind of responsibility laid on you which you can never hope to discharge. – But I also get the impression that what you yourself can't bear to lose is the capacity to feel strongly, whether it's loving or hating, which makes me wonder why you didn't include <u>the Carcase</u>?

Meanwhile I'm given a kind of hope or reason for hope by <u>The Raising of the Blind</u> – not that I think reason has got much if anything to do with it.

Thankyou again and best Christmas wishes –
Penelope

27a Bishop's Road, N6
4 October [c.1997]

Dear Francis,

This is to thank you very much for <u>Dead Letters</u> and your kind inscription.

I enjoyed the book very much, although 'enjoyed' isn't quite the word, because it's such a sad book, Francis. It's sad not just because of the Principe, he's doomed from the start and for him the story is an elegy, but because you make us like Steve so much, (as always, you have the art of letting us get to know these people so quickly, a paragraph or so is enough –) anyway I loved Steve because he was so patient and efficient and because he had no idea who Prince Myshkin was and wanted to climb higher and get some fresh air, and tried so hard to keep straight with the money – and then you gradually and quite relentlessly show him as a loveless man, 'someone who does not want to think about it'. It's true that you say he's given the Lampedusa figure 'the will to carry through to eventual triumph', but if that's to be the justification for Steve's life then that's putting art above humanity with a vengeance. – You didn't ask me for my opinion, and you mustn't think I didn't appreciate the book's construction – indeed I did, and I thought it was a wonderful book – being sad is nothing against it.

I wonder why you didn't put <u>Yesterday Came Suddenly</u> on the list of <u>Also By</u> – that puzzled me.

Thankyou again and best wishes for everything – love Penelope

[c.1997]

Dear Francis – Thankyou so much for Olympia, who cheered me up – I was so very sorry to miss you at Virginia's and it was very good of you to write. Let me seize the opportunity to tell you about my symptoms, and say my gout isn't at all the socially-historically sort which Roy Porter lectures about but the result of poisonous chemicals given me by the Whittington Hospital to make my heart work a bit better. – I don't like the way doctors take out their materia medica nowadays and look anxiously through it before writing out yet another prescription – they used to <u>pretend</u> to know, and pretences have their value –

love and best wishes Penelope

27a Bishop's Road, N6
19 November [1997]

Dear Francis,

Thankyou for your letter, and I should be happy to be interviewed about what I've written, that is if you quite honestly think anyone would want to come and listen, (always a worry). Only, please, could I have a kind, tolerant interviewer, as I've never been able to remember the names of my characters (can you honestly say you remember all yours?). Andrew would be very good I'm sure although he is always immensely busy.

Feeling very low after the last days of the BL reading room – love Penelope

27a Bishop's Road
London, N6
19 October [*c*.1998]

Dear Francis,

Thankyou so much for your invitation for October 26th – I should have loved to have come, but, most unfortunately for me, I'm irrevocably committed to help with an (alleged) literary dinner at the Highgate Institution. It was very kind of you to think of me – and I was deeply impressed by the equatorial schoolgirls on your card, writing on the earth, without any need of a teacher it seems,

love Penelope

27a Bishop's Road
London, N6
28 October [*c*.1998]

My dear Francis,

I won't apologise any more for being the lingering guest, because you didn't make me feel at all like that, indeed I'm sure no-one ever does in your house.

I would really have liked to ask you about everything <u>you</u> were doing, and say how much I admired your alterations to the house, and ask whether you designed them yourself, but instead of doing this I talked about myself. Not that I had much of interest to say.

I get depressed at times – I suppose it's ridiculous to regret the Liberal party, the Church of England, Lyons tea-shops, Carter Paterson, telegrams and so on, but so many of them seemed to disappear at once. I had a letter from Edward Blishen (who I don't think is too well), saying that he'd always suspected it might be a mistake to get into your seventies.

But then after a delightful dinner party, like the one you gave last night, (delightful in every way, because the dinner was so delicious and I very much enjoyed talking to everyone there) I can't remember why there should be anything to be depressed about. Thankyou so much – love Penelope

[March 1999]

Dear Francis – This is just to say how absolutely right you are about the north and south of Europe, and yet no-one seems to have said it before.

It was so nice to see you at International Writers Day. It reminded me of old days – such a long time ago.

On no account answer – it was just a thought – love Penelope

27a Bishop's Road, N6
1 September [1999]

I'm just reading The One and Only and enjoying it so much and partic. the absolutely right pre-war details. The 1 and only thing I question was whether you could <u>flick</u> Hatter's Castle, as I remember it, across the room. But this of course doesn't matter, the atmosphere is marvellous, many congratulations love P.

Norah Hartley*

25 Almeric Road
London, sw11
15 July [1981]

Dear Norah – Just one more letter of many! I was rung up by Hamish Hamilton last night to tell me that you had authorised a biographer for Leslie – I've been so dreadfully slow (and still haven't collected all the material I wanted, or managed to see Mary Wellesley) that I expect people have given up any hope of me getting anywhere – but if you should want me to help him (that's the new biographer) then please tell him so.

Meanwhile we are having rather a sad year, because my daughter's baby that we were all looking forward to so much was born in May and is a darling, a boy with large blue eyes, but after a week or so it turned out that he had an incurable muscular disease, it's difficult for him to breathe and they seem to think (always 'they'!) that he can't live for much longer than two years. My daughter and her husband have decided to give up teaching and run a little sub-post-office and shop in the depths of Somerset and look after the baby there, and they said will I come and grow the vegetables – but I shall have to be in London part of the time to earn a bit of a living – so what will become of us all I don't know, so life goes on.

Thankyou so much for all your kindness –
Yours affectionately,
Penelope

---

* L. P. Hartley's sister, who gave PMF a great deal of help in her research into her brother's life.

Mary Lago*

25 Almeric Road
London, sw11
24 March [*c.*1978/9]

Dear Professor Lago,

When I was in Oxford the other day I went to see Mary Bennett,** who mentioned your name and told me about your work, and I hope you won't mind my writing to you about it? She told me (and in fact I think John Christian told me this as well) that you were in the process of editing the studio diaries of T. E. Rooke, and this interested me very much, as I read them carefully a few years ago when I was writing a biography of Burne-Jones.

At the moment I am trying to collect material for a book about Georgian poets, craftsmen and publishers and this has also given me an interest in Rothenstein, who in some cases was their only portraitist.

I should so much like to meet you some time just to talk about these subjects, and wondered whether you would be free at any point in the day? I'm teaching, but only three days a week –

Yours sincerely,

Penelope Fitzgerald (Mrs)

* Professor of English at the University of Missouri. She edited E. M. Forster's *Letters* and wrote on Edward Burne-Jones and Rabindranath Tagore. She and PMF met every year during Professor Lago's research visits to Oxford and Cambridge.
** Principal of St Hilda's, friend of PMF's since undergraduate days (as was Barbara Craig, Principal of Somerville).

25 Almeric Road
London, sw11
30 September 1979

Dear Mary,

You'll wonder why I am sending back your stamp! Well, it's a token, because I can't bring myself to use it when I'm not able to answer your question – I am ashamed to say that I don't know Mrs Gaskell's dates and indeed only got the age difference from EBJ's letters to her. But the person who <u>would</u> know is Robin Bagot (her great-nephew) at Levens Hall, Cumbria, who gave me permission to quote from her correspondence &c. If by any chance he's died in the last 5 years, the Bagot family is certainly still at the Hall.

I heard from the Ormonds that your work was nearly ready and should like to congratulate you, we all look forward to it. – I've had to take to writing novels at the moment to finance trips to Texas where all the world's mss seem to be gradually collecting! best wishes with all your projects – Penelope

25 Almeric Road
London, sw11
12 July [*c.*1980]

Dear Mary,

Just to thank you very much for the tea, and to say how much I enjoyed seeing you again. It was so interesting to hear about your projects that I didn't even notice when the doors were opened and we were allowed out again (I feel the staff thoroughly enjoy these moments of power, by the way).

The bookseller who specialises in the Poetry Bookshop (and the bibliography of Malcolm Lowry) is J. Howard Woolmer of Revere, Pennsylvania, and the man who's doing B/Jones selected letters is Michael Case of Arizona State University, but, although he hopes to publish soon, he's only doing it for his doctoral dissertation, and I can't help wondering whether he realises how complicated the Pre-Raphaelite field is. Incidentally, he says he's already had, as part of his doctoral exams, 'an oral test' on the biography I wrote on B/J, which

I realise <u>now</u> (though of course I didn't <u>then</u>) is full of things which
ought to be put right – but perhaps he'll find this out as he goes along!

Please give my respect to the Master of St Edmunds – Valpy (my
son) is working 10 hour sessions at a time in Nicaragua, trying to train
the staff of their new Ministry of Economics, all on strict Christian-
Marxist-Cambridge principles, as far as is possible.

Best wishes for your E.M. Forster

Penelope

25 Almeric Road
London, sw11
25 January 1981

Dear Mary,

Thankyou so much for your letter and news – I too think the B/J
correspondence an impossible task – I suppose Michael Case has <u>time</u>
on his side, as he sounds young, but all the same! – I understand that
he inherited the project from a man called Hosmon who collapsed
under the task, and also, if I remember rightly, wasn't approved of by
Professor Friedmann. To tell you the truth, I don't know that the world
<u>wants</u> all B/J's letters. I have just been going through all the unpublished
Cormell Price papers which have now come back to his grand-daughter
(who has to find room for them in quite a small flat) – partly with the
idea of helping Norman Kelvin, but he tells me his Volume 1 is at last
ready – and there are a large number of letters from B/J there but
mostly of the 'Dearest Corm why not take the train to Rottingdean on
Saturday' variety – what is the use of it all?

I was glad to hear that the Rookes journals are on the autumn list
and am sure you are much better off printing it over there, under your
eye and with your daughter's help – the publishers here do nothing
but luxuriate in their despair and imminent ruin, although I daresay
they will pull through as usual.

As for me, I continue to want to write about the Poetry Bookshop,
and the publishers continue to say that they would prefer a novel. The
Georgian poets, it's true, seem permanently out of fashion, and no-one
took much notice when Cape at last published W. H. Davies'

supposedly unpublishable autobiography, which he'd asked them to destroy – but I still want to write this book!

My daughter (whose house this is) is having a baby in May, wh. is a very great event, and wants us to move somewhere with more space, but I'll send you the new address if we <u>do</u> move, in the hope of seeing you this summer. My son will then be in Texas! – he's just back from Nicaragua, and the Jesuit-Marxist-popular-Christian experiment from which they hope so much –

best wishes for your researches in 1981

Penelope

25 Almeric Road
London, sw11
7 May 1981

Dear Mary,

It was very nice to hear from you, and very good news that your edition of the B/J Studio Diaries will be out this year – in a certain sense it's a triply edited edition, since (as John Christian pointed out to me) Rooke <u>couldn't</u> really have been making all these notes at the time (EBJ <u>hated</u> having notes made of his conversation), he must have written them up in the evening, and then GBJ* seems to have checked them again – but I think they are marvellous material, particularly toward the end of Morris's life and the end of B/J's own – and it will be a great advantage and pleasure to so many people to have your book.

I've just been asked to talk about Morris and his <u>women friends</u> – (not his wife Janey) and I thought this was rather an interesting subject – as Morris, that really great man, did succeed in treating women as people – but I shall have to do a lot of work, as I'm not a Morris specialist.

I really don't think we can do any more for Michael Case! As he is based on a university, he should be able to find out where the university and public collections are, and I've given him the addresses of a number of private collections to try, but he still seems defeated – and surprised that some of the owners don't want their letters published,

* Georgiana Burne-Jones.

and don't even want to see him. I believe he's coming over this summer, however.

My son was very interested to get your news about Dr Coventry. He (my son) misses Cambridge, but I think he was right to accept the Hague professorship, and indeed Dr C. told him so.

Tina (my daughter) is due to produce her first baby in a couple of weeks and now says we must all go and live in the depths of the country and run a small post-office! The simple life! But I do hope to see you in June or July – we haven't moved yet –

best wishes
Penelope

> 25 *Almeric Road*, sw11
> [postcard]
> 24 July [1981]

Yes please, I'd love to come (12.30 on July 31st). It would be a treat to see you and Mary and also a moment of civilisation as everything here is in a muddle I fear beyond repair – it took me quite a time even to find a <u>pen</u> to write this, but I was determined to do so – Penelope

> 25 *Almeric Road*
> *London*, sw11
> 1 August 1981

Dear Mary,

I want to thank you for the delicious lunch (the club has changed so much – it used to be refined and chilly and I don't ever remember seeing a man in the dining-room, now it's lovely, I wonder when the change took place?) and for the chance to see you and Mary, both Marys, and hear about all the many things you've been doing. I think Murrays have produced <u>Burne-Jones Talking</u> beautifully, even without the illustrations I could see that, and really I'd have loved to sit there and read more of it, because I've never seen Rooke's introduction before, or all these fascinating notes and extracts from his letters to

Cobden-S, &c. – however I must wait and look forward to publication day. – I do hope though I don't give a wrong idea about John Christian, I am sure it's his excessive shyness and diffidence which sometimes makes him seem strange, and he is so scholarly and so devoted to classification that perhaps he doesn't see the <u>need</u> for biography. He read my book for the publishers and was most kind and helpful, but he didn't <u>like</u> it, and he didn't pretend to! I know he's been through a difficult time, and was very glad to see that he'd done the introduction and notes to <u>The Little Holland House Album</u> (those early B/J drawings), quite recently, and that was beautifully produced and may so to speak set him free and start him off writing again, I hope so, as he is a very nice person.*

I think the studio diaries and the illustrations are going to be a revelation to a lot of people, who don't realise how witty Burne-Jones was and what a delightful wry attitude he had and how deep his human relationships went – they just think of him as ineffectual, pale and bloodless – and personally I'm grateful to you for getting the University and the publishers to see this and producing such a good book.

Mary looked so well, didn't she? An advertisement in favour of retirement, what is it that makes everyone keep working like this? Because, as she pointed out, this is her <u>second</u> retirement.

Our country address is going to be Theale Post Office Stores, Wedmore, Somerset. But I shall have to be in London during the week and do so very much hope to see you when you come back again – best wishes for Forster and many thanks, Penelope

76 Clifton Hill
London, NW8
20 January 1982

Dear Mary,

How nice to hear from you, and to get the good news about <u>Burne-Jones Talking</u>, which, I do think, is an excellent title, suggesting that it's

---

* John Christian was executor to Raymond Watkinson, the William Morris and Pre-Raphaelite scholar, a good friend of PMF's.

authentic and conversational at the same time. I'm so much looking forward to it. We had an Aubrey Beardsley feature here on BBC 2 this week and it was most disappointing, and didn't indicate the relationship between B/J and AB at all, or the all important Mantegna frescoes at Hampton Court which I dare say AB would never have seen at all if B/J hadn't suggested it. The presenter kept showing a hand making pen and ink dots by candlelight, which was hardly necessary, as all the viewers must have known he was an artist in the first place – but no matter.

I'm living half in London and half in Somerset, the very depths of the cow and cider-apple country, because my son-in-law and daughter have decided to give up teaching for the time being, and run a little shop and post-office – this is largely on account of their first baby, who, sad to say, is very delicate – the muscles that control his breathing are deficient – though he always smiles gallantly – and we've had a great deal of anxiety and still do have. We can only pray that he'll survive the winter and be better in the spring.

I haven't heard any more about Michael Case, but really I shall be amazed if he ever gets as far as anything like a complete edition as he behaves in such an awkward way – he asked Eileen Cassavetti, in fact told her, to make type-out copies of the letters she has in Paris for him, Xeroxes not being much good because he finds it difficult to read B/J's handwriting! She is kind, but I don't know whether she could find time to do it. He seems to have set out for his research without any proper advice or guidance.

I loved your description of Washington – and hope to see you in the summer when you arrive in Cambridge –

best wishes –

Penelope

76 Clifton Hill
London, NW8
26 April 1982

Dear Mary –

How nice to hear from you and just when I was going to write anyway to congratulate you on the appearance over here of <u>Burne-J</u>

<u>Talking</u> – my only objection (which was quite trivial) was to the red boards which, with the jacket, didn't make quite 'a jewel of colour', but I thought the diary came out splendidly with your notes and tactful editing, it was all so alive and attractive – I went down to the BBC to chat about it in <u>Kaleidoscope</u> – needless to say they cut out all the remarks I'd hoped might be left in, and the extracts were read in another studio, so I never even knew what they were, but no matter, they have to work in a hurry and the presenter said he'd loved the book and the notes had given him the answers to everything he wanted to know.

My family news is rather sad, as Tina's baby boy died in March, at the age of 9 months. – Tina is my elder daughter, who is running the little post office stores in Somerset with her husband. He was born very delicate, but battled on gamely, then he became too weak to go on breathing, and we buried him in the churchyard at Theale, a lovely country place where primroses grow wild. They're carrying on with the shop, and they're still young, but it was a very heavy loss.

I think Forster, from the shades, must be truly grateful to you and N. F. for this royal treatment – every week of his life! (Prof. Haight once told me that he knew what George Eliot did on every <u>day</u> of her life, but he can't exactly have meant it.) It will be a splendid collection – as to Michael Case, I'm quite of your opinion – I don't think his supervisors should have encouraged him to go out and gather letters when he's quite unfitted to do so – he couldn't get access to a number of collections, including George Hardinge's, simply because he didn't know how to ask, and as you say, he can't really read Victorian hands at all; he wrote to Eileen Cassavetti asking her to type out her letters for him, but why should she? I wish him well, but I think he's undertaken something altogether too much for him and ought to look for another subject.

I hope you're coming on July 24th and hope to see you and hear more of your news – best wishes, Penelope

76 Clifton Hill
London, NW8
9 August [*c.*1982]

Dear Mary –

I was so glad to hear from you and to know that you'd been to
Aldborough, which I remember that you were looking forward to,
and that you're settled in for a while at Cambridge. I'd also like to
congratulate you again on <u>B-Jones Talking</u> which looked so nice
and had such excellent reviews, but meanwhile of course you're
approaching the end of E. M. Forster – because I assume that if vol: 1
is to be delivered in Sept. and if you're keeping up your usual amazing
rate of work and energy, you'll be well into vol: 2 by now.

My rate of work is very slow, as I'm partly down at Theale Post Office
helping with the bantams and looking after the garden – however at
least William Morris's unfinished bit of novel is going to appear* and
I've just signed a contract for Charlotte Mew's life – Charlotte who?
everyone says, in spite of which, I'm told that several other people are
writing biographies of her as well, and there are difficulties of all kinds
about papers &c – and she is of no interest in the U.S., a terrible
condemnation, but I shall go ahead as I've signed up.

I've just been down to see Mary Bennett at Rock Cottage, she
looked so well in the lovely old house surrounded by apple trees and
pastures with sheep, poultry, rabbits and piglets kept by her god-
daughter – Mary was going through the papers of her mother's family,
sitting among piles of letters in the apple-room, I don't know what
she'll do when it's time to bring in the apples.

I note that you're very busy at the moment and I am off to the
seaside just for a while, but are you up in London ever on Wednesdays,
and if so why don't you come to lunch one Wednesday (my day off
from teaching) – the only trouble is I'm up at St John's Wood, in 2
strange little rooms (but they suit me) at the top of a house – but there

---

* Published as *Novel on Blue Paper.*

<u>are</u> ways of getting there and the 159 bus, though not as frequent as
they ought to be, comes quite near. Any Wed: in September?

best wishes
Penelope

> *76 Clifton Hill*
> *London, NW8*
> 28 September [*c.*1982]

Dear Mary – Thankyou very much for your letter and Wed. October 6
would be lovely – I asked my stepmother Mary Knox (everyone is
called Mary, but why not? It's my middle name as well) to lunch that
day as well, she's the illustrator of <u>Mary Poppins</u> and the daughter of
E. H. Shepard – Collins publishes <u>Mary Poppins</u> and they're my
publishers as well, so we all have to tramp down St James's Place * at
one time or another. I wonder what you think of them?

I'm hoping you won't find it too difficult to get here – [map drawing]

It sounds a real expedition and it <u>is</u>, I'm afraid, but I'm just hoping it
will be a fine day and looking forward so much to seeing you, about one-
ish, but do come earlier if you can. I'm on the top floor, in the old attics –
the house is falling to bits and the banister is broken, but I'm sure you'll
manage – I'm very fond of the person the house belongs to and don't like
to say anything about the banister, because I'm sure she hasn't noticed –

Excuse all this and many congratulations on finishing volume 1 –
best wishes, Penelope

> *76 Clifton Hill*
> *London, NW8*
> 28 February 1983

Dear Mary,

I was so glad to hear from you on the subject of Michael Case –
because I had been feeling a trifle guilty after writing him rather a

---

* The then Collins building in Mayfair.

severe letter – I answered some of his questions off the cuff so to speak (as I hadn't got my books with me – but they were so elementary that I could do that), but it seems evident that he can't read Burne-Jones's writing, knows amazingly little about the period or the people concerned and hasn't (for instance) got Virginia Surtees' Rossetti catalogue, which illustrates all the pictures, after all – and of course I don't mind trying to help researchers, but I feel he's bringing the whole idea of research into disrepute! and would be far better off doing something else.

I'm delighted to hear that EMF is going so splendidly, but oh dear how quickly the year seems to have passed. Please give my love to Mary (Bennett) and John, and I do hope to see you before you go. I'm still at work on my little poetess, Charlotte Mew, and have grown very fond of her, as one does – best wishes, Penelope

76 Clifton Hill
London, NW8
28 May 1983

Dear Mary,

I do hope that during the crossing,* the captain's table, the competitions, the swimming-pool, and the indexing and proof revisions, you haven't forgotten your delightful farewell party at the University Women's Club, such good company and it was a great pleasure to me to see you again, just at the last moment, because, as everyone agreed, the year seemed to go nowhere &c. I'd have liked if possible to see so much more of you.

I can remember when the club was a place of dread where one went to meet aunts who had been at Girton before the first world war – no men ever crossed the threshold, there was a strange silence in the dining-room so that footsteps sounded loudly on the parquet, all voices were hushed as though in a college library, and indeed it <u>was</u> just like the women's college dining room Virginia Woolf describes in <u>A Room of One's Own</u>. Now it's a most genial and sympathetic place,

* Disliking flying, Mary Lago always took the QE2.

men can be heard talking quite loudly, and in fact it's appropriate to
the lovely building the University Women seem to have acquired
almost by accident. Now that is a change very much for the better,
which makes me think that the world isn't altogether going downhill!

I'm just struggling to do a (very short) introduction to a reprint of
Leo Myers' <u>The Near and the Far</u> trilogy* which I've always thought a
most wonderful novel, although Myers himself was a very strange
person indeed, I notice that Forster called him 'rather cold', so I
suppose Myers didn't 'connect' or didn't want to. He took an overdose
in the end and killed himself, like my poor little Charlotte Mew.

I can't see you ever getting down to Somerset. And I can't pretend
that much goes on there – only cows standing about the fields, which
were all marshland not so very long ago, so that some of the people in
the village remember rowing to school by boat, when the floods were
out. That, and the cider apple orchards all ruined by having such a wet
spring, and Wells cathedral. But perhaps you'll come there some day.
Meanwhile it will be wonderful to see your family, wonderful for
them too.

Thankyou again and very best wishes for Vol. 2.

love Penelope

76 Clifton Hill
London, NW8
26 July 1983

Dear Mary,

How nice to get your letter and, as always, the amount of work you
get through is an inspiration to me, or should be, and I can only hope
it'll last as I seem to get slower and slower. Well, it's not 'seem', I
suppose, it's just the course of nature.

I've just come back from Cumberland, the Kirkby Lonsdale district,
surely the loveliest part of this country when you get sun coming after
rain and clouds reflected in the lakes – we went over to see Ruskin's

---

* PMF's introduction to Myers' *The Root and the Flower* has been reprinted in two
subsequent editions by different publishers.

house at Brantwood, where I've never been – indeed I didn't know that you <u>could</u> go and see it – and not many people do, they're diverted by either Beatrix Potter's cottage, or Wordsworth's – and having got back on a very slow train to Euston I saw yesterday's <u>Observer</u> poster – which read E. M. FORSTER: MY FIRST LOVE AFFAIR. I'd no idea it was going to be serialised so soon, (and my friends up in Cumberland would never dream of buying a Sunday paper) – so now I'm going to ring up one or two people and see if they've kept it. I'm so glad EMF's letters have started out on so successful a career, but they are obviously going to be just as successful, so to speak, on the 'serious' end, for students and scholars and thoughtful readers – I suppose hard work is a justification in itself, but anyway, your hard work is certainly justified now.

Thankyou for the Charlotte Mew query – she does seem to attract biographers, but it seems to me that if you're going to talk to anyone who remembers her, or about her, you've <u>got</u> to come over here – meanwhile I'll send a note to this girl, as I've just about finished all I mean to do, but if I can help her at all, I will.

I'm glad you were able to go on indexing, in spite of fog and icebergs – but I think you're truly courageous to go by boat – those endless meals, and the threat of quizzes and fancy dress. Very best luck with what remains to be done and do come to Somerset – we won't go up the Tor, just walk about the lanes and eat goat's cheese.– love, Penelope

76 Clifton Hill, NW8
5 November 1983

Dear Mary – I'm sure you've seen the enclosed from the <u>Evening Standard</u>, but thought I'd send it anyway, as Michael Ratcliffe doesn't often review for the <u>Standard</u>, only, I think, books that he'd consider worthwhile, and what he says seems to me to fit in very well with what <u>you</u> say in your letter – I thought it, in fact, a very sensible review, in a paper that reaches a lot of readers.

I'm going to admit to you that when I first read Forster, as a 15 to 16 year old <u>very</u> many years ago, I knew <u>nothing</u> about his sex life and very little indeed about homosexuality – but I responded to the novels as I read them – and I'm prepared to swear that there were many thousands of other readers like me. The bias now has altered so much that the media <u>have</u> to concentrate on his sex life at the expense of everything else, but I wonder if in the end they'll prove to be right? As you say, the 'truly literary letters' are there to be looked forward to in vol 2 and perhaps the Observer will make a better choice of excerpt next time. – I sound like one of Forster's maiden aunts, I know, all the same I do think the papers underrate their public, but I suppose they or their circulation managers haven't the courage not to.

I deeply sympathise with you about the hot summer, though I know heat in Missouri and heat in St John's Wood are not the same thing, and then you were ill on top of it.

As to us, my daughter's new baby was born a month early, but he is thriving and is a great comfort, though I don't mean that he will take the place of the little boy that died, but he is a splendid individual in his own right. My son is still in Nicaragua, I think the only economic adviser who isn't a Cuban, and I must say I'll be glad to see him and his family back in Europe again.

I'm just getting Charlotte Mew ready for press – but oh, the biography industry – I wrote this book because I wanted to – but a friend who is interested in Barbara Pym and wanted to see all the diaries &c. in the Bodleian, found she had to queue, there were so many Pym biographers there already.

So glad you'll be here in 84 and best wishes for everything – Penelope

76 Clifton Hill, NW8
8 July 1984

My dear Mary,

I've only just heard from Mary Bennett about your illness and operation, and that (as she says and as I should expect) you are 'carrying on writing regardless'. She didn't give me any more detail than that, but my husband and 3 of my uncles died of cancer, which couldn't be treated then, as it is now, and I know that age-old courage, combined with brand-new treatment, is the only answer, I mean from the human side. Please do accept my very deepest wishes for your recovery.

I'm down here in Somerset where my daughter and her husband run the little store and sub-post-office. It's the moment for making redcurrant jelly and freezing the raspberries, and although we haven't got a large garden it takes up an amazing amount of time, particularly as the baby is just reaching the stage when he can crawl and walk insecurely, as long as he's holding on to something, but these somethings tend to give way, as he's not a good judge as to how stable they are – anyway there seems to be a series of disasters every day, but all are forgotten by next morning. <u>And</u> the dog is due to have puppies.*

We've had good biographies this year, the Ivy Compton Burnett** I thought was exceptional, the Edmund Gosse[†] perhaps rather too long which is always the trouble when you're writing about someone who isn't really interesting in themselves, but only the 'friend of friends'. And it must have been a great day when Margaret Drabble finished her Oxford Companion to Eng. Lit. I very much admire anyone who can classify and arrange and keep things neat and orderly. I haven't the gift, although I know that you have.

And Forster, I don't know how you feel about him. – whether he's been a faithful companion or whether you've got sick of the sound of his name – but perhaps you've already got your next subject in mind, they seem to appear and announce themselves, one doesn't have to look for them. – love and best wishes

Penelope

---

* PMF invented the puppies.
** By Hilary Spurling.
[†] By Ann Thwaite.

76 Clifton Hill, NW8
10 August [1984]

Dear Mary,

Thankyou so much for your letter – strangely enough I'd just
written to you at your Missouri address, having heard from Mary
Bennett about your operation – it was a 'get well' letter, and I'd no idea
that you would be able to go ahead with your plans so soon – but I'm
delighted that in fact you <u>have</u> – you've got the better of everything, as
I might have known, and arrived over here to finish off Forster – many
congratulations and don't bother to read my other letter when you
eventually get it.

You must have collected an immense amount of information about
Forster (that strange creature) which you haven't been able to use even
in your splendid vols. 1 and 2 and I'm glad you're thinking about
writing some articles – there's a curious impulse, once you've finished
a book, almost to turn your back on it, as though it must go out into
the world now and take its chance – don't you agree? – and then to
devote all your energies to the next one, but perhaps after all this is a
mistake sometimes.

I was interested to hear that there's yet another prospective editor
for the B/Jones letters, but I'm not at all surprised that the family, and
perhaps others, are getting annoyed with all these repeated
applications (Eileen Cassavetti, for example, made copies of all her
correspondence for Michael Case, but what was the use of it?) – and I
<u>certainly</u> think it would have been wiser to get in touch with the family
first. I haven't heard from Christopher Newell, but do give him my
address and number if you care to and think I could be of help. I hope
that (unlike Case) he is able to read Victorian handwriting, and has
<u>some</u> idea of the extent of the material. To select, one surely ought to
try to read <u>all</u> there is to select from – impossible in this case.

By the way, Norman Kelvin, though moving with the slowness of
mountains, has come good, as they say, at last, don't you think? and
I'm very glad, though I don't know how long we'll have to wait until
Morris vol 2 appears. I daresay I shan't live to see it.

I'm just off to Yorkshire and the Lake District partly to give a course, and partly on holiday. Please may I ring you up when I get back, and see if you can find time to meet?

very best wishes

Penelope

76 *Clifton Hill*, NW8

18 June [1985]

Dear Mary,

I met Jock Murray at a party (one of the parties) given for the Oxford Companion to English Literature and was talking about you – and he said 'Ah! Mary Lago!' somewhat wistfully – I daresay he regrets the EMF letters, but I suppose as it's a family firm he has, after all, to watch the money very carefully. Anyway, I think Collins brought it out pretty well, and I want to send you congratulations on Vol. 2 and its success. – I too wonder 'what you will do next' – writing a novel gives you an intoxicating <u>free</u> feeling, no paper, no references, no retrieval systems, you can think it all out, on top of the bus, but at the same time I find you miss the support you get as a biographer, or an editor, from knowing that the truth is there somewhere and all (if you can say 'all') you have to do is to find it. And there's a very real worry about the characters being recognised by friends and family who think it's <u>them.</u> Still, I think it's worth trying!

I've written to Valpy (my son) to tell him the sad news about St Edmund's – I've only met Nicholas Lash once or twice but he lived next to Valpy and family at Cambridge at the time of his marriage (he's born to be the victim of a scrupulous conscience and to do everything the most difficult and delicate way possible) – and he (N. Lash) is also the godfather of Valpy's second son. He'll be deeply interested – and now his third baby, it seems, will be born in the Baptist hospital in Managua and when I shall see him, or her, I don't know. Of course, I'm hopelessly prejudiced, but I don't think Reagan and his advisers have made any attempt at all to understand this very poor and struggling but still religious and well-meaning country, which has to make friends and borrow money where it can. But they are absolutely broke, the students are all called up and the 12-year olds have to break off school and pick the coffee crop, and what will become of everything I can't see. (My two elder grandsons are coming back to go to school in the Hague. But I'm sorry to say that they're reluctant to come, because in Managua they have a real machine-gun in the garden.)

I didn't know about the Burne-Jones/Margaret letters which I'm sure will be charming, but what thousands there must be still (like Lord Hardinge's) which I suppose will come on the market one day! I think if the collected correspondence is really to see the light it will need someone much larger, stronger and better informed than any who've appeared so far. And I wonder whether it will be worth it?

Many congratulations on the Distinguished Faculty Award – and on the generosity of your university to the Shelstone – and on having a new era of foot-comfort ahead of you. I note Manchester 10th October, but do hope to see you in London –

love Penelope

76 *Clifton Hill*, NW8
16 September 1986

Dear Mary,

How nice to hear from you, but how sad to think that your sabbatical is over and I haven't seen you again – and even more annoying for me that I missed you at St Edmund's, because my daughter-in-law and her 3 boys were taking a holiday there when my son went back to Nicaragua – a wonderful holiday because they were allowed to play on the empty tennis-court and in the empty games room – and I went to see them there, but, alas, after you'd gone. How wretched about the bronchitis, or was it perhaps something even worse than that, a virus which was 'about', as they say, last summer, flourishing in the damp, I expect, and which laid low a number of people. – And so I didn't see you, and never found out what you thought of the film of A Room with a View.

Thankyou so much for the cuttings – I'm a bit embarrassed by Robert E. Hosmer Jr who is writing a thesis (I think) on female British novelists (I think), although he's very kind in coming to our defence.

I have another one out now (another novel I mean) which will be published by Holt next year, if all goes well. What a relief when something gets finished, before you know you ought to start something else – a short but precious time.

Apart from the 2 new grandsons, and the novel, which we called <u>Innocence</u> in the end, I haven't much to report – my younger daughter has moved to a large Victorian house in Highgate – apparently the ghost of a little girl in blue appears on the staircase before the occupants leave the house (not when they come to it) – it's a nice friendly place with birds and squirrels in the garden.

Congratulations on the electronic typewriter – I can't get my poor electric one repaired, they tell me it's being phased out –

very best wishes –

Penelope

76 Clifton Hill, NW8

New Year's Day 1987

Dear Mary,

It was so nice to hear from you, even though it's vexatious to think about your illness (it must have been something worse than bronchitis) and the tiresome experiments at Manchester University which you could have done without. I also agree with you about St Edmund's – when I last went there to see my daughter-in-law and 3 grandsons, who were over for a holiday in vacation time, the place looked as beautiful as ever but there was a feeling of not knowing what to do next to make ends meet and, as you say, too many conferences will drive out faithful old customers – the kitchens were closed too, which was a nuisance.

<u>A Room with a View</u> had lots of success and was said by everyone to be 'charming' – and so it was – but in any case it's never seemed to me to be a serious book – the <u>Passage</u> is, and the film was ridiculous and Alec Guinness must have known he was ridiculous as Godbole. Ought we to mind? My children tell me that it's ridiculous to relate a film back to the original book and the 2 things ought to be artistic experiences. Meanwhile I'm sitting with a 2-year old grandchild, watching a video of <u>The Snowman</u>.

I never knew that E. P. Thompson* was, so to speak, of Wesleyan descent, but how much that explains! Morris, too, was brought up by Evangelicals and a Tractarian tutor. I've just been writing a series of introductions to the novels of Mrs Oliphant, which Virago are bringing out – I wonder what you think of <u>Salem Chapel</u>, which is largely about a minister who finds his life 'too devoid of imagination'? Though, as with Ruskin and Burne-Jones, the early limitations are surely what leads to the great expansion later on. I agree about Julia Atkins (there are really, so to speak, two of them, aren't there, one researching and the cousin writing the book) – their energy (or her energy) is amazing and there can't be much now they don't know about the Ionides.** I wasn't, alas, able to help them much about 'the ugly Luke matter', and Luke himself was not a reliable witness, and hardly wanted to be. – I feel myself that I've lost the energy and resilience which you need when you set off on a new biographical trail – I wish I still had it. – By the way, I heard from Norman Kelvin at Christmas – I hope Julia Atkins went to see <u>him</u>.

I do hope to see you this summer – someone's made me a friend of the Academy as an Xmas present – and we might meet there, as it's quite central. Best wishes for the New Year to you and your family – love Penelope

Holt are publishing <u>Innocence</u> in the U.S. some time this year – but I'm not sure when. –

> *76 Clifton Hill*, NW8
> 1 May 1987

Dear Mary,

I hope this will reach you before the 19th, and if not, well, it must just wait at 231 Arts and Science until you are back again.

---

* The radical historian, who had written on William Morris, and whose parents were missionaries in India, friends of Rabindranath Tagore, the poet, on whom Mary Lago was now working.
** The William Morris expert. The Ionides family were friends and patrons of Morris and Burne-Jones.

I'm so glad you're fixed up with a nice and convenient house in the Portobello Road (I can remember when the Portobello Rd. market was very different, and there were real 'finds', artists and actors looking for old costumes and old music scores and so on, but it's still quite fun, I think?) and I hope that in spite of the transport difficulties you'll be able to come up to St John's Wood. – Just one change on the underground at Bond St from Notting Hill Gate.

I didn't know about the K. Mansfield bibliography – but I very much admire bibliographers, and accurate editors like yourself. I hadn't known, until you told me, that E. P. Thompson's father was a minister, but to me that explains so much (as it does with Beaverbrook) one has to account both for the correspondence, or sympathy, and the reaction against. – I've been hearing from our great William Morris society member, Ray Watkinson, who is writing a definitive illustrated life of William Morris, (I think Ray's father was a minister too), and I've thought so much, as I'm sure you must have done, of this two-way pressure on several generations, including my own.

We've had a new biography of the 4 Macdonald sisters and a study of Jane Morris, and as well as Ray's William Morris there will be a life and works of Ford Madox Brown. – (I don't know how far you're interested in these people, as I imagine that when you go on to a new subject you have, to some extent, to put other ones behind you). But I would say that it's been a good Wm. Morris year, and as for myself, I'm glad that Charlotte Mew is going to be published in the U.S., the biography and the poems together.

I feel as you do about novels and film versions, but have tried very hard to see things differently: what about Verdi, hadn't he the right to make Othello into Otello? But I wasn't happy about A Room with a View – from being ordinary, respectable, timid pre-1st World War people they were transformed into 'carriage folk' – Helena had a different outfit in every shot – and footmen: But I suppose the audience expect it. I felt that the weakness of the book (George's father acting as a kind of nursemaid, as one of EMF's embarrassing 'wise' characters) was even worse in the film – and to me Day-Lewis was one of the best things in it – contrasting, I thought, most unfortunately with Helena, who has never had any training as an actress at all.

Hoping to see you, and very best wishes for your new project – love Penelope

76 Clifton Hill, NW8
10 February 1988

Dear Mary,

Thankyou so much for your letter, and this is just a note to say that I very much hope to see you while you're over here, and I think I can promise not to be in quite such a muddle. The trouble about being a really good administrator and organiser though, (as you clearly are, though you don't say anything about it) is that you are ferociously overworked as a committee member and in general as a chairwoman and arranger of all things, and the problem of there being only twenty-four hours in the day must weigh on you quite often. Still, you're coming to England (unfortunately just after the PEN conference at Cambridge, but perhaps the speakers won't be worth hearing anyway).

Alas! You're right, of course, about Mrs O.'s <u>Salem Chapel</u> and her novels in general, though they do have their moments, and I'm afraid Virago haven't succeeded, as they hoped, in making her part of the 19th C syllabus. Virago have now moved to Camden Town and have given up their nice premises in Covent Garden, but they can feel free and quite independent.

I'm expecting 2 more grandchildren (from my 2 daughters), and the U.S. edition of <u>Charlotte Mew</u> although Collins have lost (that's their story) the film of the illustrations, so I'm not sure how they're going to be reproduced. Still, difficulties are there to be overcome, as we used to be told.

I had a good time in Toronto at Olympian Writers' Week ('Olympian' referring to the Winter Olympics, <u>not</u> the writers –)

best wishes for all your undertakings –

love Penelope

27 *Bishop's Road*
Highgate
18 August 1988

My dear Mary,

I enjoyed your farewell lunch party so much, it was a real treat for a jaded old English writer like myself to hear about so many new projects, and your faith – this is what struck me most, but we <u>all</u> ought to have it – in the whole process of reading and writing, learning and teaching which has to underlie the immensely complex business of administering a university. That's one of the reasons why you cheer me up so much.

I'm here in my little green room – and it <u>is</u> small, as I told you, but it looks out on the garden and the trees and I love it – beginning to sort out the so-called papers which I'm supposed to be going to sell – but a high proportion of them seem to be yellowing newspaper-clippings and letters of the perhaps-we-could-meet-for-a-drink-at- 6.30 variety – I can't believe that anyone will much want them, or these tattered mss and tss, but I shall have to see what the expert says when he arrives.

Meanwhile – and this of course is truly the point of this letter – we all felt sad, left on the pavement when the taxi rolled off into the improbable sunshine, but confident that you would be back next year, having dealt with heaven knows how many boards and committees –

love and best wishes –

Penelope

[Christmas card]
[1988]

This is my little flat in Highgate, which <u>can</u> be reached, as a bookdealer from Pennsylvania* has just been here to take away all my papers and sell them to Austin, Texas, which gives me enough room to put my

---

* J. Howard Woolmer.

shoes – but I can fit in quite well here and am very happy looking out at the garden. I feel I'm getting like that irritating character in <u>What Katy Did</u> who was always lying about on the sofa with a tray on her lap, giving good advice.

The cuts continue here and my Physiology daughter has to wait until Feb: to know whether she can have a technical assistant or not – soon they'll be taking away the chairs and tables. I hope this isn't so with you, and meantime very best wishes for Christmas and 1989 –

love Penelope

27 Bishop's Road
Highgate
15 June 1991

Dear Mary,

How lovely to hear from you and a little at least about all the many things you're doing. I find I'm getting slower and slower – not the actual movements, but I find I've <u>stopped</u> doing or even thinking what I'm supposed to and am staring idly at the birds in the garden or (to-day) at the rain. I've been knitting a cardigan (which wasn't particularly nice in the first place) for <u>2 years</u> and the last grandchild will have grown out of it by the time it's done. The trouble is that I'm one of the Booker judges this year (about 150 novels and all must be read conscientiously, at least if you're a woman, for women are conscientious). But I should rather like to write another novel.

Ishiguro <u>yes</u>! I think his first one, <u>A Pale View of Hills</u>, was his very best – quite miraculous, and I've read it through many times. You couldn't get a better example of saying things by leaving them unsaid.

I didn't know anything about C. Herringham!* But I should love to hear.

---

* Christiana, Lady Herringham, popularised the use of tempera in the Edwardian period, copied the cave paintings near Hyderabad, and was therefore held by Mary Lago to have inspired the character of Mrs Moore in *A Passage to India*. She was instrumental in the establishment of the National Art Collections Fund.

I do hope I'll see you this year. I'm speaking in Cambridge on 27th September so there might be a chance then?

love Penelope

27 Bishop's Road
Highgate
19 January [1994]

Dear Mary,

I was so very glad to get your letter, because Mary Bennett (who I saw at the rather oddly-titled lecture, The Strange Neglect of H. A. L. Fisher) was not sure quite how you were. But we might have guessed you were working away, and would soon have a new book out. The new retirement home sounds lovely. Very few of them are quite bearable over here, perhaps because there isn't enough space, and the architects haven't realised that just because people are getting older they don't necessarily want to sit about doing nothing, looking at a few rosebushes.

Your memories! I should love to have met Leonard Elmshirst.* As to Dartington, it hasn't changed much, I'm sure, since you were there – the gardens are marvellously kept up, with those great steps of turf – but they plan all kinds of extensions which, as you can imagine, has caused bitter disputes in the committee. All the meals, even the toast, come up in a van whose arrival is eagerly awaited by the course members – literary chats and discussions make them very hungry.

I could write another novel – or so I tell myself – if I stopped reviewing, but that would leave rather a gap, as it's better paid than it used to be.

All more or less well here and the New Baby, Alfie, walking stoutly about at an amazing speed. I was so very sorry to hear about your husband, but realise you are treating this with your usual courage and refusal to be downed by anything and anybody, and with the

---

* Philanthropist, creator of Dartington Hall, sometime school, art college and arts centre near Totnes, Devon.

latest remedies. It's marvellous that he has kept stable for two years.
My brother has Parkinsons, and they're trying to keep <u>him</u> stable,
I suppose in much the same way – I do hope to see you, if only for a
moment in July – love Penelope

27 Bishop's Road
Highgate
9 July [1994]

My dear Mary,

Thankyou so much for asking me to lunch yesterday – well do I
know that your time is precious, but I should have been deeply
disappointed if I'd missed you again, and among many other things I
should have gone on not knowing who Christiana H. was, and the
lunch was delicious, truly, I did enjoy it.

I forgot to tell you that we had our AGM of the Wm. Morris society
at Fulham library this year and so I was asked to speak on B-Jones and
the Grange* – of which of course nothing exists except the bell-pull
which Kipling took away with him to Batemans when the house was
pulled down because it had made him so happy to ring it when he was
a child – I felt I was talking about 'a house of air' even though there's a
block of council flats named after Burne-Jones – but it did remind me
of you, and all the work you did on Rooke's diaries.

I honestly don't believe I've got the energy and perseverance to do a
biography now. I did one, you know, of the poet Charlotte Mew, and I
never did manage to find the crucial letters or information, although
I'm sure they exist; Professor Friedmann said to me – 'if there's no
proof that a letter's been burned, <u>it must exist somewhere</u>', but I <u>didn't</u>
manage to find them, and the book fell very far short of what I'd hoped,
although I did know a good deal more about her than when I'd started.

I'll send you a copy of my poor British Museum mystery when it
comes out in paperback, although it's scarcely worth reading, and

---

* The house in Fulham where Edward Burne-Jones lived.

meantime very best wishes for all your three books in hand and once again it was such a treat to see you –

love

Penelope

27 *Bishop's Road*

Highgate

15 December 1994

Dear Mary,

This is my Christmas letter, which I am writing in rather a decrepit state as my heart seems to be beating too fast and I can't get my cough to clear up, rather like La Traviata. – But I should consider, and do consider, the courageous practical way you've got the better of something much more serious.

I am so glad that the way is being cleared for Thompson. But Mary, I'm sure you are wrong about Kipling and <u>Kim</u>. Of course it supports the Raj, but to me it has an immense understanding, which reduces poor Forster to a faint pipsqueak. I discussed it with Carrington and Angus Wilson and both came to agree that the role of the Lama was the role of Burne-Jones himself, the unworldly artist, in Kipling's life, particularly at the point where Kim has to choose between the unreal and the real. However, I wish I could come to your seminars, and support the battle against theory – almost always imposed afterwards – like the complaints I get from a Taiwanese scholar who is writing something or other about me and says I don't fit into the accepted feminist structure, which was where she had put me.

Dear Mary, very best Christmas wishes and love from Penelope

27 *Bishop's Road*

Highgate

23 March 1995

Dear Mary,

Thankyou so very much for sending me your news. – And yet in one way your letters, which I enjoy getting so much, are deceptive because it's only when I've read them, and thought them over, that I realise 1. how hard you've been working and 2. – please don't mind my saying this – how much courage you've needed, even if your family is on call to help you.

You did tell me something about your husband and the '3 good years', and it reminded me of my brother, who died last summer – he had Parkinson's, and the doctor said he could give him something that would work, but not for ever – so that at the end there was a kind of relief. He had come out of a Japanese P.O.W. camp to become a foreign correspondent all over the Far and Middle East, but although he married and had a son and a daughter he was never quite well again.

I feel deeply ashamed that (having looked out so long for your Macmillan's Forster book) I missed it when it came out. Many congratulations on your Christiana for I know she was close to your heart, perhaps because she must have been so difficult to do. I didn't even know about Mary's book on The Ilberts in India! (My own grandmother's family were served (as we used to say) in India, but then so many families could say this.) However, this too is a matter of looking for a book until I find it. I do hope to see you in Oxford although my son and his family will have left Oxford (he's at St Anthony's) for Spain by July.

Michael Holroyd (I dare say you know this!) has had a lot of trouble with his leg (middle age comes to us all!) and only just seems to have got better, so that he was able to appear and preside at Coutts Bank award to the Best British Writer (lavish food and drink and new closed circuit T.V. practically invisible because of overshadowing palms and houseplants) – prize awarded to Harold Pinter – and the PEN Writers' Day, which I felt too feeble to attend, but I don't approve of this feebleness and intend to be there next year.

love and all my best wishes – Penelope

I ought to say that I've been ill with what the doctors say is asthma, but they say everything is asthma, since last September – much too long really.

As I'm afraid happens only too often, I've left out the main point of this letter – which is that I hope to see you this summer – at <u>Alma Place</u>, which I'm sure you mean, not Thursley.

27 Bishop's Road
Highgate
24 June 1995

Dear Mary, –

Just to thank you for writing, and in particular for telling me about your illness and (thank heavens) recovery, as I daresay you're tired of letting everyone know about it and perhaps don't even much want to think about it, and yet you've taken the trouble to tell me and I do appreciate it. To me (but evidently not to you) these were terrifying experiences, perhaps the worst of all being coming round to find yourself on the floor, but how right you were to make the decision to move to Lenoir, it seems to have proved an unqualified blessing in so many ways.

I didn't know Christiana Herringham had taken twenty-five years – I suppose you'll almost miss her, or miss being on the old trail, but it will be a glorious moment when she's between covers. I like your remark 'the NACF* now remembers her' – would they ever have done if you hadn't set to work?

I have a novel <u>of sorts</u> out in September, <u>The Blue Flower</u>, but it's not really fiction as it's based on the early life of Novalis, when he was still Fritz von Hardenburg and not a famous poet at all. No-one outside the universities seems to have heard of him over here, poor Fritz, and I don't expect much sale for this book, but I wanted to write it and don't regret it. My German wasn't really up to it, though.

In Oxford or in Cambridge I'm determined to see you this summer –

love Penelope

* The National Art Collection Fund.

27 Bishop's Road
Highgate
7 December [1995]

Dear Mary,

Although I don't think the Post Office has produced at all a nice design this year, at least it will bring you my best wishes. I'm here at Highgate looking out at the snow and the children's snowman (which for all they can do never looks in the least like snowmen in pictures) and thinking back over the year and the old friends who (as one old friend has just written to me) 'have decided to go on their journey without me'. This letter isn't supposed to be melancholy though! My book The Blue Flower didn't do too badly and was named by several people as their book of the year, and although I knew it was rather an odd thing to write about, the publishers took trouble and made it look nice. – And Tina, my elder daughter, managed to sell their picturesque but damp cottage and they're so happy in their new house, miles from anywhere in the teeth of the wind on the north Cornish coast, but with enough room at last and plenty of cupboards, which I'm inclined to think are the great secret of home life. I'm more or less all right but do everything so slowly, from book reviewing to peeling the potatoes, that you wouldn't believe it.

I've just left room to say how much I hope that all goes well and to wish you a Happy Christmas and New Year – do you think we shall meet in 1996? – love Penelope

27 Bishop's Road
Highgate
15 July [1996]

Dear Mary,

What a lot of good news in your letter – you're feeling much better than last summer, tests satisfactory, Christiana out and reviewed in the places that matter. I'm so very glad about all these things.

As to the casket, I lost heart when they let the wonderful Velasquez dwarf go – I think to Washington – without a struggle. But I think, as a matter of fact, the casket, after a lot of havering and muddling, is perhaps going to stay here.

The Heywood Hill award, although I'm very grateful for it, was really fairy gold, because I'd never heard of it, nor I think had anyone much else, as it was only started last year – still, you mustn't think I'm complaining, and we had a beautiful day at Chatsworth – and it's very good of you to congratulate me – we had both a silver and a brass band, by the way, and the Mayors of Bakewell and Chesterfield, with their mayoral chains.

I should so much like to see you, and wonder (as I'm off quite soon to Italy and Cornwall with my elder daughter and her family) whether I could come to Cambridge on one of the days in the week beginning August 19th. Any day and time in the day that week, as they all seem more or less free? I know of course you have endless things to do in Cambridge, but could you send me a p.c. if anything strikes you?

love and best wishes
Penelope

27 Bishop's Road
Highgate
19 November [1996]

Dear Mary,

This is my Christmas letter and you must forgive me if it's too early. We're just having our first snow, and I'm sitting here watching it through the windows. My heart is still not going at the right pace so I thought I'd see what a day's absolute laziness (which you have possibly never had) would do for it. But the laziness makes me feel guilty for that is how I was brought up.

As far as the election goes, Mary, you've had your wish, and I can only hope your trust in Clinton is going to be justified. He seems to me a typical shiny-bright Southern politician, brought up to corruption and taking it for granted as the accepted way to get to the top, rather like Yeltsin, (who however never really pretended to have the capacity to run a huge country like Russia).

However, this is meant to be a Christmas letter, so let me think instead about your coming to Oxford next summer, something really to look forward to. Highgate is too far, but if you let me know when you have time I could come down to Oxford and perhaps you'll let me take you out to lunch this time.

The universities here are on strike to-day – just for one day, everyone from the doormen to the Principals – they were offered one and a half per-cent pay rise, which has to be ridiculous. Maria tells me that they have no choice – her own department in London University has had a lick of paint, but it is still falling to pieces, and although she's fortunate in having a high-earning, mild-tempered husband, there are a lot of academics who don't. And she agrees with you about the Associate.

Very best wishes to you for your visit to the doctor and I am so glad your husband still recognises you when you come – that means everything. Much love and Christmas wishes –

Penelope

P.S. Can hardly believe what you tell me about S.F. library. And here in London (though not in the country) they're declaring war on the public libraries – we've had to fight to keep them open 3 days a week.

P.P.S. So you have to take on the Bengalis and the Wesleyans. But I know it won't worry you.

27 Bishop's Road
Highgate
9 May [1997]

Dear Mary,

I was very glad to get your letter, and needless to say, deeply distressed at your news. To watch someone you love change from what they were seems almost more than one can bear, and the only consolation is that they themselves don't seem aware of the change. All my thoughts and prayers at this hard time, all the harder perhaps because it's spring. 'And you were a liar, you blue March day' as Hopkins says.

I ought never to have tried to argue with you about the American South, because it's only too clear I don't know enough or perhaps anything, about it. I shall just have to trust Clinton for your sake.

Many congratulations, Mary, on your award for scholarly excellence – surely the right award <u>exactly</u> and I know you will be pleased it was for Christiana Herringham, into which you put such hard and expert research. I remember thinking – what a difficult subject, however is she going to set about it?

Thankyou for the NY Book Review cover – I'm just starting with Houghton Mifflin, where I have a nice editor who used to be at Addison Wesley, and published the U.S. edition of <u>Charlotte Mew and her Friends</u> – I was particularly pleased when he told me that he and his wife had called their cat 'Charlotte Mew'. Truly, it's a good name for a cat.

I do so hope to see you this summer, perhaps at Oxford (where my son is still lecturing at St Anthony's but researching and advising all over the world). I'm so very glad to think that your daughter is with you at this time. And I'm sure she'll make you buy something absolutely new to wear (even though you've got something that will do perfectly well already) for the Awards Dinner at the end of May. – love Penelope

27 Bishop's Road
Highgate
22 January [1999]

Dear Mary,

It certainly <u>isn't</u> too late to wish each other happy New Year, and I feel so much cheered by your letter. I realised that you were feeling seriously ill last summer, nothing else would have made you go home early, and it's wonderful to hear that you have have had such encouraging results from the two new drugs. My word, Mary, you don't let anything beat you.

It's a very satisfactory feeling to be nearly at the end of one book – just giving it a quick going over – and with another one in mind, or rather more than that. E.M. Forster's broadcasts are a brilliant idea. Let's hope the BBC have them all safe – last time I asked them for a script (in connection with The Poetry Bookshop) it was mysteriously missing from the files. But they will have Forster's safe I am sure.

It's Burne-Jones's centenary year, as I don't need to tell you, and they had a big exhibition, not in London, but in Birmingham – the refreshments were horrible, they served <u>mead</u> – but it wasn't my idea of mead – and wasted much time in municipal speeches – <u>five</u> people found it necessary to speak, and then at last we were allowed to see the pictures – and the jewellery designs, and the stained glass cartoons, for it was really a superb exhibition, but unfortunately we had to leave to catch the last train.

I hope you haven't moved house, Mary, as I'm sending this to the address you gave me –

love and best wishes – Penelope

27 Bishop's Road
Highgate
25 May 1999

Dear Mary,

Thankyou so much for your letter and the cutting from the NY Times – alas! (however) I haven't been writing another book, it's just that Houghton Mifflin have decided to reprint them all, including the very old ones, and <u>Human Voices</u> <u>is</u> a very old one. However, I've no cause for complaint, and they have been very enthusiastic and – don't forget – took me to tea at the Ritz.

I'm not surprised at your story about the BBC and the scripts – everything was always getting lost or thrown away and it's worse now they're computerised, as their computers break down at frequent intervals – and then they've got this mania for moving everyone to White City . . .

I'm so very, very glad that the miracle drugs are still working for you, Mary. Just like you to worry because they're too expensive to be prescribed over here! And your book's finished! – you say (quite casually) you're going to leave it with the University Press when you go.

Yes, Maggie Drabble is a wonderful lecturer, I think that training in the theatre gave her just that edge – perhaps all lecturers ought to start on the stage. And then she always <u>looks</u> so nice. I don't mean that she isn't academic as well! Michael, as I expect you know, has written a book about his own family and relations, and his grandparents, who brought him up. I think it's out this summer. – Mary Bennett I haven't seen for a long time, but she is like no-one else, you are quite right.

My eldest grandson is getting married this August – to the daughter of a long-distance truck driver in Cordoba. I don't quite know what they're going to live on. But he is such a dear!

with love, Penelope

27 Bishop's Road
Highgate
23 February 2000

Dear Mary,

Thankyou so much for your wonderful letter, full of doing and being and going places in spite of all the difficulties, in fact you don't recognise difficulties, it seems to me. Flying! Well, I never thought I'd hear of you doing that. It must be one of the most sincere compliments Bach has ever received, because I know you hate it – no, I won't say that, this may be the beginning of a new era.

The New Yorker piece was by Joan Acocella who is really their dance correspondent, she came over to do an interview but was much less intimidating than Arthur Lubow, who also came to interview, but for the New York Times. He took down things in shorthand (but surely nobody does shorthand now?), not looking at all at what he was writing, but watching me intensely with penetrating brown eyes. I suppose it is just his professional manner. He told me he found me rather a difficult job but the truth was I couldn't think of very much to say.

What a splendid occasion the <u>Biographical Passages</u> must have been –
they really celebrated you in style, Mary – life does have its rewards,
though you've certainly earned yours.

We are all surviving – I didn't get to Cordoba for my grandson's
wedding which I think was quite a lively party as his friends cut off his
pony tail and auctioned it by the inch in aid of some charity. But I
shouldn't have been of much use as I am rather lame from arthritis – I
find this very vexatious but am ashamed to complain, as you don't –

love and all best wishes, Penelope

J. Howard Woolmer*

25 *Almeric Road*
London, sw11
28 September 1978

Dear Mr Woolmer,

I saw your advertisement in the Times Literary Supplement today and am writing to you at once although I'm afraid you may be disappointed with this letter because I haven't any Poetry Bookshop items to offer. But I am keenly interested, because I can remember both the shop (the second one) and the Monros, and I am collecting material at the moment for a book about the Poetry Bookshop and its own particular poets – Anna Wickham, Charlotte Mew and F. S. Flint.

I can't tell whether you're perhaps a private collector or perhaps a bookseller, but in either case I should so very much like to know details of your collection of rhyme sheets. The collection in the British Museum here is 'closed' – no-one can take photo-copies of it – and I have lost all the sheets that were pinned up on my nursery walls (among them the John Nash <u>Ducks on a Pond</u> and Charles Winzer <u>Leisure</u>) all lost in various disasters. It would mean a lot to me to hear from another enthusiast –

Yours sincerely,
Penelope Fitzgerald
(Mrs)

---

* Bibliographer of the Hogarth and Samurai presses, he and PMF came together through a shared interest in the publications and personalities of Harold Monro's Poetry Bookshop in Bloomsbury. He also brokered the sale of her papers to the University of Texas.

25 Almeric Road, sw11
29 November 1978

Dear Mr Woolmer,

Thankyou for your letter of the 21st – It's a treat for me to hear from anyone who knows so much, and above all in an orderly way, about the Poetry Bookshop.

Joy Grant (now Vines, with 3 children), is a friend of mine and I very much admire her work, but the situation has changed a good deal since Alida's death – and most of the PB papers, apart from those which went to America or the British Library, are, as I'm sure you know, with Mrs Luttrell, who is a delightful old lady and, as she says, a Bohemian of the old school, but can't decide what to do and at the moment won't let anyone see anything.

The rhymesheets I still find very confusing, I agree there seem to be 12 in the first series ending I think with Ralph Hodgson's <u>The Birdcatcher,</u> but I don't know if this was taken over with the Flying Fame series. Then there's the New Broadside series which contains some of the finest, for instance no. 14 Robert Graves' Finland, then The Rhyme Sheets with Monro's <u>Overheard on a Salt Marsh</u> as no. 4, but the address on these is still 35 Devonshire St., then the 1916 Blake set (the Curwen Press still have one copy of one of these) – then Series 2. Here are some more titles (in case you don't have them) from Series 2:

6. <u>Beautiful Meals</u> (written and decorated by T. Sturge Moore)
7. <u>The Vulgar Little Lady</u> (Jane and Ann Taylor, decorated R. Marshall)
11. <u>Farmer Giles</u> (W. de la Mare, decorated Philip Hargren)
18. <u>Leisure</u> (W.H. Davies, decorated John Nash)
23. <u>The White Window</u> (James Stephens, decorated Philip Hargren)

I think there were several Nursery Sheets: no. 2 was by Eleanor Farjeon, decorated by Terence Prentis. – And then there are others which have no series numbers at all.

If only I could return to childhood just for a day and get all my rhymesheets back! I've met numbers of people who feel this.

Now I'm going to ask you one more thing – if by any chance as a bookdealer you have any of the rhyme sheets on offer, particularly New Broadsides 15 (Herrick), Rhymesheets Series 2 no. 18 (W. H. Davies), or 7 (Jane and Ann Taylor), or the unnumbered <u>They Say</u> (decorated by Mary Berridge) – would you be kind enough to let me know? Of course, I don't know whether I should be able to afford to buy them, but writers are sometimes lucky! – Yours sincerely,

    Penelope Fitzgerald

25 Almeric Road
London, sw11
6 January 1979

Dear Mr Woolmer,

I want to thank you so very much for your kind present, the <u>On A Certain Lady At Court</u>. You don't know what a lot it means to me to have a Broadsheet again, (or rather I should say you're one of the few people who <u>do</u> know), and I'm very grateful.

I'm puzzled about series 2 and 3 – the titles I mentioned to you are from the series 2 examples in the British Library. The trouble is that the copyright owners won't allow them to be duplicated – but they are certainly issued as Rhyme Sheet (not Broadsheet) Series no. 2.

I've been talking to Bob Pocock who, when he was a policeman on the beat (1928–9) used to shine his torch into the window of the (second) bookshop and learn the poems off by heart. He is a bit of a character, but has a photographic memory. He gave me the following list of the sheets which were then in the window:

On Drinking	Abraham Cowley
So We'll Go No More A Roving	Byron
The Butterfly	Wordsworth
The Animals	Whitman
There is a Lady	?
Winter the Huntsman	Osbert Sitwell
Arabia	Walter de la Mare
Leisure	W. H. Davies

The Dromedary	? Campbell
The Tired Man	Anna Wickham
Journey's End	Humbert Wolfe
Heard (he means Overheard) on a salt marsh	Harold Monro
O Blackbird, What a Boy You Are	?
With Love Among the Haycocks	?
Cargoes	Masefield

He can still repeat all these by heart. One or two of these I don't know at all. And I'm still puzzled about the salt-marsh with the Winzer decorations. I believe you are right and it is no. 4 of the first rhyme sheet series.

I enclose a copy of a novel I had out this last autumn, I thought it might amuse you as it's about a (very small) bookshop,

Yours sincerely,

Penelope Fitzgerald

25 Almeric Road
London, sw11
18 February 1980

Dear Mr Woolmer –

Thankyou so much for your letter, and I'm glad your house is going along so well. It's very good of you to say I might come and stay overnight, but I feel that would be a lot of trouble and I am sure I can get to Revere, either on the bus or perhaps by car as my daughter and son-in-law hope they can rent one so we can get about a bit – I'm determined to get there anyway and will ring up if I may when we get to NY on March 29th. We're supposed to be at the Tudor Hotel, but I daresay they'll put us somewhere else, as we're all-in tourists –

Yours sincerely,

Penelope Fitzgerald

26 February [1980]

In continuation of my last – I'm sorry but my daughter tells me that we get to NY on the 4 April, not the 29 March, but, in any case, I do hope to see you –

Penelope Fitzgerald

Tudor Hotel
E.42. St.
April 1980

Dear Howard,

Thankyou so very much for your kindness and hospitality yesterday – apart from anything else it's wonderful to find someone who cares about the same kind of material as you do yourself, and I felt really happy at seeing your collection – in fact I was thinking about it while I walked back from the bus station and scarcely noticed the distance from W.41 to E.42.

It was also very good of you to give me these Poetry Bookshop items. When I got back here I read them – perhaps Ralph Hodgson only wrote a very little good poetry, but he certainly caused happiness in others – it's <u>something</u> to be called 'pleasant to know' by T. S. Eliot. – I have a few notes here by the way, and I see F. S. Flint's 2nd book <u>Cadences</u> was published by PB in paper covers with a wood-cut of a swan passing under a bridge, hand-coloured so that every copy is different. However I'll send you a Xerox of my list and any addresses which might be of use when I get home.

Don't forget to let us know if you are in London and have any time to spare, and meanwhile very best of luck with the house, the barn, and the planting, you've taken on such a lot between you but it must be worth it as it's such a beautiful place –

Best wishes

Penelope

The Post Office Stores
Theale, nr. Wedmore
Somerset
7 October 1981

Dear Howard,

Thankyou so much for your letter and rhyme sheet list. I was very glad to hear from you, although I don't quite understand what is happening to letters from the U.S. – they seem to take a very long time and to be arriving here on foot, so to speak, although we haven't heard anything about an American postal strike, only in Canada. And that's why I've been so slow in replying – also (and I know you'll sympathise with this) we have been moving from London to the depths of the country, and so many things seem to have been lost or mislaid. I do mean the depths – my daughter and son-in-law have decided to give up teaching for a while and run a very small post-office and village store, the kind that used to have a cracker-barrel, (and in fact we do have sacks of potatoes and firewood, which act as cracker-barrels) – the locals come in for their morning paper, leaving all their cows outside in the road, and they peer through the window. I have to come up to London during the week, but try to give a hand at the week-ends, and get things straight at the same time. So I understand very well how you feel about getting your office off the front porch, though I remember you always seemed to be able to find everything you wanted, which I can't.

My PB collection is at a standstill at the moment, and I've come to the conclusion that they're the most difficult things on earth to collect – I know that they're ephemeral, and were meant to be, but surely more people must have kept them? (Why didn't I keep mine from the nursery?) And I can't get anyone to see the beauty and interest of them – over here the mania is all for Stevie Smith, whose life is being done by 2 hard-working biographers from Mississippi and Hofstra Univ. respectively, Jack Barbera and William McBrien. Now I was very fond of Stevie, yet I truly think Anna Wickham was a more interesting poet. I have been seeing quite a lot of her elder son, who is retired now, and lives in Hampstead, having been a soft-shoe dancer and civil servant – and he has documents of all kinds but no broadsheets – and he can't help me with the vexed question of the numbering!

very best wishes – Penelope

76 Clifton Hill, NW8
22 September [1982]

Dear Howard,

This is to thank you so very much for the beautiful William Morris paper – all the finest and best-loved small-repeat designs, beginning with honeysuckle – they <u>say</u> to wrap things up in, but they seem much too good for that – one might paper the walls of a dolls-house, perhaps – true, all my descendants are grandsons not grand-daughters, but two of them do have dolls-houses.

I have an old friend who is writing the book to end books about Morris – so perhaps I'll take them down to Brighton to show them to him.

I rang up Joy Grant (Vines) just to see whether there were any 'ghosts' among the bits and pieces which Alida gave her when she (Joy) went to interview her, but there weren't, only unsold copies of Harold M.'s poems. – Joy sold the letters connected with her book, (including one from T. S. Eliot and one from David Garnett) to Rota's* for £200, which I suppose was not bad, as things go – the sale of letters is a strange thing, though, a very different matter, it seems to me, from books. –

Best wishes to you and Bob –
Penelope

76 Clifton Hill, NW8
9 March 1983

Dear Howard,

Thankyou so much for your letter, it was nice to hear from you, and first of all may I congratulate you on finishing the Malcolm Lowry

---

* Bertram Rota, antiquarian bookseller and literary manuscript dealer.

bibliography – in the end I think the bibliography is the most useful
thing you can do for any author, and everyone who is interested in
Lowry in the years to come will be grateful to you, and I hope that
they'll acknowledge your work.

I'm also very glad to have your complete list of the Poetry Broadsheet
titles (incidentally I see that no. 1 O what shall the man, which I didn't
recognise at all, is quoted by Sylvia Townsend Warner in the Collected
Letters (out last year) as

Oh, what shall the man full of sun do
Whose heart is as cold as stone
When the black owl looks in through the window,
And he on his deathbed alone?

This is p. 136 of her letters and she says it's her favourite! I should
have thought it was rather a depressing opening to a popular series,
but it's just like Harold Monro.)

It's interesting to see that he issued his Overheard on a Saltmarsh
twice – I think that must have been because Charles Winzer's
decoration for the first one was so unsatisfactory.

From a literary point of view there is a lot more interest in these
writers – Anna Wickham's autobiography and a selection of her poetry
are being published over here by Virago, I'm half-way through a life of
Charlotte Mew for Collins and hope to do something about that very
interesting writer F. S. Flint for his centenary in 1985, but as for
collecting, I'm meeting total failure. I consulted the Ephemera Society
and made enquiries at the recent McKnight Kauffer exhibition and
from various presses connected with Lovat Fraser, but none of them
could produce any broadsheets. It's most vexatious that one's not
allowed to reproduce the examples in the British Library, to give
people some idea of what the series was actually like.

Now I've hardly any room left to say how much I hope that you've
finished your house and garden and that it's exactly how you both
wanted it, and that all the beans, corn, squashes, vines and zucchini are
growing and flourishing. Here it's spring, but still rather cold.

Very best wishes for your PB bibliography and for all [incomplete]

76 Clifton Hill
London, NW8
U.K.
23 October 1983

Dear Howard,

Thankyou so very much for writing and for sending the two <u>Flying</u> <u>Fame</u> sheets with the Claud Lovat Fraser head and tail pieces, I love the blue dog – they are sentimental, but people were allowed to be in those days – I don't know whether it did any harm or not. The only thing I'm going to be able to send you in return is my biography of Charlotte Mew, which is going to press now and will be ready I suppose in the usual 8 or 9 months – I couldn't do the book I wanted on the Bookshop because all the publishers (though you wouldn't guess it from their appearance) say they are so poor they can scarcely carry on for another week, and in any case couldn't reproduce the broadsheets and chapbook covers in colour, which was what I wanted: still Charlotte Mew was one of the Bookshop poets and in fact helped Alida Monro to colour the first seven sheets. Meanwhile I'm still trying to get up some interest in my favourite, Frank Stuart Flint, whose centenary comes up next year, and who certainly turned himself into a poet and translator the hard way, since he started as the soap-boy in an East End barbers.

I'm trying to get them to produce my Charlotte Mew <u>properly</u>, that is, as much as possible like a chapbook, with printers' flowers and the right typeface, but will they?

I very much envy you the trip to California – I've got a note that there are 239 correspondents, many of them enraged poets I dare say. I'd also so much have liked to see the Maurice Browne/Harold Monro letters at Ann Arbor, (they couldn't send me photocopies as they said the material was too personal) and then I think the Samurai Press material is there.

It would be a real blessing if you would do a book on the period, with all your knowledge of it, and the bibliography. Otherwise one day people will wake up and try to find out about it and won't be able to.

Your house and garden must be lovely by now, and producing pumpkins I suppose, at this time of year,

best wishes,

Penelope Fitzgerald

76 Clifton Hill, NW8
1 June 1984

Dear Howard,

I want to thank you very much for the checklist of the Hogarth
Press – I'm ashamed I didn't know it before, but in any case it's very
nice to have it now. They did more publishing, and less hand-printing,
than I'd realised – and I'm always interested in the phrase 'having
taught themselves the rudiments of printing' – which is so much easier
said than done, in my experience – I'm quite sure that Leonard must
have done the inking and cleaning up and anything that needed
accuracy. I'm not accurate myself – that's why I admire your kind of
work so much.

Anna Wickham is out now under the title <u>The Work of Anna
Wickham, Free Woman and Poet</u> – by the way I expect you know Anna
Wickham's son James, who has worked like a beaver getting this
edition out, because he was the person who found Malcolm Lowry in
a distressed condition in a Bloomsbury bed-sitter and took him back
to their house in Parliament Hill, Hampstead where Anna provided
meals at all hours for writers and poets. (I don't think there's anyone
who'd do that now.) But I remember that you've sold your Malcolm
Lowry collection now, so all that's a thing of the past. Meanwhile, best
wishes for the future – Penelope

76 Clifton Hill, NW8
6 January 1985

Dear Howard,

Thankyou so much for the <u>Warning to Strayabouts</u>, which, apart
from anything else, brings the whole Eleanor Farjeon atmosphere back
to me again – (her <u>Nursery in the Nineties</u> was reprinted recently in
paperback) – they were all such an impressive family – it was enough
in the Hampstead of those days to 'know the Farjeons' – but she was
splendid, and it's no easy thing to write for children as she did.

About your very kind offer of rhyme-sheets at cost – unhappily I've
had to give up collecting anything at the moment, as although what I
write doesn't do too badly, I seem to have rather a lot of commitments.

But all the same if you ever have any duplicates of the early numbers of Series 1 (I know that this isn't at all likely) do please let me know as I would so much love to see them again.

Thankyou so much for your kind words about <u>At Freddie's</u>, and please, I hope you won't be so busy that you give up your Bookshop book altogether. There really is something <u>needed</u> there, while on the other hand there's almost too much about Bloomsbury and even about T. S. Eliot., if one is allowed to say so.

I'm glad you had such a mild winter – white with snow here in London –

Very best wishes for 1985

Penelope

Theale Post Office Stores
Wedmore, Somerset
11 May [1985]

I'm down here at my daughter's village shop and do hope you will have better weather in Cornwall than we've got here and that you and Bob will have a very successful trip. – Some PB rhyme sheets were advertised in the <u>Times</u>, but only odd numbers of Series 2, no Series 1, so I didn't do anything about them – perhaps I was wrong –

best wishes, Penelope

76 Clifton Hill, NW8
14 August 1985

Dear Howard,

Congratulations on finishing the Samurai Press* and many thanks for your PB rhyme sheet section. You don't know what a pleasure it is to me to see them listed properly and professionally, much more

---

* A bibliography of the Samurai Press, a poetry book publisher founded in 1906, with connections to Harold Monro and the Poetry Bookshop in Bloomsbury.

professionally than the Monros ever did it. I don't know how one trains to be a bibliographer, but it must need a certain temperament, I only wish I had it.

Just one or two things –

p.2 para.5 I'm sorry that I called Allingham's <u>A Memory</u> Ducks on a Pond – it's the same, of course, and I suppose the others aren't PB, although they were certainly bought there. I notice that in the diagram Alida gives in her letters to Harold of the new PB (March 1927) there's a space for 'rhyme sheet duplication and special orders', which may account for why some were issued without series numbers. –

<u>Series 1 no 3</u> I'll have to check the reference for Wordsworth when I next go down to Somerset, as most of my notes are there. I think it's on one of the lists in the chapbooks, but I'll check.

<u>Series 1 no 4</u> Many were disappointed by Winzer's decorations in which the 'green glass beads' are shown as blue wooden ones. This is not a bibliographical point, I know, but I feel that Harold Monro was always hoping to make it 'look better' by slight alterations.

My collection doesn't get on! certainly not series 1, but when I get to the country I'll send you a bit of what I do have. As to reproduction permission, I agree it's a problem. I couldn't get any answer to requests for permission to quote from Alida's letters, and finally went ahead without it. Nothing happened! – It seems to me that colour reproductions (costing heaven knows what!) would be, not essential, but a very great asset to your book, still I suppose that's only one of many decisions you have to make.

If you got as far as Plymouth you might have got to Somerset – we're only 7 miles from Wells!

very best wishes –
Penelope

76 Clifton Hill, NW8
14 January 1987

Dear Howard,

How kind of you to send me the NYR of Books notice of <u>Charlotte Mew</u>, which I certainly hadn't seen and was very glad to have – but when you say it made you feel your Hogarth Press book 'might yet get some notice' I was taken aback, as I'm re-reading V. Woolf's Diaries (a sobering thing to do if you're beginning to write another novel) where of course your book is mentioned all the time,* as it is in the Charleston Newsletter, which is sent me (although I'm not a friend) by the secretary, Hugh Lee, who I've known for more years than I like to count. I'm glad he and the trust have got such a long way with the restoration, and yet, about Charleston, I don't know, I'm just not sure. A lot of the decorations weren't up to much in the first place, and were probably done with the idea of painting them over whenever they felt like it. And then I can remember what it was once like from a visit when Duncan Grant was there – admittedly a dreadful mess – but it doesn't seem at all right either now that it's clean and tidy – the same is true of William Morris's house at Kelmscott (I don't remember him, but I do know he kept an Iceland pony in the kitchen). Tolstoy's house in Moscow I liked, largely because the curators had got out of hand and were making tea all over the place. – But perhaps I'm ungrateful to feel like this.

Thankyou for your kind word about Innocence. I thought the jacket was good – it was quite difficult getting the colour transparency from Florence, and when it came the dynamic art editor (a newcomer to Collins, with a pigtail) tore round the edge, which I thought made it look exactly right.

Siberian conditions here, and there's only one tap working at the moment, in the basement, so I have to go up and down with a bucket. That's the end of the twentieth century in St John's Wood.

I'm so glad that the Poetry Bookshop material is still on your shelves, (and my word, was there ever a more difficult subject to research?) The sign was by McKnight Kauffer, wasn't it? That, certainly, would make a good jacket.

Well, I hope to see you in the spring. Surely the taps will be working by then –

with all best wishes for 1987 –

Penelope

---

* In the Notes to the diaries.

76 Clifton Hill, NW8
3 April 1987

Dear Howard,

Thankyou so much for your letter, and for sending me the cutting. I never knew that publishers <u>had</u> a weekly, but of course they must have trade papers just like grocers and every other professional, and it was a very nice review.

PEN has just had its Writers' Day in London – Doris Lessing spoke, and rather unexpectedly said that the novel of the future would be in computer language – not the language computers use to each other, but the language computer <u>operators</u> use to each other, which she said could be 'blackly satirical'. Next year we're host to all the other countries for the International congress (it wasn't a success last year in N. York where the authors knocked each other out) and we're going to have it in Cambridge, where they can walk about and see the colleges and have real English tea and fruit-cake. But we feel nervous.

I'm glad your birds are back. The various pesticides in the country here, and the hedge-cutting, seem to have driven large quantities of birds, as well as squirrels and foxes, into London. I saw a kestrel over a church in Hampstead the other day. But they haven't started to build because of the cold.

I'm sorry I was so ignorant about your new edition of the (indispensable and invaluable) Hogarth Press book, I hadn't seen it. I suppose that someone must be at work on a bibliography of David Garnett (though I don't know anything about this either) and they certainly won't be able to manage without it.

Please do tell me when you can face coming to this cold, windy island –

best wishes, Penelope

76 Clifton Hill
London, NW8
2 June 1987

Dear Howard,

I want to thank you so very much for <u>Susan</u> and <u>After the Wilderness</u> (The Challenge Book and Picture Store must have been pretty well opposite the 2nd Poetry Bookshop and shows the kind of competition there was, I suppose) – I was so very glad to have a sheet printed by Tolmer Et Cie – they did <u>Finland</u>, didn't they, and sent out a beautiful trade card, which is in the BL.

I wish that I knew who Edy Legrand was, but possibly I could find out.

I always have to pluck up courage to go to Rota's because of the security precautions, (which I daresay they're very wise to have), which mean that bells ring loudly even after you've shut the door behind you, and more disconcertingly still, no-one looks up from their scholarly work at the shaded desks and tables, however I felt this time I'd be all right if I mentioned your name, and I was.

I have so many things to thank you for and do wish I hadn't missed you on this visit. Your kittens will have grown up by now, and you'll be considering where to hang your new pictures. I'm so glad everything's going so well. It seems a long time since you were putting up your own house from an instruction book (if I remember right).

I had a nice trip to France, but the Proust mania seems to have got much more so. They were selling madeleines (in plastic bags) outside the cathedral at Chartres to raise funds for some charity or other (not for needy writers, as I think it ought to have been).

best wishes and many thanks
Penelope

76 Clifton Hill, NW8
12 July 1987

Dear Howard –

Wonderful that you're starting to put the PB book together and even getting the illustrations, partic. the bookshop sign, (though I also

like the photograph of Harold Monro holding it up, with his usual
expression of embarrassment). As to a short account of the Bookshop,
of course I would be glad to do it and certainly wouldn't want to be
paid for it. I'm very grateful to you for so many things. But I should
like to know exactly what length you have in mind, and whether you
want footnotes and references such as Mary Galther gives in her HP
checklist introduction?

I'm glad that Shem and Shaun are doing well – I thought that it was
<u>deer</u> that caused trouble on your property, not moles, but I suppose
you are pushing back the forest frontiers on all sides –

best wishes
Penelope

76 Clifton Hill, NW8
28 July 1987

Dear Howard, I'm now trying to get on with a draft of an introduction
to your PB bibliography to send you. I take it that you don't want
much about HM's poetry? or about his life, except for its connection
with the Bookshop? – but in any case I will send you something as
soon as I can.

Meanwhile thankyou so much for the various enclosures you've
sent <u>me</u> – particularly for the del Ré articles which, as you say, have
to be extracted with difficulty from the BL. – (If del Ré had been
accepted as an assistant by V & L Woolf in 1919 (or rather as she put
it 'to relieve us of all the business of the Hogarth Press') he could
have appeared in <u>both</u> your books) – thankyou too for Alida's
announcement, and the notice from <u>Publisher's Weekly</u>, wh.
I hadn't had.

Could I just ask one or two things (four) about the bibliography itself?

1. I want to apologise about <u>Love Among the Haycocks</u> (GS). I
realise now that Housman could never have written a poem with such
a title, and that in fact it's B2: 24, <u>Song</u> by Ralph Hodgson.

2. Romney Green certainly <u>was</u> a carpenter, only surely a bit more
than that, a master-carpenter, or even a master-craftsman?

3. I would have thought that 'A Recorder' in the June 1920 <u>Chapbook</u> (D2: 12) was certainly Alida Monro herself?

4. Is it worth mentioning that Anna Wickham had an arrangement to offer any collection of more than 48 poems to Grant Richards, which is why some of her titles (e.g. <u>The Man with a Hammer</u>) were published by The Poetry Bookshop?

Well, all this is hardly worth saying, perhaps, meanwhile I can only congratulate you again on reducing the 'bibliographer's nightmare' to order, and of course I would think a dedication a great honour,

best wishes,

Penelope

P.S. I can't give up <u>Margaritae Sororis</u>! Perhaps you'll come across a copy one of these days – perhaps it was series 3 no 24?

I notice that in HM's will he directed that the PB should be closed down when he died, and I think it's rather sad that AM struggled for another three years –

76 Clifton Hill, NW8
26 August 1987

Dear Howard,

Thankyou so much for your letter and your comments on my draft – I tried hard not to repeat material that had been used before, but, of course, in many cases I couldn't help it. I know it's not a scholarly introduction and indeed I haven't the knowledge to write one. But, as you said, the PB people are not at all like the much-heard-of Bloomsbury group – they're <u>not</u> well-known and <u>some</u> biographical information doesn't seem out of place. – Incidentally I see that in your list you relaxed just for a moment, and said one of the Christmas cards was the most beautiful of the series – I was very interested, as I never knew bibliographers admitted, so to speak, that one item was more beautiful than another – only rarer.

I'm very grateful for your corrections and, of course, accept all of them. I've never seen a complete run of the <u>Chapbook</u> and, I'm afraid,

was in a terrible muddle about the numbers. In a muddle, too, about
the opening of the Bookshop. Could I take out '(published, in fact,
before the Bookshop existed)' on page 8 1.1–2, and alter the footnote to
'was officially opened'.

I don't know what to do about page 5 1.5, I suppose it does sound
peculiar. Could I change to 'In 1913 the Bookshop began to publish'
and take out 'work was extended in two directions'?

Apart from the corrections, would you like anything else done or
rewritten? I'll get on to Virago and Anna Wickham's son about quoting
the lines on page 4 – incidentally Jim Hepburn (the son) still has
Harold Monro's corkscrew, which he stole from the Bookshop as a
small boy.

The Samurai Press interests me so much. I thought James Guthrie
gave them the press – but after all, why should he?

best wishes, Penelope

76 Clifton Hill, NW8

8 September 1987

Dear Howard,

Thankyou for your letter, and as far as I'm concerned, I'm glad you're
leaving your comment about the Xmas card in – very glad, because
although I know there's an accepted way of writing bibliography,
(there has to be,) still bibliographers ought to show that they're
human sometimes.

I was sad to hear about the Curwell Press – I didn't know that it had
gone, and I'm ashamed to say I've never heard of the Stellar Press – but
if Rota's recommend it that says something.

Harold Monro's son committed suicide, but, I'm afraid, I don't
know exactly when, or anything more about his life, though I have a
notion he was a doctor (my notions, though, have been proved not
to be worth much). I'll try to find out, and let you know. – The
copyrights were left in a confused state – Charlotte Mew's for example
being left to a friend of Alida Monro's who was to take care of the
remaining dogs in her kennels – by the way I don't know if I told you
that an American publisher, Addison-Wesley, are bringing out

<u>Charlotte Mew and her Friends</u>, together with her collected poems, which will give her a modest foothold in the U.S.

Howard, if you could get the corrected introduction typed up, I should be most grateful. I'm so far behind with everything – perhaps you know the feeling –

best wishes

Penelope

P.S. I hope the building work is going along well. It's such a relief when the builders leave –

76 Clifton Hill, NW8

2 October [1987]

Dear Howard,

This is to thank you for the beautiful clean copy of the introduction and I need hardly say that you must make any changes to the punctuation you like. I haven't any double quotation marks on my typewriter, by the way.

I wrote to Jim Hepburn (Anna Wickham's son, who threw snowballs at D. H. Lawrence as a little boy because he thought DHL was after his mother – but I've just remembered that you must know Jim, because of the Malcolm Lowry connection) and he's very willing to have her verses quoted (on p. 8 of the typescript) but points out that in spite of their furious rows, Anna and Harold were really friends deep down, so that if it's possible to add, to the footnote on p. 8, ('the verses were never published in her lifetime, and there was in fact a considerable sympathy between Anna Wickham and Harold Monro') I should be grateful, but perhaps it's too late for these alterations.

I'm ashamed to say that I don't know about Smith Settle at all, although I go up to West Yorkshire most years, to teach creative writing (but what is that, I often wonder?) – But I'm quite sure that (understanding a little, as I do, how difficult it must have been to do this particular bibliography,) you're right in making sure of printers who will understand the atmosphere and the period of the

Bookshop. But oh dear, this tedious and ungetroundable problem of money –

best wishes – Penelope

24 April 1988

Thankyou so much for the cutting from <u>Publishers Weekly</u>. I hope for the best for C. Mew, although unfortunately the printers have got 2 pages in the wrong order and all has to be put right again.

I'm sorry you won't be here this spring, but look forward very much indeed to seeing the PBS book.

I suppose by now you have many generations of Burmese cats in Revere –

best wishes Penelope

27a Bishop's Road
Highgate
London, N6
25 May [1988]

Dear Howard,

Thankyou for your letter, and the portrait of your cat, though I don't see why it has to share a stamp with a Maine coon cat which I should have thought was decidedly inferior.

I'm looking forward very much to seeing the book in July. At last there'll be something to show what the Poetry Bookshop was like and why it meant so much to people, and it won't have vanished completely off the face of the earth. – Five copies would be fine, if you could manage it.

As to my papers &c, they're a bit complicated as they include all the material I collected for a life of the novelist L. P. Hartley, but haven't used, because I realised that if it was written it might be painful for his sister, who I was and am very fond of, and his great friend David Cecil (who died not long ago). So there it all sits. Otherwise it's just my own mss, letters and so on. By the autumn I should be sorted out (I'm a very slow, inefficient and tearful mover, but I'm going to a nice small flat which my younger daughter and her husband have converted out of their garage* and it will be lovely once I've got myself in order), and I should very much like to talk to you about it –

best wishes

Penelope

27a Bishop's Road
London, N6
15 June 1988

Dear Howard,

Thankyou very much for your letter. They say moving is the second most traumatic experience and although I'm going to lay my bones with my kind younger daughter and son-in-law, who have turned the garage into a little flat with wonderful ridge-tiles and finials, I feel in a state for which confusion isn't nearly a strong enough word. And then it's a duty, in fact a necessity, to throw a lot of things away – old envelopes, jam-jars and bits of string – and yet I can't bring myself to part with them.

I also feel that perhaps I've misled you, which is the last thing I should want to do, about these papers – there is nothing complete or systematic (I'm not complete or systematic myself as you know and quite failed to make a list of the PB rhymesheets) – I haven't got mss or tss of everything and I have certainly thrown away a lot of letters. As for filing them alphabetically or taking carbons or Xeroxes of them, well it never occurred to me. What I could do is try to get them together as you suggest – under the different titles, but the letters are, I'm afraid, not from famous names. Then there are note-books full of disjointed and unintelligible bits and pieces. I feel rather ashamed of all this, but mustn't give a false impression. Please do ring anyway, won't you, when and if you come to London in the autumn –

best wishes, Penelope

P.S. The L. P. Hartley material is so complicated that I'd have to explain it to you, if you felt like listening!

---

* The garage was in fact a former coach house. The house itself had been bought from the playwright Arnold Wesker and the changes he had made to it previously are amongst his papers at the Harry Ransom Center in Texas, where PMF's papers are also kept.

27a Bishop's Road
London, N6
[summer 1988]

Dear Howard –

This is just to welcome you to London – a London with no post, however, so I'll drop this in. I'm just going down to Somerset – until Monday 12th, and then I have to go down there again on the 17th and 18th, for newest grand-daughter's christening, but otherwise I'm here in Highgate, and do hope you'll find the time to ring me up –

best wishes
Penelope

27a Bishop's Road
Highgate
London, N6
1 August [1988]

Thankyou for sending the <u>Book Collector</u> piece, it was very nice, and 'scrupulous and helpful volumes' – well, you must be pleased with that.

Very hot here, and American scholars say they can't stand it without air conditioning –

best wishes, Penelope

27a Bishop's Road
Highgate
London, N6
26 August [1988]

Dear Howard,

I'm just hoping that this arrives in time (I mean before you leave, but for all I know you may be going to other places first) to congratulate you on the PB bibliography. To me it seems beautiful, and worth having for the sinner and the Christmas card alone (but I'm ashamed to say I don't know who Alistair Stewart was), and I can scarcely believe it's out at last, as at one point I was quite convinced I'd leave this earth without anyone ever having heard of the Poetry Bookshop. Joy's book was out of print, and everyone was dying, or their memories were fading.

   congratulations and best wishes
   Penelope

> *27a Bishop's Road*
> *Highgate*
> *London*
> 12 October [1988]

Dear Howard,

   This is just to say that the 4 copies of the PB have arrived now, and to thank you very much for them – and to tell you something quite absurd (for a moderately sane person) which is that, although I've been through the book so carefully, and paused over all kinds of things, and admired the colour, and speculated over whether the ghosts would ever materialise, I only just noticed the dedication, for which too I'd like to thank you so much – I never thought I'd live to see the Poetry Bookshop properly treated and properly studied, so much of what Monro produced seemed to have dropped out of memory, or in the case of the rhymesheets, literally blown away with the wind. So the dedication means a very great deal to me –
   love Penelope

Will ring up as you suggested on the 25th. Meantime have to go out with a TV crew to Highgate Woods to try and film a birch tree – all for 2 minutes in a programme – Well, I mustn't complain

> 6 December [1988]

Dear Howard – You won't think much of this receipt, but it's what I was given – I suggested to him that his firm ought to have a receipt book and he said That's Not A Bad Idea.

It was nice to see you and I hope all went well in Aberdeen and in Edinburgh, and with your house move, but I still think it's a very serious thing to leave a garden, particularly with walnut-trees in it –

very best wishes for 1989

Penelope

When I was little I used to think it would be a wonderful thing to live to the year 2000, and now I don't care a bit whether I do or not –

27a Bishop's Road
London, N6
15 January [1989]

Dear Howard,

Nice to hear from you, and to hear that the beautifully wrapped-up cases have got to Texas. I felt a bit disconcerted by Emery Freights, as, though they were amiable and came when they'd said they would, I thought it was strange that they had no receipt or invoice forms of their own – still all is well – things <u>do</u> turn up in the end – I once had a letter from Harvard which took a year to arrive – it was from a post-graduate who was reading some letters of Rossetti for me, for which he made a charge of 50 cents.

It was very good of you to buy the envelope – I told Hugh Lee that he ought not to mix up professional artists with amateurs like myself, but he gets carried away by his enthusiasm, and I've known him ever since World War 2. Really he ought to have tried to get a royalty off the new Lloyd-Webber musical of David Garnett's <u>Aspects of Love</u> – the songs sound frightful, and I'm sure it will run for many years – perhaps he <u>did</u> try, but I'm afraid without success, and now he's having difficulties with his committee at Charleston. Still, everyone has difficulties with committees.

<u>The Knox Brothers</u> was rather hard to write, for fear of hurting people's feelings. (I don't at all mind everyone taking religion seriously, but not if it means separating people who love each other. –) Yes, Dilly was deeply fond of Maynard Keynes and L. Strachey – but Somerset Maugham, (who often said very sensible things, even if he has gone

out of fashion) said that when a man gets married his wife, sooner or later, gets rid of his old friends, and Aunt Olive almost managed to do this. – It was partly that they couldn't stand the freezing cold in the house –

Thankyou for the page from the catalogue and best wishes for 1989 to you and Bob – Penelope

27a Bishop's Road
London, N6
9 March [1989]

Dear Howard,

This is to thank you for the delicious dinner which I enjoyed so much, and for the wonderful Blake's Seven Songs. I needn't tell you how much I value them, even more perhaps because as you say in the Bibliography, they're not 'coloured consistently' – <u>partly</u> I think because of a kind of Poetry Bookshop nostalgia for Blake's own plates, which after all aren't coloured consistently either, partly, I like to think, that Charlotte Mew 'hadn't finished with the Prussian blue' as we used to say when we were children sharing a paintbox.

The very first thing I'm going to do this morning is to compare them with the <u>Innocence and Experience</u> plates in the Geoffrey Keynes ed:, then try out the music on the nursery piano with one or 2 fingers. I'm ashamed to say that I don't know anything about Geoffrey Gwyther and very little about G. Spencer Watson (but I can find out). Then they have to go into a special drawer, because Tommy, now 4 and a half, came in just now while I was looking at them and suggested that <u>he</u> might fill in the bits that weren't done with <u>his</u> paintbox. But he accepted at once that they were precious and it would be better to fill in something else. I was glad, though, that he liked them so much, even though I'm only going to allow them out on special occasions. – Truly, it's a marvellous present and you can be sure I appreciate it.

Very best wishes for your trip to Athens, which I still think sounds like the beginning of a Raymond Chandler, and for the extensions to the house, and to Bob and the rockery. I wonder if he can grow <u>dryas octopetala</u>, because that's my favourite among everything they have in the rockeries at Kew –

love Penelope

27a Bishop's Road
London, N6
8 April [1989]

Dear Howard,

Thankyou so much for your letter, and for the cheque – please don't think that I don't realise what a lot of trouble it must have been to send the money in sterling, but it was a great help to me and I'm grateful, as I'm sure you realise. I see now that dealing in contemporary (if that's the right word for me) authors must be just as much trouble as dealing in rare books. I'm so glad everything turned up in the right place in the end.

I' m so glad you still like your picture. That, it seems to me, is the great difficulty of buying anything, particularly if, like me, you're not very strong-minded – you begin to think of all the other things you might have done, or might have bought, but I can see that you've learned to trust your own judgement.

The notices of the Day-Lewis Hamlet are

1. That it lasts 4 hours – (but it used to last 6 hours in the Old Vic days when the gallery cost a shilling, and we all stuck it out) –

2. That he's physically just right for the part, but his performance is a 'near miss'. I've seen more Hamlets than I dare count up, but I still feel David Warner and the Russian, Smektounovsy,* were the only ones who got it right.

Very best wishes for your Athens expedition. You ought to keep a diary – perhaps you do – best wishes – Penelope

---

* Innokenty Smoktunovsky, who played the title role in the Soviet film adaptation of *Hamlet* in 1964.

27a Bishop's Road
London, N6
16 May [*c.*1989]

Dear Howard,

Thankyou so very much for the wonderful W Morris sale catalogue, full of marvels and (to me) unbelievably high prices – I'm reading it through slowly as it's so very interesting – I see for example that the cataloguing for the Cobden-Sanderson bookbindings in the Pierpont Morgan library was done by F. B. Adams junior, the Charlotte Mew collector, now retired to a château in Chisseaux – and what wonderful illustrations, particularly of the Morris Virgil. The shameful thing is that I've never heard of the Doheny collection, but then there are so many things I've never heard of. Well, I shall treasure my catalogue, and in my will, which I haven't yet succeeded in making, I shall leave it to the Library of the William Morris Society, which is only a small one, but has some nice things including a Kelmscott Chaucer, and is much consulted and much loved. (When there was a dispute between the Trustees and the Society we had to rescue all our books from the Trustees' locked cases with a keyhole saw). The Morris house on the river in Hammersmith has now been bought by Christopher Hampton, the playwright, and we've recovered the coach-house in which Morris used to hold his Social Democratic meetings, and are about to clean it out and restore it, with the help of the (usually unhelpful) council.

I hope your 2nd Greek visit went off as well as the first. I thought it was very brave of you to go, as the whole set up, with a mysterious dying millionaire and suspicious relatives (did I make those up?) sounded more like Raymond Chandler than anything else. But I envy you, as I haven't been to Greece for so many years,

And then you have the computer to tame, though I expect that's done by now. Lovely weather here, lilac blossoms falling onto the page –

love and many thanks
Penelope

27a Bishop's Road
London, N6
22 September [1990]

Dear Howard,

Thankyou so much for your letter, and how you got hold of my book* so quickly I can't think, but I appreciate your kind words very much, as you can imagine. I'd thought, while I was writing it, that it was a bit longer than usual, but I'm already getting letters to say that there seems to be some mistake as it is so short and some pages must be missing out of their copy. It's Collins' fault for not putting The End, like we used to have at the movies in the dear old days.

Bob will tell you that there are hundreds of clematis – but you have to choose between <u>montana</u> types which flower profusely but only in spring, and the more cultivated ones which flower twice a year, but are not nearly as strong. There's a moral there somewhere I daresay. I've put in Nellie Moser and Mrs Cholmondeley, but a <u>montana</u> would have been safer.

I do so hope to see you if you come over in November. I'm going up to the Lake District on the 9th I think, but you'll be in London before that I hope –

best wishes, Penelope

27a Bishop's Road
London, N6
20 November [1990]

Dear Howard,

I'm addressing this to Revere because, you know, I never <u>did</u> get the address and tel. no. of your London flat, which was the first great mistake I made – and the second, the date when you were coming to lunch, wh. I was looking forward to so much, must have been my fault too, because you're the business man, and I'm anything but – I was very much distressed when I got back from Kirkby Lonsdale to find

---

* *The Gate of Angels.*

that you'd been, and gone – however I hoped perhaps you might come the following Thursday, which was the day I truly thought we'd always arranged, so I made an apple pie &c, though not with much hope, and finally had to tell myself that I'd missed you.

That meant of course that I never heard about your strange adventures in England, which you told me were stranger than anything in Greece, and I don't know what wonderful things you bought this time. I'm glad you like the Spencer Resurrection and the Cookham pictures – I used to be taken to see them when I was quite small, and indeed Stanley Spencer was a familiar sight on Hampstead Heath in those days with his pram full of canvases. The big exhibition is going to be next spring, I think, with a long biography coming out at the same time. No-one wanted this biography, and then someone at Collins happened to fish it out of what publishers over here call the slush pile, I don't know what they call it in America.

I've just had a letter from Father Hagreen, son of Philip Hagreen, the wood-engraver who did some beautiful broadsheets for the PB – he says he has his father's papers &c in a room at his presbytery but no time to sort them out – I feel I'm too old and stiff to do this, but will find someone.

Once again, I was so very sorry to miss you –
best wishes, love Penelope

27a Bishop's Road
London, N6
8 October [1991]

Dear Howard,

How nice to hear from you, and to hear you're coming to England, although I was a bit dismayed when I realised how busy you were going to be – and you've said nothing about time spent in buying pictures and bits of old mantelpieces, not to speak of books. However, I know how you fit things in.

I've been one of the Booker judges this year and as always there have been alarming differences of opinion, and even one walk-out, the first in its history I believe. However that will all be over on the 22nd Oct:. I'm going up to the Lake District after that until the 7th Nov:, and on the 8th I've got nothing down except 'pay income-tax' – but you will be in Paris. Is there any chance of your coming to lunch on the 12th Nov? You can be sure there wouldn't be any confusion about the day this time.

Meanwhile I'm sure you're right not to miss the Munch exhibition – the last time we had one in London it was marvellous, and they even had the extraordinary plates of wood – separate plates for each colour – that he used for the woodcuts. Still, as you say, 'walking and looking' are the main thing –

best wishes and hoping to see you –
Penelope

Sydney
[postcard]
19 November [1991]

I hoped, you know, that you might come to lunch in Highgate on the 12th but perhaps you didn't get my letter. Perhaps we're fated never to meet again, but I do hope you had a wonderful time in Paris – I'm sure you did – and still hope to hear about it one day –

love Penelope

27a Bishop's Road
London, N6
18 December [1991]

Dear Howard,

So many untoward things seem to have happened in London that I wonder you have the patience to come here at all, but then, probably as the result of doing so much travelling, you seem to take it all with astonishing calm – the only way to take it really.

I can't imagine why the locksmith took the door away – the all-night locksmith, who I've had to call in once or twice, is expensive, but produces the lock and new sets of keys on the spot. What's the use of saying this? I'm very sorry about it all, anyway.

I went to Australia because the writers of Tasmania asked me to come – they are a very lively lot of people, deeply concerned as you can imagine with saving the lakes and forests and supporting aboriginal claims to the land. They have a writer's cottage on the waterfront in Hobart and while I was there the icebreaker came back from the Antarctic to her summer moorings. It was just getting hot (which I don't like) in Sydney and Melbourne and I did find the 24 hour flight a bit much, just 45 minutes stop in Bangkok, still it's a great thing for me to have seen wallabies crossing the road and heard all those strange birds singing.

And meanwhile you didn't get my letter! I do hope you get this one, because I want to wish you everything good and prosperous for the New Year best wishes,

Penelope

27a Bishop's Road
London, N6
[1992]

Dear Howard,

Thankyou so much for the catalogue of the Katonah museum exhibition <u>Designing Utopia</u>. I saw from my Wm. Morris newssheet that the American (and I think the Canadian) branch visited it, but I hadn't a catalogue. I think they were lucky, although I can't agree with most of Prof. Eisenman's introduction and certainly not with his remark 'Capitalism improvises all sorts of modest pleasures for its workers in order that it may never have to face the socialist demand for a regime based on the principle of 'joy in labour'. ' – However we've had Prof. Norman Kelvin, the editor of Morris's letters, over here from New York, – talking to us about the last volume. – I think he feels rather strange, having finished it at last.

Hoping to see you in November –
love
Penelope

Hope Cottage
Milton Abbot
Devon
4 December 1992

Dear Howard,

Thankyou for your letter, and it was so nice to see you – this is only
to wish you well for Christmas, as apart from that I can't pretend to
have much news. I'm down in Devonshire at the moment – floods
lying in the fields and water rushing stormily down each side of the
road. This is my elder daughter's house, or rather cottage – decidedly a
tight fit at the moment when the three children come back from
school, but very cosy when we light the wood-stove.

Tell Bob I have an Alpine in the garden, still flowering – it is really I
think a very miniature geranium, with small clear pink flowers and a
great many of them – I know the name begins with an 'e', and nobody
else seems to have one – I'm afraid this isn't a very good description
but I can recommend it.

very best wishes for Christmas and 1993 –
love, Penelope

(I never managed to ask you what bibliography you were working on
now, but good luck with it –)

27a Bishop's Road
London, N6
15 December 1994

Dear Howard,

I still think it was kind of you to wish me a happy birthday on any
date – after all birthdays are like clocks, which <u>have</u> to be right every 24
hours.

This is my Christmas letter and brings my good wishes to you, Bob,
the rock garden and the Burmese kittens, now I suppose grown into
grandmotherly cats. I wonder if you have meconopsis baileyii in the
garden (it's not an Alpine, I know) as I've been fascinated by it ever
since I saw one in Sunderland, and I set myself to find out all about it.

The three grandchildren have mysteriously expanded to take over the whole house (no 27) including the staircases, which are covered with space armies and followers of the Lion King, but I suppose we were just as bad when we were little.

You don't tell me whether you saw <u>Arcadia</u> or what you thought of it? Or indeed what you're collecting now. But no matter. I note that Sara Holmes will be arriving in the New Year and hope that she will ring up. And Jim Hepburn is still going – and still looks as he did in Nina Hammett's portrait all that time ago –

best wishes for Christmas and 1995 – Penelope

[Bishop's Road]
31 March 1995

Dear Howard – How nice to hear from you, and get another assortment of amazing stamps.

It's quite true I've been ill since last September (– I can't breathe very well, which is inconvenient –) but they can't quite make out what of! I'm bringing out a book next September*– but would much rather see the desert flowers.

I'm still hoping to meet Sara Holmes, in case I could be of any use, but she has seen the Hepburns, who will probably be much more – love Penelope

27a Bishop's Road
London, N6
12 September 1995

Dear Howard,

What beautiful stamps!

Thankyou very much indeed for your kind letter about <u>The Blue Flower</u>. I'm amazed that you've got a copy, as I haven't even had my

---

*   *The Blue Flower.*

own advance copies yet, and it was very good of you to write and tell me you liked it.

I didn't mean to insult the book-selling profession, far from it, but it still seems to me that if you go into what I think of as a genuine bookshop (not so many left now) you see the proprietor sitting quietly in a dark corner absorbed not in a book, but in a catalogue. That wasn't meant to be a criticism, though.

I hope that you and Bob and the Burmese cats are well –

with best wishes –

love, Penelope

P.S. My idea of the ideal blue flower is the blue poppy – <u>meconopsis beton. baileyi</u> – although it didn't arrive here till the 20th century – I wonder if you grow it in your rockery?

27a Bishop's Road
London, N6
25 January 1996

Dear Howard,

How nice to hear from you, and thankyou again for the wondrous display of stamps.

I'm sure you will have heard by now of the sad news of Jim Hepburn's death. Margaret (who is 14 years younger) of course in great distress. He seemed indestructible, always interested in everything, and always with so much on hand, still doing the garden, arranging to record Anna Wickham's songs, everything – He went into the Royal Free Hospital and died 9 days later.

I'll tell you about the papers I've kept – I've got the ms. of <u>The Gate of Angels</u> (then called <u>The Unobservables</u>) and an ms. notebook with a draft of the ghost story from it – also the publisher's setting copy, with my corrections – and I've got the ms. of the <u>Blue Flower</u> and the setting copy of <u>that</u> – but I haven't kept any reviews or short stories, once they're published – so you see it isn't much, apart from my notebooks for the <u>Blue Flower</u>, which I suppose aren't of much interest to anybody. I don't think it would be more than a 3-inch pile of A4. –

Snowing here – and with you too I expect.

Hoping to see you, best wishes Penelope

27a Bishop's Road
London, N6
9 June [1996]

Dear Howard,

I am afraid you will think me very unsatisfactory, but I still can't get very much sense out of the (nice) doctor at the Whittington hospital and I am sure taking all these unpleasant chemicals is reducing me to a very low state of intelligence – however I've looked through my drawers – I <u>know</u> I haven't any <u>diaries</u>, and what I had went to the bottom of the Thames. As to the <u>letters</u>, they are all in envelopes, but that only gives them the illusion of being sorted, they aren't really. Some I don't want to part with, a lot I am sure are very dull, and then there are my PB sheets, most of which you kindly gave me – they <u>do</u> have their special envelope – and a collection of letters from dear Ray Watkinson, biographer of Ford Madox Brown, the Victorian artist – he is perhaps the last of the great letter-writers and many other people all over the world have a series from him and if they should ever be wanted in some selection, or other, there they are. – There are publishers' letters, quite unexciting personal letters, and then, as time goes on, obituaries and memorial-services – all things that 'have been and will be again'. One of my sons-in-law is down to act as literary executor and he would get in touch with you if need be, but I honestly think there wouldn't be any thing of sufficient interest. Such dull old things as writers are. I was so glad to see you – love, Penelope

27a Bishop's Road
London, N6
9 October 1996

Dear Howard,

Thankyou so much for your letter and the cheque for three thousand dollars – it's very good of you to send it and very <u>business-like</u> – I know that by no stretch of the imagination could I ever run a business like yours and I do admire it.

My daughter Maria (the prof of Neurobiology whose house I live in) has had to make 3 conference trips lately to Vancouver, Seattle and Nova Scotia and says that each one in turn seemed to her the most beautiful place on earth. Well, the only one of them I've seen is NS and that was in a blizzard, and I'm afraid it's too late to think of going to any of them now.

I'm just getting down to write a new entry for Charlotte Mew for the new Dict. Of Nat: Biog. The piece itself isn't difficult to do, but you have to fill in so many forms and particulars and sources that it must be worse than trying to emigrate. – It made me think about the Poetry Bookshop again, though, bless its heart –

love Penelope

27a Bishop's Road
London, N6
21 March 1997

Dear Howard,

How nice to get one of your laconic letters which say exactly what you mean and no more – and after all that's what letters are for.

But I'm ashamed to say that I've never even heard of Big Bend National Park. I've been to San Antonio on the way to Mexico, and to the Humanities Library at Austin, the only town I've ever seen without, as far as I could see, any public transport, and where the assistant who explained the wondrous systems to me said 'you mustn't think this is just Texas brag' which won me over completely – but that's all of Texas I've ever seen, except the border customs.

But I hope you have a splendid tour and (because I suppose this must be part of it) see a lot of rock plants. My Alpine violets (which don't mind any amount of cold, but can't stand damp) have just about pulled round, and they're in bud at last.

I went to the British Literary Awards last night (every 2 years from <u>Coutts</u> bank) – won by Muriel Spark, who came over from Rome to accept &c. Coutts (in the Strand) is like a tropical jungle, with far too many huge trees and houseplants, obscuring the numerous TV screens.

Thankyou so much for the piece from <u>The Publishers' Review</u>. Well, a new publisher for me,* and a new gleam of hope, of the kind that keeps the enfeebled scribbler going –

all best wishes
Penelope

27a Bishop's Road
London, N6
21 April [1997]

Dear Howard,

Thankyou so much for taking the trouble to send the NY Times. I felt it was something of an honour to be on the cover, even though the pic. of Novalis and his sweetheart weren't quite what I should consider romantic, and Michael Hoffman was very kind, specially as I know so little German and he knows so much. You will wish me luck, I know.

Household here convulsed by the mysterious death of the kitten, Sophie (grandchild's) first kitten, now buried in the garden, and we've had to get a new, tough, plebeian bruiser of a tabby kitten, but at least he looks very much alive and will I'm sure hold his own territory against the other cats, squirrels and foxes. However I fear Sophie doesn't love him in quite the same way – perhaps because he doesn't seem so helpless –

love, Penelope

---

* In the US.

27a Bishop's Road
London, N6
12 July [1997]

Dear Howard,

Thankyou so much for sending the Richard Holmes review – I
was very lucky the NYR of Books asked him to do it, and he's taken
such pains over it, I feel truly grateful – not quite so grateful to
Levine, but Houghton Mifflin say I should take it as a great
compliment, no matter whether it looks like me or not, so I have to
remember that.

best wishes
Penelope

27a Bishop's Road
London, N6
29 March [1998]

Dear Howard,

Oh, what a kind thought, and what a beautiful bottle of champagne,
all the better for being completely unexpected. 'You're in luck' said the
boy who delivered it, and that was true.

The whole thing was in fact just as unexpected as possible. My
editor at Houghton Mifflin told me about the awards* and said I'd
better prepare a few words of acceptance, but I thought it couldn't
conceivably be necessary, so he composed a few himself, went to
New York and, lo and behold, he actually had to deliver them.
Unfortunately he had appointments with agents &c &c the whole
next day, and wasn't able to celebrate. – But I have, and you must
picture me sitting round the kitchen table with my daughter,
son-in-law, and the cat, gratefully opening the bottle –

best wishes
Penelope

---

* It had just been announced that *The Blue Flower* had won the National Book Critics
Circle Award in the US for the year 1997.

27a Bishop's Road
London, N6
June 8th [1998]

Dear Howard,

Thankyou so much for the 'green flower'. My family comes very much from the Protestant north, and I married a catholic from County Cavan, so I feel I can qualify as a reader of your catalogue, very beautiful to look at, as always. And I very much appreciated the essays by Wes Davis, but what I can't understand, Howard, in spite of your very helpful introduction, is <u>why</u> the Milberg collection is confined to poets whose first books were published after the end of World War 2, with some rather eccentric exceptions, and why you're adding new things as they come out, but not earlier ones?

Don't please think I'm ungrateful – I repeat, it's a beautiful catalogue.

All quite well here. Our cat has developed an amazing intelligence in regard to everything concerning his own food, welfare &c and a total lack of interest in everything else –

with thanks and best wishes Penelope

27a Bishop's Road
London, N6
2 July 1999

Dear Howard,

Thankyou so much for letting me know about Dominic Hibberd (he sounds saintly) and the biography of Harold Monro. I'm so glad he stuck at it, and got a good publisher too. I reviewed a biog: of Humbert Wolfe the other day, which must have been even more difficult to place. Everything has to be about Bloomsbury! And I'm perhaps the last person alive who used to go to sleep as a child with a coal fire and the PB rhymesheets on the walls –

best wishes for everything –
Penelope

[Christmas card]
[December 1999]

Howard –

With best wishes for Christmas and the New Year – I won't mention the millennium as I'm beginning to regard it as unbearable.

My Alpine violets, supposed not to do well in London clay, have now taken over all the beds. On the other hand, I can't think of a short story, which my publishers say I <u>must</u> do, as then they can bring out a Collected Short Stories, and I haven't really written enough to collect.

Have been reviewing a Letters of John Butler Yeats, edited from the Hone edition. JBY was a great talker, but I think in those days Irish people accepted talking as one of the professions –

love to you both

Penelope

Richard Ollard*

25 Almeric Road London, sw11
[postcard]
12 January [1979]

This is the T/S of <u>Offshore</u>, which you kindly told me you would look at – I didn't realise when I came to see you that all the type-writers in the family had something wrong with them as a result of physiology theses, poetry, schedules &c being produced in quantity – so I had to do the best I could – I would very much appreciate your advice –

Penelope

25 Almeric Road
London, sw11
24 January [1979]

Dear Richard,

Thankyou for your letter – I'm returning the contract form but have crossed out 'non-fiction' in the options clause as you suggested. If you could ever make time however to talk about my general list ideas I should be grateful. Some of them Raleigh** told me were hopeless and I think they're not the sort of thing Collins do, but still. – Duckworths are still interested in a biography of L. P. Hartley which I'm getting together but can't get the permissions for the moment.

I also enclose what press cuttings I can find but I'm afraid I haven't many. I don't keep them usually, perhaps I ought to. <u>The Knox Brothers</u> had a good <u>Times</u> review on the day it appeared and a good

---

* Historian and editor at Collins, to whom she took *Offshore* after feeling unwanted at Duckworth. He also saw *Human Voices*, *At Freddie's* and *Charlotte Mew* through the press, before his retirement.

** Raleigh Trevelyan at Michael Joseph, who had published her biography of Burne-Jones in 1975.

notice from Malcolm Muggeridge in the TLS that week and I could check those if you wanted them. – I feel I'm letting you down here. The TLS was also very kind to the <u>Bookshop</u> and said it was a novella in the tradition of Henry James, not a selling point perhaps.

I also enclose a note on myself and a list of back titles –
Best wishes
Penelope

> 25 *Almeric Road*
> *London*, sw11
> 29 January [1979]

Dear Richard,

It was very nice to see you at lunch-time and I hope I didn't try to put forward too many notions at once, – one thing I certainly didn't mean to suggest was that I looked down on money-making subjects – indeed, I look up to them.

I enclose some more cuttings, but the TLS notice of the <u>Bookshop</u>, which was so nice, is missing. I suppose I was lucky to be reviewed before the TLS itself disappeared.*

As to Charlotte Mew, &c. I'll send you something further if I may, when it's in a fit state to be seen – yours Penelope

> 25 *Almeric Road*
> *London*, sw11
> 14 June [1979]

Dear Richard,

Please could I ask you one more thing, which I hadn't thought of when I rang you up the other day? – I've got a long list of people I still have to interview about Leslie Hartley (whose life I'm supposed to be writing), and on this list is Veronica Wedgwood – I remember (though of course she wouldn't) that Leslie took us both out to dinner once or twice, and she was exceedingly nice, but since then she has become

---

* The *TLS* temporarily ceased publication owing to a lengthy printers' strike.

very eminent and also I'm not sure how well she is and how much she
sees people. – Now it's suddenly struck me that as she publishes with
Collins and what's more writes about the King's Peace &c, you <u>must</u> be
her book-editor, so perhaps you might be able to tell me whether it
would be all right for me to ask if I could go and see her. (You see there
are difficulties – Lady Aberconway has drunk herself to death, poor
Walter Allen, Leslie's literary executor, is too stricken to see anyone,
and other people drop dead before I've reached them on My List; it's
really much better to deal with 17th century people who can't be
interviewed except by calling in a medium) –

    best wishes
    Penelope

[postcard]
11 Aug [1979]

Thankyou so much for the copy of <u>Offshore</u> – I did think it looked
nice, and it cheered me up, always absolutely necessary first thing in
the morning. Just off to the seaside for a week with bucket and spade –
Penelope

25 Almeric Road
London, sw11
9 September [1979]

Dear Richard,
    Thankyou so much for your letter, it's good of you to take time to
console your easily depressed authors – I've always had very bad
notices from the New Statesman even for biographies – I'm a total
failure where radical chic is concerned. Indeed I was going to ask you
not to send to the NS but thought it would sound like a fuss about
nothing. – The financial pages to-day say that Collins is facing
imminent ruin, but I hope this is just sensationalism.
    best wishes
    Penelope

25 Almeric Road
London, sw11.
10 October [1979]

Dear Richard

There is one other thing I wanted to ask you, although I know it isn't something you have to deal with at all – it's about TV rights – my other novel is now with an admirable free-lance TV director who, however, is hard hit by the ITV trouble and is drawing National Assistance, and I think this is so much water under the bridge, but meanwhile people keep telling me that I ought to get an agent to try to sell the TV rights of <u>Offshore</u>. I was harangued and indeed written to by Booker McConnell on this subject 'as you cannot expect the publisher to do this for you' they said reprovingly – the latest one was the C.O.I. man who started lecturing me yesterday as soon as I set foot in his recording room 'you cannot expect &c', and I <u>don't</u> expect it at all, but the trouble is that I don't want an agent to deal with publishers, but only with TV possibilities, and I don't know if there are any who would do this. Have you ever heard of any?

I also wanted to thank you for getting my <u>spacing</u> right, you may well have forgotten this, but it meant a lot to me,

best wishes for your new book

Penelope

25 Almeric Road
London, sw11
2 November [1979]

Dear Richard,

Thankyou for the Dutch notice – I do know a little bit as I once had to help take 14 prep-school boys round Holland by water and find them all somewhere to sleep <u>free</u> every night on land, as there wasn't enough room on the boat. Certainly I know enough to see that I'm said to be of the school of Beryl Bainbridge which is a good corrective to vanity, I expect.

I don't know if you've ever had a minute to look at this piece of Prof: Kermode's, which he did before the awards for the London bit of the NY Review of Books – he is the only critic, and indeed the only Professor of Eng. Lit, whose opinion I value since Lionel Trilling died, and indeed I don't think I could teach anyone anything about the novel at all if it hadn't been for his <u>The Sense of an Ending</u>. What worries me isn't that he doesn't think too well of <u>Offshore</u> – (in fact I'm very pleased that he should say anything about me at all), but that I get the feeling that he's saying I can write a single-consciousness novel (which anyone can do if they can find a pen and a bit of paper) but I'm not up to multiple-consciousness, then I just fall into bits, and that depresses me.

You must blame Sarah* for this letter as she said 'You can always consult Richard if anything worries you.' She was most kind when I came to the office – PR man obviously despairs of me, but it's no good pretending to be what you're not.

best wishes, Penelope

P.S. No reference to Frank Birch in all these 4th man + 5th man + . . . books, where will it all end?

25 Almeric Road
London, sw11
6 November [1979]

Dear Richard,

Thankyou very much for your letter and the Leclerc xerox – I love him (at a distance) as he's my faithful fan and I'm glad you've written to him. – I told the Krug operative (who turned out to be an old pupil of mine) that I'd love to be congratulated** by them, but I'd prefer it to be on the front of the <u>Guardian</u> which they agreed to, and they <u>did</u> send a sample.

---

* Richard Ollard's assistant.
** On winning the Booker Prize for *Offshore*.

I'd love to come to dinner at all times and I enjoyed it so much when I did, but unluckily for me not on the 14th as I'm supposed to be going out that evening, it's all to do with my son who is going out to Nicaragua where they've had their revolution, to do over the economy.

Sinister Dr Garlinski's <u>Enigma</u> book is coming out to-day so Dents are launching it with (light) refreshments and we're all to be allowed to see the original machine – I wish Oliver was here –

best wishes

Penelope

I've now got <u>The Image of the King</u> from Foyles and am enjoying it very much and hope you'll sign my copy one day.

> 25 *Almeric Road*
> *London,* sw11
> 13 December [1979]

Dear Richard,

Thankyou very much for letting me know about <u>The Bookshop</u> and <u>The Golden Child</u> I'm <u>sure</u> that's out of print as Colin* printed the extra copies here and sent them out to the U.S., it wasn't really published by Scribners.

My TV director is now buoyant as he's been made director of the theatre in Leatherhead, he has to open with <u>Play it Again Sam</u> and <u>The Winter's Tale</u> and has to negotiate a bear from Chessington Zoo, nevertheless he still wants to do the <u>Bookshop</u> so I am going to see Kendall D. to see if he can understand it all, because I certainly don't.

I've given up reading the papers till after Christmas, but Ria showed me the piece from Jim Callaghan about the <u>Image of the King</u>, that was really nice –

best wishes

Penelope

---

* Haycraft.

25 Almeric Road
London, sw11
Thursday [February 1980]

Dear Richard – I'm afraid this is very rough,* not only the typing, worse than last time, but bits of the story – (for example, I've not had time to go and check the Charles I statue, although it suddenly strikes me that you might be able to tell me about it, as it's an image). I'm not quite sure the end is too clear either. Perhaps none of it will do.

I'm so glad about the Silver Pen list – Sybille Bedford was talking about you at PEN the other evening, but I didn't quite follow, – I thought A Bend in the River a very fine novel, but if the Pen is for the best piece of <u>prose</u>, I think it <u>has</u> to be for you – best wishes for the house-hunting – Penelope

P.S. I don't know whether you'll like this or not, but in any case could I come in and see you for 15 minutes some time when you're back from Dorset?

P.P.S. Are you going to the Hatchards party? I don't think I can face it otherwise.

25 Almeric Road
London, sw11
[card]
20 February [1980]

Thankyou so much for ringing about <u>Human Voices</u>. I've found various small bits on the backs of envelopes that should have gone in, but perhaps it's too late to do this, I hope not though. Very best luck with the house-hunting, which is more fun than moving, so perhaps one just ought to go on looking – Penelope

---

* Typescript of *Human Voices*.

25 February [1980]

Dear Richard,

Thankyou for the corrections which I hope I've put right, along with a few other ones, and if there's to be a photo (I think the readers <u>do</u> like to see what the author looks like, although I notice you don't put one in), well I enclose the only one in wh. I look approximately human. Also, I don't know whether you are having a jacket illustration or not, but if so, I wonder if you would agree that the artist we had last time was a bit on the old-fashioned side?

best wishes

Penelope

25 Almeric Road
London, sw11
29 February [1980]

Dear Richard,

In case you find this letter too long to get through, I'd like to ask first whether you and Mary could come to dinner one day in the week of the 17th March, any day, except Friday Saturday and Sunday, my cousin Jean, the sister of James and Christopher (now I come to think of it, perhaps he was too old to have been in college with you) Fisher is coming then, she's married now to an overworked but genial High Court judge – it would be so nice if you could manage it.

I was delighted to hear that you are printing off a few more <u>Offshores</u>. I thought it had got shipwrecked altogether by so many unpleasant remarks. I'll never forget the Book Programme, I still get letters about it. – As to the jacket of this new one, of course I leave it to you, I'm always trying to meddle about with designing and getting quite properly put in my place.

Thankyou for sending the blurb for <u>Human Voices</u>, I think it's impossible to do your own and I'm very grateful to you, nevertheless could I make one or 2 suggestions. – I'd rather <u>not</u> say that it's better than any serious work on the BBC as there <u>is</u> only one, the Asa Briggs <u>History</u>, and he's been so kind to me, and apart from that it's very good and cost him years of research – I didn't re-read it before writing this novel, but I have the greatest respect for it – 2nd would it be possible to quote Thomas Hinde in the Sunday Telegraph, rather than the Observer, he is a very fine novelist and wrote me a very nice note about the award. 3rdly do you think it would be possible to make this book sound a little bit less like a historical study and more like a novel? It is really about the love-hate relationship between 2 of the eccentrics on whom the BBC depended, and about love, jealousy, death, childbirth in Broadcasting House and the crises that go on behind the microphone to produce the 9 o'clock news on which the whole nation relied during the war years, heartbreak &c, and also about this truth telling business, don't you think these might be mentioned as it would make the book sound a little more readable, I did try to put a bit of action in it? – (Incidentally, as no-one reads Heine I suppose no-one will understand the name Asra, but that's by the way.) I'm sure you're too used to the writers, as I've heard them despondently called in publishers' offices, to mind all this, perhaps I ought to have a go and then you can tell me where I'm wrong, what do you think?

Thankyou too for the contract, wh. I'm returning. This novel isn't any more libellous than my other ones, so I expect it's all right.

One other thing, I'm now sitting down to write the book you definitely <u>didn't</u> want, I must get it done, I've seen so many relatives and so many letters about the sad lives of the Poetry Bookshop poets (who are they? as you said). I realise that is not likely to be Collinsworthy but would you like to see it when it's finished?

I've written all this because I thought it would be shorter than my appearing at Collins and rambling on about my troubles, such as they are,
     love
     Penelope

25 Almeric Road
London, sw11
6 March [1980]

Dear Richard,
     Please don't think I'm ungrateful, I am sure you know I'm not, but I'd rather not make this appeal to those who knew London in 1940 as

this would mean that the readers, if any, were all in sight of the end, as of course I am myself. What worries me a bit is that having taken a check (really just for interest's sake) over four VI forms I find very few of them know that there wasn't any TV or commercial radio in 1939–45, although they have 'done the war for O-level'. They can't conceive of such a thing. You see, I think both the versions you kindly did are a bit too grand, they make it sound more like a thesis, and it's only a story I'm afraid, no more than that. However I enclose what I'd like to put and hope to see you next Thursday. Sarah said it would be all right if I came round a bit before 5, love Penelope

> *25 Almeric Road*
> *London, SW11*
> 14 March [1980]

Dear Richard,

Just to thank you for taking me to the party, I should never have had the resolution to go otherwise and indeed I noticed many people, obviously female novelists, standing about looking at a loss, and I was grateful not to have to do this. I enjoyed it very much and you were quite right (naturally) about the Martini Terrace. In Piccadilly, afterwards, I had the experience of seeing Philip Z* run for a bus, what a turn of speed he has, or turn of foot, as the Daily Express Racing puts it, it's amazing.

I feel I shouldn't have complained – though it wasn't quite meant as a complaint, – about what you'd put on the jacket, only I know you're tolerant about such things, indeed about everything. When you said Charles Monteith was not <u>very</u> nice, I made up my mind never on any account to try to see him.

love
Penelope

* Ziegler.

P.S. I meant to say that these various festivals &c I'm going to aren't I think of any interest from the book selling point of view, except that on May 17th I've got to go to Brighton – to discuss Men As Women Writers See Them with Susan Hill and Jackie Gillott, pity me –

And the organisers asked wd. <u>Offshore</u> be on sale in Brighton, well, I just don't know.

Also, I've just had my advance from Glasgow, thankyou very much for putting it through so quickly

> *25 Almeric Road*
> *London,* sw11
> 4 September 1980

Dear Richard,

Thankyou for your letter and I was very pleased to see the copies of <u>Human Voices</u> – my family tell me that I was getting above myself anyway in objecting to the jacket and it serves me right that I've turned dark blue on the back flap. The great thing is that the book has been made to look a bit longer and for this I'm very grateful to you as indeed I am for all the trouble you take.

I'm also glad to hear about Japanese publisher &c, I'm deeply pessimistic and never expect anything nice to happen so am always pleased if it does – and perhaps you would thank Sarah for me for letting me know about Kaleidoscope and The Critics though I shan't listen as they were so unpleasant last time and I find I get less and less resilient as time goes on. That is natural I suppose.

I am struggling on with Charlotte Mew although everyone in the business (by which I mean lit. biography) seems to want to write about her even apart from Robert Gittings,* who I now find is known as the Arch Weevil. However I won't go on about this but will just wish you a wonderful holiday in France –

love
Penelope

---

* The biographer.

25 Almeric Road
London, sw11
11 October 1980

Dear Richard,

Thankyou very much for your letter and for sending me the notices, sp. <u>The Listener</u> – no-one seems to like Howard Newby but he's encouraged me and voted to give this trouble-creating Booker Prize to <u>The Bookshop</u>, and his remarks are very just, I think – I couldn't quite get <u>Human Voices</u> to hang together, but it was the best I could do.

By the way I don't know if you noticed at the strange PEN meeting (but they're <u>all</u> strange – however, not all of them start with a man holding up a beadwork purse, just like the old Missionary Sundays) that Tom Burns, who seemed to be in genial mood, as usual, said he hadn't had a review copy for <u>The Tablet</u>, but perhaps Collins wouldn't feel this worth it?

There were a number of series missing in the Waugh letters – Mark Amory asked about Ronnie's letters but none could be found although Ronnie himself kept everything – presumably EW,* as Ronnie's literary executor, destroyed them, and all I could turn up was one, not at all interesting, to my father.

Sarah kindly let me know about the NFS,** but I hope this is not the kiss of death as Martyn Goff, in his supremely tactless speech at the new Book House, pointed out that the NFS was for high quality novels which could only expect a very low sale, so let's hope things pick up later. But I do like him and sympathise with his difficulties, Book House being so much more suitable for a seaside hotel, or the Town Hall it once was – the heating failed completely last week and the vast room was freezing though this in turn made it easier to stay awake during the Modern Novel lecture – these lectures are very well attended though, I'm glad to say.

As far as my Poetry Bookshop is concerned I do realise that you've turned it down, kindly but firmly 4 times so far and I expect I had better do a treatment of it and try Faber, which was what I think you

---

*   Evelyn Waugh.
** The New Fiction Society.

suggested, in fact, particularly as it is going to be difficult as regards permissions.

I do so much hope that by now you've navigated past or through the Beatty trustees – I can't <u>believe</u> you will be held up at this point over a formality, it would be entirely unjust.

I would be very glad to meet William, I'm sure he will make a splendid journalist, if only he is ruthless enough –

best wishes

Penelope

25 Almeric Road
London, SW11
20 November 1980

Dear Richard,

Thankyou very much for your letter and enclosures and for all you've done, and I'm sorry <u>H. Voices</u> won't sell as this makes me feel guilty, though I daresay it's not a very good season for anyone except the most popular. I'm afraid, also, that it's not in my nature to be spectacular or panoramic and I'm never likely to be accepted in the U.S., they just don't like these short novels (defended by Colin* in the TLS in an unconstruable Latin couplet) – even Beryl B.** doesn't sell well over there.

My trouble – or one of them – is that I'm always influenced by the last person who gets hold of me, and at the moment I've been asked to look at a mysterious chestful of Pre-Raphaelite papers, also the question of William Morris's unfinished novel† has come up again – by now it has sunk to the bottom. Perhaps I'm better employed doing this and my endlessly complicated Poetry Bookshop than in writing novels, I don't know. I'd love to ask you one of these days – meanwhile I've had a nice notice from Frank Kermode (admired by me but not by you) in the London R of B, and received a Dundee cake from the University of Dundee, and these things make me feel a bit better. It would be better to

---

 * Haycraft.
** Bainbridge.
 † Which would be published in 1982 as *Novel on Blue Paper* with an introduction by PMF.

write long novels and short letters, but I must just say that I hope the Beatty complications turned out all right, I'm sure they must have done by this time, but copyrights and permissions are altogether nothing but a misery –

best wishes – Penelope

[postcard]
27 November [1980]

Thankyou so much for writing, I'd love to come in on Thursday 4th – I could come round at about 5.15 unless you tell me not to.

The PEN club is so DIFFICULT TO GET TO and miles from anywhere, at least for the shabbier members –

Penelope

25 Almeric Road
London, sw11
12 February 1981

Dear Richard,

I was really glad to hear from you as to me you've become something of a mythological figure, partly because of the saga of the move, related to me by Sybille Bedford, I do hope and pray it's all settled itself by now – and partly because of items in the daily press in which you figure as handing out £200,000 contracts &c – one thing after another – but I should very much like to come for a drink on the 24th, I'll come round to Collins about 5.30, unless told not to –

best wishes
Penelope

25 Almeric Road
London, sw11
25 February 1981

Dear Richard,

I so much enjoyed seeing you yesterday – I was a bit worried as you didn't seem to be looking as well as, for instance, when you came back from France, but it's not to be wondered at I suppose – however there is a point with living conditions when things <u>have</u> to get better – I felt this when we were awash in the Thames – and I am sure you and Mary have reached that point.

I'm just enclosing 2 letters about the Morris ms. which as you see suggest a leisurely uncommercial atmosphere, but that's all I want for this kind of thing. I don't care if only one person reads what I've done, as long as nobody else has written it.

Well, I've got my backs of old envelopes out of the drawer to see what I can make out of them – thankyou very much for your advice –

Best wishes, Penelope

25 Almeric Road,
London, sw11
[card]
11 March 1981

Thankyou for letter, will turn up about 3.15 on the 18th (which may give me a chance to discuss Lady Di's dress with Angela) – Uncle Ronnie's memoir by Patrick S/S is not much, he was forced to write it by these dreadful Grenfells, Asquiths &c, –

(The book on Julian Grenfell a couple of years ago, I can't remember who by, suggested to me that Patrick S/S was victimised by them as well –) have nothing to do with these people, they'll destroy you sooner or later, as Malcolm Muggeridge warned me – but Ronnie was fatally attracted by them – best wishes P.

25 Almeric Road
London, sw11
16 April 1981

Dear Richard,

Please do you think you could write what the Keeper of Manuscripts at the Fitzwilliam calls a 'letter of recommendation for our files' to say

that I'm working on an edition of an unpublished MS of William
Morris and so am a fit person to read the letters from Jane Morris to
W. S. Blunt – which the Syndics have just released, (or whatever you do
to old love letters). I know of course that this really has nothing to do
with Collins, and what's more I perhaps never <u>shall</u> edit this ms. as
nothing can be decided till the Soc. of Antiq. have a meeting at the end
of April (they could easily decide the whole thing in 5 minutes but they
like to have these meetings – and ordinarily I wouldn't trouble you as
we all write these letters for each other at the Westminster Tutors, but
as it's vacation time I'm venturing to ask you as they say).

I feel rather under pressure as my daughter and son-in-law, (baby
due in 5 weeks), have suddenly decided that they don't want to teach
any more but would like to keep a small post-office in the depths of
the country and they've kindly asked me to go with them to dig the
vegetable patch – it is very good of them and indeed I've no option
as I think they've sold this house (apparently to the Marquis of
Bath who came round here and tottered up and down the stairs) –
and I personally can <u>only</u> write in London, I love the noise and
squalor and the perpetual distractions and the temptation to take an
aircraft somewhere else, so I'll have to see what I can get finished
before we go the sub post-office. (Of course if we kept hens they
would make a noise, but it's one of my vows <u>never</u> to keep
hens again.)

Very best Easter wishes to you and Mary,

Penelope

[postcard]

24 April 1981

Thankyou very much for writing to the Fitzwilliam for me – I <u>have</u>
read there before, but I expect I've been lost out of the files – in fact I
feel I'm going under altogether, but would just like to do this Wm.
Morris subject. I hope you've got the house you wanted by now? I'd

love to come in and have a drink on Tuesday 5th, about 5.30 if that's
all right –
    Penelope

I put Collins as my address for Who's Who as I never really <u>have</u> an
address – I'm sure they won't notice.

> *25 Almeric Road,*
> *London, sw11*
> [card]
> 10 May [1981]

You won't mind me sending you one more document on this subject.*
I can't think why this man doesn't go away and publish something
else! I won't send you any more of this correspondence, I promise, but
it was very good of you to take an interest in it. Soc. of Antiq: still dizzy
at all the activity and say they must 'brief a reputable literary agent' as
though they usually employed disreputable ones –
    Penelope

P.S. Just off to Somerville High Table, jugs of water and cream crackers
I expect.

> *25 Almeric Road,*
> *London, sw11*
> [card]
> 2 June [1981]

Please are there any spare <u>Offshores</u> lying about the office, it's all these
charity auctions for the disabled &c which seem to have got
completely out of hand, I can't send any more because I haven't got

---

* William Morris.

any more but if you are clearing out the bookcase and find some, could you v. kindly let me have them?

Penelope

25 Almeric Road,
London, sw11
[card]
14 June 1981

It's so kind and helpful of you to send the books – I know very well I'm not due for any more and I suppose if I'm going to be charitable and save my soul I ought to buy them in future, so I won't ask again – incidentally I see <u>some</u> of these people aren't disabled but dyslexic and the book auction has to be called an Orcshun, it seems to me if they're trying to help the dyslexic they'd do better to teach them normal spelling –

However, thankyou again and best wishes

Penelope – Just off to do this creative writing course, which I don't look forward to.

25 Almeric Road
London, sw11
27 July 1981

Dear Richard,

Thankyou so much for your kind letter which had a good effect on me as I'm all in pieces. I take it you'll let me off this questionnaire if I'm not coming out till next autumn* and all the information, photograph &c is at Collins anyway – it's all driving me mad, I had a 'researcher' here <u>all day</u> for one of these American Directories of Modern Writers, I pointed out that I wasn't published in the U.S. but apparently this doesn't matter, they just like reading Directories for their own sake, and then they were annoyed because someone

---

* With *At Freddie's*.

(not me) filled up my recreations in <u>Who's Who</u> as growing orange
and lemon trees, and there weren't any to show, as I've reluctantly had
to part with them as I'm moving, a great loss to me as I shall never
have the heart to start them again.

This is really to say how glad I am about the house, I am sure you
and Mary will find it was worth waiting for, it wd: be wonderful if
you would come to the Post Office one day and advise me on the
vegetables – nothing has been done to the garden for 8 years and the
nettles are 8 foot high – also to send my addresses if Sarah would put
them on file, or tear them up if I've sent them already –

best wishes, Penelope

I'll send a suggestion for the book-jacket as I know from experience
how tactful you are at getting rid of things you don't like!

Theale Post Office Stores
Theale, nr. Wedmore
Somerset
23 August 1981

Dear Richard,

You won't thank me for writing to you when, if I've got things right,
you and Mary are just in the middle of the move, and no-one can
sympathise as much as I do perhaps as I'm now irreparably divided
in 2 and don't know where everything is, not even my typewriter,
however I do want to ask you whether you couldn't (or could) manage
to get <u>At Freddie's</u> out in the summer, I'm sure it would make no
difference to Collins because as you said to me hardbacks can't be sold
anyway, I just feel I shall lose heart if it's got to wait till next autumn.
Barbara (Pym) always used to come out in June, (in fact I think this
next (last) one of hers is going to) and <u>you are in her group</u> someone
said to me firmly the other day <u>you either have to be in hers or Beryl's</u>.
This made me vow <u>never</u> to go to a literary party again and I shan't,
either. – But please if you can find a moment do see if you can shift me
back from the autumn

best wishes Penelope

Theale Post Office Stores
Theale, nr. Wedmore
Somerset
28 August 1981

Dear Richard,

I'm so sorry I haven't answered the right letters, I did write from Whitstable but fear that didn't arrive. I find it rather difficult living in quite so many places at once. As to the sub-post-office stores, ones like this that still sell sweets by the ounce &c, I know they are open to criticism but do you know you only get £50 bonus for resisting armed robbery, it's not much really is it?

I return contract blurb &c and agree to everything only I wonder if you could take out <u>is an Oxford graduate</u> on the jacket as I think it sounds peculiar. The photograph is horrible, but I don't know if there are any other ones, perhaps they're all horrible. If Sarah says it's all right, I expect it <u>is</u> all right.

In respect, as they say, to the jacket,* I can't find <u>anything</u>, rulers and so on, it's not like an ordinary move because the shop had to open straight away to keep the goodwill of the village, so we haven't got anything sorted out and I wonder if we ever will. I've just got the books I've got to teach out of next term – I rescued those – but I'll tell you what I would have liked to do – all my books are before the 1960s as this was the last period when anyone was stopped from doing anything for moral considerations, and this one is 1963, I think, and the style was early Hockney, not what he's doing now but the nice clean drawings with predominant blue violet and yellow, just as neat as a Caulfield really, and I wanted a high wall with a broken basket of fruit at the bottom of it, having evidently fallen, one of the Covent Garden baskets. That gives some movement, because it's evidently fallen from somewhere. I did think of the stage children as to some extent expendable products, like the fruit. Now I'm sure you follow me, Richard, what do you think of it?

Best wishes,
Penelope Fitzgerald

---

* For *At Freddie's*.

[postcard]
16 September [1981]

This is to thank you for such a very nice dinner which made me feel considerably less defeated and I was glad to hear all the good news of your move and the family.

I'm definitely not up to living here* – a parcel has arrived but the Temple Steward has tied it to the outside door with a special knot which he uses for briefs &c and I don't know if it's etiquette to cut it off with scissors.

Will come to office next Wed – P.

76 Clifton Hill, NW8
[postcard to Sarah]
[autumn 1981]

Just one more change of address (from Mondays to Thursdays!)
Penelope

This is a kind of attic, overlooking the tree-tops, with gold wallpaper. It's rather strange. I was moving an arm-chair wh: had no bottom, so people fell through it, and found some valuable jewellery wh: had been lost for 25 years.

76 Clifton Hill,
London, NW8
20 November 1981

Dear Sarah,

Thankyou for the proof of the jacket – it's much more like the idea I had of it, & I want to thank you for the efforts you and Richard made on my behalf. I don't know why the jacket seems to matter so much, but it does.

* The Inner Temple where she was staying with her friend Jean Fisher-Talbot while she looked for a London base.

Incidentally the <u>London Review of Books</u> say that if I'm going to produce anything, could they have it in very good time as (possibly because it only comes out once a fortnight) they're always way behind with their reviews –

best wishes, Penelope

[postcard to Sarah]
23 January [1982]

I'm sitting in a cubicle at the Bristol Hospital for sick babies,* among plastic mobiles and blue elephants – thankyou so much for sending the copy of <u>At F.</u> – I thought in the end it looked right – if any more arrive, then please could they go to 76 Carlton** Hill? best wishes, Penelope

Theale Post Office Stores
Theale, nr. Wedmore
Somerset
13 April [1982]

Dear Richard,

Thankyou so much for your sympathetic letter, I admit I was upset by Paul B.† in the <u>Standard</u> as there seemed to be so much personal dislike in it, and also an unpleasant suggestion of copying, out of some biography or other of Lilian Baylis (which I've never read), whereas all the characters are taken straight from life, whether successfully or not. However, I've been reading my Uncle Wilfred's marvellous addresses to the theologians of the Order of the Good Shepherd, on 1. forgiving hostile reviewers and 2. not feeling morally superior because you've forgiven them. – But I do feel rather daunted and wonder if it's a good idea to go on, if the going is to be quite so hard. I did think that (largely

---

* Where PMF's grandson, Fergus, was being treated.
** She meant Clifton Hill.
† The novelist, Paul Bailey.

owing to efforts made by Collins) I was getting on a bit with <u>At Freddie's</u>, as it seemed a good thing to be in <u>Cosmopolitan</u>, but well, I don't know. – At Christmas time when Scribner's asked for another crime story you advised against it and I'm sure it was good advice, but, as I say, I don't feel now that I know what to do. – And worst of all I can't decide whether 'the danger of frost is past' as the seed packets express it so poetically, and whether I can plant out my marrows or not.

I did like the Japanese ed. of <u>Offshore</u> very much, though. I liked being in the Have a Nice Read series –

best wishes

Penelope

[postcard to Sarah]
18 April [1982]

Thankyou so much for encouraging words, v. necessary to faint-hearted writers.

I'd be very grateful if you could send the Financial Times review if it should come to hand – (needless to say I don't take the FT) Penelope

Theale P. Office Stores
nr. Wedmore
Somerset
23 April 1982

Dear Richard, Thankyou so much for kind thought, I mean about extracting £££ from the Arts Council – but as you say I'm not allowed to apply for anything (not that I ever have) for the 2 years while I'm on the so-called Literature Panel. What I'm entrusted with however is the other end of the business, reading typescripts and 'classics' wh: the publishers (called 'clients' at the Arts Council, as at a solicitor or fortune-teller) send in large quantities in the hope of subsidies. It's rather interesting to see their breakdown of costs.

I do wish you the very best of luck with your applications – perhaps 'luck' is not the right word, but I'm sure you understand me,
   best wishes
   Penelope

I never seem to have the time to write anything except bits and pieces, and must now go and negotiate to borrow a <u>goat</u>, to eat down the nettles on the verge of the road. There are several goats in Theale, and one goat-cheese maker – P

[postcard]
17 June [1982]

Thankyou so much for the lunch, it was lovely to see you on Wed: – meanwhile I'm afraid you won't think too highly of my researches into your father's lectures and sermon – I take it that if it's for the Newman Conversion (perversion, my grandfather insisted) centenary it must have been 1945, but he doesn't seem to have been doing anything then, except revising the 3rd ed. of his <u>Dictionary of Church History</u>.
   And the centenary lectures themselves all seem to be published by Burnes Oates, which won't do. – So you see I am a failure – but perhaps I've got the details wrong –
   best wishes P.

76 Clifton Hill, NW8
13 July [*c.*1982]

Dear Richard – I'm just sending you this Charlotte Mew (remember?) piece, which was well-received by the editor, and rather wildly, but loyally, cut down by my sub-editor, however, this is one more (the 7th) attempt by me to get you to think about a biography of CM. – I had a nice letter from Carmen C. about the article, but DON'T tell me to go to Virago, as they are so close about the £££.
   Perhaps you're on holiday, in which case forgive me.

Sybille Bedford a tower of strength at the PEN picnic. But she said she couldn't give her approval to the vino garibaldino – however, I enjoyed the party and Oliver spoke so well, and there was a feeling of success about the whole thing, I thought.

I do so hope everything is going as you want (Jasper R. says he's reviewed it for the TLS, but hasn't had the proofs yet). – best wishes Penelope

P.S. (quite irrelevant) I was talking to Raleigh's Raoul at a dinner-party last night and it seems he, too, once got into Buckingham Palace, as he was a friend of the flunkey in charge of the silver, who smuggled him in for a week to help during a busy period when 'some monarch' was staying. Perhaps people are walking in and out the whole time?

> *The Post Office Stores*
> *Theale, nr. Wedmore*
> *Somerset*
> 16 July [1982]

My dear Richard, Thankyou so much for your kind letter – just at the moment I'm down here for a while as term is over, trying to repair some of the flood and storm damage (though we can't alas put back the one apple on our 1st-year Bramley) so that it seems to me I'm further from Ashley W. Ho.* than when I'm in London, the S. of England being so extensive, otherwise I should have loved to come, and indeed we should love you to come here and see the shop, though, actually, it's the kind of stone-built cottage with low doors where tall people hit their heads, and are felled, but it's a nice sleepy place all the same. – Meanwhile (I mean during the strike) the coaches make an interesting study, they sell unlimited tickets and you can get them pretty well anywhere (at the Army and Navy for instance) and they promise to get you there somehow, but they brought out or rented everything that can crawl on 3 or 4 wheels,

---

* Richard Ollard's house in the country.

there are coaches starting out from Victoria called the Buffalo and the Llanberis Flyer, and some of them look as if they hadn't been in action for years but they get them all away somehow. The police have much reduced the confusion by making everyone come in through the main exit, and out through the entrance. It's amazing what a calming effect this has on the maddened tourists.

I really started to write this letter to thank you for reading through my g. grandfather's life – I'm sure you're one of the few people who could have done it and I perhaps shouldn't have asked you – I'm sure you're right and that apart from perhaps the end which is a classic I think it's not reproducible – worse still I've just sent you <u>another</u> letter about Charlotte Mew – I can't help it, it keeps coming over me as they say, I still feel her life is interesting in its way – and she did write at least one good poem, how many of us can say that? –

best wishes Penelope

76 Clifton Hill, NW8
13 September 1982

Dear Richard,

I'm sorry to worry you (I really do mean this) but I don't quite know who to ask now about these small matters 1. is that I wonder if anyone can tell me the ISBN for the large-print ed. of <u>Offshore</u> (this is for the Public Lending Right of course which I daresay is driving you crazy as well) – I <u>did</u> have some copies but gave them to the Red Cross 2. I never had a copy, a copy for myself, I mean, of the Charlotte Mew contract so I wonder if this book has got swept under the carpet?

best wishes
Penelope

P.S. Jasper R. <u>does</u> understand the PLR* and is bringing out his next book on June 29th to save the cost of re-registering.

* Public Lending Right.

76 Clifton Hill, NW8
25 May 1983

Dear Richard,

You remember Charlotte Mew? Well, I'm going to ask whether you can help me about one of the illustrations. It's the frontispiece to the Duckworth collected edition of her poetry (out of print) and it shows Charlotte Mew and her nurse, but the BL won't reproduce it for me, because the permission I've got from Duckworths consists of the scrawled words 'Yes, do. All the best, Colin.' This _is_ a permission, however, and I really can't ask Colin to write another tidier letter, so could Collins reproduce this photograph for me do you think? It would mean getting a copy of the book from the London Library, though, and I'm afraid I'm not a member. More difficulties all the time.

Hoping to hear your PEN address on Pepys but I believe there's no room – which is a good thing in itself –

best wishes
Penelope

I had to address the PEN conference in Venice on L. P. Hartley and I found I couldn't remember anything about him, and now I'm struggling with an introduction to L. H. Myers' The Near and the Far, and find I can't remember anything about <u>him</u>. And altogether I think as you grow older you understand more, but remember less.

Theale Post Office Stores
nr. Wedmore
Somerset
8 October 1983

My dear Richard,

Thankyou so much for your letter, I was most disappointed to miss you, but am lying here like a bit of craft patchwork, however it's promised that the stitches will come out next Monday. I didn't know it was possible to hit yourself in quite so many places. The hospital did not believe in the ladder, and clearly think we're a gypsy family who've

been having a 'disagreement'. (The next case brought in after me was
an O/D-M/D – overdose, marital disagreement.)

In respect to <u>C Mew</u>, I still have the notes to do, though they're not
all that many, I don't like nos. in the text for a book of this sort but
prefer the notes the way they're done in Quentin Bell's Virginia
Woolf biography – and I also of course have the introduction,
acknowledgements, bibliography (not serious) to do. There are quite a
few errors in the text, I'm afraid, (apart from putting 'Boswell' instead
of Pepys wh: seems a Freudian slip of some kind) but it wouldn't take
me at all long to put them right, if only I can stop falling off things.
(Apart from everything else I'm missing all my Arts Council
committees and I can feel as I lie here that they're deciding everything
the way I don't want. It's very hard when you think of all the work I
did for that committee.)

To return: Marjorie Dawson Scott has to be handled very very
carefully, for many years she has refused to show her CMew letters to
the biographers, American and otherwise, who asked her about them,
and Marjorie can be very discouraging when she tries. She wouldn't
show them, for instance, to Val Warner who was editing the <u>Collected
Works</u>, and she wouldn't show them to me, but then one afternoon she
suddenly handed me the correspondence in a paper bag. Even then she
kept changing her mind and saying she wanted to write it all up
herself, so I consulted the kindly (though shady?) Brian Elstob who
said 'photostat them all, my dear, and I'll keep Marjorie in play' – I
didn't like to do that, but I certainly copied a number of passages.
Subsequently I was shown her ma's diaries but she didn't let me <u>hold</u>
them so I had to read as much as I could upside down which I'm
fortunately quite used to, and memorise all she said without making a
note, which I find much harder than when I was younger. Let's hope
she won't suddenly object to everything again. Such are the sufferings
of primary biographers, Richard. Meanwhile I'm still very worried
about <u>Mrs Luttrell</u>. She won't let anyone reproduce the Nat. Portrait
Gallery photo of <u>Harold Monro</u> without her permission and apart
from all that there is permission for all my quotations from the BL
Add. Mss. Monro papers. I'd be deeply grateful if you could write to
her <u>again</u> as she never answered your first letter and do you think it

ought to be registered or do you think that will make her hostile? It's no use my writing or ringing up as she has refused to answer me for years, since she still thinks she is collaborating with Patric Dickinson on a book to end all books. Patric says he's just resigned to the way she is, and I daresay he doesn't care too much whether anything ever comes of the collaboration or not. Please do help me, Richard, I'm frightened to go ahead just on the strength of one letter that never got answered.

Sydney Cockerell, as you well know, was an old shit who was charming when he wanted to be a fairy godmother or cultivate famous people, although I'm afraid I haven't been as successful in indicating this as Robert Gittings was in his <u>Hardy</u>. (Incidentally, Cockerell's executor, Wilfrid Blunt, was so ill when I went to see him that he just gave me verbal permission, but I've known him do this before.) In any case no-one is interested in Cockerell, the interesting things about CMew are that 1. she was a poet, otherwise I shouldn't bother to write about her 2. she was a lesbian 3. she was unhappy 4. she has a curious lifespan as a writer, from the nineties to the 1920s. The two people who encouraged me were Michael Holroyd, who wrote one of the first biographical essays on Charlotte Mew, (I mean one of the first ones after the collected edition of 1953) and Carmen C.* who is a Mew fan and of course still hopes to sell out the Virago <u>Collected Works</u>. I suppose there aren't such luxuries as proof copies now, otherwise these two are the people who should get one, I don't think they need to be asked to do anything, they will understand well enough.

I fear none of the papers would be interested in an extract about a lesbian who didn't make it, but I can't manufacture evidence, unfortunately! (Poor Charlotte features in the <u>Penguin Book of Homosexual Verse</u> without any evidence at all.) The interest, to me, is that she's a divided personality who had to produce so many versions of herself at the same time. Perhaps we all do.

This letter is getting rather long, but Richard please do get Collins to make this book look nice. They made the Proust letters look decent and the Forster letters (which admittedly are sold to the <u>Observer</u>) are

* Callil.

also going to look nice, I'm told, and I want CMew to look nice. It's not just the cover, it's the whole shape and lay-out. You remember you <u>promised</u> to scatter the photographs, and I enclose 2 copies of Monro's <u>chapbook</u> (which I implore you not to lose as they can't be replaced) to show you the right printing, if you'd look at Gerard Meynell's ad: in the back pages (vi) of August 1919 – and I do want <u>printer's flowers</u> in between the sections which is right for the period. <u>Chapbook May 1921</u> has these (though I really sent it as I thought you'd like the 'fragment' on p 24 – this is quite irrelevant) and the format ought to be this 9 by 7 – don't say, it can't be! I know Collins will print 1031 and a half copies or whatever the mystic commercial minimum is, and sell 237 and cast it into limbo so it might just as well look nice in the first place, to give it some sort of chance. Don't tell me I don't understand commercial publishing, after 18 months of looking into their horrible secrets, costs, alleged costs and advances, I <u>do</u> understand it, but hoped this might be my lucky break. I'm sending this to Ashley T. as I can't make out what happens at 8 Grafton St and don't want it to disappear for weeks on end, but perhaps injuries are making me morbid. Yes I think they definitely <u>are</u>, but I do mean what I said about the make-up.

Michael Schmidt of Carcanet said he wd: like to put an extract in PN Review but I am ignoring this completely as it has no circulation and doesn't pay.

Please forgive me if there are any feverish expressions, love to Mary, best wishes for the garden, mayfly and Clarendon – Penelope

76 Clifton Hill, NW8
14 November 1983

Dear Richard – This is only to say how sorry I was to miss you at Collins last Wednesday, I did hope to talk to you for a moment, (not I must admit about anything in particular) but Angela said she thought you were in the post room, and I couldn't find you there and got lost (temporarily) in the basement. – I think it's very strange that the jackets and the book design are done separately, even if the 2 ladies are in adjoining coops – surely that's no way to get nice-looking books?

I tried to explain to Erica what 1920s Poetry Bookshop design was like, but didn't have much luck, as I could see she had no idea what I was talking about. I did show her some examples, but she looked at them with dismay, I thought, well, we shall see.

While I was recovering from my dispute with the ladder, and Michael Church was in Frankfurt, the rest of the Arts Council grants committee came close to ignoring the all-important principle which Michael Holroyd got the Arts Council to accept last year, that history and biography (<u>not</u> only literary biography) were literature, just as much as fiction and poetry – however, we were both back last week and have got things straight again, so all is going well, I think.

Just back from Somerset – the baby is thriving and all the broad beans have come up – but the hens keep getting out, nothing, it seems, will keep them in. Committees and hen-keeping are terrible time-wasters I think –

Hoping to see you one of these days, best wishes to you and Mary – Penelope

> *76 Clifton Hill,* NW8
> 9 December 1983

Dear Richard – Please excuse this A4, I'm never in the same place as the things I want.

Thankyou very much for taking this trouble about the I. of W. photograph, it would be a great improvement to have one – I'm not sure when the illustrations are supposed to be in, and am having great trouble getting Sydney Cockerell out of the National Portrait Gallery, who are always very slow. I'll never do a biography again! In any case, I've rather lost heart over Charlotte M. since I was told it's got to come out in the ordinary format, the jacket of course having been designed for 9 by 6 and will look dreadful, and Vera I think was disappointed as she had taken a lot of trouble over the right type, &c but now we're back to Baskerville and the usual depressing mediocrity – I know of course that the book will lose money for the great firm but I hoped for once they might let themselves lose a little more.

Perhaps I might see you on the 14th? when the council are parting with a few sandwiches somewhere or other. I'm horrified that you should thank me, as obviously, if there are to be grants, you <u>should</u> have one, – the trouble was to persuade Charles that history and historical biography are literature, and it was Michael Holroyd who did this, before he departed –

best Xmas wishes to you and Mary – Penelope

> *76 Clifton Hill,* NW8
> 13 March [1985]

Dear Richard,

I was so glad to see you again, and want to thank you so much for giving me such a delicious dinner, as well as your advice, which I always need. I felt ashamed that I hadn't a better grasp on Lord Louis,* but I've reached a stage where the train-journeys, the chickens (not laying), the winter broad-beans (laid low by the second great frost), the dear grand-children &c seem to have stupefied me, perhaps my intellectual life is pretty well over, although this of course is my fault and not that of the beans, the grand-children and so on. But I'm truly glad that you've brought out Lord Louis so well and it must have been a wonderful day at Broadlands. – (I think that when the Cowper-Temples were there they supported the Temperance movement, but I daresay there have been a lot of changes since then.) As to Leslie Hartley, when I look through my interview books, (and also the list of people who refused to say anything) my heart fails a bit. – I had a letter this morning from someone who said 'when you look at your PLR, don't you feel sorry for your biographies?' and this is absolutely true, it's the fiction that keeps us all going. – In any case, I shall write to Lord David and (not mentioning any financial considerations) put him off in the politest manner I can manage.

---

* Philip Ziegler's biography of Lord Louis Mountbatten.

And now I find that I didn't ask you for your new address, which was lost with my address-book during my Christmas burglary, so I'll have to send this to Collins, and it will have to be a test-case, to see how long they take to forward it – but when it arrives, it's to thank you and send all my best wishes to you and Mary –

love
Penelope

76 *Clifton Hill,* NW8
28 March [1985]

Dear Richard,

Thankyou so much for writing – I thought afterwards that I could have got the address from Oliver, but no matter, it was nice to hear from you and I still hope that you and Mary may pass by the Theale Post Office one day.

I was pleased to have the award* and delighted to share it with <u>Edmund Spenser, Poet of Protestantism</u>, it's all so completely typical, an award that no-one's ever heard of from a body that no-one's ever heard of for 2 books which I fear not many people have heard of either, but I didn't say this to R. Schlesinger or J. Chapman as I thought it was kind of them to write, and didn't want to seem ungrateful, and in any case it means so much to me to have a record of my poor Charlotte Mew in print.

Meanwhile the daffodils are all out and I must write to Lord D. – While on this subject, I am glad your beans are showing, but they <u>can't</u> be winter broad beans – that's the glorious reckless gamble of it all, to keep them at 6 inches high all through the winter and have them in flower before the black-fly comes, I'm sure you'll agree – and this is the first winter I've failed in our little post-office garden – wh: I'm afraid is symbolic of something – love Penelope

* The Rosemary Crawshay prize from the British Academy for *Charlotte Mew.*

76 Clifton Hill
London, NW8
13 January 1986

Dear Richard,

Just a note to say that I took the t/s of this (potential) novel* round
to Collins, where Angela was sitting with her head in her hands,
looking as if she was contemplating suicide or early retirement, and
Stuart says he will send you a copy, (I wish he'd made a few more,
but mustn't be ungrateful, and perhaps he's not supposed to) – he
sounded so excited about his New York holiday, like the spirit of
youth itself. I hope he won't get above himself and that all will be
well, as he works so very hard. – Also that you had a good Christmas –
some of our tiles came off and there was trouble with the drains, but
Xmas would be nothing without that to a country-dweller –

To revert to the T/S, perhaps you'd let me know what you think** –
love Penelope

76 Clifton Hill
London, NW8
30 May [1986]

My dear Richard

Thankyou so much for your letter, it was nice of you to write – you
don't know how often I wish you were there, back in St James's Place† –
for example I've just had a letter from R. Schlesinger, saying he's now a
literary agent – perhaps that's what he was before? – but surely he <u>can't</u>
want to represent the Collins list, and go back to negotiate at dreaded
Grafton St, it seems so strange? And I would have liked to ask
you what you thought about it. – Meanwhile, in spite of his
disappointment over his high-powered girlfriend being too afraid of

---

* *Innocence.*
** Richard Ollard had now retired and Stuart Proffit became her new editor. PMF contin-
ued, however, to send Richard Ollard her manuscripts and to seek his editorial advice.
† At the old Collins premises. The company had just moved moved to larger premises in
Grafton Street.

the Libyans to go to Rome, Stuart has done all he possibly could for <u>Innocence</u> – a title which <u>does</u> fit on to the jacket and I can't help feeling the pig-tailed man is a great improvement on the defeated-looking Ron and the cover is the nicest-looking I've ever had. How Belinda got hold of the picture I don't know, but then, she's an amazing girl.

I haven't seen Patty or Oliver since they set off to stay at the Plaza NY, for the wedding. I am sure Camila is very nice, and I'm sure she is very rich, I think it's the relatives you have to look out for with L/American girls. I don't know how strong-minded Dilly* really is. I wonder now whether he'll ever be allowed to leave the U.S.

I would like to write to Simon King,** referred to by Private Eye as 'the Scottish supremo's hatchet-man', but I don't know what to say to him quite. I have a contract for Innocence to come out in this Flamingo series, but I wonder whether in fact Collins will go on with their Flamingos if they don't make money. – The truth is I can't manage the publishing world. Addressing the Virago, Hogarth, Chatto &c sales reps at the Drury Lane Hotel at 8.15 in the morning laid me out completely, and then Carmen goes on all day and takes these dreadful people out to a dinner dance in the evening. How can she?

I'm so glad Clarendon has gone so well, but the last stages of such a big book must be a terrible undertaking. I wonder if you'll be sorry to part with it, or glad.

I hope Mary and the family are well – Valpy came back to Holland for a while and it was lovely on the ice with all the canals frozen – now he's going back to Nicaragua, one book behind with Macmillan, one with Heinemann and 2 with the C.U.P. but he says it won't matter – Tina's baby is my great anxiety but I shall know the best or the worst at the end of July – love Penelope

---

* Oliver Knox's son, Dillwyn's grandson.
** Managing director, Collins Trade division.

76 Clifton Hill
London, NW8
10 December 1987

My dear Richard,

How I wish you were here to explain Collins: The New Concept, all on such beautiful paper, much better than they ever use for the books, but am glad to see you figure so largely, so too does my cousin once removed Crispin Fisher, while others seem to have sunk rapidly downwards and totally new names (to me) have appeared. But I'm told the Maclehose baby has to be a boy, because the Ms are really a publishing clan, like Collins itself once was – so that may affect the new concept.

Stuart says he'll do the photocopying so I'll take my bits and pieces in – I still want someone to put all the Italian refs. right and it seems a lot to ask anyone, I know Maurice Cranston is retired, but perhaps he didn't count on spending his retirement in reading other peoples' m or tss.

They say the BBC is getting ready for the 1688 celebrations already, I expect with your assistance,

love to you and Mary
Penelope

27a Bishop's Road
London, N6
1 February [1989]

Dear Richard,

Just to thank you for giving me good advice during the epic struggle – I hope the Chapmans were able to recover at the Health Farm – and 'after all' as Angela put it the other day in reception 'it was only the board who had to resign'. Stuart had seemed sad about the takeover but now on the contrary appears to be even more energetic and cheerful than ever, perhaps there's a moral in this somewhere. I hope he gets his biography series, and then I'm told Collins is going into the movie business, I suppose to make soap operas for the box of tricks Murdoch has invested in.

All well at Watchet except that Paschal (the second little boy) is very slow at learning to talk and I think has hearing problems so that it's hard to explain any thing to him, it's painful to see how puzzled he is. He's 2 and a half, and the doctors are doing this, that and the other thing and everyone in Watchet has advice to offer. Meanwhile he's invented a sign language of his own which is quite adequate for day-to-day purposes, and probably wonders what we're making such a fuss about.

Best wishes to Mary and the family and whatever you're writing or whatever is 'allowing itself to be written by you' as AEH* put it –

love, Penelope

27a Bishop's Road
London, N6
16 February [1989]

Dear Richard,

I think perhaps our letters crossed, but whether they did or not I want to thank you for yours, and for sending me the kind remarks of John Verney (surely the <u>Dinner of Herbs</u> man?) and the Lincolnshire Old Churches leaflet which is very elegant and effective as you say (I wonder if they've still got the Sanctus bell at Bottesford wh: my grandfather mysteriously recovered from The Society of Antiquaries).

Meanwhile I gather from a letter from Ian that he knew he'd got no hope of surviving from the start but that he intends to go on publishing (surely not on his own?) – so <u>Private Eye</u> are wrong in saying that 'Macbeth is accepting his silver watch', I should have expected him to be sick of the whole business, but I suppose he's an indestructible Scotsman.

I don't know how long it is since I've seen Dickie Walker, or even been to Knill, but if there's ever a chance to see him again, it would be nice. His father was rather strict and didn't like it when, during a charade, someone came in wearing Wolsey's underwear (do you remember it?) from which the Walkers earned their £££.

* A. E. Housman.

I hope Stuart is allowed to do his biography series – also that you saw T. Wogan interviewing R. Murdoch on TV. That I did enjoy –
Love and best wishes to you and Mary –
Penelope

Poor S. Rushdie, or rich S. Rushdie, whichever you like, that was a publicity campaign that went dreadfully wrong. I don't think he ought to go into hiding, though. My local Patel grocery on the corner tells me that it is not a dignified act.

> *27a Bishop's Road*
> *London, N6*
> March [1989]

Dear Mary and Richard,
    Thankyou so very much for all your kindness and hospitality at the week-end – I knew it was a beautiful part of the coast, but not quite how beautiful, and also, it seems, health-giving, or in any event it has had a wonderful effect on me. And what good luck it was to have the right weather and be able to see the sea like that, in the sun with cloud-shadow later.
    It turned out that Stuart's extra bag was full of <u>running</u> things, in case it turned out too cold to walk, this made me even more grateful that the weather was so clear. He had to keep awake in the train so that he would sleep well at night, and to be able to psyche himself up for Monday morning at Collins. So we had to talk rather than read and Stuart (who says he's 28) believes that the world is really going to be clear now of the shadow of war, of world war at any rate. Maria says the same, and I wish I could dare to believe they're right. – He also spoke enthusiastically about Mary's cooking and there, certainly, I agree with him.
    Really I was glad to see him so much better than when he arrived, in spite of all the mishaps (which reminded me of the stories which we used to get in the Boys Own Paper where someone always 'lost the right path' as darkness fell) – I'm so fond of him and he is a tremendous book editor.

Very best wishes for the conversion of the barn, and for Fisher and Cunningham (I know this isn't and couldn't be the right title, but I very much enjoyed hearing about it) and thankyou once again for asking me to stay

love

Penelope

27a Bishop's Road
London, N6
5 October [1989]

Dearest Richard,

Very many congratulations on the arrival of Hermione (who was as tender as infancy and grace, if I remember right). It must have been a terribly anxious time for you and Mary, but now there's a wonderful new stage of total slavery opening for you and I'm delighted on your account.

Only your arm, Richard, I'm afraid that must have been a really hard knock – Richard Cohen (how does he know this?) tells me it was a riding accident, which makes it more distinguished, but just as painful.

I can only hope you're out of plaster soon, because plaster is tedious beyond words.

Thankyou for your kind words about the review – I always think I'm going to dash them off in an evening, and they take weeks. (Now they've sent me the latest Adrian Mole!) Mary is <u>of course</u> right about the Glynne language, but I weakened because I shd: have had to explain who they were and I couldn't get it into the sentence, a terrible confession for a reviewer. – You were very kind by the way about John Carswell's Algernon Sidney, if only you'd come to the party I could have asked you who he was – nobody knew – I don't think Jock Murray knew, and I thought by the way that he might have given the party at <u>his</u> place, but the Carswells are always v. kind and hospitable.

Tina and family have moved into a cottage at Milton Abbot – an old cottage, not one of the model Lutyens ones – and Paschal is going to a special school for deaf children in Plymouth – or rather he's had 2 mornings there and been very happy and now he's going to be staying for lunch, and see how that works – he's very well able to make people understand what he <u>doesn't</u> want, it's hard to find a school like that now so it makes the move from Watchet (which was sad in itself) worthwhile.

I would have loved to send you a Burne-Jones, but didn't think he was the right century for you – I had to fight to get the photograph I wanted on the cover and they have coloured it rather strangely, but it's a good portrait to my mind because you think 'What are they saying?'

Meanwhile I wonder how Xtopher S. Stevenson is getting on, and at least he's started up, but I don't know about the Chapmans. How confusing it all is.

It was very kind of Stuart to take me to <u>The Magic Flute</u>, which I loved, and home in his rarely seen car. I didn't like to ask him about Suzanne, because I consider myself a granny figure, and Stuart has a granny already, to whom he seems much attached. But I can't think it would be a good thing for him to go to the U.S. when he has worked so hard and done so well where he is. The great thing now is surely for him to prove that he didn't pay too much for this Bullock book,* and I'm sure he will, too. I did write to him of course but he replied that it was all his fault. But nothing is ever all anybody's fault.

It would be only right for Dilly to go into the DNB, but Olly of course wd: have to write it. – Most of my notes have been sold to Texas Humanities and have disappeared for ever into the air-conditioned interior where daylight never penetrates.

I'm a (small) part of a series of biographers on Radio 4 wh: is going out in December so I have another chance to say a few words on Charlotte Mew! I sent a copy to Hermione (now Hermione the inferior) as she is doing some collection of women poets, she tells

---

* Alan Bullock's *Hitler and Stalin: Parallel Lives.*

me, and I want CM to be properly represented, she was in the Gay and Lesbian anthology, but I <u>don't</u> consider that enough.

love to you and Mary

Penelope

27a Bishop's Road
London, N6
23 November [1989]

Dearest Richard

I'm sorry to have been so slow in thanking you for reading my untitled, illegible and incomprehensible T/S.* Maria usually gets them moonlighted for me in the Anatomy Dept of University College, but she was away, and I thought it would save trouble to get the processing done elsewhere, but it didn't.

I did check 'stow it' and it is said by Partridge to be <u>cant</u> in the 19th C. and <u>low colloquial</u> in the 20th, though not very low, I should have thought.

More important, I tried to decide from your writing whether your arm was really quite right yet and decided it wasn't – I hope I'm wrong.

Stuart seems to have a large staff now, inc: a boy assistant, who looks about 16, such as Sexton Blake used to have – but I suppose there will be room, for all, in the dreaded Fulham Palace Rd** –

love to you and Mary

Penelope

27a Bishop's Road
London, N6
24 August [1990]

Dearest Richard,

Thankyou so much for your kind letter, written I don't know in the middle of what new and difficult piece of work – but in any case I was

---

* *The Gate of Angels.*
** The location of the new HarperCollins building in Hammersmith.

very glad to hear of the illustrated edition of your Pepys – not quite so glad to hear about your back – but perhaps that was only a way of describing the heaviness of folios – I hope so.

I dread the transference of the BL to St Pancras. I met Dilly there the other day, looking just as handsome and spiritual as ever, although he tells me that it's not rhetoric that he teaches now. I'm sure I'll never meet him by chance at St Pancras, as I so often do at the BL, simply because the catalogue won't be circular.

Stuart kindly took me for my publication day to a restaurant with beautiful macaws and parrots in cages, where he took Suzanne for her birthday, and I know he can't say more than that. – I know he worked and got the Collins PR department to work, to try and get this last novel off to a good start.

Meanwhile I've been on holiday in Devon, where my little grandson who's deaf is making what they call significant progress. At least he always says 'Don't cry' when any of them in fact do cry.

Now for Christopher S-S's* great launch – I don't see how a life of Dickens written by someone who has no sense of humour whatever can be a success, but I daresay it will be, and everyone I'm quite sure wishes Xtopher S-S well –

love,
Penelope

27a Bishop's Road
London, N6
12 August [1991]

Dearest Richard – I admit I'm writing to ask you to help me, but not to read anything and not to try and get anything published – it's to advise me on the case of a friend of mine, Antonia Southern, who used to run the Westminster Tutors in its better days, and who has written a book about Col. Rainbarrow (perhaps Rainborough? She always calls him Col. R.) and the Levellers. She tried the Windrush Press, wh: I've never

---

* Publisher, Christopher Sinclair-Stevenson.

heard of, and they sent it back, saying there were too many Times, and not enough Life, which may well be the case, I don't know. Anyway, she says she once had an encouraging letter from Robin Deniston and will I write to him introducing her – the trouble is I don't really know him, it was only that he once long ago asked me to write a life of his father, which I had to say I was not competent to do – but I wondered if you could tell me whether he's still at OUP, or whether he's retired, and whether he really did take orders in the end in which case I suppose he ought to be addressed as the Rev.

Antonia also asks me whether it's true that Lawrence and Wishart specialize in books on the Levellers – I thought they were an old-fashioned Marxist concern – do you know anything about them?

And am I right in feeling that there are an awful lot of books about the Levellers? Hadn't she better concentrate on Colonel R.? But she's an historian and says she still hasn't lost faith in her book as history.

Meanwhile I feel that if Angela has gone and mice have got into the air-conditioning the Harper Collins palace must be almost untenable. But I'm so glad that Stuart's Big Book* after many worries is proving such an enormous success – what energy he's got! If he gets this place in Herefordshire I suppose he will have to arrive up at week-ends and put together the roof and chimneys and then walk miles over Hay Bluff &c for exercise, but I expect that will be as nothing to him.

The Booker reading is stupefying me I'm afraid – but I do hope to see you when you come to Highgate in the autumn. Just off to France for a week – I do hope the barn and everything else is going well – love to you and Mary – Penelope

27a Bishop's Road
London, N6
26 August [1991]

Dearest Richard – this is just a note to thank you for your very real help about Colonel Rainborough, all of which I've passed on to

---

* Bullock's *Hitler and Stalin: Parallel Lives.*

Antonia Southern, who will be more than grateful to have it – I did however leave out Duckworths as I went to Colin's farewell party at The Old Piano Factory before they moved the offices to Hoxton Square, it was just the same as in the old days, everyone introduced as geniuses and Beryl loyal as ever, only asking to be stopped getting too drunk to take a taxi to the airport – but as all the furniture was gone the refreshments had to be put on the floor and the authors' coats (most of them had come from Oxford and Cambridge in their best sherry-party clothes) had to go in what were once the packing rooms and were thick with dust and bits of paper. I hated to see it all go, and was glad to be able to wish him luck, but I can't think he'll be able to publish anything for a while that hasn't American money behind it. I thought he had the Piano Factory on a council mortgage, but it seems it was a council rent, which has been immensely put up.

I also must put right the impression that Stuart is to become a Herefordshire landowner, it's a ruinous cottage he saw FOR SALE somewhere near Hay Bluff and it's not even certain that the owners can be bothered to sell it, and quite certain that it needs all manner of repairs, but he hoped it would be nice for his family to come to from Bolton, and particularly his father, and he wanted to be able to leave Collins on Thurs: evening taking his TS's to read with him and walk over the hills at the weekend and these he says are the nearest hills to London. All are welcome at the cottage, and I'm sure he means this. But I'm ashamed to say that I can't make out which of the girls he went to Italy with (certainly not his secretary who is so nice, but takes 2 months to forward correspondence). There were 2 girls at dinner the other night, but Richard Holmes talked with such Coleridge-like profuseness and charm that I couldn't hear anything they said. Now Mary would have identified the right one immediately. But of course these things can change. Anyway it's so much better without Suzanne who seemed very demanding, and the Parallel Lives, thank heavens, seems established as a great success.

I'm so glad your lovely barn is converting so successfully. About Fisher and Cunningham I don't understand, as Oliver said something about reviews he knew were coming out, and hoped to get some reference into them, I'm not sure how, to Mavis Batey and Uncle Dilly and Matapan. – But Churchill and the navy – surely you've got the best subject of the whole book there.

Just back from the nouveau art hunting lodge, with stuffed fox in the hall, near the Dinan coast, with wonderful sunshine ripening the maize – no architecture except Mont St Michel, now a nightmare*, on the way back, but beaches with the 3 children and tarte aux pommes every tea-time –

with many thanks again for your advice – love Penelope

* so, too, is the Booker list! I'm in favour of The Van, but there are a lot of dead weights (in my opinion) to get rid of.

> *27a Bishop's Road*
> *London, N6*
> 3 March [1992]

Dear Richard,

It was one of the nicest parties I've ever been to, and you could see that everyone thought so. Your 'few words', in particular, seemed just right, and that can't have been so easy to do, in spite of your experience of these things. Surely there can't have been a friendlier evening, even at Great Tew. (No women there, of course) and it was a great treat to meet Patrick O'Brian –

With many thanks
Love
Penelope

I'm so glad Mary was able to come.

> *27a Bishop's Road*
> *London, N6*
> 25 January [1993]

Dearest Richard,

Thankyou so much for your kind invitation to the Painted Hall at Greenwich – I should love to come, as I don't need to tell you, but I wonder if it would be possible to arrange it later in the year, perhaps when you and Mary have got back from your summer travels, when I hope that though I shan't be any younger I may be a little less decrepit?

At Oliver and Patty's party, Derwent May, who is always in wonderful spirits and so usually cheers me up, was talking about Frank Kermode who seems to be a great friend of his and the sad incident of F.K. giving all his notes, his life's work, to the demolition man – 'he just can't manage, he just lets life get the better of him.' – and my heart sank because I felt I was just the same (although that wouldn't have worried me if I could write like FK). – All this sounds like self-pity, which is hateful, but I've got a much nicer heart specialist at the Whittington now, who doesn't keep menacing me with warfarin as he knows I don't like the idea of it, (the idea of rat-poison I mean) and so I am hoping to get into better condition. It comes and goes rather.

Snowdrops out at last – I began to think they were going to miss a year –

love
Penelope

27a Bishop's Road
London, N6
12 January [late 1990s]

Dear Richard and Mary,

This is to thank you so very much for finding a taxi for me last night, (something which looked almost impossible when we got out of the Ivy, and clearly <u>was</u> impossible to the overwhelmed doorman) and a nice archetypal driver who told me 1. that he'd often picked up stage folk from the Ivy and they didn't look nearly so good close to 2. that the homeless all had their own cars waiting for them just round the corner.

Lovely to see you both and many congratulations on the birth of Hughie. I'm sure he will do great things –

love Penelope

Lovely too to see Oliver and Patty so truly happy – and they've had their ups and downs – and surrounded by so much true friendship and affection and as Ol. said, by their wonderful children, all in safe harbour at last.

27a Bishop's Road
London, N6
14 September [1994]

Dearest Richard –

Thankyou so much for your letter and needless to say I was very glad to have your editorial suggestions, although I feel it quite wrong that you should have to bother with literals. It's already been back for 2 retypes to University College London, where Ria gets it moonlighted, but the operative doesn't know either German or English and my German isn't up to much either.

All this really began when I tried to find out who really discovered the blue poppy, meconopsis baileyi, as it seems not really to have been Colonel Bailey at all, and one thing led to another, but never mind that now.

It would be lovely to see you and Mary. I thought there might be a chance of your coming to Anne's party on the 24th, but I expect you'll still be in France, wonderful to go there in the early autumn,

Why has Stuart grown this beard, and where will Harvill go? Up here in Highgate, where we've now got a large fox curled up in the sun and not even bothering to take cover, I don't know these things –

love,
Penelope

27a Bishop's Road
London, N6
29 November [1994]

Dearest Richard,

I am so sorry I didn't ring earlier about the DNB lecture. I did want to go, and (after all these years) still felt I was sure to be all right, but now I have Cornish flu on top of all the other kinds, (this is my 4th consecutive go) and would not do for decent company. There are so many things I wanted to do this week, (including, sadly, a funeral, and what I suppose is the last lunch party at the Independent*), but I particularly looked forward to the lecture, and to seeing you.

Well now I suppose there will be Christopher Maclehose Books as well as Richard Cohen books and how many others, how can they all survive? Everything seems to be getting too much for everyone. I was very sorry about Colin. They managed to kill him off between them.

This flu is very lowering.

I hope you will forgive me for asking you something – I can't ask Stuart, what with one thing and another, indeed many others, to do anything more about this not-quite-novel I've written, but I do need a German, not any old German but one who is at least somewhat interested, not in the Romantics, but in the Early Romantics, just to read through and say what's wrong, particularly in the titles people used, or did, when they spoke to each other, – Years and years ago Michael Joseph got in an expert to read a life of Burne-Jones I did and he altered almost every line, and it turned out that he objected to the biography of artists in principle and this one in particular.

Thankyou very much for <u>your</u> corrections, Richard. I know you have a lot to do.

I spent the week-end at the riding stables and sorting through the angels and shepherds outfits at the church, and trying to find a Jaeger dressing-gown (do you remember them?) for Joseph, and now here I am –

Best wishes for everything
love, Penelope

27a Bishop's Road
London, N6
2 November [1996]

Dearest Richard,

Thankyou so much for your letter – I couldn't make up my mind about the DNB lecture, but I'll write now and see if they've got a ticket

---

* PMF was one of the judges for the *Independent* Foreign Fiction Prize.

left and if so I'd love to met you there. I haven't been to any of them
since the H.A.L. Fisher – Mary (Bennett) was a little disappointed by
that one as she felt not enough was said about H.A.L.'s work at New
College, very difficult to come straight after the Spooners, sp.
Mrs Spooner.

The trouble is that after having flu, quite 8 weeks ago, I've found it
very difficult to breathe, rather a handicap really, and everyone is, I
feel, getting very sick of me and my disabilities. I think I made a mistake
in going to the Cheltenham Festival, but I'd promised. – But surely I
ought to be able to manage a bit better by Dec. 1st

Lovely here and a large fox taking a short nap in the sun in the
garden. Cats terrified of it. – Pretty well everything in Highgate is now
run by Anne, with complete calm and efficiency. I'd love to be like that,
but we must be satisfied with our lot – love to you and Mary –

Penelope

30 September [1998]

Dearest Richard,

I was looking forward so much to hearing you speak and perhaps
seeing you at Anne's on the 22nd, and when I realised the dreaded
Booker dinner was on that evening I hoped I might not be needed
there, but now I see that because there's been so much trouble about
the judging (and I feel that I'm in more trouble than anyone in some
ways, as Irish papers keep ringing up and saying, we see you're
supporting this fellow Doyle, did you know his family were jumping
round the kitchen when they heard he was on your list, and is it true
this lord (i.e. Nicholas Mosley) has been upset by Doyle's language?) I
shall <u>have</u> to go, although I wanted to tell you, with a heart and a half,
as we used to say, that I'd so much rather hear about Pepys. I'm truly
glad that the new edition has come out so successfully.

This would have been a great opportunity to see Mary too, and to
hear about Hermione, and all I can do now instead is to send my love,
which I do – Penelope

23 October [1998]

Thankyou v. much for p.c. – it <u>would</u> have been nice if you could have come to PEN – but Andrew Wilson did nobly, I hadn't realised he had a new baby and was up half the night with it.

What I do deeply regret is that I can't come to the Royal Soc. of Lit. for your keenly looked-forward-to talk on A.L.R.* but I have been committed for a long time to a parish meeting in aid of the collapsing (of course) spire, where the vicar is going to show his collection of <u>cigarette cards</u> – you are one of the few people who will understand why having promised I have to go, although I'd so much have liked to hear you speak –

Love Penelope

[undated]

Dearest Richard – Thankyou so much for your letter and I hope to see you in Highgate – I don't really hold with sending about photographs as everyone has too many and doesn't know what to do with them, but I thought you might like to have this as you've got such a kind (though rather abstracted) expression love Penelope.

---

* A. L. Rowse.

Stuart Proffitt*

27a Bishop's Road
London, N6
11 June [1990]

Dear Stuart,

Thankyou for the <u>Bookseller</u> – I <u>did</u> ignore the front cover as you suggested and looked at the splendid 2 page advertisement of the <u>G of Angels</u> – and I also want to thank you for the cards – you sent such a lot of them, it reminded me a little of <u>Eliza</u> – 'why don't you have some visiting-cards printed for the cat, he knows more cats than we do people –' but don't think I'm not grateful, I am, and they too are splendid.

By the way, the NYTimes rang up to ask me not to review a book they were sending (a relief really, as it was a long novel about the death of Tolstoy) because it was published by Holt, and it's a rule of theirs – they asked whether I was still published by Holt or not, and I said I thought I wasn't, which I suppose is correct, more or less –

best wishes
Penelope

27a Bishop's Road
London, N6
24 June 1990

Dear Stuart,

Just one or two things which I forgot to say on Friday, which is not the right way to go on talking in any case – I felt depressed at being discarded by yet another American publisher, even though Marion

---

* Took over from Richard Ollard as PMF's editor at Collins. Unfortunately, we do not have the correspondence relating to *Innocence* and *The Beginning of Spring*. He remained her editor for *The Gate of Angels* and *The Blue Flower*, after which he left the firm for Penguin.

Wood's manner did seem to get increasingly strange, but there you are, it can't be helped. I'll tell the <u>NY Times</u> when they next ring through, as they do every now and again, (although I thought they wouldn't after my article on Canaletto, about whom I know nothing). On the other hand I was very pleased about the <u>S. Times</u>. Now I have to brace myself up to judge the 1st novels for the Whitbread, the worst job of the lot, but of course if you agree to do something you haven't the right to complain –

    best wishes

    Penelope

27a Bishop's Road
London, N6
8 August [1990]

Dear Stuart,

Surely it's not so hot today, though? The magpies have stopped coming to drink out of the children's paddling-pool.

I'd love to come out to dinner on the 23rd, but I think <u>Tosca</u> might be wasted on me as I am so fond of it, and Jonathan Miller is so silly. They encourage him to be silly.

I was going to ask you two things which I have asked you before. I wondered if you could send a review-copy of <u>The G. of A.</u> to <u>Libération</u> (though I suppose <u>The B. of Spring</u> would have been better) and also if you could send one to Richard Holmes, not that I know him at all, but he wrote the only thing worth reading about M. R. James (the 2 biographies of him are dull beyond belief.)

Jane Bown just came to take some pix for the Observer, where they've got air-conditioning, as I suppose you have in Hammersmith. She tells me that when Lord Snowdon came to photograph Anita B.* he pinned her at the back with clothes pegs and she was justifiably upset –

    best wishes

    Penelope

---

* Brookner.

27a Bishop's Road
London, N6
24 August [1990]

Dear Stuart,

Thankyou so much for the dinner on Thursday, which was quite delightful and quite different from anything I do or anywhere I go usually, and thankyou once again for all the work and all the care you've taken over <u>The Gate of Angels</u>. If I seemed to criticise the Island of Mull, or mussels, or Goethe, then you must forgive me, and I daresay I didn't really know, as often happens, what I was talking about. But many thanks once again, Stuart, and best wishes –

Penelope

27a Bishop's Road
London, N6
7 September [1990]

Dear Stuart,

Thankyou so much for your letter and for saying that if I write another novel you would be ready to come to its assistance as you've so kindly done before. It (that's to say the novel) might have to be a bit longer this time, I suppose, as there are so many complaints about the 160 pages.

I'm going to ask you about 2 things that worry me a little – one is that Ria sent various people from her labs. to buy the Gate of A. but they said they hadn't got it and didn't know when they would as Collins was very slow answering, but I'm sure they must have some really, and the other, which I don't want you to laugh at me about, is that I'm supposed to be giving a talk, or something of the sort, at the Cheltenham festival, on the 18th Oct, and some of these talks are sponsored and some aren't, but mine is down as being sponsored by Nuclear Electrics, who are surely responsible for the pressurised water reactor at Hinkley Point, which I most strongly don't approve of, and

I can't believe you do either, they never said anything earlier on about
these sponsorships, what do you think about it?

best wishes

Penelope

Karen* is endlessly polite and patient – she must be very tired of hearing
the same 'few words' time and time again, but she never says so –

[postcard]

15 September [1990]

Thankyou so much for your note – this is the 5th short list our poor
book** has been on, and I don't see how it can do much against
J. Updike, but luckily I've got too old and worn-out to expect
anything.

Who is 'Nibby'? I'll ask you when I next see you,

meanwhile best wishes – P

27a Bishop's Road

London, N6

24 October [1990]

Dear Stuart,

Thankyou so much for your letter, (also for the beautiful p.c. of
a pink-and-blue Prague, under a pink-and-blue sky). In spite of
everything – in spite of poor Simon King's foot, and poor Richard's
stomach-upset (the pike mousse, I'm sure) and in spite of feeling so
sorry for agonised-looking Michael Holroyd, who I suppose had to
pick up the pieces – I enjoyed the Booker dinner really, and so did
Ria, and it was worth going even if it was only to hear the round of
applause when Shakespeare was mentioned – that must have been the
Loseley ice-cream and Norwegian fish-oil contingents, the first writer's

---

* Karen Duffy, PMF's publicist at HarperCollins.
** *The Gate of Angels.*

name they recognised, I daresay. – Beryl rather under the weather, perhaps, but she's the only one who really gives the idea of a proper old-fashioned Bohemian, which I suppose is what is needed at an alleged writers' dinner.

I don't think I ought to be either on the short or the long or any other Whitbread list as technically I'm a judge, but as Michael Ratcliffe is one of the fiction judges I know that he's loyally put me forward – the other 2 judges in my category are Sybille and the dread Malcolm Bradbury, who won't let me go further in any case. But I don't mind that a bit – this is what we all feel – by 'we all' I mean the enfeebled old scribblers themselves, who I was talking to last Thursday at the R.S.L., where Pat Barker was giving a wonderful lecture on ghost stories. – However most of them were also complaining (William Cooper in particular) that their publishers did nothing for them, and there I <u>certainly</u> didn't join in. I think you've done marvels for the sales of <u>The Gate of Angels</u>. I've just had a letter from someone going back to the U.S. on the Q. Eliz 2, who tells me 'of course, your book was in the ship's library' but – of course – there's no 'of course' about it. To revert to the Whitbread – it is all run by one of those superior competition firms, which means going down to Notting Hill Gate and being locked in to a white-painted drinks-and-lunch room until you come to a decision. – the faintly sinister organiser told us he'd been responsible for the Young Guitarists' Competition and that when he'd asked how long each competitor was to play – and they'd come at their own expense from every quarter of the globe – Segovia replied 'For one minute only, that is sufficient.' – Anyway, you couldn't want nicer fellow-judges than Lynne Truss and Rob Carr-Archer, although (of course) I didn't agree with them, so we were left with a majority decision, which I suppose I'll have to announce at some future lunch or other.

I'm lying flat on my back, looking at a book on painting in East Anglia since 1880 – (this is an entry for the Llewellyn Rhys prize by the way) and there's a nice Stanley Spencer of Southwold beach, which doesn't, as it happens, give me the idea of Southwold, but <u>does</u> give me the idea of Stanley Spencer –

so many thanks, and best wishes –

Penelope –

27a Bishop's Road
London, N6
6 November [1990]

Dear Stuart,

Thankyou very much for The Haunted Study. I thought it was very good – all Peter Keating's books are good, and since you say I can keep it, I'm glad to have it. The cover picture I shd. have thought was very difficult, because it isn't about The Haunted Study at all, or even about the phantasmagoric town, it's really, as he says, about 'the business of letters', (and the attendant alarming business of university studies) – I suppose you really want a dark study with a window looking out at the bright light of popularity, sales returns, chief reps., and so on. – I expect you've solved the problem by now, but am just sending a p.c. of Andreyev in <u>his</u> study – certainly no-one would be likely to identify <u>him</u>!

I've just crawled back from the first Whitbread judges' lunch. Malcolm Bradbury said a few kind words to me about The G. of A., and I felt like throwing the pale green mayonnaise over him. I'm not sure that all these tests of character aren't too much, as one gets older.

I'm sorry that <u>The B. of Spring</u> has to go, but that's something I <u>am</u> used to, there's no room really here for my books (I mean books I've written), but still I would like 2 copies if convenient.

My American book-dealer has arrived in England and wants the manuscript of the G of A, but I simply can't remember where I've put it –

best wishes
Penelope

[postcard]
22 January [1991]

I do wish the pbk. of <u>The Gate of Angels</u> didn't have to wait such a terribly long time to come out. Couldn't you put it in a bit earlier, as it's only a little one, then perhaps they could sell a few at some of these so-called festivals and alleged conferences –

best wishes Penelope

27a Bishop's Road
London, N6
2 February [1991]

Dear Stuart,

Thankyou very much for lunch yesterday and I was so glad to see you and should like to say again how much I appreciate your finding yet another American publisher for me. I'm sure it can't have been easy, still, you did it.

I still feel bemused by the palace of glass.* It's perhaps designed to bemuse the authors, the elderly ones at any rate, but Mary** was wrong in thinking there were no books to be seen, there <u>are</u> a dozen or so floating like disembodied presences in the atrium. Meanwhile, I was reading the Ruskin you kindly gave me in the underground going back to Highgate. It's not really a biography, is it, but the story of his ideas. I was disappointed at first because I always make my first estimate of a book on Ruskin by what the writer says about <u>Proserpina</u>, and he evidently hadn't read it, as he says it's about geology, but having got over that, and the quite unwarranted appearance of Goethe, (but then it's a German book so he has to come in somewhere) I did think it was very good in the way he stuck to his main thesis and indeed to the title all the way through.

Well, you didn't ask for my opinion: By the way, it was Aubrey de Vere, not perhaps a great authority, who thought listening to FD Maurice's sermons was like eating pea-soup with a fork, but Jowett said 'Well, all I could make out was that to-day was yesterday and this world was the same as the next' – but I hadn't got room for that.

If I get an idea worth asking you about, then I will.

best wishes
Penelope

---

  * The new HarperCollins building in Hammersmith.
 ** Ollard.

27a Bishop's Road
London, N6
4 March [1991]

Dear Stuart,

Thankyou for the Flamingo catalogue – I quite see that the cover
is contemporary, having had over 100 new novels in this room (all
cleared away now thank heavens) and <u>all</u> their jackets were like that.
You don't tell me, though, what a 'generic dump-bin' is, but I expect
the booksellers know.

If there is a spare copy of G. M. Hopkins do you think I could have
one? I can't give any good reason for asking because I've told Isabel*
she must get one of her formidable Jesuits to review it – she says they
always write far too much, and don't like being cut – but I should so
much like to see it.

I realise now that you can't get hold of Malcolm Bradbury, he seems
to be made of some plastic or semi-fluid substance which gives way or
changes in your hands. That's what I felt at King's Lynn.

And now dreaded Writers Day is coming round – terrible to see so
many writers in one place, and they've transferred it to Olympia,
surely not very sympathetic –

best wishes
Penelope

27a Bishop's Road
Highgate, N6
19 March [1991]

Dear Stuart,

I'm now half way through Professor Martin's <u>Hopkins</u> – by my
calculations, it must have taken him about five years, and he is kindly
and protective, and so unsensational (<u>doesn't</u> put in the story about
finding a pair of eyes in the nettle-patch at the seminary), so

---

* Isabel Quigley, literary editor of the *Tablet*.

painstaking and level-headed that you can't help feeling the deepest confidence in him. I don't think there's really any evidence at all that GMH was in love with Dolben, but I wish for the Professor's sake that there were. Well, I'm enjoying it very much, though I don't think that he (the Professor) probably as a result of having to live for years in Hawaii – has any ear for GMH's poems at all. Here he is plodding through <u>Felix Randall</u> and he doesn't seem to notice the nicest thing in it, 'being anointed and all', (which is just what they say in Liverpool and Southport, and I shouldn't think GMH ever heard 'and all' until he got to Liverpool) – right in the middle of the sonnet. But the description of St Francis Xavier's is very good.

2 of my grandsons were educated by the Jesuits for 2 years in Nicaragua – they had no equipment and had to do long division (I suppose you never had to do that) and sums from a blackboard, and then go out coffee-picking, I think, however, that the pope excommunicated them all on his pastoral visit.

I've <u>never</u> had a word of a novel on paper when I signed the contract – I suppose some people do. My trouble is that now the Booker books will be arriving, and I don't know how soon I could undertake to do anything –

best wishes
Penelope

[postcard]
[summer 1991]

It was very nice to see you at the South Bank last night, I felt it was quite like old times. And thankyou for the pbk jacket of the <u>Gate of Angels</u>. Many people have told me how much they liked it, and one customer said the jacket was the best thing about it. Good wishes from N.York –

[postcard of Tasmania]
19 January [1992]

Thankyou so much for your card – I was very pleased about <u>Human Voices</u> (perhaps David arranged it, I don't know) and very pleased (incidentally) that Kendall is now a director.

Must now pull myself together and go and queue for the Mantegna as I see they have sent over one of my favourite pictures of all pictures The Death of the Virgin from the Prado. I only really went over to Spain last Feb: to see it, and now I'll be able to see it twice in just over a year.

Martin Gilbert is coming to speak at the Highgate Inst. on Tues. so must see that there are some respectable sandwiches. I couldn't go, alas, when Richard came.

very best wishes for everything – Penelope

[postcard of Brugge]
[1991]

Dear Stuart – The American jacket,* well, after the jacket on my poor Knox Brothers I feel I oughtn't to be upset by anything – the German jacket, showing Moscow in the height of summer I thought feeble, and I don't really like the American one but I've written to Nan A.T.** to say that I <u>do</u> (which shows how much I've gone downhill as I never used to tell lies on business matters) and that it's striking, wh: I suppose it is. What's the use of arguing with her, I thought.

I hope it was lovely in Italy, I'm sure it was.

I'm dreading Bath† as they've put me in the Royal Crescent, but I expect I'll be in the attics – best wishes Penelope

* Of *The Beginning of Spring.*
** Nan A. Talese, PMF's American publisher.
† The Literary Festival.

27a Bishop's Road
London, N6
16 August 1992

Dear Stuart,

Thankyou for your letter – I haven't been ill really, but it was kind of Richard to think I might be. And I hope you're well, and not on a diet any longer.

I don't know about <u>The Golden Child</u> (the title I wanted was <u>The Golden Opinion</u>). I can't forget the embarrassment of sitting through a long post-Bakhtian analysis of it at Alcalá, the book was only a joke, such as I used to make then. Of course, the Russian part is terribly out of date, and things have got a bit better now even at the British Museum.

I must have had a contract at some point in the Piano Factory days. I had a long talk with Colin the other day on the Northern Line and he showed me a case full of affidavits, part of his courageous fight with Rowntrees. He says he's bought back 71% of the firm, but, unfortunately, can't pay for it, while Anna is writing a book about Ireland. 'All this religion' Colin cried. I told him he might look to it for help. All this makes me wonder if he has much interest in his long-ago titles.

I'm surprised, by the way, that you consider 'tricky' and 'charming' as opposites, it would be much easier surely if they were.

I really was glad to hear from you, it was a voice from the past – best wishes for everything
Penelope

27a Bishop's Road
London, N6
10 January [1993]

Dear Stuart,

Thankyou so much for letting me know about <u>At Hiruharama</u> – the British Council made us all write stories (needless to say for practically nothing) which went into an anthology to be imposed on the unfortunate natives of other countries, that must be how the

Norwegians got hold of it. However, it's gone out on Radio 4, 2 or 3 times.

I heard the story from a New Zealander when we were being rebaptized in the Jordan (or one of its sources, the one the Methodists favour anyway) marvellous wild cyclamen on the banks. It's most vexatious that you were stopped and I shouldn't feel as calm about it as you are.

I should be very grateful if you would write to Mette Fjeldstad for me. The story is totally unsuitable as an example of modern English, but no matter –

best wishes
Penelope

27a Bishop's Road
N6
10 November 1993

Dear Stuart,

Thankyou for your letter – I'm in bed with flu, like 1 in 4 of the population, so no-one wants to hear my symptoms, but it makes me feel better to hear from you.

I was glad that Stock* took The Bookshop. I don't think they've been able to do much with the other two, but no matter. I don't understand the rights issue either. I did ring up Jim Holden as he is so kind and does so much and I'm still no clearer. He says, 'Can't we get hold of this Gerald Duckworth?' not realising that he is asking for the spectre of a shit. I'm getting on with my ms. but think it more than possible that you won't much like it, then I have to rewrite it all and find someone who can read my handwriting, or indeed any handwriting.

Well, you survived, and it all went marvellously –
The Fulham Palace Road Years –
best wishes
Penelope

* The French publisher.

[postcard]
6 May 1996

Thankyou for the PW* and the telesales brochure, we shouldn't have known what to do with such a splendid publication in the poor old Sole Bay bookshop. – I feel I've been given every chance and hope for the best. – Howard (N York bookseller) coming tomorrow to acquire mss. although I feebly tell him that I haven't got any – best wishes
    Penelope

[postcard]
10 September [1996]

Thankyou for the pbk. sales figures, and such a kind letter from the Hubert in the RSC <u>King John</u> about <u>At Freddie's</u> – admittedly as they're playing it uncut he must have plenty of time for reading behind the scenes –
    best wishes
    Penelope

[postcard]

Dear Stuart – This is just to thank you very much for sparing the time, wh: I very well know is precious, to come to the dreaded ICA – Christopher Hope** is very nice and a very brilliant writer and reader-aloud, but, like all serious S. Africans, a little off his rocker, so I had to do the best I could, and felt very encouraged to see you.
    Best wishes, Penelope

---

*   *Publisher's Weekly*.
**   Whom she interviewed for the video series on contemporary novelists.

[Postcard]
16 January [1997]

Dear Stuart, Thankyou for your letter – you notice I'm sure that the Declaration of Editorial Independence (this sounds like my History notes at school – we had to have 3 causes for everything and 3 results) is in fact not quite that, but what you say is very kind and encouraging.

Addison-Wesley now say they're bringing out C. Mew in paperback, not of course because they've sold so many hardbacks, but because they've sold so few. (This isn't exactly how they put it.)

Hope to see you next Tuesday – it was very nice to meet Suzanne – love Penelope

[postcard]
14 February [1997]

Thankyou for the proof of the jacket for <u>At Freddie's</u>, I think Watteau's pathetically knowing little boy comes out very well on the dark background. I'm also returning the proofs of <u>The Bookshop</u> corrected intelligibly I hope although I've now got three quite different lists of signs, but perhaps the printers have given up noticing.

best wishes
Penelope

All my papers have now arrived in Tokyo, misread by the air freight company for Texas. It wd. have been quicker to send them by sea.

27a Bishop's Road
London, N6
24 February [1997]

Dear Stuart,

Thankyou for the proof of the <u>Bookshop</u> jacket – you mustn't think I'm complaining but I did think the young Cicero had come out rather high in colour, (although of course the original has faded a lot), his

socks are really pale rose and everything else is keyed to that, but anyway
I think you're much to be congratulated on the whole set. – By the way
I thought it was kind of Tom Aitken to send a little letter to the
Independent about Human Voices.

Meantime back on the ranch, after the takeover of Addison-Wesley
my high-minded book editor has had a moral and aesthetic
confrontation and has had to take his leave, although he's allowed to
finish the publicity. I suggested to him that he might try and get a job
at Holt's, as Marian Wood seems just as nice, and just as crazy, as he is.
But New York seems rather a bright, unkind place for him to go –
    best wishes
    Penelope

(2 comments on proposed blurb, which quotes the Washington Post
on Innocence: 'as civilised and intoxicating as a shot of aged brandy',
this I do think is nice, as if I've got to be aged I'd rather be brandy than
almost anything. –)

I've just thought of something else, which is that when the
paperback of Innocence was advertised, they didn't put Now in
Paperback – and yet these seem to me to be important words –

27a Bishop's Road
Highgate
London, N6
27 May [1999]

Dear Stuart,

Thankyou for your letter and I hope all goes well at Hay. I suppose
you have an operative, by the way, to turn your Aga on before you
come, otherwise I can't think how you manage?

I'm afraid Arthur Lubow drew a complete blank on his interview –
evidently he is a superior Greenwich Village (not SoHo) gay and
specialises in interviewing gays and colourful people generally. Ria and
I were fascinated by his taking notes in shorthand which nobody does
nowadays, while still never taking his eyes off your face. Meanwhile the

German television people are supposed to be coming, so I'll have to straighten the place up again.

I was amazed to hear Monty James mentioned, because I remember a very long time ago you told me you'd never heard of him, and I thought well, that's it, Monty James is as dead as the dodo, as well as being unbelievably n.p.c., indeed, so are ghost stories, of that kind anyway. But he seems to have survived.

Surely Richard Holmes, (as it happens) knows a lot about him, and wrote a piece about him, it must be all of twenty-five years ago?

Just crawling off for a week's holiday –

best wishes

Penelope

James Saunders*

185 Poynders Gardens
London, SW4
2 May [*c.*late 1960s]

Dear Mr: Saunders,

Although I know that this kind of letter is a great nuisance to an author, I am asking for your help – partly because I believe you were a teacher yourself and possibly you still are – please would you stop my A level classes from coming to blows (I can't call it a discussion) by letting us know whether all the characters in <u>Next Time I'll Sing To You</u> are 'inside' Rudge, that is, different faculties of the mind, or are they his 'creations' in the sense that he's made them up?

We should be very grateful indeed if you could find time to settle this point for us –

yours sincerely,
Penelope Fitzgerald
(Mrs:)

185 Poynders Gardens
London SW4
15 May [*c.*late 1960s]

Dear Mr Saunders,

Please may I thank you on behalf of my embattled classes for your letter, explaining my point about <u>Next Time I'll Sing To You</u> (that is, why Dust should feel that Rudge had 'created' him). It was very good of you to spare the time to write, and we shall all, needless to say, listen to the June 10th broadcast –

yours sincerely,
Penelope Fitzgerald

* The dramatist.

Graham Chesney*

27a Bishop's Road
Highgate, N6
27 January [1995]

Dear Graham Chesney,

Thankyou for your letter, which has just arrived from my publishers.

I'm afraid I can't be of a great deal of help, because I've never lived in Cambridge myself, but my uncle Dillwyn Knox was up at Kings from 1903–7, returning as a fellow in 1909, (and later becoming the most brilliant code-breaker at the Admiralty) and when I was writing the biography of my family (The Knox Brothers, 1977) I had to do a good deal of research into 'his' Cambridge. Then later on, when I wanted to write The Gate of Angels, about the early days of nuclear or rather atomic research, and whether Mach was possibly right in thinking it was a misconception, I used the notes I had already made.

Maynard Keynes was perhaps my uncle's closest friend, although I didn't bring him into The Gate of Angels.

I had to search for quite a long time, by the way, to find a possible site for a (possible) small and ancient college,

best wishes for your book –

Penelope Fitzgerald

* Wrote for help in his research into Edwardian Cambridge.

A. L. Barker*

27a Bishop's Road
London, N6
20 January [1994]

My dear Pat – I just had a note from Sally – the Lavender Lady – to tell me that you of all people have had a stroke – I say 'of all people' because you seem to exist like a bird on almost nothing, and indeed there's almost nothing of you to <u>have</u> a stroke, yet it happened, and I'm very distressed and deeply sympathetic – but the cheering part of Sally's letter was that you were <u>better</u> and recovering, though she couldn't tell how long it would take – and she even thought you might have an idea for another book – without which you could hardly be said to be yourself – but you <u>are</u>, thank the lord.

Dear Pat, I'm just off to see my elder daughter and family in soaking Devonshire, but will ring up when I get back. By my count you have had <u>too many</u> illnesses in the last few years – but then, you've written some wonderful things!

love and best wishes
Penelope

Doctors can be very irritating – one has to remember that they can't help it – but perhaps yours isn't.

27a Bishop's Road
London, N6
23 February [1994]

Dear Pat,

You know how much we all want to hear you're better! Or rather, I know very well that every day you get a <u>little</u> better – I know that, and

---

* The short-story writer and novelist, known as Pat to her friends. PMF taught fiction-writing with her for the Arvon Foundation.

perhaps that's the way it will be, a matter of 'in front the sun climbs slowly, how slowly' so that you get better without quite knowing how.

Dorothy says she is trying to cope with calls from publishers and agents – which I agree is a great worry – but what an encouraging feeling to <u>have</u> them – I think my publisher has given me up, though he doesn't precisely say so, as I never get round to producing anything.

In your last few books you've been so much concerned with story-telling in itself – are writers talking to themselves, or are there always listeners who need stories? And now you've been forcibly propelled into this situation – the story-teller cut short (though not for too long) and finding (when set free again), an absolute wealth of words – a hospital novel I hope – although I know you were in the middle of something else.

I've just been watching a video of the consecration of the first woman bishop of Washington D.C. She had a special crook sent from the Yorkshire dales as her crozier. In his Christmas letter Jim Carr said he was all in favour of women priests. I'm sure he'd have enjoyed this video.

Must now see to the pancakes
best wishes and love
Penelope

8 March [1994]

Dear Pat,

Just a note (I know one <u>shouldn't</u> start letters like this) to say how much you were missed at Francis' party – I'm sure you'll have had a lot of letters on the subject, but no matter. I was sorry in a way that it had to be transferred to the Polish Hearth, but of course that comes of being generous and asking so many people. Just as I came in and was going to take off my anorak and hand it to the grand flunkey, the zip stuck – and then in came Peter Day, and kindly and efficiently put it right again – what a wonderful putter-right he is – I've only once been to his flat (not the present one) and was stopped by an old lady, a total stranger, on the stairs who told me, quite without prompting 'how good he has been to me'. – So I got my anorak off and went up to the

pale green drawing-room where poor Francis was worrying because
the food hadn't arrived, but then it suddenly miraculously did, on
large dishes. I was able to get more news of you, encouraging, from
Penelope Bennett, and I saw people I hadn't seen for a long time,
including the amazing Raoul, I mean Raleigh Trevelyan's Raoul –
amazing to me because having spent so many years I think as a waiter
in Morocco, he has mastered all the writers, all the names of their
books, all their life-histories, and all their reviews, and never lets one
slip. But there were so many kind hearts and such goodwill in that
room – my only disappointment was that I had to go early, and so
didn't hear Peter's speech.

When I think how ill Francis and Josephine were – how long was it
ago? – and how they looked at the party, I can only marvel and say let
us be indestructible. And you too, in particular, Pat.

I'm so sorry the Festings are leaving, but I suppose it is his job? I
love her book on Lavender. We used to live in Battersea, near Lavender
Sweep, and I used to try to imagine what it used to be like when it was
all lavender fields.

Everything is moving. The poor TLS have to go out to Docklands
and they are being computerised. 'They are taking away our pencils
and rubbers' I am told 'we shall have to watch screens, we shan't know
how to manage.' I think the computer terminals are going to be the
death of some of the assistants at the London Library too.

And Maura Dooley off to Swansea. She's going to be in charge of
making it into the City of Poetry and Literature for 1995, but she'll be
much missed. She's got a nice flat, I believe, down by the harbourfront
which has been converted, like all harbourfronts, into experimental
theatres and flats which no-one will buy – and David will follow as
soon as he can, but of course he's still with the BBC.

very best wishes
love
Penelope

27a Bishop's Road
London, N6
25 September [1998]

Dear Pat,

I heard your news from Sally Festing, and I do hope that you are
back home again by now. What I'm quite sure about is that you've had
all your life's share of illness and bad luck and it must take a turn now
for the better and indeed the glorious best.

Alas! I don't get down to PEN nowadays, it's such a very long way
from Highgate, and then I must admit I've got lazier, and much more
addicted to sitting in the garden not doing very much – the squirrels
have long since given up taking any notice of me. However, I was on
the Booker committee (still am, for that matter, because we've only got
to the short list stage) this year, so had to rouse myself a bit. All the
books (115, I think) are standing in piles on the floor of my small
sitting-room. Now I'm wondering who I can get to take them away.

The chairman this year was Douglas Hurd, who is certainly, as
might be expected, a marvellous hand at managing a committee, but
he admitted that his idea of a novel was a good read with a strong
ending. Perhaps he's right, Pat! He was also an amazingly rapid and
efficient <u>eater</u>, I suppose from attending so many banquets all over
the world – the difficult things, such as the little <u>bits</u> of green salad
disappeared in a flash and he was ready to continue the discussion.

As usual, I didn't agree with anyone, but it was altogether a
strong-minded committee. Nigella Lawson looked stunning, and it's
marvellous how she carries on working while her husband is so ill.
He's just had <u>another</u> operation for his mouth cancer, and in the
middle of it all, her nanny left, saying she didn't feel up to the stress.

It seems such a long time ago that we were at Arvon. David Hunter
is still on the management committee, and he still goes on lecturing in
Yorkshire and Devonshire, although he's been working for ages now in
BBC radio drama – one of the few people the BBC haven't sacked, it
seems.

This is really just to send you love and all best wishes –
Penelope

Harvey Pitcher*

76 Clifton Hill
London, NW8 6JT
6 March 1988

Dear Harvey Pitcher,

Please may I tell you (I'll make it as short as I can) that I've just finished writing a novel about Moscow,** or rather set in Moscow in 1913, and (I suppose) it will come out with Collins some time this year. – The idea of it came from a Swiss friend whose father was a business man in Moscow and continued to live there and to sell flowers from his greenhouse all through the revolution and into the twenties, although (as happens when you're writing a novel) the greenhouse has disappeared in the final version.

To get some idea of what Moscow was like at that time I read the Times Russian supplements from 1910 to 1913, but I also read, among other things, your <u>The Smiths of Moscow</u>, which I enjoyed so very much. I'm writing to you now to ask if I can use (if, of course, I acknowledge it properly) your story about the bear who ran riot in the dining-room, though not with the ending which you give it in your book, because that was truth, and mine is only fiction.

I should be very grateful if you could let me know what you feel about this.

Yours sincerely,
Penelope Fitzgerald

* The novelist and writer on the British in Russia in the nineteenth century.
** *The Beginning of Spring.*

76 Clifton Hill
London, NW8 6JT
15 March [1988]

Dear Harvey Pitcher,

Thankyou very much for <u>Lily</u>. I thought you managed the (very difficult, I should think) backwards narrative marvellously, only letting it go <u>once</u>, on p. 117, when Sergei thinks 'The Moscow Arts Theatre still lay years in the future' – and that, of course, doesn't matter. I did, as you say in your introduction, come to understand the characters better, but not Lily, because she's inexplicable, and to me the most successful thing of all about the book is that you've brought to life this delightful but not quite normal and not quite comprehensible person – no-one is sure of her, either in England or in Russia, and she has to remember that she's supposed to be dying – without inventing any kind of explanation for her, because there <u>is</u> none. I felt very fond of Lily. But nothing will ever make me fond of Olga Knipper.

Thankyou too, very much indeed, for letting me use a version of your bear story. I'm afraid, though, that there are a lot of errors in my Moscow novel, so am sending you one I wrote about Italy,

with best wishes
Penelope Fitzgerald

76 Clifton Hill
London, NW8 6JT
18 April [1988]

Dear Harvey Pitcher,

Thankyou for your letter and your kind word about <u>Innocence</u>. I read <u>Lily</u> quickly because I was so much interested, but also because I thought that if I was going to follow the narrative backwards it would be much better not to have too many breaks. You're asked to hang on, I thought.

I was surprised, though, at what you said about biography. It seems to me that (particularly if you have the letters, and if you knew the subject yourself or can get hold of someone who knew the subject) you can know him or her at least as well as anyone you meet in real life. The trouble is that it's rather difficult to shake the people off when the book is written, and to return to yourself. They're not to be got rid of so easily.

We used to live in Southwold, down by the harbour at Blackshore (as it was then) but I never knew there was a Mrs Knox in the town. – And certainly I never dreamed there might have been a Morris window in Moscow. I've had a chance now to look at A. C. Sewter's <u>Catalogue of Stained Glass of William Morris and his circle</u>, which includes the firm's foreign orders and there's no mention of it there, unless some more information has turned up since 1975, so I'm afraid St Andrews never had any. – Morris's great friend Cormell Price (Kipling's headmaster) went to Petersburg as a tutor to the Orloff-Davidoff family from 1860–3, but found the job a 'purgatory' – I expect English governesses were more satisfactory, on the whole, than tutors,

best wishes
Penelope Fitzgerald

27a Bishop's Road
London, N6
9 June [1988]

Dear Harvey Pitcher – Please forgive me if I've sent you my change of address before, as I don't deny that the move is getting me a little bit muddled, though not too much I hope. – I was very much interested in what you said about The Book Den. Surely running a bookshop, in England at least, is one of the most difficult businesses imaginable, people can come in all day and turn the stock over and read bits of it (which is equivalent to biting the fruit at a greengrocers) and go away having bought nothing, but that 'traditional practice'. – I have a terrible suspicion that you don't <u>like</u> Burne-Jones (about whom I wrote my first book!) or Morris & Co. windows. That is a distress to me –

best wishes, Penelope Fitzgerald

27a Bishop's Road
London, N6
16 December [1988]

Dear Harvey – This is just to say that during the process of moving I
<u>did</u> find another copy of <u>Burne-Jones</u> and would be glad to exchange it
(as you once suggested) for a copy of <u>When Miss Emmie was in Russia</u> –
on the other hand I think (as far as I can make out anything that
publishers say) that <u>B-Jones</u> is coming out next year in paperback (of
course in a smaller and more miserable form) so perhaps this wouldn't
interest you any longer.

In any case very best wishes for Christmas and 1989 – Penelope

I've had a number of complaints that Red Square wasn't called that
before the First World War – but surely I'm right about this, if about
nothing else?

27a Bishop's Road
London, N6
12 January [1989]

Dear Harvey,

Thankyou so much for <u>Miss Emmie</u>. Although I can hardly believe
it, it's the first time I've read it – hardly believe it, I mean, because
there are innumerable details in it which I had to find out with painful
slowness from the <u>Times</u> special Russian supplements and Motoring
supplements – but never mind that, what I'm thanking you for is the
wonderful way you've collected the stories and arranged them in their
historical pattern, also their human one, of course. Interviewing your
governesses must have made the whole thing worthwhile in itself. –
'You see, I've grown old since then – very foolish of me, but I couldn't
help it' – how could you better that?

What a commentary it is, too, on Pasternak's <u>Povest</u> – reading this
I've always felt sorry for the unfortunate Mrs Frestein for having taken

on such a very unsatisfactory tutor and companion, she'd have done very much better with English ones.

I enclose <u>Burne-Jones</u> with all its faults – the bibliography is now hopelessly out of date and the illustrations were always dreadful, but nothing can be done about it now.

with very best wishes for 1989 –

Penelope

P.S. The Muir & Murrilees <u>flag</u> – I had no idea they <u>had</u> one, and took it from the Arding & Hobbs flag – I always look to see if it's flying when I go through Clapham Junction as it indicates a sale – (but they lowered it for some reason when Lord Mountbatten was murdered, and perhaps on other sad occasions). I very much look forward to your book.

I'm glad you went to see Lorraine Price – it's hard to know what to do about Cormell Price – he <u>is</u> interesting but not quite interesting enough for a biography, it seems.

I expect you know Felicity Ashbee, C. R. Ashbee's daughter, who has such a wonderful set of photos of 'Russian types' – but now I'm hesitating because I can't remember whether her family lived in Moscow or Petersburg wh: would be no use for M & M.

27a Bishop's Road
London, N6
5 July [1989]

Dear Harvey,

Thankyou so much for your letter, and I was relieved to find that you don't object to Burne-Jones, at least as a designer of windows. Yes, he was a great admirer of, and correspondent with, young women (one or two of whom bowled him over completely). If the Muirs settled in Holland Park, then they would have been near 'the Greeks', the celebrated Ionides family, and Watts studio, and Eva Muir became Mrs Richmond, didn't she? The <u>Memorials of Edward Burne-Jones</u> by Georgiana Burne-Jones (vol 2 p 206) reveals (what I'm sure you know) that the brown bear had to go to the zoo, and that Eva (addressed as Dear Bearwarden) promised in 1890 to take B-J to see it, but didn't – because he was too old, he claims, but adds 'never by any chance let the old interfere with plans, never for a moment let them be in the way. They are so soon pacified.' B/J's only contact (which can't be called a contact) with Russia was when he was a young man and his friend Cormell Price went in 1860 as a tutor to the Orloff-Davidoff family (having answered an ad. in the Times). He (Cormell Price) wasn't happy, however. His great-grand-daughter has his Russian diaries, but they aren't as informative as they ought to be.

Ellen Terry <u>may</u> have been an angel at the first night party for <u>Helena in Troas</u> – and she certainly <u>was</u> an angel, but it may well have been Ellen's daughter Edy, who appeared as an angel in the last act of the Lyceum <u>Faust</u> – interesting that Oscar W. appeared with straight hair, as I think he only began to have it curled in 1883.

I'm very sorry to tell you that I have no <u>Burne-Joneses</u> left, and indeed I sometimes wonder if there are any copies left in the world. Americans sometimes write reproachfully, saying they've had to Xerox the whole book – not my fault really and if only there were enough of them (the Americans I mean) perhaps it might be reprinted.

I was very interested to hear about my 3rd cousin Andrew, because he must be the grandson of Frederick, who rebelled against his father and nearly bit right through his hand. – As to Southwold, I think it's kill or cure in that east wind. My dear old friend Phyllis Neame who ran, as I told you, the Sole Bay bookshop, survived, and only died this January, though not quite 109 I think, and she was asking about new books until the last. It was from her that I learnt about 'stickers', and I can hardly believe that <u>Lily</u> is one – only there's one thing I <u>have</u> noticed, and that is that the writer's favourite book is scarcely ever the same as the public's – let me take an example, Shakespeare only published his sonnets under his own name, didn't he? and evidently relied on them to make him immortal – and they've got used, too, to your doing something else, another kind of book –

best wishes
Penelope

27a Bishop's Road
London, N6
15 September [1992]

Dear Harvey,

Thankyou so much for sending me <u>The Search for Maud Macintosh</u>.

Of course I remember Ronald Chapman's <u>The Laurel and the Thorn,</u> which was a much more sympathetic book than Blunt's, I thought, and I was very sorry to hear that his eyesight had failed. But he's lucky to have you to take over this particular interest of his, when he must have lost so many other things.

The trouble (if it <u>is</u> a trouble) with this totally fascinating story, or reconstruction, is that it has so many attractive diversions and byways. The Sterling Mackinlays, for example – I remember Jean's performance so well and she used to come round to schools – and Viola Garvin – and the whole strangely oppressive atmosphere of the Watts gallery where I spent so long reading the Watts correspondence when I was trying to find out about Burne-Jones. I thought I was working hard and indeed I was, but I'm overwhelmed by the skill and patience you and Ronald Chapman have put into <u>your</u> researches.

But the question you ask is 'Who then is M.M., and who was buried in Nuthurst churchyard?' and so I had to put aside a lot of the deeply interesting things you say about the Watts household and about Lily herself, as in a sense not strictly relevant. Among other things, the <u>letter,</u> I believe, full of (rather odd) character though it is, seems to me to have nothing to do with the case. Anyone can see that the writing is not the General's, no matter what any number of graphologists say, and it's impossible that in Dec 1879 he should make no reference to the pregnancy. Nor was Chelsea a 'right' address for a retired military man and his wife in the 1870s – nor was the general's name Lew. I shouldn't have thought the letter was addressed to Mary Fraser-Tytler either. You say she 'circulated freely' in the seventies, but I don't think more so than, say Frances Graham (the first of these girls to be allowed to act as hostesses to her own parties) and she (Mary) would have been in the same class at the Slade as Kate Greenaway. However, there the letter is, but I can't think it will help in the matter of Maud.

Now let me tell you my story, to add to all the other versions.

The name Maud, still more Maudie, Macintosh, strikes me at once and very forcibly as a stage name. The trouble about trying to trace her through Mander and Mitchenson would be that even they can't do anything if there are no reviews, notices, playbills, or photographs, and Maudie's career must have been very short if she took up with the General, say, in 1877. But I am sure she was an unsuccessful, pretty, only just respectable young singer ('a singer' because of Lily's inherited love of music, and the influence on Maud of those hymns) – I should think she appeared, or tried to, in burlesques, comediettas and subscription concerts, but then met the General, and became his 'annuitant'. The relationship between Maud and the Rev. McCarogher is absolutely typical of the period. (To take an example, which I'm getting from Claire Tomalin's marvellous The Invisible Woman – in 1879 the Rev. William Benham (the Margate clergyman to whom Ellen Ternan later confessed her 'affair' with Dickens) invited a friend to give a sermon on the importance of establishing links between the church and the theatre.) Where did Maud and McCarogher meet? In Freiburg or Baden Baden. Maud had been sent there at the General's expense to have the baby, but after meeting the McCaroghers, and receiving spiritual help and advice and Christian friendship, she decided to go back to England with them and stay at the Rectory with them in Nuthurst until the birth, I don't mean that Maud's repentance wasn't sincere. I'm sure that it was.

But of course, although she was still an annuitant, she couldn't, as a penitent, go on living as the General's mistress. What an awkward spot he was in, with two London addresses to pay for, two sick women on his hands, and, at the age of 63, another child to provide for. No wonder he sent for his son, who seems to have behaved admirably, and the General too did his best. There is real affection in his 'dear Maudie'.

As to the grave: the General evidently came to Comeragh Road when Maud was dying, and it was most likely then that she gave him her New Testament, and told him that she would like the burial to be entrusted to her kind confessor, the Rector of Nuthurst. The memorial inscription I am sure she chose herself. It's the choice of a Victorian penitent. She was at rest at last.

Let me remind you that you are a novelist too!

I am sending your T/S back rather than showing it to anyone else because I believe that handing papers round is a sure way to lose bits of them, and I'm sure that every copy of The Search for M M is precious.

very best wishes

Penelope

P.S. The passage about the bear from The Beginning of Spring was set for A-level prose appreciation by the Associated Board last year. So I suppose I'm getting on little by little.

27a Bishop's Road
London, N6
22 June [1995]

Dear Harvey,

Thankyou very much indeed for Muir & Murrilees. I only wish I'd had it before I tried to write about Moscow in 1912, instead of trying to manage with the Times Russian supplements – but never mind that, it's a marvellous piece of research and I should imagine you feel rather sorry to finish it, with Meta and Stuart Hogg lying in their quiet churchyard.

The comparison with Whiteleys worked extremely well – I wonder by the way why Selfridges made such a point when they opened, of there being no admission fee? Surely none of the department stores had one? Perhaps Marks and S. did though, at their Penny Bazaar.

When The Beginning of Spring was on, I think, 2 of the A-level syllabuses, I used to go round and give little talks (quite uselessly, as the candidates always told me I couldn't be right because it wasn't what they'd got down in their notes). I used to tell them about M & M's carpet department.

Hollyer's beautiful photographs stand out as always. The hands in the portrait of the 3 Muir sisters are so well placed, and 'the girls' in their Liberty dresses might well be going down B-Jones's The Golden Stairs (which he did in 1863).

Surely you have to write next about Maud Macintosh? I never did see how the General could be thought of as writing the 'sweet and bonny' letter, but I also don't think that 'you won't love me as I most wish to be loved' – the meaning of which is only too plain – <u>can</u> be interpreted as 'you share this prejudice against cousins marrying &c' – in that case, surely, it would have to be 'you <u>can't</u> love me' – wouldn't it?

(To judge from the papers at the Watts Gallery, Mary Watts was a great goer-through and crosser-out of letters, but that was in later life, of course.) – Meantime I think you only need a stroke of chance or luck, such as often comes the way of patient biographers, for the whole mystery to come clear, and I don't see how you can possibly feel a sense of failure when you've got such a long way already. – What is so odd is that the people concerned, it seems, both did, and didn't, want to conceal everything.

I am sending what I am afraid is only a wretched proof copy of my (short) book due out this September – but they will have to change the jacket as the story is based on the early life of Novalis and if the artist wants to put handwriting all over the place it should be German gothic and <u>not</u> English looking-glass writing – perhaps he thinks there's not much difference –

with thanks and best wishes – Penelope

Frank Kermode[*]

25 Almeric Road
London, SW11
2 November 1979

Dear Professor Kermode,

I hope you won't mind my writing to you, partly because I've relied so long and so much on <u>The Sense of an Ending</u> in trying to teach university candidates something about fiction – most of them, too, with a half-finished novel of their own in a drawer back at home – but also to thank you for what you wrote about me in <u>The London Review of Books</u>. Could I make one comment – you said in passing that the 'apocalyptic flood' at the end of <u>Offshore</u> wasn't a success and I expect it isn't, but it isn't really meant as apocalyptic either – I only wanted the Thames to drift out a little way with the characters whom in the end nobody particularly wants or lays claim to. It seems to me that not to be wanted is a positive condition and I hoped to find some way of indicating that. – I realise too that the danger of writing novels, even very short ones, is that you get to take yourself too seriously –

Yours sincerely,

Penelope Fitzgerald

25 Almeric Road
London, SW11
20 November 1980

Dear Professor Kermode,

I hope that you won't mind my writing to you once again to thank you for your remarks in the London Review of Books, on my own behalf and, if it's allowable, on William de Morgan's too – all my 2-volume copies of his novels went to the bottom of the Thames

---

[*] The literary critic whom PMF most admired. He reviewed several of her novels, and wrote the introduction to the posthumous Everyman collection of her work.

except for <u>It Never Can Happen Again</u>, which I've always liked because
the characters quote from <u>The Haystack in the Floods</u>* but are also
worried by their motor-car which won't go because 'a certain hexagonal
nut' is missing – that is diachronic in a sense, I suppose. – At least de
Morgan's novels were entirely <u>his</u>, whereas he had the pottery made for
him, and only decorated it himself.

   Yours sincerely,
   Penelope Fitzgerald

27 Bishop's Road
Highgate
3 October [1995]

Dear Sir Frank,

   I hope you won't mind my writing to thank you for your review of
<u>The Blue Flower</u>. I started from D. H. Lawrence's 'fatal flower of
happiness' at the end of <u>The Fox</u>, having always wondered how DHL
knew it was blue, and never quite managed to find out all I wanted to,
partly because Novalis' letters to Sophie have disappeared, buried in
her grave I daresay.

   I was so glad you defended Novalis against Carlyle. The person who
really understood him, it seems to me, was George Macdonald, but
nobody reads <u>Phantasies</u> now.

   I don't know whether you'd agree that writing, like teaching, produces
considerable spells of depression and moments of great happiness
which seem to justify everything – that's what I felt, anyway, when
I read the LRB this week –

   with thanks and best wishes –
   Penelope Fitzgerald

---

* The poem by William Morris.

Hilary Mantel*

27a Bishop's Road
[postcard]
[1995]

Dear Hilary – For some reason I can't account for I got an invitation to your Hawthornden Prize giving several days after it had taken place – which of course doesn't matter, but I <u>do</u> want to congratulate you on the award, and say how much I enjoyed <u>An Experiment in Love</u> – and so did my daughter – and so I'm sure will <u>her</u> daughter in a few years time – best wishes Penelope (Fitzgerald)

27a Bishop's Road
[postcard]
[1997]

Dear Hilary – I wish I could agree with you that death is the least of the things that divide people, but I do want to say how good I thought <u>Terminus</u> was, and how moving, all the more so from the distance, or strangeness, that you've put between the narrator and the reader, although we feel brought together by the very last sentence –

best wishes
Penelope (Fitzgerald)

---

* The novelist, who reviewed PMF with great insight and appreciation.

Bridget Nichols*

27a Bishop's Road
Highgate
London, N6
26 February 2000

Dear Bridget Nichols,

Thankyou very much for your letter, which I'll answer as best I can.

Certainly you are quite right in thinking The Gate of Angels is about the questions of faith and generosity, and also that Dr Matthews is a portrait of Monty James. I set my novel in the Cambridge of 1912 because that was the height of the so-called 'body/mind controversy', with the scientists of the Cavendish in controversy with professing Christians, championed by James who was then Provost of Kings, and made an unforgettable comment on the situation in his ghost story 'Oh Whistle and I'll Come to you, My Lad'.

St Angelicus was not a real college, but I calculated there would just be room for it if I made its back wall run down Jesus Lane, and kept it very small. Dr Sage was based on Maudsley, the great alienist for whom the Maudsley Hospital in Denmark Hill is named.

Best wishes for your work –

Penelope Fitzgerald

---

* A reader and fan of PMF's work.

Alyson Barr*

27a Bishop's Road
Highgate, N6
27 March [c.1995]

Dear Alyson,

Thankyou so much for the Stanley Spencer p.c. – a terrifying scene, and yet he was so kind and gentle, walking over the Heath with his easel when I was a child.

I've been ill with what I'm told is asthma, but I'm not at all sure that it is, since last <u>September</u> – I was down staying with Tina and found I couldn't walk up to the village shop (the village is on the edge of Dartmoor, but it isn't <u>very</u> steep) and had to sit in the churchyard while the children went on to get their sweets – well, anyway, this illness has gone on so long that everyone is sick and tired of hearing about it and I am still creeping about the place and finding it hard to get up hills and steps – me, who was brought up in Hampstead NW3. Other people, however, seem to be getting mysteriously ill and Ham (Hugh) even in hospital, though he seems to have cured himself by sheer will power – (I thought it was so characteristic of him that he had thought of a number of reforms and reorganisations which would improve the day-to-day running of the hospital while he was there as a patient). I'm so glad that he's better, and able to get down to Devonshire.

It makes me see how time passes when I think that I first suggested an Iceland trip goodness knows how long ago, but with <u>ponies</u> – now I don't think I'd be able to stick it out in a coach, but I still think ponies would be the right way to do it. I wonder if you're going on the N. France coach trip? It doesn't tell you who is doing the guiding, and if it's John Purkis, amiable as he is, you do sometimes get more

---

* A friend and fellow member of the William Morris Society, to which PMF devoted much time and energy.

information than you can manage. I suppose, as Morris said, one ought not to grumble at this?

I <u>would</u> like to put a few stitches into the Banner, but it seems you have to go to Haworth to do this. But who designed it? I must go to the AGM to find out these things – I thought last year the finance committee was getting rather high-handed and there was a distinctly hostile element in the hall.

I avoided reviewing Fiona (McCarthy's) biography, as in spite of the glorious illustrations there were some things I wasn't sure about. And Ray (Watkinson), struggling with his review for the Journal, isn't sure either, I think. To me it's a bit of a tragedy that he won't ever finish his own Morris book now.

I would have liked to go to the WM Birthday, but it was Mothers' Day, and various preparations had been made here, and I suppose anyway you would have been in N.Z. Besides, Ursula once pointed out to me that the Birthdays are the dullest WM occasions of all. I haven't seen <u>her</u>, either, for such a long time. But I'm determined to get a bit better by the centenary –

love and best wishes

Penelope

27a Bishop's Road
Highgate, N6
28 December [1999]

Dear Alyson,

Thankyou very much for your letter and your very kind words about <u>The Knox Brothers</u>. I wanted to write that book, although there was a great shortage of documentation, because after all the time was coming – and indeed it has almost come – when nobody alive would remember my uncles, and I felt they were worth remembering. (Evelyn Waugh worked hard on his life of Uncle Ronnie, but never got any real idea of what the family were like) – The trouble was, of course, that there was so much to be said about the history of the Church of England, which was once of intense interest to so many, and now isn't. – And so, certainly, it's out of print, although it's due to be reprinted by a small U.S. firm called Counterpoint, which, it appears, is run by an eccentric millionaire who doesn't mind if nobody buys it. Surely there can't be many millionaires like that, even in Boston. – But I consider myself very lucky to have a reader like you who understands my attempt to give the atmosphere of those long-ago times, – the zeitgeist, as you say – which I have to admit I do just remember myself.

Your story about your father and the scholar who treated him as a son is truly heart-warming, there's no other word for it, it's strange to think that he must have been at Corpus just when that same Evelyn Waugh was at Hertford declaring that the noblest thing Oxford had to teach was how to get drunk without a hangover the next morning! – I never knew you had a younger brother, though. You must look forward to seeing him when you go back to New Zealand. – I'm the only one of my family left now (although there are plenty of cousins).

best wishes for the New Year and love from

Penelope –

Dorothy Coles*

76 *Clifton Hill,* NW8
1 December [1987]

Dear Dorothy – Just a note, which I'm sure you'll excuse – to say that although I think the Morris poetry readings are a good idea and much more than that, (Morris's poetry ought to be read and heard as much as possible) I don't think that I personally ought to try and make a selection or suggest a subject until the late spring or early summer of 1988, as the new grandchild, the novel (about which Collins are getting very pressing) and a possible move (which will mean painting, wallpapering and getting a bed, mattress and cooker) are all weighing me down at the moment. I've done 20,000 words of the novel, but have to manage 60,000, and I suppose they have to make some sort of sense. – Also, I ought to say that I'm not at all an expert on the Earthly Paradise – it's the lyrics, from first to last, that I love, so I mustn't have ambitions beyond my station –

best wishes
Penelope

27 *Bishop's Rd,*
Highgate
5 June [1992]

Dear Dorothy,

Thankyou for your letter about the poetry reading. To put last things first, do you think it would be all right if I brought some sandwiches for lunchtime, if I don't leave any crumbs.

Secondly, I should prefer anything I say to be inserted into the readings, rather than the readings being inserted into the talk.

* Weaver, designer and expert on William Morris's poetry.

Thirdly, I take your point about ending with a longer dramatised poem, but could I suggest something rather different. Above all, I don't want to finish with Sir Peter Harpdon's End. It is bad, like all Victorian versions of blank verse tragedy, and you get lines like 'Moreover take this bag of franks/for your expenses' – and there's the perpetual danger you get with Morris (remember Georgie Burne-Jones had to stab herself with pins!) that it may be more fun for those who are reading than for those who are listening.

What I've noted down is – <u>not too much narrative verse</u>, as there'll be such a lot in the afternoon, I imagine.

<u>Don't attempt a chronological order</u> – that is, don't start with <u>The Willow and the Red Cliff</u> or <u>Blanche</u>.

1: I should like to begin with <u>The God of the Poor</u>, even though it appeared in 1868, and in my experience, such as it is, it would be best if everyone who has a copy reads a verse in turn, which will wake them up. Only this once, I wouldn't let them do it again. Perhaps we should have <u>The Haystack</u> in here, and <u>Winter Weather</u>. I should then like to go on to the lyrics, which in my opinion are far the most important part of WM's poetry. If I could keep them I would cheerfully sweep all the sagas and Earthly Paradises under the carpet.

2: Wearily, Drearily
Summer Dawn
Christ Keep the Hollow Land
I know a little garden close

3: I wouldn't have thought <u>a lot</u> of biographical refs, was wanted, but as you get on to 1870, it can't be avoided altogether, and wasn't even by Mackail, so I'd like to end with this group

(Earthly Paradise)
Of Heaven and Hell
June
September
November
Prologue to Grettir the Strong

My main idea is not to wear people out in the morning by making them listen to anything very long. Much better, I'd say, to have the lyrics read over twice, so that they really hear them.

Now you very likely won't agree with any of this, but perh: you'll let me know? Someone is hammering at the door – I'm afraid it's some books for review, which in a way I don't want at all, but it's such a temptation to say you'll do them, and then there's no time for anything else –

love, Penelope

27 Bishop's Rd,
Highgate
8 September [1992]

Dear Dorothy,

Thankyou so much for the programme for Oct 17th. As far as I'm concerned, I'd rather say something at the beginning, and, if wanted, at the end, rather than keep intervening between the readers.

I could do the first line of the Odyssey! but mustn't offer to read more than that as it's so long since I learned Greek and I should get muddled with the quantities and should imagine Mackail* being very severe, as indeed he is on Morris's translation. <u>Beowulf</u> I could do, although my own copy has disappeared, I fear. No-one has the slightest idea how it was pronounced, though they pretend they do, so it's everyone for themselves.

I'll go to the BL as soon as I can (rather a lot of pressure at the moment) and look out the Ordène de Chevalerie and send you a passage – though they've now taken to saying they can't issue some titles, because of the move – it's enough to drive anyone to despair. We still have 5 weeks, haven't we?

New grandson Alfie, short for Alfred, what a name! is now a month old and a wonderful peaceable baby,

love – Penelope

---

* John W. Mackail, Burne-Jones' son-in-law, and official biographer of Morris.

[card]
23 September [1992]

Just one more word about W. Morris and his poetry – Ray writes to say that surely <u>Deus est Deus Pauperum</u> is too long to read at one go, and of course he is quite right, and I suggest the last 17 verses (The western sky was red as blood onwards) would be quite enough – it only needs a word or 2 of introduction, 'the story so far' – love P

27 Bishop's Rd.
Highgate
18 October [1992]

Dear Dorothy,
    Just to congratulate you on the Poetry Day yesterday – real interest, and real lovers of poetry, and some of the audience knowing such a lot about WM's poetry – and it was so nice (although in a sense it had nothing to do with it) to watch interested people outside looking up at the house,* and gradually approaching the sacred door to the basement steps. I thought the lunch went very well, and it was a happy thought of Lionel's to bring all that fruit, which gave a lavish I-am-the-ancient-Apple-Queen effect.
    I just got home for the treasure-hunt at Thomas's party, as I'd promised, but was very sorry not to stay for the last part. I realise now I did not do the excerpts from <u>Beowulf</u> right. – I had thought you wanted just a few lines of the original, to give an idea of what it was like, but really I think you wanted a <u>long</u> extract, with WM's version after it – I'm so sorry, I should have thought more clearly.
    Everyone looked so well, including of course yourself. Perhaps we'll be like Ursula and Ralph in the Well at the World's End and stay just as strong after four generations have passed –
    love
    Penelope

---

* Kelmscott House, headquarters of the William Morris Society, formerly his London home.

27 Bishop's Rd.
Highgate
5 November [1992]

Dear Dorothy,

Thankyou so much for your letter – I must say once again that Poetry Day was a great success, and as Ray wrote to me 'Dorothy was justified by her children'! I'm so glad the Beowulf went well – a man's voice is much better, in fact now I come to think of it, essential for Anglo/S poetry. Professor Tolkien, who taught it to me centuries ago, also insisted on the 'Hwaet!'* although really of course we've got no idea how anyone pronounced anything in those days.

Thankyou for your deeply interesting, in fact absolutely fascinating, account of the Eurydice. Of course, you are right, I think you <u>must</u> be, although I never thought of it before, (although I'm a great GM Hopkins reader and have quoted the line from <u>The Loss of the Eurydice</u> 'And you were a liar, you blue March day' to myself often on those lovely days when some dreadful thing or dreadful loss happens and seems even worse because of the blue sky). Charlotte Mew was still going for holidays to the I. of Wight when the frigate went down, and couldn't have failed to hear about it. She was odd about her I of Wight family, being partly fond of them and partly I think, with the 'ladylike' side of her, being rather ashamed of them.

It's most interesting that one of your ancestors was one of the crew, and you tell the story so well – it's so terrible that she went down with all hands, and all her lights showing – coastguards <u>always</u> say that 'she was carrying too much canvas' or making too much speed especially if there are Navy personnel on board, they can't help it, but I still think it's a mystery. I haven't got the Collected Letters, (I wish I had) so I don't know what WM said** – however I shall get them one of these days.

---

* The bardic clearing of the throat in *Beowulf*, to obtain silence.
** He wrote to his daughters that he had noticed the 'sudden gust of wind' which reportedly sank the *Eurydice*. The tragedy of the wreck, in sight of land, haunted Charlotte Mew.

Family well, and Baby Alfie wreathed in smiles at the sight of anything resembling another human being –
Little does he know!
love
Penelope

J. L. Carr*

27a Bishop's Road, N6
10 January 1990

Dear Jim, Thankyou so much for sending William Cowper – but Jim, where are the <u>morals</u>? <u>The Dog and the Waterlily</u> (No Fable) has lost 2 verses and the <u>Retired Cat</u> has lost 'Beware of too sublime a sense' &c – to lose <u>one</u> moral might be a question of space, but to lose <u>two</u> 'looks like carelessness', or I suppose it might be that you don't like morals. Anyway, I love Cowper dearly and the book is beautiful like all your books.

    <u>Very</u> glad you're going on with Harpole & Foxberrow, Publishers, and best New Year wishes –

    Penelope

I do like the Latin Toll for the Brave upside down – just to show –

27a Bishop's Road, N6
18 December [c.1992]

Dear Jim,

    Thankyou so much for the Reeve's Tale.

    A few years before I stopped teaching – I don't know if it was the same with you – the London Board took the daring step of setting it (and the Miller's tale) for A level, which they'd never done before, and it was amazing how easily the class got through it. Now they've decided Chaucer is too difficult for everyone, even at university, but you've evidently felt that it isn't, although you've encouraged them with an amazing selection of decorations wh: I enjoyed very much –

---

* PMF first met the novelist, J. L. Carr, at the Arvon Foundation, where they both taught fiction-writing.

the only thing is, I'd have expected JLC on the back of the van, but you
can't make room for everything.

I also liked D. Bancroft's piece, but I think it's very broad-minded of
him to call it 'a gracious house'. I think Lycett Green might have
spoken to him more than <u>once</u> in nine months.

I enclose another little book about Cambridge,* shrunk down by
the publisher for some publicity scheme or other,

with best Christmas wishes –

Penelope

                                                        27a Bishop's Road, N6
                                                        23 December 1993

Dear Jim –

You will forgive this paper, as everything except tangerines seems to
have run out at the moment. Thankyou for Mark Amory's letter. He
is nice, but I don't think many or any of us can have got such a letter
even from the nicest literary editor. You can tell that he really means it –
that is what I like about it. And he's a hard worker himself, and had a
difficult job, I think, editing the Evelyn Waugh letters.

Only I didn't realise that you were ill. They didn't tell me so when I
went to Kettering to talk to the Wheelchair Association, but that was in
October. I do wish you weren't, Jim.

I'm so glad you were converted by the Burne-Jones west windows in
Brum Cathedral, they were put in while my grandfather was (suffragan)
Bishop, but he had no aesthetic sense whatever (although he was a
wonderful organiser and Feeder of Sheep) and, I think, scarcely noticed
them. I'm told they have had to put wire over them, which is a great
pity.

Maura and David (once of Lumb Bank) have at last had a baby,
after many trials and tribulations – a daughter, Imelda.

I still have my 'little books'. And now I see someone has republished
Jane Austen's History of England, apparently believing that no-one else
has done so.

* *The Gate of Angels.*

I'm getting too old to write novels. But I wish I could say, as you can, that you've written everything just as you wanted to and it's all come out absolutely right.

love and best wishes for everything –

Penelope

Sybille Bedford*

27a Bishop's Road
Highgate
21 September [1989]

Dear Sybille,

Please may I be one of the many 100s to congratulate you** –
I wasn't at all surprised, but I did feel very pleased –
best wishes
Penelope (Fitzgerald)

27a Bishop's Road
Highgate
14 July [1996]

Dear Sybille – Thankyou so much for writing to me about the Heywood Hill Prize.† It was fairy gold, really – I didn't know the award existed, and in fact I think it <u>didn't</u> until last year, but that perhaps made it all the better. And thankyou too for your kind word about <u>The Blue Flower</u>. –
with best wishes –
Penelope

* The novelist and doyenne of PEN International.
** On being shortlisted for the Booker Prize with *Jigsaw*.
† For lifetime achievement in literature.

Julian Barnes*

27 Bishop's Road
Highgate
23 March 1993

Dear Julian Barnes,

Please don't think I've forgotten that you once (politely and kindly) turned down the idea of lecturing at the Highgate Institution, because you said that, apart from anything else, you didn't like giving lectures. However, we still hope you might come to give a reading and say something about your books – would that be possible, do you think? The Highgate shop would send along copies, and we shall have the roof mended by 18 January 94, which is the date I'm hoping might possibly suit you – I won't apologise for its being so far ahead – as I'm sure you're only too used to it –

Yours sincerely
Penelope Fitzgerald

27 Bishop's Road
Highgate
8 April 1993

Dear Julian Barnes,

Thankyou very much for your kind letter. I admit I'm the one, or one of the ones, that writes novels, which is one of the reasons why I particularly hoped you might come and talk to us, but so of course do all the Highgate dwellers.

Would it be all right if I put you down entirely provisionally for 18 Jan 1994 (I agree it's difficult to imagine that we will ever get there)

---

* The novelist.

and write to you again nearer the time, and if it doesn't suit then, it
will be my fault and no-one else's –
   Yours sincerely
   Penelope Fitzgerald

                                                 27 Bishop's Road
                                                 Highgate
                                                 5 January [1994]

Dear Julian Barnes,
   I couldn't get you on the telephone, but I do hope that you will be
coming to read whatever you prefer to us at the Highgate Institution
on the 18th. I know that you couldn't commit yourself, and also that
you might possibly be in the Argentine, but we're allowing ourselves to
look forward to it just the same.
   with best wishes –
   Penelope Fitzgerald

                                                 27 Bishop's Road
                                                 Highgate
                                                 3 April [1994]

Thankyou so much for <u>Letters from London</u> and indeed for
remembering how much I wanted to read your Lloyds piece. – I
admired it very much indeed, not only for the information and
explanation but for the exactly right <u>tone</u> you've managed to get, or
perhaps I should call it a never quite unsympathetic point of balance,
something classic anyway –
   best wishes Penelope

27 Bishop's Road
Highgate
26 September 1999

Certainly I was am and always shall be an admirer of Brian Moore,
The Answer from Limbo and Judith Hearne perhaps still the best, after
all these years. Would love to come if my back doesn't hurt too much
though I do note that seating is limited.

    best wishes, Penelope

27 Bishop's Road
Highgate
16 October 1999

Dear Julian,

    I'm so sorry but my back is too bad at the moment to allow me to
crawl out in the evening – I ought never to have accepted in the first
place, but I did and do like Brian Moore's books so much – I'm
returning this ticket you sent me as it says seating is limited and so it
might be needed elsewhere – anyway enough of all this and best
wishes for the evening – Penelope

Michael Holroyd*

76 Clifton Hill, NW8
18 September 1984

Dear Michael, I just want to thank you most sincerely for writing about <u>C.Mew</u> in the Good Book Guide, and also (since it seems to me that all biographers apply to you sooner or later) that although it's true that I've been collecting material for years on Leslie Hartley, and knew him well, I don't know that I shall ever be able to write his life, so if anyone else wants to have a go (and this is the answer I give them when they write to me every few months or so) they are welcome, but they won't find it easy. This is because: 1. Leslie's sister who breeds deerhounds and is in every way delightful, but much firmer than Leslie, won't consider giving permission for the use of any material which might reflect the slightest discredit on her brother, or suggest that he died of drink 2. a mysterious paternity case was brought against him towards the end of his life, which was heard by a judge in chambers, so I can't see the papers 3. Leslie, who was very interested in ghosts, appears to be <u>haunting</u> his old home near Bath, now a leisure and canoeing centre called 'Misty Waters'. And so on, and so on.

best wishes
Penelope

27a Bishop's Road, N6
31 January [*c.*1988]

Dear Michael,

Thankyou so very much for your kind words about Charlotte Mew and myself in the <u>Telegraph</u> – and indeed to the BBC as I think you suggested, perhaps in passing, that she might figure in their <u>Visiting</u>

---

* The biographer and autobiographer. He and PMF worked together for the Royal Society of Literature.

Lives. Partly as a result of that the book is going to come out in trade paperback and that's another step forward from 'said to be a writer'. I can only hope for a little at a time, and I'm sure you know how grateful I am for your help,

    best wishes,

    Penelope

27a Bishop's Road
Highgate, N6
21 February 2000

Dear Michael,

    I am truly sorry to make you read the same letter twice, particularly when you have (always) so much to do, but I'm writing once again to resign from the committee of the RSL* because arthritis (although I'm told the word means nothing) makes it such a business for me to get from one place to another. At Hyde Park Gardens I even had to appeal to Mark Amory to open the front door for me (which he did of course with the greatest politeness), but I felt then that this wouldn't do for a committee member.

    You asked me to be one of the judges for the Heinemann and Holtby prizes and I will finish doing that, of course. Meantime, all good wishes for the move and all your other undertakings. And surely you couldn't have found a better place for the society to start its new century. – I've sometimes thought you looked a bit tired, but never in the least defeated – not for a moment –

    with best wishes

    Penelope

---

* Royal Society of Literature.

27a Bishop's Road
Highgate, N6
5 March 2000

Dear Michael,

Thankyou for your letter and I'm sure you've come to the right decision about the history of the RSL, which perhaps the Society would never have undertaken if they'd known what a business it was going to be. I didn't know, of course, that poor Isabel was ill, and I don't know how much she minds about the history, except that it's impossible not to feel fiercely protective about anything one writes.

I think I went through the possible nominations for honours with Mark before. Do you remember, you were away, and we tried to take the opportunity to get your name on the list, but in vain.

Thankyou for saying I can stay on the committee in my rather unsatisfactory condition. You never believe the time will come when you can't walk everywhere, but it does –

best wishes
Penelope

Alberto Manguel*

27a Bishop's Road
Highgate, N6
12 July 1998

Dear Alberto Manguel,

I can't tell you how pleased I was to have that copy of Max Beerbohm's lecture on Lytton Strachey.

I remember giving it to my father. – He came up to London as a young man before the first world war with the idea of earning his living by writing, and one of his ambitions was to meet the great Max Beerbohm. At last he summoned up courage to ask him to lunch. Thankyou very much for your kind and generous thought –

best wishes
Penelope Fitzgerald

27a Bishop's Road
Highgate, N6
14 September 1998

Dear Alberto Manguel,

Thankyou so very much for your kind letter, and I'm so glad to have your approval for The Blue Flower, which took me a long time to write because my German is so slow. I had Novalis' complete letters &c. out from the London Library for two years, and they never asked for it back, much to their credit, I think.

If you would like to use a line, any line, as an epigraph, I should consider it an honour, although I think that particular one was mine, in imitation of Novalis, or rather of his Fragmente. I was very much interested to learn that Borges asked to have Heinrich von Ofterdingen read to him during his last illness. There is something 'noble' about it, perhaps that appealed to him.

---

* The novelist, anthologist, translator and critic.

At the end of your fine book you say that 'The history of reading has no end.' I treasure these words and can only pray they're true. I am assistant-judging the Booker Prize this autumn, and one of the novels sent in doesn't even exist – it has to be downloaded from the internet –

With all my best wishes for whatever you're undertaking –

Penelope Fitzgerald –

Masolino d'Amico*

27a Bishop's Road
Highgate, N6
6 January 1999

Dear Masolino d'Amico,

Thankyou for your letter, and I'm delighted to hear that you are translating <u>The Beginning of Spring</u>, but the terrible thing which I have to confess to you is that I don't know the answer to your question. In fact, although I have done a bit of amateur hand printing, I'm afraid there are several things wrong with this passage. On p. 41 I've got 'T. spent no time in distributing the print from the reserves' when it ought to be 'back from the reserves' and now there's this matter of washing the dirty type – it would be inked, of course, but not dirty, unless it had been dropped on the floor, but that I'm sure T. would never do.

However, I'm quite sure that by 'slip' here, I meant a long straight holder or container, onto (or into) which he put the type while it was still damp from washing. But <u>why</u> he did this I can't think, although I must have got the idea from somewhere. You are the only person who has noticed, and I feel deeply ashamed of this. The German translator, Christa Krüger, has put 'Messinglineal' for 'brass slip' i.e. a brass ruler. Do you think that would do?

Please accept my apologies and best wishes for the New Year – Penelope Fitzgerald

---

* The Italian translator of all PMF's fiction.

27a Bishop's Road
London, N6
10 June 1999

Dear Masolino d'Amico,

Of course I should have loved to come to Italy, as would anyone in their right senses, but alas! I am too old.

However please do come and see me if you are in London at the end of June and I'll do my best to give a satisfactory interview –
best wishes
Penelope Fitzgerald

27a Bishop's Road
London, N6
[postcard]
27 July [1999]

Thankyou so much for sending me your interview. I feel very proud to be on the front page of the Stampa supplement, and very grateful to you for your translations.

What a relief it will be to get to the seaside and leave Rome to the tourists and pilgrims for a while –
best wishes – Penelope

Richard Holmes*

27a Bishop's Road
London, N6
20 July 1997

Dear Richard – This is to thank you so much for your very kind and very discerning review of <u>The Blue Flower</u> which reminded me that I only 'started to write' (as they say at the University of the 3rd Age) as a result of reading your piece about Monty James in the <u>Times</u>, so many years ago. I've still got it, although it's almost falling to pieces –
    very best wishes
    Penelope

---

* PMF's review of Holmes's biography of Coleridge is one of her finest critical essays – and his review of *The Blue Flower* the most learned and interesting account of it so far.

Mandy Kirkby*

27a Bishop's Road
Highgate
19 May 1995

Dear Mandy,

Thankyou very much for the page proofs of <u>Blue Flower</u>, which I'm returning as you ask, and thankyou too for the most helpful yellow stickers (and for your note about the jacket). I believe now we ought to have had a <u>map</u>, as Stuart said, but I'm not capable of making one, and didn't like to take one straight out of someone else's book.

The ghost at the Southwold-Walberswick crossing is said to be a mother waiting for her child who was supposed to be coming back on the last ferry. The white dog, which I have actually seen, was something to do with Dunwich, I think, and the poltergeist** was horrid.

Still doggedly going on with the Independent Foreign Fiction awards, only to find that one of the books we've got on the short list has been pulped by Macmillans already – the whole book business is getting very depressing –

best wishes
Penelope

27a Bishop's Road
Highgate
25 April 1997

Dear Mandy,

Thankyou very much for the cover proofs – delighted to see the child Cicero† in his rose-coloured socks again, I once used to live quite near the Wallace and it's then that I saw him so often.

---

* PMF's editor at Flamingo/HarperCollins for *The Blue Flower*, *The Means of Escape* and *A House of Air*.
** As featured in *The Bookshop*.
† Fresco known as *Boy Reading Cicero* by Vincenzo Foppa in the Wallace Collection, used as cover for *The Bookshop* in its Flamingo edition.

I also want to congratulate you on biking (but surely not all the way?) to Standen.* I love the house (Webb designed everything, even the electric fittings) but can't understand what you say about the garden. What <u>can</u> they have done with it – it should be full of flowers at the moment, specially narcissi. As my little book says, Webb quarrelled with the landscape gardener over the layout and then 'Margaret Beale took the planting into her own hands and her notebooks record a typical amateur's enthusiasm for an abundance of colourful and unusual plants at variance with the quiet, restful effect Webb would have hoped for.' Surely the National Trust can't have got rid of <u>everything</u>. The flowers were mostly in the lower garden, of course. –

Don't do too much cleaning, nobody gives you proper credit for it – best wishes Penelope

> *27a Bishop's Road*
> *Highgate*
> 17 June 1997

Dear Mandy,

How nice to hear from you, thankyou for the paperback covers. I like them, although I wish there wasn't an Egyptian artefact on <u>The Golden Child</u>, as I took such pains to make it <u>not</u> Egyptian, but I've now begun to see (and about time, too, you may say) that one mustn't make a fuss about nothing. (By 'nothing' I mean something that no-one cares about except oneself.) I'm very glad they're being reissued, anyway.

I'm struggling, at the moment, to answer the deeply learned questions of the German translator of <u>The Blue Flower</u>, who has a doctorate in Early Romantic literature. She knows so much more than I do that I feel deeply ashamed. There is a conference, too, this summer,

---

* Arts and Crafts house in West Sussex, designed by Philip Webb for the Beale family.

somewhere in East Germany, on Novalis, and Professor Schulz (from Australia, but one of the five editors of Novalis' Collected Works, and I think the only surviving one) is going (not to complain, as I feel I truly deserve, about my omissions and errors) but to make a presentation, whatever that means, of <u>The Blue Flower</u>. He writes in such a kindly, old-fashioned German-scholarly way that I feel taken back in time, and, once again, that I can't live up to it, although I once could.

I hope you have had a great time in Dublin. I haven't been there for a long long while – my husband's aunt used to be Mother Superior of the Dominican deaf-and-dumb school out at Cabra –

all best wishes
Penelope

27a Bishop's Road
Highgate, N6 4HP
7 October [1999]

Dear Mandy,

I was so glad to see you again, and didn't feel I congratulated you enough on your decision (which you announced so calmly) to buy a house. It's such a proud moment to stand on your own doorstep, however tired you feel.

Here is a list of my short stories:

The Axe (Times Anthology of Ghost Stories, Cape 1975)
The Prescription (London Review of Books. New Stories 8, Arts Council 1983)
At Hiruhamara (British Council New Writing Minerva 1992, also The Oxford Book of Short Stories OUP 1998)
The Means of Escape (British Council New Writing 4, Vintage 1995)
Desideratus (British Council New Writing 6, Vintage 1997)
Not Shown (Daily Telegraph, also on Telltale Tapes, but I can't find the date)
Beehernz (The BBC paid for this in August 1997 but I'm not sure when it appeared. It was commissioned by their music mag. And reprinted in one of their publications)

The Red-Haired Girl (TLS paid for it Oct 30 1998 but I'm not quite sure (again!) when it appeared).

I'm sure there are a few others, but I can't lay my hand on them.*
I must apologise for this miserable list, and can't believe they could really be turned into a book. Anyway, one of them, Desideratus, was my 'sleeper' – editors always ask to see more than one, and I used to send it out so they could reject it and keep the other one. At last I had to part with it, though, as I had nothing else left – **
with best wishes
Penelope

27a Bishop's Road
Highgate
London, N6 4HP
10 November 1999

Dear Mandy,
Thankyou very much for your letter (8 Nov) and I should be happy for you to publish my short stories although I'm afraid they are rather an odd collection, only there's just two things 1. I'm very slow at writing them, so I don't know how long it would take me and 2. I already owe HarperC money although I'm not sure how much as it was paid on July 11 1997 (according to my notes, which are not reliable) but must have accumulated interest since then. I'd love to do something about this debt – what do you think?
best wishes
Penelope

* 'The Likeness' (published in *Prize Writing: A Booker Anthology*, 1989) and 'Our Lives Are Only Lent to Us' (an early story, published in Granta) were added to the paperback edition of *The Means of Escape*. Two stories remain uncollected.
** 'Desideratus' was, in fact, one of PMF's three last stories, all written to commission, in 1997–8.

27a Bishop's Road
Highgate, N6 4HP
23 December 1999

Dear Mandy,

Thankyou for the 2 copies of the contract form. There are just two points I'm worried about – one is at the bottom of page 3 – the work <u>has</u> been published, and in what territories I've no idea. The other is on page 7, par: 8 – about the option on my next (entirely notional) work of fiction – do I have to sign that one?

I hope you have a really restful Christmas with no troublesome authors, no trouble either with the drains or the rubbish collection, just plenty of beautiful snow –

all best wishes
Penelope

27a Bishop's Road
Highgate, N6 4HP
19 January 2000

Dear Mandy,

Thankyou so much for your letter and the new contract form, I was rather disappointed that it now says: illustrations, none. Although at one point I think you did say something about wood engravings, or at least wood cuts – not specially done, I don't mean that – but maybe they got swept under the carpet. – I still hope to write another story for this collection, which wouldn't of course be 'previously published'.

Still I mustn't make a fuss about nothing, although as I hardly need to tell you, what seems nothing to the publisher is often immensely important to the writer.

I'm so glad you had a restful Christmas – mine wasn't at all, it was an electronic Christmas – Ria had a new laptop and the children all had things which flashed and made irritating half-audible noises. But I had a wonderful time just the same.

Do let me know about the illustrations, Mandy. It seems to me the only hope for this book is for it to look nice. I did an introduction for Penguin for a new edition of Jim Carr's A Month in the Country and

it's printed now and looks quite dreadful, in tiny print fit for mice
to read –

with best wishes
Penelope

27a Bishop's Road
Highgate, N6 4HP
16 March 2000*

Dear Mandy,

I'm sorry I've taken so long to thank you for sending me the
photocopies. The trouble, but I ought not to call it that, is that Chris**
has gone through The Knox Brothers so carefully and made so many
queries that I'm hard put to it to answer them. I can't help feeling that
it makes things more difficult that he's now back in Boston and
Counterpoint are in Washington, but no matter.

The letter was not from S. Vickers but from a woman in Sandbach
who was distressed because she'd thought of opening a bookshop and
having read The Bookshop now felt she ought not to. Perhaps she's
right – in any case Miss Garnet's Angel has come out looking really
nice and I hope Clare Alexander, who I used to teach and who, I now
remember, was the first person to write to me about it, will be pleased.

Janet Silver† has been ringing up and although she speaks very
clearly I find what she says rather confusing. She says she wants to call
the Houghton Mifflin ed. of the short stories The Means of Escape,
which I've no objection to, and that this is 'the theme of them all',
(perhaps it is, I don't know) and that it (I mean the American edition)
can't have any illustration because that wouldn't be consistent with the
other titles, which don't have any. She seems rather upset, and in a

---

* This, with a letter to Chris Carduff, is one of PMF's last letters – she had her first stroke
a few days later.
** Carduff.
† PMF's editor at Houghton Mifflin. Chris Carduff was no longer with the firm.

great hurry, says everything must be ready for their catalogue by Monday. Do you think <u>The Means of Escape</u> might go first in the Flamingo ed., as it's the longest story anyway?

I'm supposed to be going away from April 15th to 29th, but hope to send you another short story before then to see what you think about it. But it's of no use mentioning it to Janet as she wants everything ready by Monday. I feel there's some kind of pressure on her, but I don't know where from, certainly not from me. Meanwhile I'm letting her down because I haven't been asked to appear at the London Book Fair (?), in fact I didn't know that it was on, or even what it was. She tells me Peter Ho Davies is coming over for it specially. I'm a bit vague about him too.

I won't ask you again about your house, but just hope everything is going well –

all best wishes

Penelope

Chris Carduff*

76 Clifton Hill
London, NW8
12 September 1987

Dear Christopher Carduff,

Thankyou very much for your letter and the two admirable biographies you sent me, (not to speak of the others which you said you might send later).

I'm very glad that Charlotte Mew should be in such a series, she <u>is</u> a 'timeless woman', I think.

1. May I ask you something? When you reprint, I do hope the illustrations will still be scattered, as I'm told it's no more expensive than putting them all together in the middle in the old way, even if they don't come out quite so clearly, and I'm sure it's much more encouraging for the readers, particularly if they don't know much about the subject.

2. I'm afraid <u>Ethel</u> Oliver appears as <u>Edith</u> Oliver in the index and throughout the text, except on p. 33. I've had quite a few letters about this, but I don't see how it can be altered now –

3. The poems – they are all out of copyright now, except for those which Carcanet/Virago printed for the first time – The following are reprinted <u>complete</u> in the text of <u>CMM and Her Friends</u>:

Exspecto Resurrectionem, Sea Love, Péri en Mer, The Farmer's Bride, Fame, A Quoi Bon Dire?, The Shade-catchers, Fin de Fête.

* PMF's American editor, who brought out *The Blue Flower* with great success for Houghton Mifflin and subsequently published or republished all her other fiction. His new edition of *The Knox Brothers* appeared in the autumn of 2000, and he co-edited her essays, known as *The Afterlife* in the US.

I suppose they wouldn't need to be reprinted again in appendix? (Normally a biography wouldn't quote so much, but I couldn't rely on the readers knowing them at all.) Apart from these, my list would be:

The Changeling, In Nunhead Cemetery, Ken, Madeleine in Church, The Quiet House, Rooms, Saturday Market, Domus Caedet Arborem, Here Lies a Prisoner, The Call.

But I have to leave that to you, and of course as you say it would have to depend on the exact page count.

4. The foreword – Margaret Drabble is a splendid writer, very kind and helpful, and a well-known name, and Michael Holroyd – also kind and helpful! – was certainly an early supporter of Charlotte Mew – but they are both very busy at the moment (and indeed always) – the Bernard Shaw biography having at last got under way with Volume 1 – I'd much rather you wrote to her, as I only know her slightly and it would come better from you! – If she can't manage the time, then, possibly, the poet Patric Dickinson, who is a great expert on early 20th century poets.

5. The cover – Unfortunately I have never been able to discover a colour-photograph or painting of Charlotte Mew, and the (black-and white) sketch we had for a frontispiece was said (by Mrs Marjorie Watts, who knew her well) not to be at all like her! I see that you got someone to colour the engraving of Margaret Fuller – but don't know what to suggest. The 1923 Photograph, opposite p. 191 of CMM and Her Friends has a lot of character, I think – but that wasn't what you were asking for. The chief collector of CMM items is Frederick B. Adams – but he hasn't got a colour picture either.

Thankyou again for Cassatt and Fuller, which I'm now settling down to read, and for your kind and encouraging remarks about authors and publishers. You'll let me know, won't you, if I can do anything –

Yours sincerely

Penelope Fitzgerald

76 Clifton Hill
London, NW8
17 October 1987

Dear Christopher Carduff,

Thankyou so much for your letter and for telling me how Charlotte
Mew is getting along. I'm glad the illustrations can be placed in the
same way, as I think they help to 'tell the story', always a difficulty when
you're trying to write about somebody who is not at all well known,
and give an idea of their character and their background – it's quite a
different problem if you're writing a life (as a friend of mine is doing at
the moment) of William Morris – or of Emily Dickinson. I was also
very interested to hear about the layout you're thinking about for the
poems – they're a printer's nightmare, I know, with their long lines –
but the way you suggest doing it would give the feeling of the original
Poetry Bookshop editions – and that, I think, would be just right.

The selection of poems I leave to you, of course, with great relief,
and I think that the Ethel/Edith is the only error that needs putting
right.

I hope you're successful with Margaret Drabble! I did see her for a
few minutes the other evening, but didn't like to mention this
introduction –

best wishes
Penelope Fitzgerald

76 Clifton Hill
London, NW8
7 December 1987

Dear Christopher,

Thankyou so much for your letter. I was a bit dashed to find that
Collins had lost the film of the C. Mew illustrations, and I consider it
very forgiving of you to say that such things happen in this business,
although perhaps they do in all businesses.

I'm sorry about Margaret Drabble – but it was really Michael Holroyd
who knew all about Charlotte Mew – and I think Brad Leithauser,

whose article needless to say I appreciated very much, will be just the right person particularly as he's a poet himself.

Who will say a word on the back jacket? Well, I think Robert Gittings <u>might</u>, as I know he is interested in Charlotte Mew, since she was a friend of Florence Hardy's, and he even thought of writing about her himself at one time, I know. He's always kind and generous to other writers.

As to the note on myself, I'm answering your letter at once but have only just got it – we've been having a postal strike – so I'm afraid it's too late – but anyway, I'm a niece of Ronald Knox and published a biography of my father (who was editor of <u>Punch)</u> and my three uncles (<u>The Knox Brothers</u>, American ed. Coward, McCann and Geoghegan 1977). I also write novels (on the whole I think you should write biographies of those you admire and respect, and novels about human beings who you think are sadly mistaken) – and two of them, <u>Offshore</u> (Booker Prize 1979) and <u>Innocence</u>, came out with Henry Holt's in 1987.

The jacket with Dorothy Hawksley's portrait sounds beautiful and I'm very much looking forward to seeing it – and much regret the extra work you've had to do – with best Christmas wishes

　　　Penelope

76 Clifton Hill
London, NW8
3 January 1988

Thankyou so very much for the delightful Christmas card and kind message. I was also very glad to get the jacket design for <u>Charlotte Mew and Her Friends</u>. The water-colour is so much better in colour. Whatever happens to the book, I'm sure it's in good hands – best wishes for 1988 Penelope

76 Clifton Hill
London, NW8
22 February 1988

Dear Chris,

This to thank you for the proof copy of <u>Charlotte Mew and Her</u> <u>Friends</u>, and for all the trouble you've taken over it. I thought the introduction was just right, and I'm very glad that she should have a chance to find friends in America and to find, too, such a helpful book editor –

all best wishes –
Penelope

76 Clifton Hill
London, NW8
[1988]

<u>Charlotte Mew and Her Friends</u> has just arrived, looks magnificent, but at the same time it's just right for a very unmagnificent and genuine poet. Thankyou so much, I feel proud to have your edition –

best wishes
Penelope

76 Clifton Hill
London, NW8
24 April 1988

Dear Christopher,

Please forgive this unbelievably battered air-letter form, but it is Sunday, and this is the only one I have left. How it got like this? I really can't tell.

I'm sorry about the pages 112/113 trouble in <u>Charlotte Mew and her</u> <u>Friends</u>, and altogether I'm afraid the book has given you a lot of extra work, and it's very good of you to say your heart is in it. Thankyou for returning the photographs – they too, I'm afraid, have been another cause of difficulty, but I very much appreciated the piece in <u>Publishers' Weekly</u> which suggested there might be new appreciation for Charlotte M 'after years of inexplicable neglect'. Whether or not that turns out to be so, I'm grateful to Addison-Wesley for giving her, so to speak, the chance.

I sympathise with you about the need for growing something out of the earth. It's strange but I used to believe that Americans didn't feel this need (and called their gardens 'yards'). Robert Frost, when he was over here, gardened by going out and digging up wild flowers, which of course refused to grow when he and his wife brought them back to his garden. But I see that nowadays anyway, I'm wrong –

with thanks and best wishes
Penelope

New address: As from June 10th, (if you should ever wish to get in contact with me again!):

27a Bishop's Road
Highgate, N6
26 May 1988

Dear Christopher

Thankyou for your letter and you are absolutely right about moving, said to be life's second most traumatic experience, and thankyou, too for the <u>CMews</u> which have arrived safely – also the reviews, which of course I was very interested to see.

About people who it would be useful to send copies to I am afraid I'm not going to be of much use, although I should like to be – the reason is that they were sent copies of the original biography, (without the poems of course) – otherwise I should suggest an American in France, Frederick B. Adams – as he is one of the chief collectors of Charlotte Mew letters &c. best wishes, Penelope

27a Bishop's Road
London, N6
15 June 1988

Thankyou so much for the notices of <u>Charlotte Mew and Her Friends</u>, particularly the kind words from Gloria Fromm. I'm sure that you've done everything possible for the book, and hope there may be a chance of seeing Copenhaver Clumpston.

<u>All</u> moves are dreadful and one's possessions become hostile and seize the opportunity to disappear however carefully you've packed them, but I hope to be settled one of these days –

best wishes, Penelope

27a Bishop's Road
London
4 August 1988

Dear Christopher, (no, Chris)

This is to thank you for the notices of <u>CMew and Her Friends</u> which have just arrived, and to say how sorry I was to have missed (at least, I'm afraid I've missed) your art director.

I'm trying to get Camden Council to put a plaque on Charlotte Mew's house (which now belongs to the council) – I should so much like to see it there – but Camden, like nearly all the other London authorities, is hopelessly in debt,

best wishes
Penelope

27a Bishop's Road
London, N6
15 October 1988

Dear Chris,

This is to thank you for the <u>American Scholar</u> and in general for all the kind attention and help you've given to <u>Charlotte Mew and Her Friends</u>. I would say that if anyone counts as one of her friends, it's yourself.

I'm so glad that you're allowing yourself a week-end – although that doesn't seem very long – in Maine, and if you really take my Russian novel with you I shall feel flattered – best wishes Penelope

> 27a Bishop's Road
> London, N6
> 17 January 1989

Dear Chris,

Thankyou so very much for your letter and the copy of Doris Grumbach's review, and for letting me know about the paperback of <u>Charlotte Mew and Her Friends</u>. I needn't say how pleased I am about this, and it would be wonderful if with the paperback we could reach some more readers. You're right, readers of poetry (and, I might add, poets) aren't usually rich, but, in my opinion, they're important.

<u>Burne-Jones</u> was the first book I ever wrote and I think I'd do it very differently now – it needed colour illustrations, which of course no-one could afford – however I think it's proved useful to people who wanted to study the period, although the bibliography is now seriously out of date. Hamish Hamilton, however, are re-issuing it as a paperback (with even fewer illustrations, I fear) later this year. The editor in charge is called Rosalind Sanderson, and Hamish Hamilton are now at 27 Wright's Lane London W8 – This is just in case you're interested in asking them about it. But although there's a very large Burne-Jones in the Museo at Puerto Rico, I don't think he's ever been a success in the U.S.!

best wishes, Penelope

> 27a Bishop's Road
> London, N6
> 24 February 1989

Dear Chris,

Thankyou so much for your letter and I should like to congratulate you on two counts – on your new fiancée, and secondly on the stand you've taken over your profession – when I saw that Pearsons had taken over Addison-Wesley I felt that changes might be on the way, and I think you had not only a literary but a moral choice to make (I'm not talking about my book! something much more than that) and that you've chosen right and it must turn out well. I do hope your interviews have been successful. I wonder if you went to Henry Holt's who courageously brought out some of my novels – Marian Wood, who is my book editor there, seems to have some of the same ideas as you.

Needless to say, I was very glad that you are going to write the copy for Charlotte Mew, in spite of everything. I see that a correction is necessary about Netta Syrett (although I've checked, with the only person I can find who knew her, that she (Netta) did more than talk about sex –) and I've written to Elizabeth Skinner about this and hope that my letter will arrive in time.

My Edward Burne-Jones is being re-issued in paper-back by Hamish Hamilton, and I hope that a few copies may make their way over to the U.S.

All my very best wishes for April 8th – surely the best date in the year for a wedding –

best wishes Penelope Fitzgerald

27a Bishop's Road
London, N6
24 February 1989

Dear Elizabeth,*

I had a letter from Chris Carduff giving me his news, and enclosing a page of corrections from the proofs of Charlotte Mew and Her Friends on which, I'm afraid, there's an error which has been pointed out by a reviewer.

This is page 63. In line 23 (down from the top), could we change 'uncle' to 'friend'? it ought to be 'friend of the family', as he was a good deal older than Netta Syrett, but I fear that can't be fitted in.

* Carduff's colleague and wife-to-be.

Please may I congratulate you and wish you all possible happiness on the 8th of April

Penelope

27a Bishop's Road
London, N6
25 March 1992

Dear Chris,

Thankyou for your letter – I can remember so well when you left Addison Wesley and married, but since then Emily has been born and you have your new job and I should like to congratulate you most sincerely on both. (I'm expecting my ninth grandchild in August and consider that there's nothing like them.)

I should like to thank you too for the copies of The New Criterion and say how pleased I am that you've printed the Bruce Bawer piece and how honoured I feel to have my work discussed in your very worthwhile magazine, I'm absolutely in sympathy with what you say about the 'common reader'. We just <u>have</u> to assume they still exist – the common readers, I mean – Emily mustn't inherit a world without them.

Harvill Collins have brought out Charlotte Mew and Her Friends in trade paperback now – the book for which you did so much. You don't say anything about your election! And I shan't say anything about ours –

with best wishes – Penelope

27a Bishop's Road
London, N6
23 April [1992]

Dear Chris,

Thankyou for your letter. What a beautiful word-processor you've got! As a matter of fact there <u>is</u> one in this house, up in the spare bedroom, though it's by no means as beautiful as the New Criterion one, but I still find it easier with pen and ink and I think they will have to last me out.

I should be happy to write something about <u>Punch</u>, but I'm afraid it would have to be recollections and reminiscences rather than any kind of formal account, with just a paragraph about the paper's decline, because, to tell you the truth, I haven't read it for a good few years. (Last year Punch gave a party to celebrate the 150th anniversary, but I couldn't bring myself to go to it.) I think my best course is to send you something in good time for June 22 and see what you think of it.

The election! Well, I'm a Liberal, but my party was abolished, once and for all, while I went out into the kitchen to make a cup of tea, and I can't give my heart to the parties who are supposed to have inherited the name.

Keep the faith, is all I can say –

Best wishes – Penelope

27a Bishop's Road
London, N6
14 May 1992

Dear Chris,

Here is a piece about <u>Punch</u> – not its complete history, and certainly not an attempt to say whose fault it was that the paper had to close – just a few thoughts.

I hope you and your wife and daughter are well – my ninth grandchild is due in August but believe me it's just as exciting as if it was the first –

best wishes
Penelope

27a Bishop's Road
London, N6
15 June [1992]

Dear Chris,

Here are the page proofs which only seem to have one correction, on p 2, and even there I'm not sure of the title of Mark Twain's book. It seems to have several titles.

The contributor para. is fine. It still surprises me, after all these years, to think I've published anything.

The Charlotte Mew paperback is not going too badly over here. About her I've never changed my mind – I still think that at least sometimes she was a great poet.

I hope you and your family are well –
best wishes
Penelope

27a Bishop's Road
London, N6
16 September 1992

Dear Chris,

Thankyou very much for the copies of the New Criterion, and the cheque. Still no hope, I'm afraid, for poor <u>Punch</u>, although there is a publisher who produces selections from Punch for Canadian dentists' and doctors' waiting-rooms, and he says he might like to take over – dear, dear – but anyway I was very glad to have a word about it in print.

I have a new grandbaby in the house – my ninth – and as a connoisseur you will know how I feel –
best wishes
Penelope

27a Bishop's Road
London, N6
[17 December 1992]

Dear Chris,

This is really to send you and your family all my best wishes for Christmas and 1993. I hope you got the snow. I remember the Rockefeller Centre, if it's the one people skate round in their lunch hour.

Yes I should like to do the Larkin letters, if you could ask the publisher to send them. I think Anthony Thwaite had quite a hard time making the selection.

A new grandson here, just four months old – a handsome baby, and a great philosopher –
best wishes
Penelope

27a Bishop's Road
London, N6
29 October 1996

Dear Chris,

How lovely to hear from you, even quite apart from anything to do with books or publishing – I certainly <u>would</u> love to know, if time ever allows, how you and your family are – the last news I had was of no. 1 daughter, as the Chinese would say, but I'm so glad that everything is going well.

About corrections to the text of the <u>Blue Flower</u> – Thankyou for the ones you sent, and if possible I should like to add 4 more:

1. p 122 line 18 from top – read 'has' for 'had'
2. p 129 2 lines up from bottom – read 'undertook' for 'understood'
3. p 148 line 10 from top – read 'spending' for 'sending'
4. p 164 4 lines from bottom – read 'worldliness' for 'wordiness'

Unfortunately I didn't manage to get any of these put right in the paperback edition over here. Also unfortunately, I have never had an original photo of Novalis's ring – we reproduced from the <u>collected works</u> (Kohlhammer Verlag), and very unsatisfactory pictures they are, although I think by now the Weissenfels museum must have better ones.

Thankyou so much for all the work I see you must have done on the book and for telling me you liked it, which is the most important thing of all.

Meantime we (my 3 children and 9 grandchildren) haven't too much to complain of, and my youngest daughter, now a professor of neurophysiology, is just back from Seattle and tells me that it's the most beautiful place she's ever been to (like all scientists she spends a good deal of time at conferences). Now I never knew that Seattle was beautiful, and as so often, feel appalled by my ignorance.

However, I have the new entry for Charlotte Mew in the Dictionary of National Biography, and am glad to have the chance of putting the record straight a little –

with all best wishes,
Penelope

27a Bishop's Road Highgate
London, N6 4HP
New Year's Day [1997]

Dear Chris,

This is to thank you for the proof copy of The Blue Flower, without its misprints, which were my fault and no-one else's. I, of course, didn't know about your Mariner imprint and I feel very pleased to be one of its early titles. Best of luck to it in any case – 'The stars are with the voyager wherever he may sail.'

This was our Christmas card this year, a picture of our resident policeman, who is now aged 4, the very youngest of my grandchildren. I do hope you and your family are well and that Boston suits them.

Once again, thankyou for all you've done for my book, and very best wishes for 1997

Penelope

27a Bishop's Road
Highgate,
London, N6 4HP
2 March 1997

Dear Chris

Thankyou so much for your welcome letter and the before-publication notices of <u>The</u> <u>Blue</u> <u>Flower</u>. Over here, you know, racehorses that don't do well are said to 'disappoint their connections'.

I do so hope I shan't do that, because you've given me such a good start.

Thankyou too for the corrections to <u>The Bookshop</u>. I've come to the conclusion (or rather, I came to it some time ago) that I would <u>never</u> make a decent proof-reader. I'm never good enough, for instance, for the New York Times Review of Books. I'm just doing a piece for them now, on Muriel Spark, and I've been over it time and time again, but I know that they will ring up and (with the greatest politeness and kindness) point out my errors here and there – As far as I can see I don't want to make any further alterations to <u>The Bookshop,</u> and I apologise for not having any more reviews, but it was my first straight novel, and I think the ones Flamingo quoted were all I could expect.

I did appreciate the Houghton Mifflin catalogues – they treat books seriously and with appreciation of what books mean and, as I see it, will always continue to mean in a human society.

You kindly say, 'are there any books here that you would like for yourself?' and I have to answer (because I don't think that I can get it over here for myself) that I would very much like a copy of the Mariner <u>Wild America</u>. I understand of course that it's a commemoration of Roger Peterson, but James Fisher was my cousin, and I've so often driven about with him (when he was working at the London zoo) with the zoo's first Chinese panda in the back of his car, together with a supply of bamboo shoots,

best wishes
Penelope

27a Bishop's Road
Highgate
London, N6 4HP
2 April 1997

Dear Chris,

Thankyou so much for the 2 copies of your edition of the <u>Blue Flower</u>, which arrived here with the spring, just as our pear-tree came into blossom. Let's hope that's a good sign, and meanwhile let me

thankyou again for all the care you've put into the book before
publication – believe me I appreciate it, with best wishes, Penelope

27a Bishop's Road
London, N6
25 April [1997]

Dear Chris,

Thankyou so much for your letter and for having done so much for
<u>The Blue Flower</u>. Someone must have done it! I've never been so well
looked after as I have at Houghton Mifflin, and I'm sure it was right to
start with paperback, and I'm very happy about the reviews. I'm also
so happy to think that you and your family are back in Boston, where
you started from and wanted to be. Sometimes something does go
right in this world after all.

Once again, many thanks and best wishes – Penelope

27a Bishop's Road
Highgate
London, N6
[10 May 1997]

Dear Chris,

Thankyou so much for the draft cover for <u>The Bookshop</u> which I
thought very impressive (although as you say the books suggest an
antiquarian bookshop and we weren't anything as grand as that – alas,
the shop in Southwold is closed now and two others, I think, have
taken over). I think it must be very exciting to work on a new series
like Mariner, with all your future in front of you.

I very much appreciated your card, a beautiful blue flower although if I
could get hold of that wily but generous old William de Morgan I would
like to point out that these are <u>not</u> pansies and indeed I think the design is
based on William Morris's Larkspur. No matter, they made a splendid tile.

And now I also have a Houghton Mifflin bookbag – the first I've
ever had since Interchurch Travel gave me one in Jerusalem – and
that's long since disappeared – but I shall look after this one carefully –

Once again (or ever and again, as Henry James signed his letters) thankyou for all you've done – love Penelope

27a Bishop's Road
Highgate,
London, N6
2 June [1997]

Dear Chris,

Thankyou so much for the proof of the Mariner edition of <u>The Bookshop</u>, and your corrections. There's only one more I should like to make – that's on p. 112, 7 lines down, where <u>petolaria</u> ought to be <u>petiolara</u>. (It's that climbing hydrangea with large flowers like white lace.)

I like the cover very much, because, or although, it's much less sedate than the old one, and was delighted about the kind word from Maurice Sendak. I'll never forget first reading <u>Where the Wild Things Are</u>.

As to Kesselfleisch, I've never had any myself, but it never ceases to amaze me that the Germans could (at the end of the 18th century) eat the things they did and still produce the loveliest music ever heard by the ear of man. Perhaps it oughtn't to surprise me, but it still does.

love and best wishes
Penelope

27a Bishop's Road
Highgate, N6
8 June [1997]

Dear Chris,

Thankyou very much for the copy of <u>Wild America</u>. I've read it of course but never possessed a copy of my own and it reminded me of how things were so many years ago, apart from being a beautiful book in its own right. You say you can't think (by the way) how they set about it – Roger Peterson and James, I mean – but they managed it by separating the two diaries and maintaining the distance between them, in spite of what became a great friendship.

Thankyou too for <u>The Bookshop</u> – I appreciated the cover copy and don't think <u>any</u> of it <u>OBJECTIONABLE</u> (your capitals) – particularly glad of the reference to Balzac, because he was the presiding genius of this little book,

best wishes,
Penelope

27a Bishop's Road
Highgate, N6
6 July [1997]

Dear Chris,

Thankyou so much for sending Richard Holmes's review from the NYR of Books. He's always so thorough, and yet so interesting, but I never thought I'd have the luck to be reviewed by him, particularly as I think he's at last got well into the daunting task of Coleridge Vol: 2.

About the names of flowers, I suppose the Latin does at least give consistency, but the 'Name That Blooms'* wouldn't necessarily agree with each other. For example I don't think that Blue Bonnet, which I think is the official state flower of Texas, is called Blue Bonnet anywhere else –

love
Penelope

27a Bishop's Road
Highgate
London, N6
12 August [1997]

Dear Chris,

Thankyou so much for the two copies of <u>The Bookshop</u>. You don't know how glad I am to have it in an American edition – it takes me

* Popular Flora books.

back a very very long way – even the house we were living in when I was working in the bookshop in Southwold has disappeared completely – it was an old oyster warehouse and one day it simply fell down flat – and the bookshop itself, which was the only one in town, has closed. – But on the other hand, my Mariner adventure, as you quite rightly call it, has started, and I do want to congratulate you on the sales, as up till now all my books have sunk without trace in the U.S.

I was also delighted with Jill Krementz's photographs. They make me look thoughtful, which I've always wanted to be. But I haven't her address, so have had to write to her at Random House and hope that it reaches her.

Best wishes – Penelope

27a Bishop's Road
Highgate
London, N6
2 September 1997

Dear Chris,

Thankyou so much for your letter and the reviews – I can't help feeling particularly glad to read these kind remarks about <u>The Bookshop</u> after all these years. It seems like another world. You're so right in saying that Mrs Neame (name of the original proprietor, now dead, alas) would have been horrified at the idea of on-line bookselling, and so would the customers, who thought of the shop as the one place to go on a wet day (and the weather can be very bad in Southwold). They would hang about for <u>hours</u> and go away without buying anything – or perhaps one greeting card – but we never complained, that would have been against the tradition of book-shop keeping.

I must say I should be very sorry to see the bookshops go.

I'm glad that you liked the Jill Krementz pictures. She is a generous person. – best wishes, love Penelope

27a Bishop's Road
Highgate
London, N6
29 January 1998

Dear Chris,

This is just to thank you very much for the books, which arrived to-day. – I haven't read Maeve Brennan's stories yet – I'm ashamed to say I don't know them, but at least that means I have them to look forward to, and meanwhile I appreciated the just-right introduction by William Maxwell and should like to congratulate you on the beautiful appearance of the whole book.

This is quite an anxious time for us in Highgate as Maria (my younger daughter) is down with pneumonia and has had to take some quite horrible antibiotic, so that although she's a professor of neurobiology at London University, she is lying in bed looking much as she did when she was ill as a little girl. Meanwhile <u>her</u> three children (like all children) are getting rather impatient, though sympathetic, and think it's quite time she got up again. Mothers aren't really supposed to get ill –

With all best wishes –
Penelope

27a Bishop's Road
London, N6
25 February 1998

Dear Chris,

Thankyou so much for the copies of <u>Offshore</u> and <u>The Gate of Angels</u>. I do very much appreciate the cover design for <u>Offshore</u>. All writers, or most of them, any way, are impossibly difficult about their covers, but I did dislike the photograph of poor <u>Grace</u> as a trim houseboat in a backwater, whereas she had served an honourable career at sea and still had part of her mast – the only trouble was that she was beyond repair. The new design has just the right rust-and-open water colouring.

I don't think I have any corrections for <u>Innocence</u> or <u>The Beginning of Spring</u> (I asked a visiting delegation of teachers from Russia about this and they declared everything was all right, but of course this may just have been politeness).

Beautiful spring here and all the daffodils up, but it is <u>so dull</u> having to hear about the millennium dome, it seems to be just a competition in how much money they can waste. – And everyone is <u>ill</u> – but not you and your family I do hope –

best wishes –

Penelope

27a Bishop's Road
London, N6
14 March 1998

Dear Mindy,*

Thankyou for telling me about the error on p 22 of <u>The Blue Flower</u>. I have to admit that it <u>is</u> a mistake – not the only one in the book, I'm afraid – but I have to consider myself lucky that someone should read my novel carefully enough to want to put it right.

If I had the chance to change it, I could take out the line 'Lucklum, October 1787' (9th line from bottom on p 22) and leave the dates of Fritz's visit unspecified. That's the trouble of trying to combine biography and fiction, even with the best intentions.

I'm glad the books arrived safely. At the last moment, when everything was sealed and stuck up, the despatch company said they wanted to open them all to make sure there weren't any dangerous devices in them, but they relented and let them through.

Best wishes

Penelope

---

* An editorial assistant at Houghton Mifflin.

27a Bishop's Road
Highgate
London, N6
14 May [1998]

Dear Chris,

Thankyou so much for sending the cuttings. I see that a lot of
people felt that I shouldn't have been awarded this prize* – which is
only to be expected – but I still feel it's a tremendous honour and I'm
truly grateful to you for all the work and worrying you've done.

Thankyou too for Sarah Orne Jewett book – now I've got stories
that I've never even heard of, and <u>A Country Doctor</u>, which I <u>had</u>
heard of, of course, but I've never been able to get hold of a copy. And
it's such a treat, Chris, to have a book with sewn bindings. However, I
must guard against thinking everything 'used to be better'. I find it
hard to say why I think so highly of 'The Land of Pointed Firs'. It's the
restraint, I think – all the things that aren't said.

The Booker is a dreadfully slow process. First the long short list (20
books out of 150) then the short list, and we're not finished till
October. Also Booker plc's profits have declined this year, so they've
had to make economies, and we haven't even been given folders and
pencils –

best wishes to you and the family – Penelope

27a Bishop's Road
Highgate
London, N6
3 December 1998

Dear Chris,

I'm writing to you now because I thought you would probably be
going away with your family for Christmas – perhaps to the in-laws
who took charge of your cat – so I've tried to send this in good time.

It's such a relief to have the Booker judging over – it's always the
same, you make up your mind to remain calm, dispassionate and

---

* The National Book Critics Circle Award.

civilised and then as the meetings go on you become increasingly heated and quarrelsome. The book I wanted to win, (Magnus Mills's The Restraint of Beasts) didn't win, and I felt like weeping. And everyone complained, as they always do, that the judges must have lost their wits anyway.

All reasonably well here, and two of my grandchildren down in Cornwall are in their local church silver band – one plays the baritone horn, and the other plays the cornet.

Thankyou so much for all you did for me, Chris, you can be sure I never look at one of my books without thinking about you, and I do hope all your new enterprises are going just as you wanted.

love and best wishes for Christmas –

Penelope

27a Bishop's Road
Highgate
London, N6
9 January 1999

Dear Chris,

Thankyou so much for your letter and for what you tell me about Richmond, where I've never been, but I'm particularly interested in it because I've just been reading The Langhorne Sisters, and I'm particularly interested, too, in what you tell me about Charlotte Mew because our experience with Eddie is quite different – reared on dry catfood and water, (because that's said to keep them healthy and eliminate many problems), he too was allowed turkey and milk as a supposed treat at Christmas, but he wasn't used to it and wouldn't eat it. He catches quantities of shrews and, I'm afraid, young birds in the garden, but he won't eat those either.

I was fascinated by the photographs of Weimar and Leipzig, about 1904–6 I should say – the one of Schiller's house is amazing as the photographer evidently intended a poetic contrast between the nicely dressed ladies and the market women with their shawls and dreadfully heavy baskets, but the effect is quite oppressive and frightening. Perhaps it's on account of the weak lighting, I don't know, but anyhow I was very glad to have them. The Lutheran nun who sent me photographs of Schlöben (where the community had succeeded in keeping their hidden chapel going through the whole of the war) told me that she trusted me to send them back, so of course I did, but perhaps you'll let me keep these ones. I'm sure you'll be happy to be back with the New Criterion. I felt that was the place where you were really at home. The Counterpoint Press and the North Point Press I, of course, have never heard of. Do you think they're <u>safe</u>, Chris? But then you're young, and quite rightly don't consider these things; you left Houghton Mifflin* on a point of principle and I expect you'll go on the same way.

My youngest grandchild Alfie, aged 6, has just beaten me at chess, but says that I am not bad for a beginner –

love to you and your family – Penelope

> *27a Bishop's Road*
> *Highgate*
> *London, N6*
> *25 May 1999*

Dear Chris,

To begin with, thankyou for sending me the piece about Carroll and Graf, I was never very happy at being published by them as they had a pornographic list – Venus in the kitchen &c. – but I think I had better steer clear of the law-suit.

I very much appreciate your suggestion of reprinting (or republishing) <u>The Knox Brothers</u> but do you think people in the U.S. would want to read it? There's so much about the Church of England, which has become an exceedingly dim subject, and <u>Punch</u>, too, an important paper in its day, has been reduced almost to nothing (I'm glad my father didn't live to see it) and has finally been bought by Al Fayed. My uncle Ronnie was once a very well known figure, but I was sent an article the other day titled Who was Ronnie Knox? I'm not complaining about this, not at all, time passes, but with <u>The Knox Brothers</u> I think that constitutes a real difficulty. I'm also a bit doubtful

---

* PMF meant Addison-Wesley.

about revising and correcting it, as I no longer have the letters and photographs I borrowed. (I did correct it for the Harvill-Collins paperback in 1991, and what happens to the copyright I don't know. Perhaps it reverted to me.)

This doesn't seem a grateful or polite answer to your kind suggestion, and I know you will understand and accept my apologies in advance. Even while I was writing it I thought what a closed chapter of history it was, but I didn't mind, because I wanted to leave a record of it before it was too late. But by this time I feel it's barely intelligible. And the bibliography! Someone did do Ronnie's, I think, for a thesis, but Dilly destroyed all his papers.

with love and best wishes – Penelope

24 August [1999]

Thankyou so much for your card – but it's a sad fact that by my calculation this is the last day of your holiday – so glad it was such a success. I do wish I liked lobster – this has landed me so many times in awkward situations – and I feel the same about oysters – but I know I must be wrong as no-one else in the world agrees with me – love Penelope

27a Bishop's Road
Highgate
London, N6
28 September [1999]

Dear Chris,

This is just on the subject of The Knox Brothers, which may well have gone right out of your mind, but just in case it hasn't, this is to say that Harvill Press have written to me to tell me that all the rights in this book have reverted to me, for what they're worth.

I've never got to the state where I don't care if I never see another book, but I sometimes allow myself to think that there are too many of them in the world. Now I've agreed to be a judge for two prizes given by the English Speaking Union and that means about a hundred large, heavy new books arriving and where they're to go I can't think, for I really have no room at all, and I know I shall have great difficulty in getting anyone to take them away afterwards. I've decided that my prize-adjudicating career, such as it is, must draw to a close, but it's a fact about life that you never do get completely to the end of anything.

One of my grand-daughters is getting confirmed – she is <u>eleven</u>, and wants to wear a long, tight black skirt, which she can't kneel down in without alarming sounds of stretching and ripping. But there you are, she's a good girl and plays the cornet with the local silver band –

all best wishes

Penelope

27a Bishop's Road
Highgate
London, N6
13 October 1999

Dear Chris,

Thankyou so much for your letter, and I'm quite willing for Counterpoint to be the exclusive publisher of <u>The Knox Brothers</u> in the U.S. and Canada and the terms seem all right as far as I understand them, but whatever is 'the retailer's freight-pass through allowance'? I ought to know, I expect, but I don't, but perhaps it will all become clear in the contract, or perhaps I'd do best to leave it to you as usual.

(I feel this paragraph makes me sound stupider than I am. But I'm just no good at business.)

Thankyou, too, for the cuttings – we've had two enormous bookshops open here this month, one in (on?) Oxford Street and the other in Piccadilly where Simpson's used to be. (I must say I miss Simpson's – not that I've ever bought anything there for many years. They were the first people in London to sell Daks – but I'm afraid you'll never have heard of them.) Anyway, these bookshops are said to be going to stay open till all hours, and serve coffee, and put the little places out of business. Let's hope not.

Good luck to your daughter with the Irish step dancing. But I don't think you ought to speak of 'Michael Flatley's Riverdance' as he had an almighty row with them and formed his own company, in which he can still jump higher than anyone else.

I'm so glad there is going to be another Maeve Brennan. HarperCollins did ask me to do an introduction to the first one, but I couldn't see it was possible to have any introduction except William Maxwell's. It just couldn't be bettered, and I'd have had to take all the information from it anyway –

best wishes

Penelope

27a Bishop's Road
Highgate
London, N6
11 November 1999

Dear Chris,

Thankyou so much for your letter, and for the photograph of Charlotte Mew – you say 'in her prime' but she looks quite old, although absolutely ready to defend her corner. Our Eddie looks much less aristocratic – Charlotte Mew has a proud, delicate expression. – Meanwhile my elder daughter is in real trouble, as she had 2 cats from the same litter, much prized by <u>her</u> daughter Jemima – Tina had a day off teaching and undertook to mow the lawn, or a bit of it – and there in the long grass she found the stiffening body of Rosie, one of the two cats – Jemima came home from school and Tina missed the moment and didn't tell her that she had just finished burying Rosie in the orchard – and now she has to keep up the deception somehow, and even, at Jemima's suggestion put up an advertisement in the local shop – LOST, GINGER CAT and so forth – I suppose one should never tell a lie, even with the best intentions.

(Please thank your mother-in-law for her kind message.)

You may feel I haven't tried very hard with the questionnaire but I promise you I've done my best. At least I've been able to suggest a photographer. But I have to admit failure with the reviews of

The Knox Brothers, but equally certainly I haven't any now. You say 'if you feel you can trust me and the post-office with the originals' – well, of course I could but I haven't any. I feel the same inadequacy as I did when Texas (who have all my mss) said they would like some diaries, but I haven't kept any diaries.

I seem to remember that Malcolm Muggeridge wrote quite a nice notice, but alas! he's dead now.

I'm having to save up The Rose Garden as nearly 200 books have arrived, to be judged for the Heinemann award. Really, the publishers seem to have sent anything that came to hand. I can't believe Charlotte Mew was the first book you edited. I thought you'd edited dozens, from the calm, experienced way you took it on. Well, that's an honour for me – love, Penelope

27a Bishop's Road
Highgate
London, N6
5 December 1999

Dear Chris,

Thankyou for your letter, and the contract for The Knox Brothers. I don't feel sorry to have written it, as all the evidence and the direct witnesses were disappearing or dying or losing their memories, but oh dear, it seems to belong more and more to a vanished era – I never dreamed of a time when Punch would have been bought by Mohammed Al Fayed, and Bletchley would become a museum. However, I've got great confidence in what you call your familiar m.o., though I don't quite see how you manage now Counterpoint has moved to Washington? You've never had the time to explain that.

I was very interested in the story of your family's old tortoise-shell cat. It's the element of time again – the secret had to be kept so long that when it did come out you weren't sorry either for Chat or yourself, but for your mother. Let's hope the same thing happens to Tina's daughter, Jemima, but they are still at the painful stage of advertising in the local papers.

This letter seems to have got rather melancholy, but it was really intended to thank you for all you've done with the Knox Brothers – love and best wishes – Penelope

P.S. Books still pouring in for the Heinemann. The poetry collections are slender, as usual, but the biographies have reached vast proportions, and the novels are almost as bad.

> *27a Bishop's Road*
> *Highgate*
> *London, N6*
> 13 January 2000

Dear Chris,

Thankyou so much for your letter and I'm glad everything goes so well at Counterpoint (can it really be nine months?).

When you say 'new poems' by Geoffrey Hill, I wonder if you mean The Triumph of Love or something since that?

I was rather dismayed by what you said about my short stories. I didn't know Houghton Mifflin were thinking of bringing them out – they didn't tell me anything about it, and although Harper Collins did suggest it, they wanted me to write at least one new one, which I'm afraid I haven't done, and I couldn't even produce a list of the old ones, as I haven't kept one. I sent them the titles I could remember. That doesn't sound much like a book! I did tell them (Harper Collins) that short-stories don't sell, but they, I suppose, know that. (I don't mean Maeve Brennan! She is a classic.)

I do congratulate you on your Christmas presents. Putting what you say about the Smithfield ham together with what you previously told me about the lobster-kettle on your Maine vacation, I take it that you're an expert cook, (although there is one trouble with hams, which is however to finish them up).

And it's splendid to think that you're coming to London. I myself don't go out much, particularly in the evening, as I've got rather lame lately (said to be arthritis, but really I think just old age) but perhaps (although Highgate is rather a distant suburb) you could make time to come and see me?

Love and best New Year wishes –

Penelope

27a Bishop's Road
Highgate
London, N6
31 January 2000

Dear Chris,

Please forgive a short letter as I have to catch the post (that's what they always said in Victorian days but it's much truer now than it was then).

What you've written about <u>The Knox Bros</u> is splendid, except that my grandfather was Bishop of Manchester – he <u>had</u> been Bishop of Birmingham, but the height of his career was in Manchester.

About <u>Not Shown</u> (not my title) I <u>have</u> actually now signed a contract for this book, but I was taken aback because all I'd done was to produce a list, not at all complete, of short stories, but it <u>is</u> due to be published by Houghton Mifflin, I think the publisher. The trouble is that I don't really seem to have got a particular editor, at Harper Collins, since the departure of the much-missed Stuart Proffitt, who has gone to Penguin, and I find this rather confusing –

Love, looking forward to seeing you –

Penelope

27a Bishop's Road
London, N6
5 February 2000

Dear Chris –

Thankyou so much for the New Yorkers. I hadn't read one for a long time and at first I thought – How it's changed. But then it occurred to me – perhaps <u>I've</u> changed. In any case, I liked Joan A's piece very much –

love and best wishes

Penelope

27a Bishop's Road
Highgate
London, N6
15 March [2000]

Dear Chris,

If this wasn't as near as I can get to a business letter, I would say what a great treat it was for me to meet you, but let me at least thank you for the amazing amount of hard work and care you've taken over this book. Believe me it's appreciated and gives me a wonderful feeling of trust.

My arthritis (about which I'm afraid you've already heard too much) is a bit overwhelming at the moment and I can't quite face typing. Will you forgive me returning your letter with the answers written in – the same for your corrections.

I don't really want to alter anything in the book. One of my troubles was to say as little as possible about my aunt Ethel and my nephew Christopher, who were both (in varying degrees) not quite normal, and about the vexed question of Uncle Ronnie's Money which he left to us, but we never got anything except a small plaster bust of Shakespeare, which I still have. So it's really the opposite of the usual tell-all biography.

My main worry, though, is about the foreword. You kindly say that my uncles' world must have been a great inspiration to me, but the truth is that (like most children with conspicuous relations) I tried to get away from them and do my own thing. I didn't realise until much later, indeed until after my father's death, how much there was to find out about them, and by that time it was almost too late. Isn't that your own experience?

I don't think I could write three or four pages of introduction that would be in any way satisfactory, and I certainly don't want to say anything about Al Fayed, let us hope he fades away like the nightmare he is. What I would like is to break off the existing foreword at line 12 'one humour and one mind' and go on:

They gave their working lives to journalism, cryptography, classical scholarship, the Anglican church, the Catholic church. Since I wrote this book twenty-three years ago all these professions, all these worlds, have changed. If the four of them could be reborn into the twenty-first century, how would it treat them? I can only be certain that they would stand by the (sometimes unexpected) things they said. Evoe, my father, muttered to me, on the way to my wedding 'the only thing I want is for everyone, as far as possible, to be happy'. Dillwyn: 'Nothing is impossible.' Wilfred: 'Get on with it' – also 'why should we not go on, through all eternity, growing in love and our power to love?' Ronnie: 'Do the more difficult thing.' I miss them all more than I can say.

Then the acknowledgements could start 'I should never have got any way at all . . . ' (Most of these acknowledged people, or at least some of them, are dead, and I haven't got their addresses, so they must stay where they are.)

I want you to have a line to yourself, <u>please</u>, so 'I am most grateful to Richard Garnett' must shove up into the paragraph above, and then could you put 'Finally, for this <u>Counterpoint</u> edition I should like to thank Chris Carduff for his energy, inspiration and patience' – or if this isn't the right thing to say, put whatever <u>is</u> the right thing.

The bibliography is a real problem, especially Dilly's – now that the files at Kew have been opened there have been quantities of books on Enigma (and an appalling play, in which Dilly figured as a kind of fall guy), and it would be a daunting business to bring it up to date. When my <u>Edward Burne Jones</u> was reprinted by Sutton (for his centenary) there was the same problem, and I just had to do the best I could, but it wasn't very satisfactory. On the other hand, an out-of-date bibliography is not of much use to anybody. But you have to have them.

so many thanks for all you've done

love and best wishes

Penelope

27a Bishop's Road
Highgate
London, N6
21 March 2000

Dear Chris,

To start with, I feel terribly distressed by your remark about Herbert Morris's poems, that you hope I'll find them more interesting than I did when you were describing them. I don't remember your describing them at all, or perhaps it was to somebody else, could that be it? Let's settle for it being someone else. I haven't even read <u>What Was Lost</u> yet. Evidently it mustn't be read in a hurry, and I have to review Saul Bellow's novel first, and I'm such a hopelessly slow reviewer. I'm also saving up <u>The New Criterion</u> which is always so elegant-looking, such a pleasure to see.

I don't know what to say about the photograph of my father with the Punch marionette. I've always thought he looked so desperately embarrassed in it. Prof. Peter Mellini was here last week – I'd always pictured him as Italian, but he is a German from California with a bushy beard and a flat cap. He's just on the verge of retirement and has been writing a history of Punch since 1900, for years, but can't really grasp any thing in the nature of a joke – He gives an audible sigh of relief when he gets back on the business side.

The difficult thing is really to get photographs of Dilly, who didn't much like having his picture taken.

I never did thank you for your letter from Durrant's Hotel, which made me wonder if you oughtn't to be writing yourself.

I'm glad the maple tree is out, but horrified at the arrival of the Canada geese. They've given up hibernating – the ones that live over here, anyway – and stay right through the winter, multiplying at an alarming rate

with best wishes
Penelope

27a Bishop's Road
Highgate
London, N6
29 March 2000*

Dear Chris,

Thankyou so much for your letter and the further notes and queries. I've <u>never</u> had such a careful editor, not even in the long-ago days when there were 'printers' readers'.

You've been most successful in tracing these various clerics, though they may all drop dead while your back is turned, and that's also true of practically every one in the foreword. Do you think it's enough to put 15 March 2000 at the end? I expect you've come across this problem quite often. Really it would be better not to thank anyone, but they did go to so much trouble.

And so have you! 'patient to a fault' is just about right, but at least Dilly's birth-date is right now. His own son, my cousin, Oliver, didn't know it. In fact, I'm not sure Dilly knew it himself, because I'm certain he said the lunch at the Spread-Eagle was for his 50th birthday, but he was wrong.

I'm supposed to be going away from April 25th to 29th – Ria says I must go because she must have my walls repainted. I'd hoped they might last me out, but she says not –

love and best wishes
Penelope

---

* This is one of the last letters PMF wrote. The first of her strokes took place a day or so later. She died on 28 April.

The Kitchen Drawer Poem

1. The nutcracker, the skewer, the knife,
   are doomed to share this drawer for life.

2. You cannot pierce, the skewer says,
   or cause the pain of in one place.

3. You cannot grind, you do not know,
   says nutcracker, the pain of slow.

4. You don't know what it is to slice,
   to both of them the knife replies,

5. with pain so fine it is not pain
   to part what cannot join again.

6. The skewer, nutcracker, and knife
   are well adapted to their life.

7. They calculate efficiency
   by what the others cannot be

8. and power by the pain they cause
   and that is life in kitchen drawers.

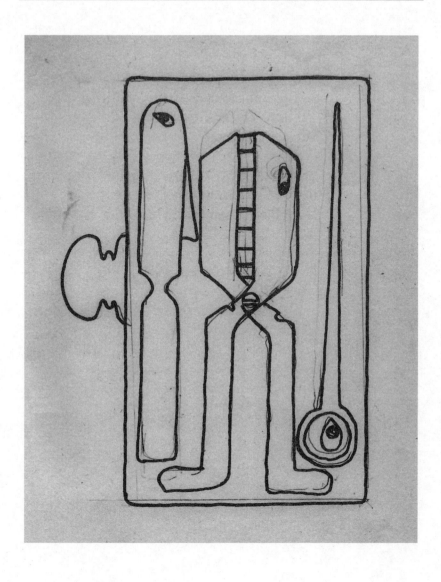

The Father and the Mother

Here are two individuals who
have reproduced their kind
and each of them possesses both
a body and a mind.

They sit upon two separate chairs
they sit between four walls
and it was a mistake to call
them individuals.

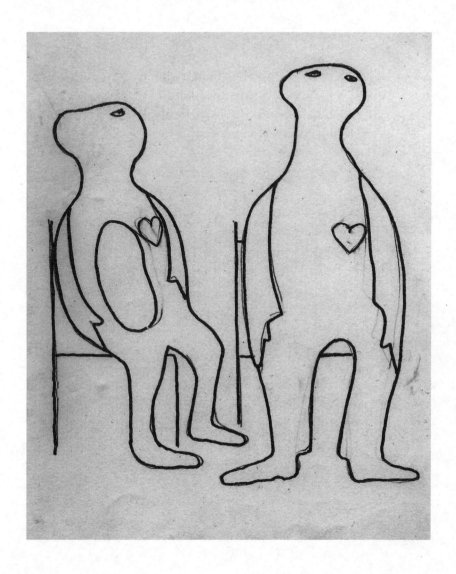

ACKNOWLEDGEMENTS

My grateful thanks are due to all those who kept their letters from Penelope so carefully, and so kindly contributed them to this book: to Hugh and Penny Lee, Maryllis and Anne Conder, Elizabeth Barnett, Chris Carduff, Howard Woolmer, Mavis Batey, Helen Knox, Harvey Pitcher, Michael Holroyd, Alberto Manguel, Stuart Proffitt, Alyson Barr, Dorothy Coles, Richard Holmes, Heulwen Cox (for J.L.Carr), Bridget Nichols, Masolino d'Amico, Graham Chesney, Maria and Tina.

Also to the archivists and librarians who have been so helpful in granting me access to their collections: John Rylands, Manchester (Norah Hartley), Senate House Library (Colin Haycraft/Duckworth), Macmillan publishers (Richard Garnett), HarperCollins (Richard Ollard, Stuart Proffitt, Mandy Kirkby), Wheaton (Malcolm Muggeridge), Huntington (Hilary Mantel), Princeton (Sir Frank Kermode), Missouri (Mary Lago), and the Harry Ransom Humanities Research Center, Texas (Francis King, Sybille Bedford, A.L. Barker, Richard Ollard, James Saunders, Julian Barnes, Mary Knox).

I would like to thank HRHRC most especially for the two temporary research fellowships they've given me, and for their excellent continuing care of Penelope's archive.

Mandy Kirkby and Philip Gwyn Jones of Flamingo commissioned this book, Nicholas Pearson and Catherine Heaney of Fourth Estate took it onward, and Mandy Kirkby and Mark Richards have prepared it for publication with tact and devotion. Last and first my thanks to Maria, Valpy and Tina for their help, advice and support.

INDEX